THE SCOTTISH MOUNTAINEERING CLUB JOURNAL 2020

Shelter Stone Crag. Photo: Jon Read.

THE SCOTTISH MOUNTAINEERING CLUB JOURNAL 2020

Edited by Peter Biggar

Volume 48

No. 211

THE SCOTTISH MOUNTAINEERING CLUB

THE SCOTTISH MOUNTAINEERING CLUB JOURNAL 2020
Volume 48 No 211

Published by the Scottish Mountaineering Club 2020
www.smc.org.uk/

ISSN 0080-813X
ISBN 978-1-907233-27-2

Typeset by Noel Williams

Printed and bound by Novoprint S.A., Barcelona, Spain.

Distributed by Cordee Ltd, 11 Jacknell Road, Hinckley, LE10 3BS.

CONTENTS

EDITORIAL

In his resigning editorial my distinguished predecessor Noel Williams wondered what changes I would oversee during my time as Editor. The obvious one, suggested by Robin Campbell, was the change to a hardback format. Like the earlier change from a plain blue cover to a coloured pictorial one, acceptance of this change was not a foregone conclusion, and I was pleased when the AGM of 2015 voted for it by a substantial majority. Apart from the practical advantages the hardback enjoys, being stronger and more enduring, it also means that we have been able to abandon a system, inherited from the past, in which two or more editions of the Journal went to the making up of a volume so that an edition might start, confusingly, on page 327. Now each edition starts on page one, is a volume in its own right, and can be referenced simply by its year. Campbell's suggestion has resulted in an improvement.

The other happening of note on my watch has been the reintroduction of a steady trickle of Accident Reports from teams belonging to Mountain Rescue Scotland and the Independent Teams represented by Cairngorm. It has taken a great deal of persuasion to bring about these modest results and I can only hope that the current trickle will grow into a stream presently. The trend is in the right direction. The Reports are a valuable supplement to the Statistical Report which we also publish: they give it a human dimension and hill people are influenced by them.

I have one small disappointment as editor: the Journal does not receive many articles from younger people. There are notable exceptions, two of which can be found in the current issue, but generally the mountains are seen from an older viewpoint. This imbalance reflects the Club's imbalance in its membership. Perhaps, for the future good of the Club and its Journal, a way could be found of incorporating the young and promising as well as the exceptionally talented young climber?

If editing the Journal wasn't a difficult job it wouldn't be worth doing. Trying to do it well is a wonderful challenge. In this I have been supported by a splendid team with a wide range of talents without whose enthusiasm and dedication the Journal could not be produced. They know who they are and I thank each and every one of them. I also hope that they will remain in place to smooth the path of my talented successor.

In *Porterhouse Blue* the satirical novel by Tom Sharpe, dramatised on television, the Dean of Porterhouse remarks:

They can improve things as much as they like, they never make them any better.

Amusing in context this seemingly cynical aphorism nevertheless hints at a truth: the current edition of the Journal has seen vast improvements which the first Editor, Joseph Stott could hardly have imagined, but in terms of their essential value there is no difference between them.

When I was about to be made Editor the late Des Rubens remarked: 'We don't choose our Editors, it's a bit like the Dalai Lama, we find them.'

Des was joking of course, but again in his humour was an element of truth. I can honestly say that even before I was made Editor I was sure who my successor would be – and I wish him every success.

P.J. Biggar

NOT YOUR REGULAR CUILLIN TRAVERSE

By Will Rowland

Finally finished school

In the Summer of 2008 two tired teens arrived at Sligachan Hotel. Clive was waiting at the bar, we joined him and immediately a pair of pints, crisps and Snickers bars were thrust in front of us. For Fran and me this was our first proper introduction to the ridge. We managed the traverse in a day and were exhausted. The thought of an extension of this route seemed impossible to me at the time and I thought anyone pushing further or indeed faster was a freak. Without a full licence and too tired to drive, our 'chauffeur' took us back to Glen Brittle, Cuillin FM blasting out loud. The rain bounced off the tent for the next week, but that didn't matter to us...

Ten years later

Despite a friend having some issues leading to a 10 a.m. start on Sgùrr nan Gillean, I managed a solo winter traverse during the exceptional conditions of 2018. Skipping along the bogs to Glen Brittle in the dark, I wondered what a Greater Traverse would be like...

Skye is always on the mind

2019–20 was another big winter with many storms and few benign days. Having missed the best week of the season I was very keen to have some big days to make up for lost time. From my home in Fort William

I headed east to climb some Cairngorm classics with my good friend Rob. Unfortunately, with Coronavirus spreading and school closures

Early morning light on the start of the north–south traverse. All photos: Will Rowland.

Looking back to Sgùrr nan Gillean, An Caisteal in the middle distance under cloud, Bealach Harta bottom right. Heard and Reynolds on North Peak of Bidein Druim nan Ràmh. Taken from Central Peak of Bidein Druim nan Ràmh.

imminent, Rob was unable to join me due to increased responsibilities at work and home. I had intended to head to the Cuillin so this simply meant I would go a little earlier than originally planned and I could help the folks out with some DIY.

I was sure the conditions could be great on Skye but without any current information it was a bit of a gamble. I lay in my van trying to sleep, hearing hailstones rattle the roof, I wondered if a traverse was a good option. 'Ach well,' I thought, 'it'll be a good couple of days either way.'

Leaving Sligachan at 3 a.m. it was cold and clear, the stars were magnificent. A few lights were on in the car park and other climbers were readying themselves for a big job of their own. Walking in I wondered if I'd meet other teams, if there would be much of a trail and how the snow would be. There was only one important question and I would find out soon enough.

Keep it in the family

I decided to follow a similar route to the line my Dad took when he did a summer traverse of the Black and Red Cuillin in the 1980s. Having only climbed Pinnacle Ridge in summer I thought it would be a nice way to start the ridge in winter. If the conditions weren't ideal for a full traverse I would at least get to do something I'd not done before.

Pinnacle Ridge was great fun, but in full winter condition it's definitely a serious route. I stood on the summit of Sgùrr nan Gillean at 6.45 a.m.

Looking back from the flank of Sgùrr a' Mhadaidh's first top to Bealach na Glaic Moire with the Central Peak of Bidein Druim nan Ràmh on the right.

The full length of the ridge lay ahead of me – it was breath-taking. The crest was virtually untouched, I couldn't believe that people hadn't been up here. I bumped into a team at the start of the West Ridge, had a little chat and continued on my way. The snow was generally good but there was plenty of soft stuff to plod through and there were some cheeky, slabby surface layers that liked to pop when you really didn't want them to. I knew I was in for a long day and I had to be particularly careful with such variable snow – especially when descending and down climbing. Unsurprisingly, after abseiling King's Cave Chimney from Am Basteir, the most time-consuming section seemed to be between Sgùrr na Bhairnich and Sgùrr Dearg where there is the most continuous route finding and down climbing in addition to the constant ascent and descent. It was in this middle section I noticed some other climbers make good use of my trail. I shouted across to ask them if they wanted a 'shot out front', but they politely declined stating I was doing a grand job and that they would soon stop for lunch.

I plodded along with my thoughts for company. No footprints and no abseil tat…was I really on the Cuillin Ridge? I was glad I brought enough disposable slings and cord as there were so few abseil points where you'd normally expect them. I watched eagles jousting in the distance. I'd never seen so many together in one place. Their large talons indented the snow where they landed on the ridge, taking a break between soaring, riding thermals, true masters of their trade.

A view down the Druim nan Ràmh to Coruisk and Sgùrr na Stri, Blàbheinn and Clach Glas far left.

I surprised a lone walker on Sgùrr na Banachdaich and met another approaching the bealach descending north from Sgùrr Dearg. It was strange seeing people after having the place to myself – I have no doubt the other lone walkers felt the same. I arrived at the Inaccessible Pinnacle and there was a crowd of people (six in total) scattered around the iconic rock. After completing a quick loop – up the east ridge and down the west – I met my friends Peter Heard and Louisa Reynolds. It turned out that they were the pair following me. What a small world. We had a good craic and then went our separate ways. I think the other climbers were glad at the return of peace and tranquility.

The sun had really softened the snow and it wasn't easy-going breaking trail to Sgùrr MhicCoinnich. Fortunately the abseil was in-situ at the top of King's Chimney but it was typically messy and well buried in snow. I quickly linked everything together with a wee sling I'd found along the way, just to be sure. Certain risks can be easily avoided. Soon I was at the TD gap and strangely there was no in-situ tat. A final abseil into the gap followed by some down climbing into Coire a' Ghrunnda led to the final stomp over the southern hills. I followed the pinnacled ridge across to Sgùrr Dubh Mòr where my friends caught me up. We then retraced our steps, picked up a trail at Bealach a' Garbh-choire and continued over Sgùrr nan Eag and along to Gars-bheinn chattering away. The views were spectacular in every direction, nothing can compare.

I watched my friends drop down the screes on Gars-bheinn's southern

The Inaccessible Pinnacle, Rum to the right and S. Alasdair, S. Theàrlaich, S. Dubh na Dà Bheinn, S. MhicCoinnich and S. Dubh Mòr to the left.

flank with a Hebridean back drop. I could have sat at the summit all night, but I didn't really know where I was going and had some rough ground to cover. I descended Coire a' Chruidh to Loch Coruisk and out towards Loch Scavaig. The land here feels enchanted and timeless even with the presence of the JMCS Hut. Hearing the waves lap the shore gave me the impression that I would soon be at the new Camasunary bothy but the trip around the Bad Step seemed to take forever. This is often the case when walking tired in the dark.

I checked the map I'd acquired from my old man. I headed up-stream to the bridge, crossing the river running out of Glen Sligachan. In the darkness I could see the concrete pillars of the once great suspension bridge. But that's all that remains. There were no cables, no walkway. Nothing. I backtracked to the shore and crossed the river at its widest without drama. I suppose that's what happens when the map has more years than the user. Walking across to the new bothy I rationalised the constant upgrading and revisions made to maps: although the hills may never change – everything else does.

Arriving in the bothy I was welcomed by local father and son team Alasdair and Duncan who were good craic and very welcoming. It was 9 p.m. and I was gasping for a brew and something hot to eat. I got changed out of my wet gear, into some dry bivi socks and trainers – aaaaah! I looked for the fireplace to dry my kit but strangely the new bothy had no such luxury. What is the world coming to?

This view from Marsco, showing Gars-bheinn distant right to Blàbheinn distant left, gives some idea of the distance travelled.

The following day I set off up the long ridge of Blàbheinn. I looked across to the hills I did the day before, fresh in my memory and my legs. I stopped just before the summit to change out of my trainers. Forcing my feet into frozen socks and boots I remember Alasdair asking me in the bothy 'What was the hardest part of the journey?' Now I knew.

Running down the névé towards Clach Glas soon got the blood flowing and my cold toes warmed up nicely. I had only been on these hills once before on a miserable day and I didn't really have a clue where I was at the time. It was great to see this corner of the Cuillin in all its glory! After abseiling the classic 18m chimney off Blàbheinn, Clach Glas was in good condition and I needed my crampons for most the ridge. I didn't need to hurry and just enjoyed the route making sure I took the best line. The ridge has plenty of tricky steps and isn't to be underestimated.

Leaving the summit of Garbh-bheinn seemed like a milestone. I was relieved to be on my way back north even if I had plenty of up and down yet to come. The wind was horrendous as I plodded up the shoulder to Marsco's summit. It seemed to be funnelling through the glen and accelerating up and around the hillside – it almost got the better of me. Following an old fence line brought me round to the north-east side of Marsco and out of the wind. The old snow was bullet hard and a joy to run down. Immediately sheltered from the wind – everything went quiet allowing me once again really to appreciate where I was and what was around me. I stopped at a burn, it was the first for a long time and the last before the final hurdle.

The gruelling screes of the Red Cuillin are well known – great for running down but not so great for going up. My big boots had not long defrosted and my feet felt quite safe on the rough ground whilst carrying a big bag. I got the head down taking each hill in my stride and eventually I stood on top of Glamaig. I didn't see anybody all day and I was relieved a hill runner didn't skip past me on the Red Cuillin for I looked totally out of place with all the equipment I was carrying.

Standing on the last summit I tried to take a picture, but my battery had died due to the cold. With nothing else to do I began stomping down the frozen screes, I couldn't wait to get onto the softer terrain below. Relieved to be on friendly ground I wriggled into my trainers for the final march across the bog.

I made it back to the van in good time (6.45 p.m.) and charged my phone to let people know I was safe and sound. A message came through from a good friend 'Everything is closing – free beer at the pub!' This was just what I needed. Frantically messaging Iain back, he immediately responded, 'This was last night bud, everywhere's shut now!' It seemed that in just two days everything had changed, and I was oblivious, just running around in the hills.

And all of a sudden it was Spring! Blàbheinn, watercolour by John Mitchell.

FIFTY YEARS, JIMMY HENDRIX AND ARRAN

By Graham Little

MUSIC AND ROCK CLIMBING have always had an esoteric connection and they have been, and continue to be, two of the great pleasures of my life. In the late 1960s a burgeoning interest in climbing was gradually supplanting my childhood passion for fishing and this was accompanied by the music of 'progressive' bands such as Pink Floyd, Jethro Tull and The Jimmy Hendrix Experience. Jimmy Hendrix, in particular, captured my imagination: his energy, his charisma and his ground-breaking guitar playing struck a chord in a somewhat shy and repressed teenager. I loved the 1966 story of Hendrix, newly arrived in London, asking to jam with Cream (a super-group before the term was invented). Eric Clapton (the then guitar God), on hearing Hendrix play, walked off stage in disbelief, uttering the words 'you never told me he was that fucking good'. Someone commented that Clapton was a great guitar player but that Hendrix was a 'force of nature'.

After some scrambling initiations, a friend and I started to rock climb with little skill but plenty of enthusiasm on Ayrshire and Galloway crags. We just climbed what took our fancy with no concept of the naming and recording ritual that goes with new routing. In retrospect, it was the purest form of exploration: a fun and ego-free baptism.

In 1968, after a wet weekend on the Cobbler and a midge plagued week on Skye, I decided to check out Arran. On my first visit I soloed a number of routes, including *Sou'wester Slabs*, and fell in love with the island. In March 1969, Jimmy Dykes and I climbed *South Ridge Direct* on the Rosa Pinnacle (kicking steps up a snowfield to the foot of the Layback Crack!). Returning over the ridges to Brodick the fine profile of the Full Meed Tower caught my eye.

In September 1969, after a long hot summer surveying in the Cairngorms, I returned to Arran with Jimmy and climbed the front face of the Full Meed Tower. The start of the first pitch presented the classic Arran challenge of crumbly granite and vegetation, which I aided with a few pegs, but thereafter the climbing was on solid rock in splendid situations. The belays were just as fine as the climbing; the first one on a small rock ledge on the very edge of the tower, the second in a 'sentry box' slot on the face. Wearing clumsy boots, carrying an awkward sack and equipped with a limited rack, I found the climbing quite gripping but the high that it delivered more than sufficient reward.

Jimmy shared my enthusiasm for Hendrix so we named our route *Voodoo Chile* ('Chile' being an alternative spelling of 'Child'), a side-A track from the much acclaimed 1968 double album Electric Ladyland (which had, what was then regarded as, a scandalous album sleeve depicting nineteen naked women). We graded *Voodoo Chile*, VS, the highest available grade in Scotland at the time.

Full Meed Tower: Voodoo Chile takes the pillar half in shadow slanting towards the centre of the picture. Photo: Graham Little.

In 1970 Eric Clapton bought Hendrix a left-handed Stratocaster as a present but it was never to be delivered. Jimmy Hendrix died in September 1970, aged 27, from barbiturate-related asphyxia. As with climbers who die young, there was the inevitable speculation as to just what heights Hendrix would have achieved had he lived.

Many climbing (and musical) partnerships seem to have a natural 'end by date'. However, a premature ending becomes a double loss. Firstly we grieve over the lost one and then grieve again over the lost relationship that, at its best, was or could have been so much more than the sum of the parts. And yet there is a strange irony here: friends who die young stay friends for ever; we never have to experience that gradual decay or the harsh words and actions of an abrupt ending.

I repeated *Voodoo Chile* in 1979 with my brother Rob, reducing the aid points to four, but it was a dull day with a heavy sky and lacked the magic and innocence of the first ascent. In 1993, the route was free climbed by Robin McAllister and Mike Reed at a modern grade of E2 5c.

Moderating my addiction to winter climbing was a pragmatic response to changing professional and family commitments but I decided to stop completely in 2003 after having a serious fall whilst soloing a new route. In a similar vein, my last high mountain expedition was to the Indian Himalaya in 2007 – as well as a drop off in high altitude performance, I sensed that my luck was running out. My climbing energy and enthusiasm were then re-directed into rock climbing and in particular new routing, with a strong focus on Islay, and occasional trips to Morocco and the Balkans.

The desire to climb *Voodoo Chile* a third time came to me out of nowhere in December 2017 during an icy walk on the Border hills but it was obvious that I should wait until 2019. To really appreciate five full decades of passing time would require patience!

I had planned to repeat the route with Carl Schaschke but a misunderstanding over dates resulted in a last minute call to Geoff Cohen to see if he was game for a quick dash to Arran on 21 June. I'd first climbed with Geoff in March 2019, enjoying nine days of warm Moroccan rock.

Nostalgia and anticipation are in the air as Geoff and I cross the Firth of Clyde, talking of past trips and planning new ones. Age and Innocence was the last new route we climbed together in Morocco and it seemed to summarise aptly our entry into the eighth decade of life. We had been around long enough to know better, yet still pursued a child-like delight in risk and adventure.

The weather forecast promised a dry and sunny afternoon but Arran has different plans. Standing below the initial pitch, with rain and grot dribbling down the crumbling, vegetated corner, I have an abrupt reality check. Even in dry weather this is never going to be enjoyable climbing. Today it is madness.

Reassuring Geoff that the upper pitches are on superb clean rock, I move round the corner and launch up *Full Meed Chimney* with the intention of gaining the top of the first pitch of *Voodoo Chile* by traversing right from the chimney. Following much messing about on rock and steep grass (that seems much harder than the grade) we gain the platform on the edge of the tower.

After a few moves upwards, pitch two involves a right traverse using a combination of slime-oozing underclings and palming damp breaks until unstable greenery provides a tenuous pull up into the sentry box belay. My memory of this belay is of a perfect, clean-cut, granite slot. The reality is a dank, mossy cave roofed by two dubiously jammed blocks.

Pitch three gives a hard start and as Geoff braces one foot against the jammed blocks, a large chunk breaks off and grazes my arm on its way down. I reassure him that, despite the blood, the damage is superficial. After the move right from the inset block Geoff spends what seems an age figuring out how to climb the crux chimney-crack as I grow colder and colder in my damp and dingy recess. Eventually he cracks it (leaving some skin behind) and carries on up the chimney line, going over rather than under the big chockstone, to a ledge at the top of the difficulties.

The sun's warm caress welcomes me as I clamber over big blocks to the top of the tower. Clouds roll away revealing the island's fine peaks and ridges in sharp relief. We are both well bloodied and liberally smeared in that black gunge that the nooks and chimneys of Arran specialise in producing. I apologise to Geoff for putting him through such an ordeal,

The author relaxing after the climb. Photo: Geoff Cohen.

claiming, in my defence, a double dose of false memory syndrome. 'I really enjoyed it.' Geoff replies. 'You must be the only person who's climbed (or will ever climb) this route three times', he adds wryly. As we pack the gear, we talk fondly of lost friends, the process of ageing and the pleasure of being in the mountains.

In the still of the evening, we traverse the ridge over Beinn Nuis occasionally glancing back at our tower. Nursing aching knees, the long descent to Brodick is rewarded with a much needed pint of Arran Blonde at the Ormidale Bar.

Boarding the last ferry, we re-cross the Firth in the dimming light of the longest day. It has been a full-on experience: a great line, if not a great climb, a test of our minds and bodies and, for me, laying to rest the ghost of nostalgia.

The final track on side-D of Electric Ladyland is 'Voodoo Chile (slight return)' and the lyrics include:

> *If I don't meet you no more in this world*
> *Then I'll meet you in the next one*
> *And don't be late, don't be late*

The soundtrack of my early life lives on and the 'return' was indeed slight. As for other worlds, I'm keeping an open mind. Whatever lies in wait, I'm hoping to be (unusually) late, hanging on in this one for another decade or two; just savouring the pleasures of islands, rock and music.

Full Meed Tower on the ridge of Beinn Tarsuinn. Photo: Geoff Cohen.

NOTES:

Voodoo Chile, as it was originally climbed, is a striking line but doesn't warrant any stars (it is given two stars in the current guidebook). The first pitch is probably best avoided.

Voodoo Chile (slight return) 90m E1 (perhaps HVS when bone dry.)

1) 25m 4c Climb *Full Meed Chimney* until moves right give access to the platform on the edge of the tower

2) 15m 5a Climb up to twin roofs, traverse right between them, then move up to a sentry box belay.

3) 35m 5b Quit the sentry box on the left and climb to an inset block. Move right and climb an off-width chimney-crack (crux) then the continuation chimney-line above to easier ground.

4) 15m Scramble over blocks to the top of the tower.

SCOTLAND'S LANDSCAPE
Our National Scenic Areas at 40

By Bob Reid

*(The author reflects upon our Scottish landscape protection –
National Scenic Areas – in the year of their 40th anniversary. He also
focuses upon the role W.H. Murray played in their origins.)*

LANDSCAPES ARE BACK on our screens again: pixelated, granular, inspiring. They really are everywhere. Social media is cluttered with images culled from the glorious landscape of Scotland. It seems we've all become budding Ansel Adamses. Although no subtle monochrome here. Colour saturation set to maximum, to amplify blues and browns to levels of intensity rarely seen in nature. What would Bill Murray have given for this level of exposure when campaigning to protect our mountain landscapes in post war Scotland?

This thought follows me as I take my daily exercise – in this time of Covid-19 cycling through Grassic Gibbon's Mearns. No yellow broom yet. This has been a winter like no other in living memory. The Aberdeenshire landscape can be as cruel as its underlying grey granite. 'This is the East coast with winter written into its constitution', wrote north east poet George Bruce ('Praising Aberdeenshire Farmers', in *Poetry of North East Scotland*, Alison, J. (ed.) 1976). It is a cruelty spelt out in the new reality of 'social distancing'. The daily ritual of a walk in the park, let alone climbing Tower Ridge should never be taken for granted. Modern technology can broadcast images of the North Face of Ben Nevis in real time, all wedding-cake, sugar-coated, ice climbing perfection. Yet there's nothing this technology can do it seems, against this Covid-19 virus, which would allow us to climb into our landscapes any time soon.

The parallels to the time when Bill Murray was a prisoner of war in Italy, in Czechoslovakia and then in Germany may feel stretched, but there are parallels none the less. Denied access to the hills Murray loved, he wrote about their beauty and their impact upon the human condition. Yet *Mountaineering in Scotland* was published in 1947 with hardly a mention of the circumstances in which it was written. Others have covered this backdrop in much greater depth, not least Bill Murray himself in his autobiography *The Evidence of Things Not Seen*, 2002 (see also *The Sunlit Summit*, Lloyd-Jones, R. 2013). However, it is hard to separate the circumstances, from the deeply philosophical themes Murray explored. If ever there was word written about mountaineering that has depth and conviction, it remains the prose that Bill Murray scribbled on toilet paper in a prisoner of war camp. It was his preoccupation with spirit and landscape that led to a post war role that might arguably be seen as his greatest legacy. I speak of the protection of the landscape of Scotland.

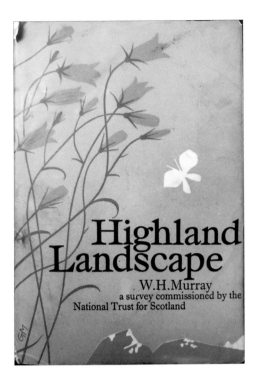

The cover of WH Murray's seminal survey published in 1962.
Photo: Bob Reid.

When we look back on 2020 with the hindsight this particular year should invoke, we will inevitably and sadly remember the circumstances of disease and death. However, 2020 also marks the 40th anniversary of our National Scenic Areas [NSAs] in Scotland. NSAs that protect our forty most precious landscapes; an oft forgotten defining characteristic of our nationhood and psyche: mountain and river, island and loch.

I would suggest it is not only a significant year for landscape and mountain protection in Scotland, but also for Scottish Mountaineering Club history as well. Because it was the culmination of a campaign commenced by Bill Murray, Percy Unna and many other club members immediately after the war, that finally found its way onto the statute book forty years ago. NSAs are not just a planning designation, more a conviction that our mountains are important and worthy of protection. Murray said, 'Mountaineering is important, the mountains even more so'.

When we commemorate, perhaps we should also reflect. Have NSAs had any real effect? Have Murray's efforts been in vain? It is also hard to ignore the fact that the origins of NSAs were partly about a reticence to have National Parks in Scotland. The 1945 Ramsay Committee actually recommended eight National Parks in Scotland and the enactment of the 1949 National Parks Act in England must have looked tempting from north of the border.

The origins of NSAs actually date back many years before they came

The north facing cliffs of Ben Alder and the conical Lancet Edge frame the Bealach Dubh and its burn. Ben Alder Forest was meant by Murray to be included in the National Scenic Areas but never was. Photo: Bob Reid.

into effect. To discussions and writings in wartime prison camps, in committee rooms in the 1950s and in the early1960's surveys. It was largely because of the authority Bill Murray had gained through his writings that the National Trust for Scotland commissioned him to carry out a survey of Scotland's landscape. He travelled far and wide across Scotland, walking, camping and visiting most of our core mountain areas. The result was a report called '*Highland Landscape – a survey commissioned by the National Trust for Scotland. 1962*'. It was published as a small but beautiful, hardback book. It was only illustrated with charming, hand drawn maps. Bill Murray's prose served to qualify his selections. Famously he chose to use 'beauty' as the defining characteristic which would justify inclusion in a list of areas worthy of protection. 'With bracing boldness, [Murray] elected 'beauty' as the chief principle of evaluation, defining it as 'the perfect expression of that ideal form to which everything of its kind approaches' – hardly the kind of language that would survive the crushing-machine of contemporary planning policy' wrote Robert Macfarlane in the foreword to *The Sunlit Summit* [ibid]. I have to say on the basis of forty years of planning practice, there is much to agree with in this statement. In 1962, the threats were from hydro electricity, large scale afforestation, roads and power lines. Perhaps little has changed.

It took until the mid-1970s for work properly to commence on Scotland's alternative form of protection to National Parks. Famously the birches and the shining loch, it soars to the sky, a sharp and perfect cone. Loch Tummel is best seen from the Queen's View on the north shore near its east end. Its far-stretching waters are framed by forested capes and grassy points, and by the tree-tops of the nearer wood. Far beyond are the bare moors of Rannoch and Schichallion. The River Tummel appears to best advantage at the Linn of Tummel, near its confluence with the Garry. Although of small height, the falls are justly renowned. They burst in rapids and plunge through wide-set rocks into the still waters of Loch Faskally below. Pinewoods flank the scene, and larch, with a sprinkling of birch. One of the best points from which to survey the whole length of the Tummel Valley is the hill of Craigower, 1300 feet, which belongs to the National Trust for Scotland.

SURVEY NO.17

The Range of Ben Alder

INVERNESS-SHIRE. One inch O.S. Sheets 36, 37, 47 & 48. Area 90 square miles. The range includes the two deer forests of Ardverikie and Benalder, and Loch Ossian of Corrour Forest. They lie between Lochs Laggan and Ericht in Badenoch.

BOUNDS. The region defined is bounded on the north by Loch Laggan; on the east by the River Pattack to Loch Pattack, whence a line is drawn east to Benalder Lodge and south-west down the middle of Loch Ericht to Alder Bay; on the south by a line up the Alder burn to Bealach Cumhann, thence south-west through Meall na Lice, 1912 feet, to the railway at Corrour; on the west by a straight line from Corrour to the foot of Loch Laggan at Moy Lodge.

ACCESS. From the north by road to the head of Loch Laggan; from the east by rail or road to Dalwhinnie; from the south by road to Loch Rannoch, thence on foot up the River Ericht; from the west by rail to Corrour. Private roads lead into the interior from Dalwhinnie, Kinloch Laggan, and Corrour.

¶ From south to north through the region stretches the Ben Alder range, a magnificent chain of eight mountains, 17 miles long and linked by high bealachs. Ben Alder, 3757 feet, stands at the south end above Loch Ericht. Its north and east faces are caverned by great corries. From these corries and their several lochs, rivers drain north-east to Loch Pattack, and thence to Loch Laggan.

58

The southern part, named Benalder Forest, is entirely deer forest, almost treeless save for scattered capes at the Lodge and Loch Pattack. The old forest on the north shore of Loch Ericht has been felled. The Forestry Commission are now operating there. The loch has long since been dammed at the south extremity and a wide scar marks the shore. The loch has good fishing.

The northern part, named Ardverikie Forest, is most beautifully wooded along the whole length of Loch Laggan, and around the foot of Lochan na h-Earba which runs parallel to Loch Laggan in a narrow fold of the hills. The old forest along the shores of Lochan na h-Earba has been felled. The finest view of this Forest is to be had from the road towards the upper end of Loch Laggan. Ardverikie House is seen from there standing at the water's edge amid a well-grown wood. Close behind rise the pointed mountains of Binnein Shios and Binnein Shuas whose craggy flanks, clothed in pinewoods, are most like the Canadian Rockies. The unusual beauty of Ardverikie won the admiration of Queen Victoria, who considered its purchase.

The western part falls within Corrour Forest, and comprises Lochs Ossian and Guilbinn, the rivers that feed the latter, and the mountains of Beinn na Lap and Beinn Eibhinn, 3611 feet. This western sector has been included entirely for the sake of Loch

59

'...the Ben Alder range, a magnificent chain of eight mountains...Ardverikie Forest...most beautifully wooded along the whole length of Loch Laggan...' W.H. Murray. Why has it never been a National Scenic Area? Photo: Bob Reid.

Countryside Commission (both Bill Murray and Donald Bennet were commissioners) concluded 'we do not recommend that national parks in the internationally accepted sense are necessary to conserve landscape as such in Scotland' [A Park System for Scotland, Countryside Commission for Scotland (CCS), 1974]. Officialdom continued: 'there is a school of thought that the mere act of designation without the most stringent control policies effecting development and visitor use contains the seed of destruction of the very resource it has sought to protect.' Indeed.

Nevertheless, with Murray and Bennet still involved, by 1978 the CCS decided that certain areas which contained landscapes of 'unsurpassed attractiveness' should be conserved as part of our national heritage. CCS duly published a report called 'Scotland's Scenic Heritage' defining 40 NSAs in Scotland. With due ceremony in September 1980, the Scottish Development Department finally published Circular 20/1980 bringing the protection of forty Scottish National Scenic Areas into effect.

1980 was also an important year for the author, as I qualified as a town planner at Liverpool University and chose to follow the path well-trodden (by G.G. Macphee among others) and head north to the Ben. It wasn't so many years later that this young planner, by then working for the former Grampian Regional Council dared to challenge Bill Murray and ask why he hadn't included parts of Scotland's North East coast for protection, such as Pennan and Gardenstoun (made famous in *Local Hero*), the Bullers of Buchan (mentioned by Samuel Johnson), or Dunnottar (of Civil War fame and surrogate Elsinore for *Hamlet*). The admonishment I received has stuck with me ever since; 'but Bob, I never went there'.

Bill Murray had been commissioned only to look at the mountains by the NTS and not at the coast or islands at all. The CCS stretched the definition to include islands and even to include the Borders. So began something of a landscape protection campaign (of sorts) that has continued to the present day. It was well within Grampian Regional Council's role in the1990s to seek the designation of parts of its coast as National Scenic Areas. However, unbeknown to many at the time, the ability to amend or designate new NSAs had accidentally (we are told by way of explanation) been deleted from the 1991 legislation which merged Nature Conservancy Scotland and CCS to become Scottish Natural Heritage [SNH]. It took concerted action by many to enact revisions to NSA legislation through the 2006 Planning (Scotland) Act – once more enabling variation and new NSAs. Nevertheless, there were still legal flaws.

The spread of windfarms across Scotland's windy countryside is both awesome and devastating. When I started work in Grampian in 1993 there were only two turbines in Scotland. One was Maitland Mackie's ice cream factory in Aberdeenshire and the other was the test turbine on Orkney. Today we have in excess of 4000 turbines across the country and the ability to power the whole nation on wind alone. We even have turbines in the sea off our coast. A confession: I have approved many, refused some and continue to oppose a few. Renewable energy is important. Yet, we now see the sickening phenomenon of millions of pounds paid to windfarm owners not to produce electricity because there's too much electricity for the national grid to carry south; so-called 'constraint payments'. Against this backdrop I worked on a legal challenge to try to stop a windfarm which was all-but climbing the slopes of Ben Klibreck. The legal challenge was against the Scottish Government, so the chances of success were slim and needless to say it failed.[1] Nevertheless, Lord Boyd of Duncansby, in his 2017 decision, shone a light on the inadequacy of certain words in the legislation which made any protection provided by NSAs equivocal at best. So in 2019 today's landscape protection stalwarts, carrying on the traditions of Bill Murray, Adam Watson, Bob Aitken, *et al* took this story forward once again, working with sympathetic MSPs, to get the Planning (Scotland) Act 2019 amended and finally create a statutory duty on local government 'to preserve and enhance' our NSAs. This gave them equivalence, at long last, to our urban conservation areas in terms of the letter of the law. Already positive decisions are being made that reflect that change.

As part of the work to oppose the Klibreck windfarm, research was also

---

[1] See Bob Reid, 'I Fought the Law and the Law Won', *SMCJ* 46/209 (2018), pp.208–9 (Ed.)

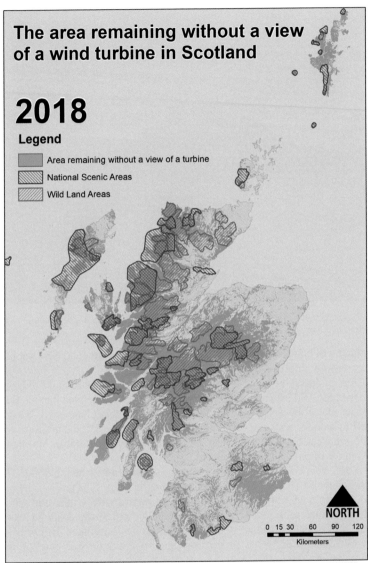

The area remaining without a view of a wind turbine in Scotland

2018

Legend

- Area remaining without a view of a turbine
- National Scenic Areas
- Wild Land Areas

NORTH

0 15 30 60 90 120
Kilometers

Mapping and amalysis by Wildland Research Institute (2018) © Crown copyright and database rights 2019 Ordnance Survey (100025252)

commissioned by, among others, the John Muir Trust. Dr Steve Carver, Geographer at Leeds University, and previously published in these pages, has done work mapping the visibility of windfarms in the landscape of Scotland. The above diagram shows the impact that our NSAs have had over the last forty years. There is enough of a correlation for Bill Murray to have been pleased. All too evident on the map, however, are the areas

A closer view of Lancet Edge: part of Murray's '...magnificent chain of mountains...' The scenic qualities speak for themselves. Photo: Bob Reid.

which will be the next areas of contention. Our strengthened NSAs could yet play an amplified role.

A conundrum remains for the future which will involve more digging in the past. Bill Murray's *Highland Landscape* recommended that the Ben Alder massif be designated. To this day, this has never happened. We are left to wonder why and challenged once more to search the archives for the answers because I suspect the latter-day NSA imitator, Wildland Areas, will have a limited shelf life.

Forty Years on – have we reasons to be optimistic? Is the job done? My own view is that you can never let these matters rest. This is also why the journal of a Mountaineering Club should record why, where and when these actions took place, lest they are forever lost in the dusty pages of Hansard or Parliamentary Record. They must be illuminated. Bill Murray would have wanted us to do this; and to continue our care of the mountains.

HIGHLAND ENVOI

Before you sleep for good, remember this:

the moss-soft bridge within the dripping wood,
the wild catch of sea air blown on high;

night-climbing up, through ice-storm, to the cornices,
the starlit snow-peak shining in night sky;

the slopes you charged, when young, because you could;
and summer's sunlight on your hills of bliss.

THE VISION

Do not expect it in the green of May.
No cleanness in that growth that parturition
as pure as clean as death.

Nor in the bland and flyblown August sun,
in hot banality upon a balding lawn,
in non-event of sweltering desiccation.

Ignore October's blustering warm winds,
rain-rotted fruit let clog the orchard paths;
it brings no insight eaten.

But when the bloodline's thin as mercury
when ice flowers white on wood and stars the stream
then head up through the beeswarm of the snow
then climb the Hill of Vision.

Sophie-Grace Chappell

TAKING THE EASY WAY?

By Mike Jacob

... the fiends that plague thee thus

I AWAKE FULL OF gloom, in the small hours before sunrise. I have no choice but to lie there, stilled by the presence of the malevolent voices in my head as they whisper to me of failure and underachievement. My dawn chorus is a muttering of contemptuous jeers and taunts, of waste and colourless monotony. These are devils' thoughts. Another part of me tries, unconvincingly, to parry but, like a buzzing cloud of black flies, they part and bide their pestering time. Some will say that this is all part of the ageing process and a consequence of declining hormone levels. Perhaps. My only weapons are memories of the good times and, in an illogical sequence, I am walking with Phil Gribbon from Inchnadamph towards Ben More Assynt.

I try hard to concentrate, to re-create the day in my imagination. On the leisurely, ambling approach we skirt Dubh Loch Mor, sheltered from the wind as we kick steps in the wet snow up this steep western flank of the mountain ... and then the mental adjustment required as the weather turns unexpectedly from scudding clouds, sunshine and April showers into a full-blown blizzard on the narrow south-east ridge. Matters turn abruptly from relaxed to serious. We grope for protective clothing in our sacs as

Dubh Loch Mor under the South-East Ridge of Ben More Assynt. Photo: Tom Prentice.

The south-east ridge of Ben More Assynt from the Glen Cassley side.
Photo: Grahame Nicoll.

the wind roars up the hidden corrie to our right and then we head northwards. I sidle on a snow-plastered slab over a murky drop ... slip ... heart in mouth ... held by an ice-axe pick in a shallow crack ... phew. It becomes apparent that this is no passing shower as we choose a way over and round looming rock barriers.

We are barely aware of each other in the squally gloom, leaning this way and that in silent, buffeted accord until eventually the summit cairn appears. This is followed by another staggering struggle over ankle-twisting stones to reach Conival. Accurate navigation is impossible as the snow turns to penetrating sleet; the map a desperately flapping fish, demonic toggles on my hood trying to whip my eyes out as I concentrate on the iced-up compass in my frozen mitt, relying more and more on gut instinct. Should we alter course and run with the wind at our backs although that tactic will mean a wearisome detour? No, stick with it, stick with it, we decide.

The forces of Nature are tangible and can be counted; they can be battled against until victory is won or lost but, as we gradually lose height, the nature of the fight alters. The sleet changes and becomes marrow-chilling rain, relentlessly invading waterproof shells, violating jealously preserved havens of dryness ... and still it comes down, not in drops but like strands of wire although at least we are sheltered from the all-powerful wind. There's no escaping, it is hopeless to resist; stoically, it has to be tolerated, just like this insidious murmuring which trickles

A perfect day on Arran. The South Ridge of Cir Mhòr. Photo: Tom Prentice.

> *Through caverns measureless to man*
> *Down to a sunless sea.*

But behold! A ramshackle wooden shed with ancient agricultural implements and a floor of dry sheep-dung. So we pause, hunting in our sopping sacs for emergency rations, until we shiver uncontrollably and have no choice but to continue. I am brought, metaphorically, to my knees and I want to give in ... The refuge of sleep has deserted me. As the night slowly fades I listen for the songbirds' joy of a new day but all I hear are the mocking croaks of the corbies, gathered in the skeletal boughs of a wintry ash tree, twigs curled against the half-light like beckoning bony fingers.

Sunlight percolates through the curtains which slowly turn orange, like the closely-woven cotton fabric of my old Vango Force-Ten tent. Ali's hand reaches out of his sleeping bag, followed by a strong, tanned forearm, and the zips of the door are opened to reveal the golden glow of a dry Arran rock-face. It is going to be a perfect climbing day of well-oiled sinuous movement and an easy fitness that could eat up any number of rock-miles. If I tell you that there wasn't a midge in sight as we balanced from diamantine crystal to mica blade and as the world held its breath then you'll know yourself that this was one of those rare Spring days of warm climbing on a magical staircase to heaven. But now it all seems so distant, so remote that I have to question if it ever really happened?

I could have been at the CIC hut or a far-flung bothy. I had the chances

'...a magnetic, bleak winter day...' on the hills above New Abbey in Galloway.
Photo: Mike Jacob.

to go but I couldn't raise the enthusiasm, finding pathetic excuses; now salt is about to be rubbed in my wounds as I imagine others reaping the mountain rewards that I have helplessly abandoned. So I set out, belatedly, to walk up a nearby hill by the most convoluted route that I can contrive and thus find myself struggling clumsily through unimaginably-awkward ground. The heather and bog myrtle, ungrazed for generations, are waist high and conceal cleughs and gulches of glutinous peat and slimy moss. A damaged, arthritic joint starts its grinding, whining ache and I've not even travelled a couple of miles.

It's a magnetic, bleak winter day of scudding grey cloud and shafts of light, plantations of bronze larch and a distant silver Solway textured by the darker, sandy shallows of the ebbing tide. In the far distance, barely visible in the haze, are the snow-capped Lakeland fells, a captivating world away. A solitary mute-swan powers purposefully home towards its reed-fringed loch; although the bird is silent its rhythmic wingbeat drummed a favourite Dylan song …

> *Where black is the colour and none is the number*
> *And I'll tell it and think it and speak it and breathe it*
> *And reflect it from the mountains …*

There's a heavy squall of rain heading my way like a galleon in the sky, full-square before the wind. I attempt to race it to the triangulation-point but am reminded by my breathlessness that I have another, more-intractable problem. Just yards from the top, a wee black dog appears

Criffel with snowy Lakeland Fells in the distance. Photo: Mike Jacob.

from the overworked path on the other side of the hill, to be followed by a middle-aged woman in smart crimson Gore-Tex mountainwear. I groan, my desire for solitude is about to be thwarted by trite pleasantries. She scrutinises my scruffy attire and comments that I must have reached the top by, oh, the easy way and I guess from her manner that she's the bossy matriarch of some dog-training group or somesuch. I keep quiet but want to remark that

> *Her jacket is red and her breeches are blue,*
> *And there is a hole where the tail comes through.*

For the first time that day I smile inside and cannot restrain a chuckle. She takes a couple of wary steps away as the rain arrives and asks where I'm going next. I wave my hand vaguely through all the points of the compass as she prepares to return down her hard way. I head off through the heathery undergrowth towards the top of some small crags where a pair of peregrine falcons nest. Somewhere, in my own down, this indifferent encounter has triggered an emotional reaction. In the gathering gloom I stumble heavily over a tussock and automatically look over my shoulder. Fortunately, she is long gone ...

> *And the Devil did grin, for his darling sin*
> *Is pride that apes humility.*

*

And that's where my story, for what it's worth, would have ended, somewhere in the dusk above the wooded loch and the forestry carpark where they found his car. It was to be an absolutely vile night of torrential rain and gales which blew down massive trees, demolished power-lines and was unabated the following flooded day. Did he, a doctor with a young family, after leaving his surgery as normal on that Tuesday evening, choose his time because of the imminent storm?

He made one final call before removing the SIM card from his mobile phone and placing it in the glove compartment. Decision made, easy, the way clear. To be honest, the decision was probably made days before. But easy? There is no easy way or hard way. There's just the only way. Then he started his grim walk into the darkness.

I've now removed most of the fluttering blue and white strips which delineated search areas on the hillside and amongst the conifers. They had become yet more superfluous plastic litter; intrusive reminders of a tragedy. I had assumed that he took a large overdose, washed down with alcohol, and set off up the hill and onto the moors or swam out into the suffocating embrace of the waters of the loch, eventually to succumb to the numbing effects of the drugs. It took over a week to find his body. He died somewhere not far from my home and where I slept through his pain, oblivious. I never met him, I didn't know him – but he has unwittingly put my own dejection into perspective.

Note: quotations taken from the works of Samuel Taylor Coleridge (1772–1834) unless otherwise stated.

HEROICS

By Geoff Cohen

I HAVE ALWAYS FELT a bit uncomfortable when people talk about courage in climbing. Probably we all have known times when only a supreme effort of self-control and the marshalling of all our physical and mental resources has saved us from falling off, or enabled us to escape an appalling blizzard. And these are perhaps the achievements we treasure most, when somehow one part of the self kept it all together while another part of the mind was desperately on the edge of panic in the face of an apparently impossible situation. Yet to me this kind of courage, a mental mastery over our own responses to rock or mountain or weather, is secondary to the courage required to face up to danger from other people, to remain steadfast, fair and optimistic in the face of anger, hatred or despair. That kind of courage may be needed in a crisis in any walk of life but is rarely called on in mountaineering.

Somewhere in *Mountaineering in Scotland* Bill Murray comments on how many unsung heroics must have taken place high on mountains, unwitnessed by any save a climbing partner. This thought has always appealed to me, the more so since the advent of a somewhat narcissistic climbing culture. Yet I am also conscious of a paradox at the heart of Bill Murray's observation. For by its very nature the first kind of courage is only truly known to the individual concerned. As a climbing second we may marvel at our leader's success on some desperate pitch that we could never have got up; but if as a leader we are complimented on our success we may feel that actually the heroics being praised required less true courage (self-control) from us than some other climb where we had to dig far deeper into our reserves than our second realised. Be this as it may I want to pay tribute to a few 'heroics' by some of my closest climbing friends, events that I feel grateful to have had a part in.

September 1965, Thirlmere Eliminate

I was just 18 and had been climbing for a couple of years. Gordon Macnair, a little older, had already completed his first year at university and I was much in awe of the climbs he had achieved. I found the first two pitches of our climb hard enough and was belayed to some rather uninspiring pegs on a sloping ledge below the final pitch when the downpour really started. This crux pitch has an overhanging start and continues up a steep corner. Within a short while it was literally streaming with water. Gordon made several attempts to surmount the overhang, and I even tried myself, though I was in no way a mature enough climber to cope with what lay above. The torrents continued but Gordon persisted and finally got himself above the first few moves. The climbing remains very sustained for 30 or 40 feet and we were still in the age when protection consisted of line slings and the odd hexagonal nut found by

Gordon Macnair on Thirlmere Eliminate, a more recent ascent, in rather better conditions. Photo: Geoff Cohen.

the roadside – none of which had any chance of being used here.

How Gordon managed to stay composed and adhere to the rock I will never know. It must have required not only the strength of youth but also a ferocious concentration of will and discipline to force himself to stay cool, to keep bridging and to have faith that his PAs would not slip on the slimy ribs and knobbles that constituted the only footholds. I stood below in my army surplus combat jacket which acted like a sponge and was now so sodden that the pockets bulged with water and when squeezed emitted goodly spouts like a generous tap. I shivered and watched in trepidation, willing him to reach what appeared to be a good spike on the right wall about two-thirds of the way up. When he got there it wasn't, of course, as good as expected, but provided a brief respite before he continued with grim determination to the top. Although in later years we went on to do other perhaps equally hard climbs in the wet, this was undoubtedly one of the finest leading efforts I ever witnessed. The standard of climb we were attempting was pretty much unknown territory for me, and to a lesser extent for Gordon. The strength of character he displayed in getting up it with virtually no protection in the foulest of conditions was a great example of what a disciplined will could achieve.

July 1971, Gavarnie

The first climbing day of a long awaited holiday has a special magic. You have made your preparations, enjoyed or suffered a long journey, established your camp and finally you wake up to a new morning and are ready to climb. The mountains are there, inviting you up, full of secrets to be unravelled and offering you the opportunity to re-establish your faith and joy in the life that is found upon them.

It was on such a morning that Rob Archbold and I found ourselves in the Cirque de Gavarnie in the heart of the Pyrenees. All around were noisy waterfalls cascading down huge limestone cliffs set in tiers above a verdant corrie. We had done no research and had little idea what the area had to offer as we thumbed our way through a newly acquired French

Mur de la Cascade: the route described goes by the pillar left of the double waterfall. The trouble occurred on the obvious ledge one pitch from the top where Rob and Geoff went under the waterfall to the right and up the muddy chimney. Nowadays the recommended route is by a long traverse along the ledge to the left. Photo: Geoff Cohen.

guidebook. As a starter we selected a route of Difficile standard, about 750 feet long, that took a clean attractive pillar on rock that looked sound and dry. The guidebook seemed to recommend 'une très belle escalade'. The approach was short and we ambled pleasantly up six or eight pitches with no especial difficulty till we reached a lunching ledge about 150 feet below the top. Here we realised that a large waterfall was just above to our right and immediately ahead was a bulging rotten wall with no features. Looking again at the guidebook I made an unwelcome discovery. The preamble to the description had been quite complimentary about the climb, but I had neglected to turn the page! Overleaf was a final paragraph. Up to the present time, it said, no-one had succeeded in climbing the direct finish up the rotten wall. The alternative suggested was to traverse behind the waterfall on a ledge and climb 'une abominable fissure mouillée et boueuse'. We knew not the meaning of 'boueuse' (muddy) but we were soon to be enlightened!

Having tried and failed to make headway on the direct finish we ran the gauntlet of the waterfall, getting a thorough shower, and emerged, still under a heavy spattering of drops, at the base of a repulsive, slimy, yellow, wet chimney. It was Rob's lead (I having footered pointlessly on the unfinished direct), and as I shivered on my uncomfortable stance he disappeared up the said loathsome fissure. I waited and waited till, finally, cold and numb I got the call to follow. It is hard to estimate the difficulty, especially after so many years, and no clear memory of the moves remains. But what does remain is a powerful impression of a challenging pitch which must have required real courage to lead each move. Advancing into hideous rotten rock with more or less steady spouts of water drenching you is bad enough; but it was compounded here by the awkwardness of the rucksack in a constricted chimney and by the awesome friction of wet moleskin breeches, a delight unknown to younger climbers. Somehow the pitch was breached, and followed by a further traverse back across the cascades and up into grassy terraces. It was still light when we reached the top, but we had yet to find our way down. A long series of explorations of the cliffs was required before we finally reached the tourist path descending from the Brèche de Roland, and it was well after dark when we stumbled back to our tent. Like so many first days of a climbing holiday it had been a bit longer than intended. But for Rob's steadfastness in the abominable chimney I felt I might still have been standing there, by now entirely saturated if not dissolved!

April 1980, The Pilgun Gad

Dave Broadhead and I had spent four weeks alone on the Khatling glacier in Tehri Garhwal, engaged in a variety of explorations and minor ascents. Our walk-in to the glacier had been up the beautiful Bhillangana Valley, but for our return we decided to cross a col and head westwards to the Uttarkashi – Gangotri road. We had ridiculously heavy sacks: with base camp tent and cooking equipment, clothing and climbing gear for ascents

The Pilgun Gad.
Photo: Geoff Cohen.

up to 21,000 feet, and numerous other useful paraphernalia, accumulated during several months in India, that we were loath to leave behind. The one thing we had little of was food, as we chose to abandon as much as possible at base camp (the shepherds would use it later in the season).

Our crossing via the Shastru Tal col involved three days of pretty heavy work, climbing through thousands of feet of forest on minimal tracks, wending onward over high grassy ridges and easy snowfields, then descending an open rocky valley into thick forest again. It was on the fourth day, (when we had anticipated reaching villages), that we realised we were pretty well lost. That is to say, we knew where we were, in the Pilgun Gad, but could find no semblance of a path and were confronted by miles of thick forest dropping down steep hillsides into a busy Himalayan torrent. Progress was painfully slow; we probably spent ten or more hours covering no more than two or three miles that day, thanks to the roughness of the terrain and the wretched encumbrances on our backs. After a night spent in a tiny bay by the water's edge, our readily edible food was down to a few polo mints (the last of a blessed food parcel Dave had received from Mungo Ross some months earlier). A view of big crags further down the gorge convinced us that, like it or not, our only alternative was to lug ourselves and our sacks up perhaps 4000 feet of steep forested hillside to reach a ridge above the trees and from there, hopefully, find a way down.

Logic is one thing, but finding the inner determination to push interminably up pathless forest carrying a huge sack while not really knowing whether the effort would pay off, is another. Dave, in his quiet way, was the inspiration to continue. I'm not sure how I would have found the willpower to persevere had he not pushed on steadily. It was crucial really not to waste our meagre remaining resources of energy on contouring the craggy hillsides. We had no choice but to climb up, yet I wonder if I would have stuck single-mindedly to the uphill line of greatest effort had it not been for Dave's example. Finally we emerged out of the trees onto a grassy ridge but had only followed it a short way before it plunged downwards into the forest again. Dismayed we were forced to career down, in the right general direction, but not knowing if we should meet with steep crags barring the way. The stars were with us and weaving down leaf beds and around craglets we descended all the way back to the Pilgun river where we could at least make ourselves a drink, there being apparently no side streams in the forests. After another bivvy we reached a village late the next day, and the main Uttarkashi road on the following day. I shall always be grateful to Dave for his staunchness on this most memorable trek.

July 1991, Chamonix

Hamish Irvine and I had risen early and after a long wait for the telepherique to Plan de l'Aiguille had walked over to the Nantillons Glacier to climb the Cordier Pillar on the Aiguille de Charmoz. Leaving our rucksacks, boots and axes on the snow at the foot of the route we donned rock boots and started up, still in cold shadow. The first few pitches were damp and steep but we climbed steadily through the day, maybe 15 to 20 pitches, passing a memorable off-width crack at two-thirds height. It was quite late in the afternoon when we completed the climb and breasted the east ridge of the Charmoz. Keen to reach the summit we traversed along quite difficult and exposed rock for a fair way. Eventually, at the striking gendarme known as Baton Wicks we realised there was no time to go farther, and so we retraced our steps as rapidly as we could and began abseiling down about 6 p.m.

All went well at first but after some six abseils we made a slightly poor choice of route and lost precious time. After this mistake abseil points became harder and harder to find in the gathering gloom. It was probably about eight or nine p.m. when, having abseiled one of the steepest and most indirect pitches, and reached a point only three or so pitches from the bottom, the ropes well and truly jammed. We were on a good ledge and though we had no spare clothes we were still quite warm from moving. The thought of prusiking up this steep pitch in the dark was too much for me. I was tired from our long day, and ready, somewhat unrealistically perhaps, to sit out the night on the ledge. Hamish, however, was full of buoyant spirits and prepared to launch himself up the rope. The start of the pitch being diagonally up a ramp it was obvious that the

Geoff Cohen on belay on pitch 2 of the Cordier Pillar. Photo: Hamish Irvine.

first bit of prusiking would involve an alarming swing, but Hamish took it in his stride and slowly disappeared into the night, leaving me clutching one end of the rope and beginning to shiver as my warmth evaporated.

I could see the lights of Chamonix 6,000 feet below, and while my eyes wandered between that haven of comforts and the dark glacier sensed just a few hundred feet under me, my ears caught the sound of music. My slow brain, attuned to the quiet dark rock all around, revolved idly around the question, who would bring radio or tapes up to a bivvy? Only a long time later did it dawn on me that it was the fourteenth of July, and the sounds I could hear were the distant revelries down in the valley, not the amusement of an invisible pair of climbers close by. After what seemed like an age, but was probably not much more than an hour, a comforting shuffling announced Hamish's reappearance above me (having had to split the abseil). By now it was really black and moonless, and we had foolishly left our torches in our sacks at the bottom. With Hamish staunchly prepared to continue it was a matter of casting about on the rocks by feel to find a suitable abseil point and then gingerly lowering into the murk. One abseil was made thus, then another, at the end of which we thankfully reached the snow, naively thinking our troubles ended. It was about midnight.

In my tired mental state I couldn't quite make out what was wrong, but something didn't seem right as I came off the abseil. Slowly it dawned: with the melting of the snow during the day our boots and sacks, with all their contents (including the precious torches), had fallen into the

On this early pitch of the climb the rucksacks are clearly seen on the dubious bergschrund in the background. Photo: Hamish Irvine.

bergschrund. Without a convenient rock ledge we had just placed them on a snowy platform which must have rested on the corniced lip of the bergschrund. Here again my mental fortitude was lacking – I was just too tired to think what to do – but Hamish, with great generosity and spirit, volunteered to descend into the 'schrund. Fortunately we had not yet pulled the ropes through from the last abseil and there was enough slack to descend, and, even more fortunately, the schrund was not very deep. While I slithered on the snow in my rock boots, toes getting colder and colder, my intrepid partner dug into the snow at the bottom of the schrund with his bare hands and one by one retrieved each of the four precious boots, the rucksacks and the ice-axes. By the time he was up again on the surface it was 2 a.m., and we blundered down the glacier with, as it turned out, only faint light from fading torches.

The night seemed to go on and on; that familiar scenario where having lost time earlier in the day, fatigue and dark make us lose more and more time the later it gets. At some point we lay down on a flattish boulder for a short nap, then roused ourselves, staggered off the snow and got down to Montenvers. Half way down the track we rested outside a little locked auberge, dreaming of hot drinks – by now it was light again. Of a sudden the hearty patron opened the doors and we were welcomed in to meet our dreams. Thus fortified, by 8 a.m. we were trudging into our apartment, another 24-hour Alpine ordeal over! That it had not been a lot longer and colder was entirely thanks to Hamish's indomitable spirit.

A PASSION FOR FLINTY

By Helen G S Forde

Whilst crossing the Minch, I Googled my grandfather. I wanted to check the details of his obituary, printed in the Linlithgow Gazette which read, after the bold headlines, *John Wilson Dougal BSc, Ph.D., chemist, businessman, inventor and geology pioneer*, a small but interesting fact which led to this sea crossing, my first visit to the Outer Hebrides. It involved a monument to his memory that had been erected by the North Lewis islanders after his death in Edinburgh in 1935.

John Wilson Dougal on North Uist, the Isle of Maddy in the background. Photo: Forde Collection.

Throughout my childhood I had heard stories from my mother, Grace, his youngest daughter, about his life, but had never visited the Long Island to try and locate it for myself and indeed find out if it still existed or had succumbed to the elements like many a croft on the windy headlands and peat bogs, and become forgotten boulders among the sweet smelling machair.

A chance discovery which further spurred me on to make this journey was a search in the attic which revealed, to my delight, a foxed copy of a book written or rather put together by a family friend, Alasdair Alpine

Macgregor, himself an author, after my grandfather's death. JWD's intention had been to devote himself to publishing his scientific findings and also to arrange in book form many of his personal experiences during a long and intimate association with the Outer Hebrides. These had been published in various newspapers over a period of years. AA Macgregor quotes in the foreword of the book, entitled *Island Memories,...As far as possible I have left his text unaltered so these chapters are essentially in the form in which the author set them down and I now send them forth with no small sense of affection for a man I knew well and greatly revered.*

I read the book through several times which clarified to me why he should have had a compelling reason to leave his family and business to make the then long and arduous journey from Edinburgh to the Outer Hebrides from c1900 for over thirty years. A brief biography reveals that he was educated at Daniel Stewart's College where he excelled in science and graduated in that faculty at Edinburgh University. In 1907 he founded the Dunedin Chemical Company, a business employing manufacturing and analytical chemists of which he remained in control till the time of his death. The family home was St Ann's Bank House, Edinburgh with his business in the nearby Abbeyhill area. This enterprise prevented him from pursuing his scientific studies as he would have liked but he arranged his work in such a way to enable him to devote some weeks each year to his geological researches in the Hebrides.

There was a family connection in Lewis which may have been of help in providing a base for JWD's geological wanderings on the islands. His wife Emma, my granny, was a school teacher, as was her sister Mary Helen who taught at the Nicholson Institute in Stornoway. Mary married the head teacher of Barabhas (Barvas) school near the NW coast of Lewis. I have no dates for this but as a fairly young woman she fell ill with consumption and died but the Dougal family stayed close to the Smiths. For many years Barvas school house provided a welcome place to stay. Over the years there were expeditions made to the uninhabited islands of North Rona and Sulisgeir. The former expedition, which in 1927 included a landing party of fourteen people who accompanied my grandfather, is recorded with photographs in the Scots Magazine of February 1985 under 'Letters to the Editor', thus provided more evidence of the memorial.

Dear Sir

In 1927 I was one of a party which sailed to North Rona from Stornoway to enable J. Wilson Douglas, a geologist from Edinburgh, to make certain that the vein of flinty-crush which runs down the western edge of the Outer Isles does not touch North Rona. In my collection of photos of the period I find two taken on North Rona at that time of JWD, J. Cunningham of Scalpay who owned and skippered the boat and McFarlane of the Mill, North Tolsa who owned the sheep on the island. I believe that a memorial erected by the boats skipper to JWD still stands on the cliffs near the Butt of Lewis...

My grandfather made preparatory visits to mainland Munros including

JWD on left: a later picture with two men of Lewis.

Photo: Forde Collection.

climbing the Torridon hills amongst others, to study and obtain rock samples. The oldest rock formation was found on Beinn Alligin which is composed of quartz-capped Torridonian sandstone and the ridge of Liathach with its broken quartzite spires – the Fasarinen Pinnacles. During his annual visits to the Outer Hebrides he became closely acquainted with the island's mountains and glens in all weathers, filling his rucksack with samples. Whether coming off the hills of Uig or Harris, either Mealisbhal, with its views of St Kilda, or the towering Clisham, he was glad when a welcome farm cart would pass and carry his increasingly heavy rucksack.

As a result of his perseverance in the field of geology he discovered what is known to geologists as the flinty-crush belt, first noted by him in 1905. Subsequent years were devoted largely to tracing this flinty crush belt throughout the length of the Long Island – a distance of more than a hundred miles. His laborious researches in this region, extending over a period of thirty years were nearing completion when his death occurred. Some measure of public acknowledgement came to him in 1928, when at the meeting of the British Association in Glasgow, Dr Craig of the Geological Department University of Edinburgh referred to him in the following terms:

Happily we have with us, in the person of Mr Dougal, the man who was the discoverer of the great flinty-crush belt of the Outer Islands. He was the pioneer – a pioneer of the finest type – and it is a reproach to the professional geologist that this work should have been done by an amateur.

In the same year JWD received from the University of Edinburgh the Degree of Ph.D. in recognition of his contributions to geological knowledge.

Below is an edited copy of the last chapter of *Island Memories* describing the last uninhabited island he visited when he would have been around 65 years old:

Voyaging from Ness to Sulisgeir – Rock of the Solan[1]

The lonely island of Sulisgeir, 40 miles north of the Butt of Lewis, is the most north-westerly island of Scotland. From Sulisgeir, the Flannan Isles are 70 miles south-west and on the same line lies the St Kilda group 120 miles distant. In sight of Sulisgeir is the island of North Rona twelve miles to the east, in the seas, termed of old, the Caledonian Ocean. Sulisgeir is famous as a gannetry, where a great colony of gannets, or solans, find a habitation with colonies of lesser sea birds. The island is seldom visited except by Ness men making annual visits of seven to ten days or several weeks in pursuit of the geese in poor weather conditions. To visit in a small boat is an affair not undertaken without concern for weather conditions and provisions of food and water.

Our journey was made in a scow converted into a motor-boat by a small petrol engine, manned by a crew of four men generally engaged in fishing and crofting. Accompanying us was our old friend Angus MacDonald. Of the six of us, only he knew the one landing place on Sulisgeir and like the other four Ness men, was expert in the currents and winds of the north-west Atlantic.

The men left their harvest fields to prepare for leaving Ness harbour breakwater by mid-night. JWD with his sack of provisions walked a mile in dense fog through which a full moon struggled to appear. A lamp's glimmer 30ft below the breakwater showed the tiny craft being loaded with oil, spars, ropes, provisions and a barrel of water. A course of NNE was set into the open sea.

To our stern, the Butt lighthouse gave a directive beam for some miles. A watch was set for 'blind trawlers' which poach the fishing banks and, as the Ness fishermen know, are dangerous obstacles on dark nights. Clear of this area, the engine was primed for a seven hour run to a point between the islands of Sulisgeir and North Rona. Two hours had taken us beyond the far-reaching lighthouse beam steering now into ever increasing darkness. A flicker of the hand-lamp showed the crew discussing the course in Gaelic. A now cloudless sky showed brilliant constellations, the pole star holding its place while moving worlds circled through the immensity of space,... (a revelation in cleanness and beauty that ranked as one of the rare sights that JWD had seen in thirty years acquaintance with the Long Island.)

From the moment of leaving Ness at midnight until we returned to Lewis twenty hours later we never sighted a trail of smoke nor a sail throughout our passage of 80 miles in the Old Caledonian Ocean. The boat was dipping and

[1] John Wilson Dougal (ed. A.A. Macgregor), *Island Memories*, Moray Press, Edinburgh and London, 1937.

rising from basin to basin sometimes with a rending slap on the bow that made more than one of us look involuntarily to see if one of the bare planks had sprung. There was no pretence that our scow had a trail boat or even a lifebelt. We were more sensibly loaded with chains and ropes for use when we reached the island.

As light broke we were disturbed by a lively pod of porpoises, a royal escort to Sulisgeir. In tens, sevens and threes they plunged around us rushing with speed beneath us so near you could touch their dorsal fins.

Sulisgeir became more imposing as we approached, waves breaking into spray at the base of the high cliffs, rising sheer and stark from the sea. From the whitened cliffs, clouds of solan geese rose in flight. In mid-island, a bay of rocks facing the south narrows to a geo, which leads to a deep cave. Towards this breach we steered. This is the only landing place round the sea-cut walls of this island. The boat was kedgered by a dropped anchor and a stout chain with a bowline on a rock sixty feet high. Watching the flow, a jump was made to a six inch ledge and ascent of a steep cliff of over one hundred feet brought us near the centre of the island – Bealach an t-Suidhe – the Valley of the Sitting Stone. The chief prominences lie southwest where the young solan geese congregate. To the southeast the dark cliffs of Temple Rock rise hundreds of feet from sea level. The island is deeply indented by three baylets of forbidding and precipitous cliffs.

We were fortunate within ten minutes of landing to discover the abundant presence of Flinty Crush rock probably connected by undersea reefs to the great belts of the Long Island and fishermen tell us of fishing lines held on undersea reefs running NNE. These belts form an interesting feature of geology in the Outer Hebrides.

Hornblende gneiss, granite gneiss and a great belt of red pegmatite resemble Lewisian features. Torridonian pebbles were evidence of the extensive area of the ice flow. The examination of rock specimens from Sulisgeir will provide interesting notes to add to the records made of Hebridean specimens collected in the Western Isles over many years.

The elation of reaching the island – the desire of many years, helped to sustain us against the soaking showers of rain which beset us as we ranged, hammers in hand, over the rough rocks with Angus. During the period of our visit some of the men were journeying to the heights stocking-footed and brought back to the boat several bagfuls of solans for their own use.

Among the living things of Suilisgeir there is an abundance of interest for the expert botanist and ornithologist which would require more than the four sodden hours which we had. Here sea pinks do not flower abundantly and the few sea-pinks appeared to have a grey fungus, but closer inspection showed that the down from the young birds had blown in the wind and encircled the leaves and the stems, changing their natural appearance.

Apart from the colonies of gugas, or lazy fellows in Gaelic, the young solans in autumn weigh about seven pounds relished by those who acquire a taste for the oily flavour and dark flesh. During the Great War (1914–1918) shell practice by warships led to the island being deserted by the birds.

The most joyful bird we saw on Suilisgeir was a St Kildan wren which hopped near while we were about our work. On neighbouring Rona, pretty crossbills had been seen, which was remarkable as their usual food is seeds from ripe pine cones in Central Europe but on Rona they were feeding on the seed of the sea-pinks.

12 o'clock mid-day and the seamen called us to return against a breeze, still south easterly and an uncertain element in the pall of heavy clouds before us.

We knew that the solans were relieved by our departure but hope there was a little grain of regret with the wren of the glad eye and the happy flick of his tail. We feel he will welcome us again.

Down the cliff of Phuill Bhain, slippery with the grease and blood of the last solan slaying, into the boat we jumped and she cleared for her eight hours home. For long hours we repeated our night's rise and fall in hidden dips of agitated water without sight of sail or life but lonely puffins and a few fulmars on powerful wings and solans searching the waters.

Six hours elapsed ere much gazing and guessing brought us to view the Muirneag Hill, a mariner's sure landmark and the exiles last farewell. In turn Tumpan Head, Tolsa Head, the goring rocks of the Butt of Lewis with its lighthouse, stood out. From the shore lee one may see the Dune Tower with its sweet memories and the ruined dwellings of centuries ago, even before the time of St Ronan or of the Norsemen. The weather had moderated and smoother water went with us, the sun cut through a break in the clouds. Ness had glorious harvest weather. We could see its fields dotted with reapers working to late hours.

At last the wind had dropped. The waters became still as we reached the stark cliffs. The evening sun left its glowing colours on the horizon, a ruddy gold melting into a blue canopy. When we reached the peaceful haven of Ness, friendly hands welcomed us home to some comfort after our adventure in lonely northern seas.

Back to the present day, crossing the Minch are a party of two, the SMC President, John Fowler and myself, who are now approaching Stornoway to try and find the elusive memorial. On arrival we drove westwards armed with climbing gear, fishing rods and painting materials to camp at Bhaltos. From the very first, the Long Island enchants my senses. The light on the sea lures me across endless stretches of sand to a distant place among wind-blown marram grass, looking seawards, where a blue rowing boat at anchor finds itself included in my painting.

Today the search begins at Barvas school. I talk to the present head teacher who is very interested and immediately when told of the Dougal connection says there are two pupils at school who are descended from the original family and still live in the schoolhouse where my grandfather stayed. I am encouraged to call in to the house which is a handsome two-floor stone building with mature trees in the garden. I knock but there is no-one in – a disappointment. North-eastwards we go to Port Nis (Ness) where we visit the Historical Society who know of the memorial and are extremely interested in our quest. As regards its condition they tell us that a man from Port Sgiogarstaigh still ventures across the moor every few years to spruce it up and protect it from the elements. Now progressively eager to get going, knowing that there is definitely something to see, they point us in the right direction. We are now off-road and walking through peat bogs but with a pleasant light breeze – the going is not too bad. I know we are heading seawards and expect any moment to see a glimpse as we plod up and down in the peat hags. 'I see it!' shouts John who is taller. I speed up, heart racing.

There on the headland of Meall Geal stands a three metre white painted obelisk with steps up to it and metal plaque bearing the words JOHN WILSON DOUGAL 1866–1935 and a bas relief geologist's hammer. On the top is a peak composed of what resembles for-all-the-world a pile of potato shaped stones – these were his passion – Flinty Crush!

The aspect was stunning, looking across the sea to the far off Suilven and the mountains of the north-west on a lovely clear day, the turquoise sea below and the headland air smelling fresh and green. There was no more beautiful place to stand and feel so connected to a grandfather who died before I was born. I could feel the strong family ties and pride in his achievement. John was impressed by both the memorial and the glorious outlook from the headland which marks where the line of flinty crush enters the sea. Eventually we left with not a few backwards glances.

His bones may rest in Edinburgh, wrote an Isle's man, but if by chance his spirit should walk it will not be in the thronging city streets – he will be found communing with the wind on the mountains of Harris or his voice will mingle with the sea-birds' cry on some solitary northern isle.

The author and the memorial to her Grandfather at Ness, Isle of Lewis. Photo: John Fowler.

NORDWAND IN TRAINERS

By Noel Williams

I SIT HERE IN LOCKDOWN staring up at Ben Nevis from our front living room. The weather has been superb for over a month and the Ben has looked magnificent for most of this time. A late dump of snow in March transformed the North Face and even now at the end of April much snow remains. Fresh green leaves have started to appear on the trees. It's my favourite time of year and I recall that just twelve months ago I enjoyed a wonderful week on Skye.

At this time of year the late evening sun starts to catch the North Face of Castle Ridge. This huge triangular face is the most prominent feature we see from our house – that and the more distant North-East Buttress on the left-hand skyline. Climbers tend to hurry past this face on their way to do battle on other parts of the mountain. If you venture onto it, however, it has a surprisingly Alpine feel. You perhaps wouldn't guess this from our guidebooks. In the 1936 Ben Nevis guide, Graham Macphee says:

> the climbing on this face is unsatisfactory and no definite route has been made, although it has been climbed by Harold Raeburn alone on 31st December 1907, and J. B. Russell on 18th July 1931, among others.

Macphee was also fairly dismissive in the 1954 Climbers'Guide:

> Indeterminate scrambling on steep rocky buttresses alternating with grassy ledges. At one place there is a huge overhang, well seen from Castle Ridge climb.

I first climbed on this face back in April 1978. I had a surprise visit from John Fleming, a fellow Jacobite MC member and student with me at Moray House. A bit late in the day we decided to set off for the North Face and since it is one of the most accessible routes on the mountain we plumbed for *Nordwand*. This was graded II/III and given two stars in the little Cicerone guide (60p) which was our bible at the time. The climb had been done in 1959 by a party of five, which included Ian Clough. We noted that it was said to have 'a genuine, grim nordwand atmosphere.'

The early leftwards traverse was rather thin, but we eventually broke out onto easier ground on the face proper. As we gained height the size of the face started to become more apparent. The name *Nordwand* was well chosen.

We stomped up soft snow for some distance, but we then realised that the route continued by a long leftwards-rising traverse on rather steep snow. At the top it appeared to be capped by a much more serious wall of steep rock. In view of the hour we were both wondering if we really wanted to commit to this upper section when we spotted a line of fresh, deep steps heading off rightwards. Wimps that we were, we decided to follow them. They took a devious up and down line along a string of snow

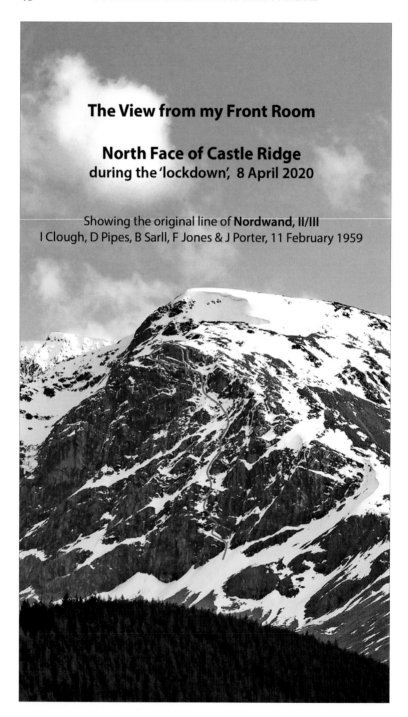

The View from my Front Room

North Face of Castle Ridge
during the 'lockdown', 8 April 2020

Showing the original line of **Nordwand, II/III**
I Clough, D Pipes, B Sarll, F Jones & J Porter, 11 February 1959

ledges, but eventually exited onto the flank of Càrn Dearg. Whoever had found this escape route, not long before us, must also have been intimidated by the upper part of the route.

It's interesting to note that Jimmy Marshall gave *Nordwand* grade III in his 1969 guide, but in modern guides it has crept up even further to grade IV, mainly because the original Clough start has been forgotten.

I remember describing our experience to Con Higgins who was living in Fort William at the time. He was familiar with that part of the Ben having done *Lobby Dancer* with Alan Kimber the previous winter. He agreed that the whole face had a certain atmosphere. Con went on to do *Last Day in Purgatory* with Mike Geddes the following year. The route was misnamed *Purgatory Wall* when it originally appeared in the Journal, and it was only corrected the following year. I was amused by the accompanying comment by the Editor, Bill Brooker, who added. 'We hope this puts Higgins out of his misery.'

Skip forward to the summer of 2002. I set off on my motorbike with another biking friend for a walking holiday in Switzerland. A mutual friend had bought a holiday home in Adelboden and the plan was to travel out there and meet up with him, his brother and their 80-year-old father. This was the first time for many a year that I'd deliberately left my climbing gear behind. It felt pleasantly relaxing to know that nothing desperate was planned.

In former days I would have scoffed at walking from valley to valley over high passes, but it proved to be a delightful holiday especially since the weather was so good.

We set off from Grindelwald with the intention of working our way back towards Adelboden. The scenery on the route was truly spectacular and it made me realise there was more to mountaineering than just climbing.

The first afternoon we had a pleasant easy walk up to Männlichen. The whole time we had ever-changing views of the North Wall of the Eiger. The tourists disappeared by late afternoon and when we booked into our very modern accommodation we found that we had the whole place to ourselves. As the sun started to sink we had magnificent views of the Eiger and the Mönch.

The next day Charles took his father by cable car and train down to Lauterbrunnen, while the rest of us jogged down. We were feeling good and went at quite a lick, so weren't all that far behind them at the bottom. I remember thinking it was good training for the Ben Nevis Race.

We then took a funicular railway up out of Lauterbrunnen (which has since been replaced by a cable car), and then walked south to Murren.

Exactly where we spent the following nights is all a bit hazy, but I do recall having good views along the way of the north face of the Gletcherhorn – one of the best adventures of my youth. I think we stayed a night at Griesalp and from there headed over to Kandersteg. I only

The North Wall of the Eiger, July 2002. All photos by the author.

mention all this because I was pretty fit by the time I got home and returned to the chalkface.

I was working on *Highland Scrambles South* at that time and I had been wondering for a while if there might be a worthwhile scramble on the North Face of Castle Ridge. I knew there were a couple of winter grade IIs on this face called *The Serpent* and *The Moat*, and routes of that grade can sometimes give good summer scrambles.

I set off from the house with a light sac and jogged up to the foot of the face in just under an hour. I thought I'd keep my fellrunning trainers on to start with as they're nice and light. The pyramidal studs aren't much good for climbing though, so I planned on changing into my scrambling boots as soon as things got more interesting.

I sauntered up to the start of *The Serpent* and was delighted to find an easy ledge leading right. I followed this until it broke out onto a large terrace. I then cut left and was pleasantly surprised to find a hidden grassy terrace leading back right again. I was starting to enjoy myself and began to think that this face might indeed offer a pleasant summer scramble.

The terrace started to narrow down as I approached a broad recess where *Nordwand Direct* comes up in winter. It suddenly became a bit more than a hands-in-pocket amble. There was a big drop to the right, and the ground became rocky and quite exposed for a short section.

Once past this section the way ahead was slightly steeper though it was again mainly on grass. I eventually reached a broad vegetated rock rib,

North Face of
Castle Ridge

* slimy fist-jam move

The route taken on 25 August 2002.

but there weren't any ledges so I had to keep my trainers on. I carefully worked my way up and left towards a shallow runnel with more rocky ground straight ahead. I soon reached a groove with smooth slabby rock walls, but again no ledges where I could change my footwear. The groove continued straight above me to much steeper rock which looked outrageous. *The Serpent* must exit here in winter, but it was out of the question for me to attempt it without a rope.

I could tell that I was now above our winter high point on *Nordwand*. The ground leading up leftwards looked every bit as intimidating as I remembered. I was braced across the groove wondering what to do. To tackle the grass and broken rock that rose steeply leftwards I could have done with an ice axe and crampons. Failing which I'd have to change my footwear. I managed to get my rucksack off, but I found I couldn't trust myself to balance on one leg to put my boots on. I soon gave up. I would have to continue in my trainers.

I set off slowly and carefully on the steep vegetated ground. In my trainers I couldn't kick my toes in very far and most of the time I had to cling to a mixture of grass and rubble. I kept hoping there might be a hidden exit on the steep headwall above my right shoulder where *The Moat* was supposed to finish. There was nowhere there that looked remotely doable.

With some relief I eventually got to the top of the vegetated ground. Although I now felt a bit more secure, the way ahead was not obvious.

There were rock steps running up slightly leftwards, but certainly no easy exit. I could see a slimy groove over to the right which is probably a straightforward ice pitch in winter, but again it wasn't an option.

I clambered up the rock steps without difficulty, but then came to an abrupt halt at a short blank wall. I eventually found a wide crack hidden under a small overhang that offered a slimy fist-jam, but I quickly dismissed that as a possible solution. I don't like hand jamming at the best of times, and slimy fist-jams even less so.

What to do? I couldn't imagine reversing what I'd done, but *in extremis* it might be my only option. I remembered that Clough and party had traversed leftwards at the top of *Nordwand* and finished up the final section of *Castle Ridge*. I moved leftwards to the end of the ledge and was horrified to see a sheer wall dropping away below me. I could see a finger ledge leading across the wall and made a couple of moves along it. However, there was nothing for my feet and I quickly got frightened and scuttled back.

I then retreated back down the rock steps and looked again at the slimy groove, but it was no more inviting than the first time. Going back down the vegetated ground also looked a complete nightmare.

I didn't have a mobile phone in those days. I was just kicking myself for not having brought my rescue team radio with me when something surreal happened. A guy on a parachute went gliding silently across the face just a few feet above my head. I didn't have the presence of mind to shout for help, and before I knew what had happened he had disappeared from view. I still don't know if he saw me.

I must have gone up and down the rock steps to the ledge at least three times. Although I couldn't sit down I knew I was safe where I was, and one option was to wait it out for my colleagues in the rescue team. However, if I was to spend the night out I couldn't be sure I wouldn't drop off in more sense than one. I had no climbing gear with me at all.

I went back up to the wall and yet again I stepped up until I could insert my left fist, palm upwards, into that slimy undercut crack. I tried to dry the crack with my sleeve, but it still felt precarious. There was nothing for my right hand until I committed to that fist-jam. I would have to lean out on it with all my weight and then stretch up for a right handhold.

The memory of that move is seared into my brain. Never has my fist been more tightly clenched than when I leant out on that jam. Once committed I managed to grab a good hold with my right hand and pulled up onto what I imagined would be a flat ledge. I thought my troubles would now be over, but the ledge was in fact a steep slab. It seemed like a case of out of the frying pan into the fire. I took some time to steady myself, then made a long step right and after a couple more moves pulled up onto easy ground. I have rarely been so relieved.

I was now in a broad easy alcove with two clean, right-angled corners straight above my head. They both looked like miniature Cenotaph Corners – very enticing lines, but not for today. I wondered about

The two corners at the top of Nordwand catch the late afternoon sun, 5 September 2015.

traversing left round the corner as Clough had done, but I noticed that an easy ledge ran off to the right. It was too good to ignore, so I headed along it and to my astonishment I popped out onto the flank of Càrn Dearg. In no time I arrived on the flattening at the top of *Castle Ridge*. Well I was up in one piece, but it hadn't been a scramble.

The weather was still fine and I was feeling good so I continued on up to the summit. Then I dropped down beside the snow in *Tower Gully* and descended *Tower Ridge*. It felt pleasant to finish the day by doing a proper scramble.

When I bumped into Ian Sykes later that year, I quizzed him about where his route, *The Moat*, had finished. I couldn't make sense of what he said apart from his comment about it being a difficult route to grade. He said that most of the route was easy grade II, but that the exit pitch was grade IV. I wouldn't argue with that.

*

By way of a footnote I would love to know where the Glasgow JMCS party went in July 1931. The report of the Meet in the Journal for that year (*SMCJ*, 19/112, Nov 1931, 302–3) gives no clue apart from mentioning an ascent of *Castle Ridge* and also the 'Geddes' route (?) – described as 'being somewhere on the west of the cliffs, the party having overshot their objective in the mist.'

TRAVELS WITH A GUN

By Tim Pettifer

MY SECOND WIFE HAS three well earned peace awards, gained in the most dangerous arenas of the world. Testimony to her work is an impressive collection of death threats. The longest of these, a whole foolscap notebook, was an excellent catharsis for the author because my wife still lives and breathes. With such useful experience her advice, when danger looms, even if a gun is pointed at your head, is to remain confident and show no fear.

The late Ian Angell examining an impressive set of polar bear tracks.
Photo: Robin Chalmers.

The same mantra works with polar bears. Remain calm! Never turn your back but give 'em a good verbal bashing, adding expletives and banging saucepans works well. *Flower of Scotland* on the pipes I would like to try, but the real decider is an exploding flare between their feet. Two members of the Club, Robin Chalmers and Bob Barton will vouch for the effectiveness of trip wires, letting rip an ever faster catherine wheel, finishing with a bang to wake the dead and everyone else in the camp when I tripped over it answering a call of nature.

It is said, and I think it is true, a party of research students were trapped in a hut by a curious, but not necessarily aggressive, bear. It's difficult to leave a hut if it only has one window and the bear comes round the corner just as you leave the door. Their mistake was not having more than a rifle, so rather than having a dead bear blocking the one exit, or a dead bear at all, they contrived an effective deterrent by jamming the door, so it would only partly open. When the beast poked his nose in to have a good sniff at the aromas of a cheap packet soup on the stove and not being a fussy eater, a great white head soon followed and it was ambushed by a double handed swipe with a cast iron frying pan.

Whatever your defences if you are the rated marksman your status as the leader of the group will be assured. Your reward will be many pats on the back and encouraging smiles when a menacing bear appears over the horizon and you go out to do battle. But pulling the trigger is a last resort because who were we to invite ourselves into their lair and put temptation in their way?

Different countries take a different view. In Greenland a dead bear is a cash bonus and they have been doing it for hundreds of years without any impact on bear numbers. Svalbard is a cash rich tourist attraction because it has many live bears and a protective management policy that favours the bears which kill on average two tourists a year. Numbers of tourists are increasing, but due to global warming bears are decreasing so Svalbard takes a very progressive view and extracts maximum retribution if you have a shoot out. This happened to a young Norwegian I met who turned himself into a tourist spectacle, speeding well-heeled guests from cruise ships round the ice on an almost authentic dog sledge. His dog team let the side down but led by an impressive husky supported by German Shepherds and lots of barking from Collies and several different varieties of large mongrels and cross breeds, the sledge ran well enough. Image is everything, so he theatrically sported a long beard and hair to his shoulders, dressed in a ragged sealskin suit, hat and mukluks, held up with a thick leather seal skin thong. He looked like the sole survivor of Franklin's fateful expedition, just returned after 170 years wandering the Arctic or the lead soprano of Roald Amundsen the Musical.

This Arctic entrepreneur was making good cash sales doing what he always wanted, imagining he was born two centuries ago. Reality kicked in when the team passed too close to an ice hummock and a surprised bear, in a spirit of self defence, grabbed hold of the husky. Our brave time-traveller ran up and shot the bear in the head with a solid-round .22 pistol, making two mistakes. A .22 pistol with a solid round would hardly do harm to a cat unless it hit bone and secondly would never get through a bear's thick skull even if it was squarely fired at point blank. Being an environmentalist at heart, our hero was concerned for the bear that had made off looking for a headache remedy and reported the incident to the Sessillman of Svalbard, a Sessillman being our equivalent of a Mayor. The young musher was found guilty by a jury of one, for the offence of 'wilfully surprising a loveable bear going about lawful and peaceful duties' and given a bill equivalent to £5000 for the helicopter and marksman sent to despatch the wounded animal. The Sessillman obviously liked things done by the book because I recall a letter I sent him before my first trip to Svalbard that was addressed to and began 'Dear Mr Sessillman...' I never got a reply.

It would be unfair to think that the bears of Svalbard are badly influenced by the aggressive persona of the residents. On the contrary, a Scandinavian welcome is overwhelming and it is where I was served roast whale, fresh from the sea when I was an active member of Greenpeace, mistaking the cook's hearty back slap and pronouncement 'We have vale for dinner' as meaning veal. Their ability to party is endless. On one occasion we enjoyed a long night of dancing, free vodka and a huge smorgasbord before our host discovered that the taxi driver had dropped us off at the wrong hotel and we were soon out on the snow!

The good people of Svalbard also very helpfully posted to my home address a bag full of frozen turds from eight people for 14 days. A mechanic finding the mislaid bag in the weasel trailer believed the tinkling sound was valuable rock specimens. Fortunately, but my enemies and many of my best friends would say unfortunately, a complicated telephone call to the sorting office in Longyearbyen, the small capital of Svalbard, sorted out the mess.

At the other side of the Arctic Ocean in the much bigger landscape of Greenland I used dog sledges as less expensive alternatives to skidoos and helicopters, to ferry food and equipment from Scoresby Sound for parties of skiers flying into Constable Point at the top of the Hurry Fjord. The big Greenland Huskies pull well on the abundance of seal and fish found around the world's largest fjord, but even at human jogging speed, crossing a wide expanse of sea ice is like watching paint dry, so we pulled into Cape of Good Hope for a welcome break. A good lady from one of the huts proudly and generously offered us raw Narwhal, full of vitamins but a taste that takes a lot of acquiring. The Huskies were refuelled with chunks of frozen Greenland shark, only fit for dogs in Greenland but served in Iceland as an expensive delicacy. A small boy sitting on a galvanized dustbin lid was being towed around by a big old husky he was prodding with a Narwhal tusk. All in all, a normal quiet Sunday afternoon until the babel of conversation took on an urgency and arms were pointed out across the ice. The dogs immediately picked this up, lunging at their traces and the noise would have put Murrayfield to shame at the final whistle with a score of *Scotland 51 England 0*. A bear had been seen!

Three huskies were released and their acceleration and speed was breathtaking. Huskies love to run! They live to run! For camaraderie, for adventure, for new horizons. A few years ago, leaving Scoresby Sound with a strong team a very pregnant bitch caught us up. She ran alongside licking their faces and wanted to be nowhere else but in the team, running. She was told to go home and in her despondency she sat on the ice and howled to the sky and anyone that would listen.

Huskies also love to fight! Especially bears, so the game was on. The young male bear hearing the dogs went direct for the edge of the sea ice, its most natural and best defensive environment but the dogs bit at his heels and he was forced to face them. He lunged for one and another would run in from behind and make a painful snap at his feet. As they

Camp on the shores of Van Mijenfjord, Svalbard, under Aspelin, 1217m. Just visible in the photo are the posts for the trip wires which give warning of the approach of a bear. Photo: Robin Chalmers.

made a grab they kept their eyes on his head, not his body or his paws and if it turned to make eye contact they jumped back. So before long the bear was confused and unable to judge the speed and distance to bring his great swiping, crushing forepaws into action.

The second sledge, short of the pulling power of two huskies, eventually arrived and an old .30 Mannlicher was pulled from under a seal skin: a sharp crack on the clear Arctic air and the bear went down. The three Huskies leapt at the corpse and started pulling it in three different directions and the tethered teams went berserk trying to share in the bounty. My Greenlander companions were thanking their good fortune, estimating its size with outstretched arms and playfully testing the sharpness of its teeth and huge claws with their thumbs. It was a tragic and violent death, but the joyfulness of the dogs and the hunters connected them to their land, as the hunters they still are, so it was not easy to be critical and then be accused of hypocrisy. They have been chasing bears for a very long time and anyone in the comfort of the West, except the homeless sleeping rough, produces more carbon emissions in a week than a whole family in Greenland will produce in a lifetime.

Unless you are high in the mountains you should always travel armed, as bears are insatiably curious and will follow up an interesting odour on the wind for miles. A rifle is often recommended but if you have done your best to deter the bear and he is still attacking, you are dependent on just one shot as your last resort. If so you are putting a bolt action weapon to the wrong use as it is designed for long range accuracy and careful sighting.

Pump action shotguns have the benefit of being a loud deterrent with rounds still available if it gets nasty. Shotguns for defence use solid, rifled rounds and although the muzzle velocity is much lower they still pack a big punch at close quarters. My preference is for a double-12 with the stock adjusted so it comes cleanly to the shoulder in line with the eyes and head of you and the bear. In double or selective single trigger it can deliver two very fast and accurate shots at a moving target. Above all, a large calibre revolver in a holster is best as it is far more easily kept close and ready for use but virtually impossible to own these days.

If a double-12 appeals, the certification process is far easier than a rifle and you can buy one for £100 and get rifled slug in the Arctic. Here in the UK you can become a marksman using bird shot cartridges and every bear will disappear over the horizon when they know who has arrived, Wild West style, just off the stage. To ensure you have done everything you can to deter a bear you must carry a flare gun. A dead bear is a violation as bad as a war crime and will ruin your day.

So here we are fully armed and ready to shout, jump up and down, play the pipes, bang on the big round saucepan and let off fireworks, and standing before us are a herd of musk oxen. They have a pleasant, friendly bovine look about them but there the likeness to Angus the Aberdeen that lives opposite our cottage ends.

Musk Ox can seem placid...

The late Bill Wallace from the Club described to me an encounter with a musk oxen in the Stauning Alps. The beast ran amok amongst tents and equipment and hotly pursued them up a rock ridge and back down again, until they made an escape in their kayaks out into the fjord.

The Danish Commandos that manned the elite Sirius Patrol, using dog teams up and down the long East Coast of Greenland, gave them a far wider berth than Polar Bears. If you flex your muscles you can persuade a bear to not even enter the ring, but musk oxen will and it will go to a knock out. They are totally ungovernable, can be bad tempered and have the inviting stillness of Eilean Donan Castle reflected in a mirror calm Loch Duich, that can suddenly change into a lighting charge if their personal space is invaded.

During an SMC expedition to the Stauning Alps, we tried a photographic stalk of two bulls sunning themselves on a prominent snow hummock, commanding a view over the wide Skel Valley. With Dave Ritchie from Luing, it was our first breathtaking sighting of these spectacular animals, as much an icon of the Arctic as bears, yet so unlike the restless activity of bears, their rock steady calmness lured us closer.

A telephoto lens shot of a lion taken from an armoured Landrover with the engine running is for wimps, so for a challenge we tried for a shot of the whites of their eyes with a wide angle lens. We got to standard lens range and they gave us a warning, menacing grunt from deep within their massive chests that shook the beautiful long guard hairs hanging down their flanks. We chanced another few steps and the closest bull began

...but don't be deceived. Photo:Tim Pettifer.

scraping up the moraine beneath the snowpack prior to a charge. I had very recently read Ernest Hemingway's *Death in the Afternoon*, recounting Spain's most famous bull fighters, alive, wounded and dead. Full of useful information, I learnt that scraping the sand is a fighting bull's body language immediately preceding the matador being tossed high up into the crowd, landing to a fanfare fit for a Royal entrance and tremendous cheers when he is pushed back over the barrera. So we quickly beat a retreat! Not undignified but definitely a retreat. Since then I have avoided musk oxen, going nowhere nearer than 100m. Consequently travelling in an Arctic fog poses a unique challenge because if you stumbled into a herd you would be glad you knew your Hemingway and every trick with a cape ever used by every matador that went into a ring facing several bulls at once.

Over a few years, working with Callum Scott from BASI[1] we had built up a good relationship with the hunters from Scoresby Sound, legally transporting polar bear pelts and Narwhal tusks back to Iceland, saving airline carriage and our reward was a surprising present. A haunch of fresh musk oxen, a bag of mixed frozen vegetables, a sack of powdered spuds and five litres of red wine, from their own vineyard with MERLOT scrawled on the recycled plastic container, revealing wide cultural differences with Scotland's standard form of appreciation: a decorated tin of shortbread and a bottle of malt.

There were no complaints. Without their generous gift we could not

[1] British Association of Snowsport Instructors (Ed.)

On ski in Svalbard. Simon Gibbs, friend and client of Bob Barton, in Nathortsland.
Photo: Bob Barton.

have survived an eight day blizzard that began the day after the hunters and their dog sledges went down the hill and left us up in Liverpool Land. Unusually for Greenland in April the pressure dropped like a stone, the wind turned to storm and delayed the helicopter lift and the arrival of our clients. There is very little imagination can achieve with just three ingredients and an MSR[2] and I can genuinely tell you I have hardly ever eaten red meat since and not because I was sickened of it. I now know how meat should taste and just how it is to eat the very best that clean, ancient land can produce.

So I propose a toast to the Arctic, its mountains, the people, the Huskies and the animals and fish that make it a great adventure. Get there as often you can!

---

[2] Mountain Safety Research stove. Characterised by Malcolm Slesser as 'My Stove is Rotten'; he preferred the good old Primus. (Ed.)

SRÒN ULADAIL
the Monsters and the Climbers[1]

By Murdo MacLeod

WHEN YOU HAVE BEEN PAID to take pictures for more than thirty years people feel obliged to introduce you as an award winning photographer. Well, I did once win an award. There was no cash prize, the trophy was made out of plastic, but the ceremony was televised. To collect my award, I had to kiss, none other than Anne Widdecombe. But that was twenty years ago, and now I give myself frights, by being a novice climber.

Geòdha Bhrataigea, climbers on What Planet Do You Live On?
Photos by the author unless otherwise noted.

A new preoccupation requires its own reading material. Last year I began to see reviews of a new publication and as soon as I got my copy I was bowled over by it. There, in the SMC guide to *The Outer Hebrides* on p.165, I was amazed to see the ancient Geòdha Bhrataigea and its freshly renamed *Orpheus Wall*. As familiar to me as my mother's face. It sits a stone's throw from the crofting hamlet where my ancestors have subsisted for hundreds of years. I believed throughout all of my childhood that a fatal incident in 1906, involving an eighteen year old at the base of this Orpheus Wall, had given me my name. But that was wrong. Maybe we'll come back to that but not now, instead let's judge this book by its cover.

---

[1] This is an edited version of the speech given by photographer and climber Murdo MacLeod at the 131st SMC Dinner on Saturday 30 November 2019 at the Carrbridge Hotel, Carrbridge. Title with apologies to JRR Tolkien. (Ed.)

Sròn Uladail. Photo: Rab Anderson.

On the cover is Sròn Uladail. On p.2 is a warning and disclaimer. I have read it: beware of loose holds, rockfall and dodgy in situ tat (to paraphrase. Ed.). Your life is in your own hands. But there is a serious omission, no one warned David Macleod, back in 2010, before he began his five hour live television broadcast entitled The Great Climb, that while scaling this edifice he might only be metres away from a monster. To get that warning you will need to lay down the SMC guidebook and consult your copy of *The Morrison Manuscript*. Teacher and Cooper Donald Morrison, known as An Sgoilear Bàn[2] was born at Loch Reasort in 1787. He died when forty-seven, having sired twelve children. He devoted three years of his life to gathering stories and histories that were fast disappearing from the oral tradition. He travelled widely and used a board across his knees as a desk. Here is how he tells us Sròn Uladail got its name:

There lived at Hushnish in Harris – a man named Dos Mór Mac a' Cheannaich (Big Dos the merchant's son). In the glen to the north, high on a hill side, in a dark cave, lived a wild beast called Ulaidh. Ulaidh would allow none to pass. Dos armed himself and, despite the remonstrations of his fearful friends, he set off to fight the creature. His friends followed at a distance.

When Dos got to the cave – Ulaidh would not come out – she was rearing a child, which she was unwilling to leave. It was not until the third day of taunting – wearing an attire of scarlet, that Dos provoked Ulaidh into a ferocious attack. Dos slashed with his broad sword, but she came back at him with double vengeance, and he was forced to retreat. For four

---

[2] The fair or fair-haired scholar. (Ed.)

hours the bloody fight continued, until they reached Ceann Loch Reasort.
Here Dos weakly climbed onto an enormous rock. The beast approached,
suffering from loss of blood. At the base of the stone she collapsed – dead.
Dos addressed his friends, he told them, to go and kill the young whelp,
which was still awaiting the return of its mother in the cave. He confessed
that his wounds were fatal, and instructed them to bury him, on one side
of the rock, and the beast on the other. The rock is known to this day as
Clach Dhois, Dos's Rock. Sròn in Gaidhlig is nose, Ulaidh is the name of
the wild beast, and Dail is norse for valley. Hence Sròn Uladail.

I visited the cave a few weeks ago, on a storm drenched day and it is a
dramatic lonely spot. It is wide fronted and at some time has been walled

Murdo MacLeod leading The Vertical Ladder at Traprain Law. Photo: Neil Busby.

up leaving a linteled doorway. The cave also features, in the original rough guide to the Hebrides: the one written by Martin Martin in 1703. He says he found it to contain two wells, one strictly for dogs, and one strictly for people. One of those survives. Dog or human I am not certain, for I did not test the dark liquid.

As a Hebridean child I was often detailed to help my head-scarfed and heavily black-skirted grandmother (Cèit Chahain) carry a large galvanised bath out onto the moor. It contained a full set of crockery, tea, scones, and a pan of half cooked mince or salted cod. I would be accompanied by a crew of aunties, enlisted as porters, this was the late 1960s and the peats were not going to cut themselves.

So how did an ungainly old man like me start climbing at this unlikely age? It was my daughter Lilidh's fault. She works as a trekking guide on the Milford track in New Zealand. She suggested that when I next visited we could together stroll up Mitre Peak in Milford Sound. It turns out it's not a stroll but a bit of a climb. What began as a mad notion, that I could learn to scale this peak with only a few hours' tuition from an instructor, was soon replaced by a growing fascination with all things climbery and jangley. But I needed inspiration, a guru, someone I could follow. That was when it came to me. There it was right under my nose. A climbing legend already in the family: David MacLeod. Cousin Dave! In Gaidhlig he is *Daibhaidh MacLeoid* and I am *Murchadh MacLeoid* both sons of Leoid our eleventh century common ancestor! We are as good as cousins.

The clan emblem of the Macleods of Lewis is a Mountain On Fire. What could be a clearer sign of common destiny. Known in the local language as *Sìol Thorcuil*[3] their reputation is well established. King James VI described them as: *sic an unfamous byke of lawles lymaris* which translates as 'a hornet's nest of pirate vagabonds'.

Benjamin Franklin may have said 'those that fail to prepare, prepare to fail' but it was Dave who said 'Resting makes you weak.' I have sat up late, wearing yellow-tinted glasses, watching Dave's coaching Vlogs – causing me to rush out, and purchase an expensive Argos pull-up bar. It is installed in the kitchen doorway, and I have started spread sheets to record my progress.

As the video played, I was taken aback to hear Cousin Dave intellectually down climb enough to quote Mike Tyson no less: 'Everyone has a plan till they get punched in the mouth'. Really? I was so shocked, I walked face first, straight into my Argos pull up bar. Looks like it's back to wearing the helmet around the house again. One day Penny my wife will sit at the kitchen table and say 'make us a cup of tea dear' and watch in wonder as I climb the hand crafted holds of the E9 route that I have installed across the kitchen ceiling and down the far wall – to put the kettle on.

It's 2002. I am seriously agitated – standing in the corridor, outside the lounge bar in a Marriott Four Seasons hotel in Manchester. Time is

---

[3] 'The Seed of Torquil': the legendary founder of the MacLeods of Lewis. (Ed).

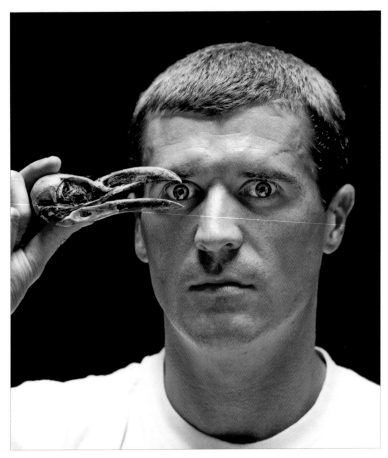

'The raven himself is hoarse...' Republic of Ireland and Manchester United mid-fielder Roy Keane after the interview.

running out. Roy Keane, having recently stormed out of the World Cup, in a fusillade of expletives – is pouring out exclusive confessions. Accounts of brutal ambushes and of inflicting injuries on fellow footballers. I am eavesdropping; the interview is liquid gold for my colleague, writer Sean O Hagan.

Timewise, I am getting screwed over, but I cannot interrupt this thunderous unburdening. Finally, Keane walks out towards me, now strangely calm, telling me we have but a few minutes. I abandon all my intentions but one. There is no time for conversation. I produce a polythene bag from my back pocket. I remove the rotting head of a dead raven. I hold it touching my face, the points of its beak framing the pupil of my eye. 'Can you do this?' I ask. He takes the raven's head, winces, it smells pretty bad. I had found it on a rainy walk near Càrlabhagh the previous week. 'Like this?' he says. The shutter falls and almost instantly time expires. 'That's my taxi now,' he says quietly, handing me back the festering head of the dead bird and departs.

On p. 39 of the Hebrides guide there is a mention of Stac Dhòmhnuil Chaim a sea stack located right in the middle of the climbs listed at Mangersta just south of the Screaming Geòdha. Named after its one time besieged resident Dòmhnall Cam – Donald Macaulay.

Dòmhnall Cam was a sixteenth century warrior in the Uig district. He employed a blacksmith called An Gobha Bàn. The smith had laboured at the anvil for seven years without any payment from the warrior. The smith expected to be paid in meal, and additionally to receive the head of any cattle killed in the neighbourhood. There came a day, that one of   the warrior's horses fell over a cliff. Dòmhnall Cam instructed his servants to cut off the horse's head and send it to the smith. The smith was unperturbed. He waited a while then invited Dòmhnall Cam to a lavish dinner.

Dòmhnall Cam was flattered and pushed back his plate – well fed – saying what a fine tasting feast it was. The smith replied 'well so it should – you are eating your own horse's head'. Dòmhnall Cam raged and stormed off. The smith calmly retired to the smithy; fired up the peaty forge and placed an iron bar in the fire. He barred the door. Before long Dòmhnall Cam arrived dressed in battle array. Murder in his eye. He thumped the door but it was solid. Eventually he peered through the latch hole – spying out his quarry. At this the smith took the bar out of the fire and thrust it through the latch hole, burning out Dòmhnall Cam's eye. The warrior fell down in agony and disarray. Dòmhnall Cam was devastated by his injury and impairment. This explains his name – Dòmhnall Cam – Donald of the squint. As Dòmhnall Cam slowly recovered, he lobbied and petitioned his peers to have the smith hanged for the GBH committed. The appointed day came and the smith was dragged to the gallows. A strange woman stepped out of the crowd, she pointed out that they only have one blacksmith in the region – no way, can they manage without one, but they have two tailors and can easily manage without one of them.

Gleibhabh an gobha crochabh an tailleir – Save the smith and hang the tailor. Whereupon Dòmhnall Cam seized the tailor and hung him facing the midday sun. After that Dòmhnall Cam and the Gobha Bàn, warrior and blacksmith, became inseparable friends.

All along this coast, every stone has a story – each metre conceals a message. *Leabaidh nan h-Aon Nighean*[4] – a young girl forsaken, brokenheartedly falls asleep on a high cliff ledge. Turns in her sad dreaming and falls down the wall to her demise. *Clach Na Gruagaich5*[5]: a mermaid is ignored but her sea cattle are captured and taken from her. Tradition tells us all the sea cows' names: *Sitheag, Caoilteag Bhan, Duibheag*[6]… but not the mermaid's. *Am Balla Gorm* – a fugitive falls

---

[4] 'The bed of the solitary (or forsaken) girl'. (Ed.)

[5] 'The stone of the fairy (or here) mermaid.' (Ed.)

Release from the Underworld? Celebrations on top of Orpheus Wall.

down a crag, breaks his leg, throws it over his shoulder and runs till he hits the coast where the pursuers catch him and hang him.[7]

This summer there came the time for me to attempt my first climbs from The Guide. I had my eye on *Rampling* at Daile Beag. It's Very Difficult. In preparation I realised I had best learn to prusik, in case a climb proved too hard. I decided that I would do this using a rope slung from the holly tree in my suburban Edinburgh garden. Brandishing a copy of *The Complete Guide to Climbing* by Peter Hills and using a couple of prusik loops – I slowly levitated, until my helmeted head, pleasingly, bumped into a branch. By now the number 26 bus had paused at the bus stop outside our gate and I was level with the puzzled commuters on the top deck.

It was, as I avoided their gaze, that I realized I hadn't read the next page. The one that tells you how to get down. I did not know how to switch from ascending to descending. *Klemheisted*. I spent some quality time, watched by the top deck of several different buses – suspended in the tree – before I worked it out.

If you go to climb the Orpheus Wall at Geòdha Bhrataigea you will pass a small cairn to your left. It sits on the debrided shoulder of heath as you approach. I thought that was the spot that gave me my name. In 1906 my ancestors rested a moment here, carrying home my eighteen year old grand uncle's body. The sea had taken days to relinquish him having

---

[6] Respectively: 'fairy'; 'fair, slender one'; and 'darker or blacker one'. (Ed.)

[7] Acknowledgement: I have grown up steeped in stories, but I have to praise Dr Finlay MacLeod, my teacher and friend, for sharing his knowledge and insight into everything Hebridean.

washed him off a rock in Geòdha Bhrataigea. I grew up believing his name was Murdo. That I was named after him to mark the tragedy. They often did that. But when eventually I researched my family tree, I found that it was Tarmod his brother that had drowned. While Murdo and the others reached out to him, with their long bamboo fishing rods the tips repeatedly broke off in Tarmod's hands and the sea took him. Murdo himself died three years later but the landscape does not tell us how or why.

> If I was the rock
> That gave you a hold
> If I was the flaw providing an edge
> If I was the belay found on a ledge
> You could pull on my ears
> Tear at my hair
> Rest your brow in damp despair
> On vague crimps in thin air
>
> If I was the rock
> Metamorphic and bare
> Providing a lip
> A touch
> A care
>
> Through the fear
> And the pain
> You'd rise
> again
>
> a note
> In the song
> Of a lark ascending
> I'd watch as you go
> An intimacy ending.

EDINBURGH IN THE EARLY SEVENTIES

By Dave Broadhead

ROBIN CAMPBELL'S REMINISCENCES about Edinburgh in the early Sixties (*SMCJ* 2018, pp.17–24) have prompted me to jump forward a few years with my own story. I arrived off the train from Liverpool in October 1971, a fresh-faced teenage Biology student with some hillwalking experience in Wales and the Lakes and aspirations to become a proper climber. Joining the Edinburgh University Mountaineering Club (EUMC) at the first opportunity, the following Sunday found me on a bus full of Yummicks heading for Traprain Law for some rock-climbing. Rob Harper, another chap from my digs claimed to have done a lot of caving and I exaggerated my previous experience, so we borrowed a 120-foot

Ken Macdonald, Salisbury Crags 1973; note Super Grattan PAs. Photo: author.

hawser-laid rope, headed to the foot of the nearest rocks and tied on. When we finally reached the summit trig point and un-roped, we wondered where everyone else had got to. Back at the bottom we discovered the crowded crag just around the corner and agreed to keep quiet about our activities. Rob stuck to caving, specialising in cave diving and in 2018 was a member of the rescue team which saved the twelve schoolboys and their football coach trapped in a cave system in Thailand.

The following weekend the bus took us up to Glen Coe for the traditional Freshers' Meet. I have already recounted my first meeting there with Des Rubens and our eventful ascent of North Face Route on the Buachaille in his obituary (*SMCJ* 2017, p. 266) and by now I was well and truly hooked. Involvement with the EUMC gave structure to student life, with a programme of meets every second week-end. For a mere one pound the heavily subsidised bus took us all over the Highlands and even down to the Lakes. Camping or bothies were the preferred accommodation and I never had space in my rucksack for a change of clothing.

Other club activities tended to centre around Graham Brown House on the corner of Gordon Terrace, the venue for meetings and slide-shows on a Thursday evening. When T. Graham Brown died in 1965, he left his Manor Place flat to the University as a student residence, preferably for EUMC members. The original flat was sold and replaced with a fine old house near King's Buildings, accommodating twelve students under the watchful eye of a postgraduate student warden, throughout my time the idiosyncratic Lynn Jones, a Welsh chemist who was also a very good rock climber, a keen ski-tourer and an SMC member. With a large black and white portrait of TGB hanging beneath his long wooden ice-axe above the fireplace and a huge map of Scotland on the opposite wall, the other feature of the large common-room was the Dempster-Wallace Memorial Library, stocked with an inspirational selection of mountaineering books and journals available for perusal or loan. The club's Kintail bothy, Glenlicht House was the venue for the New Year "Harrow" meet and was also known as the Hadden-Woodburn Memorial, so one soon got the message that things did not always run smoothly on EUMC meets. Aspiring rock climbers were encouraged to develop their skills at evening sessions on the climbing wall in Meadowbank Stadium, built by creative brickies into one inside wall of the building. This bore little resemblance to the modern version, with all routes top-roped and helmets compulsory. Unfortunately, sharp edged holds, lots of brick-dust and a lack of heating made it a generally unpleasant experience and the novelty soon wore off.

Climbing guidebooks were of course another source of information and inspiration. Soon after my first visit to Traprain I purchased a copy of the indispensable *Creag Dubh and the Eastern Outcrops* which saw plenty of use. The SMC guides at that time had a rather dated feel, with Very Severe still the hardest grade, so the publication in 1971 of the two volumes of *Scottish Climbs* by Hamish MacInnes was very timely. His topsy-turvy grades, numerical for rock and adjectival for winter caused some consternation but were soon found to be more realistic. Interspersed with dramatic action pictures, the crag photos with dotted route lines were so much more inspiring than the most carefully drawn diagrams, despite the grainy black and white production. Many happy hours were spent just browsing and dreaming. I got into the bad habit of climbing with the guidebook stuffed down the front of my jumper until one day, near the top of *Big Top* on the West Face of Aonach Dubh when Volume One slipped out. I will never forget the strange whirring noise of the pages flicking through as it tumbled into oblivion. Another significant and much perused publication was Alan Blackshaw's thick Penguin paperback *Mountaineering*, the outstanding how-to-do-it manual at the time. Packed with useful tips and life-preserving advice, illustrated by John Cleare's iconic pictures of the late Tom Patey in action, it became an essential reference for brushing up skills. Later on, publication of Ken Wilson's ground breaking *Hard Rock* caused great excitement, especially the stunning photo of Lynn Jones on *The Needle*.

With no classes in the afternoon, Wednesday featured the weekly pub lunch when we crowded into Rutherford's Bar on Drummond Street and signed up for the weekend meet. Back in the halcyon days of student grants topped up with parental contributions I had failed to budget for buying climbing gear but our Joppa digs provided a big breakfast and a substantial evening meal, so during my first year I skipped lunch to fund essential purchases. Fortunately, the EUMC equipment store was well stocked with tents, ice axes, crampons and ropes. Located in the bowels of the Pleasance Gym, items required were collected or returned after the pub lunch. During my first term I used Wednesday afternoons to try my hand at judo but soon lost interest, stiff and sore from the frequent floorings this seemed to involve. Instead, a few of us would wander down to Graham Tiso's shop on Rodney Street to browse and check out the latest gear.

The seventies of course saw major advances in climbing equipment and techniques. I had started hillwalking at school with an oilskin cycle cape, soon replaced with a thin polyurethane Peter Storm cagoule.

Standard Yummick wear was a bright orange Tiso Zip Cagoule, made of a thicker sweaty neoprene proofed material. Some people seemed to live in theirs but I preferred my warm, heavy knee length ex-Civil Defence great-coat to wear about town. Des Rubens wore a donkey jacket on and off the hill while George Gibson sported a tatty corduroy jacket and a distinctive black Homburg hat. The canvas Tiso Sac was another popular bit of kit, advertised as made to *Graham Tiso specification* and disparagingly described as *a tattie sack with straps*. I was still using mine years later trekking in India when my ex-EUMC companion and I met the legendary Joe Brown and his wife coming down from Amarnath Cave in Kashmir. Stopping for a chat he admitted 'We knew straight away you were from Scotland. We recognised the rucksacks'. Fibre-pile and fleece

Geoff Cohen on Sassenach in 1974; note Tiso Zip Cagoule. Photo: author.

did not start appearing until later, so old woollen jumpers formed one's
warm layers, along with a wool balaclava and of course Dachstein mitts.
Big leather boots were the norm for hillwalking and easy rock climbs.
Universally known as PAs, rock-boots had been around for a while and
any serious climber soon acquired a pair but it was considered a bit soft
to wear them on anything easier than Severe and similarly, excessive use

21st Birthday with Errol Meidinger at Pontresina camp site in 1974. Note Vango Force Ten and battered Tiso sac. Photo: Broadhead collection.

of runners was frowned upon. There were no cams or quick-draws or harnesses and chalk was only for blackboards, so racks tended to be light, apart from the obligatory hammer and a few pegs. The equipment-store soon phased out hawser-laid ropes and as 120 feet lengths gave way to 150 feet, 45 metres gave way to 50 metres. All full weight of course, like the popular Joe Brown fibreglass helmet, the cause of many a stiff neck.

At the start of my second year I moved into Kitchener House, just along from GB House. Thanks to the encouragement of my more experienced peers, I had climbed a few dozen Munros, cut holds up some easy winter gullies, lead plenty of rock climbs up to VS and was now considered an experienced mountaineer. I had also twice been late off the hill and missed the bus home and been involved in two rescue call outs, fortunately not as the casualty. Looking back, it is easy to see why young students are a particularly high-risk group for mountain accidents. Compared with the previous decade, climbing standards had not progressed as much as the quality of our singing, thanks to hours of practice on the bus and a regularly updated song book. Rob Griffiths summed it up neatly when he penned what became the club song: *The EUMC are a wonderful band/ you'll ne'er find a better in all of the land/ at bagging the Munros or climbing Severes/ it's the EUMC that all Scotland reveres.*

Meanwhile some of my contemporaries were becoming more ambitious. George Gibson and Ken Macdonald had both climbed at school and the latter was a particularly talented and graceful rock-climber who moved to New Zealand after qualifying as a dermatologist and gave up climbing. He rediscovered the low-level traverses and boulder problems in the quarry area on Salisbury Crags which became a regular haunt on Wednesday afternoons despite the parkies on patrol to enforce the many park rules, especially the climbing ban. On one occasion we were caught red handed but using his public-school charm Ken had a chat and to my astonishment they apologised for disturbing us and continued on their way. Des Rubens explored various railway bridges near his flat down in Leith while those of us living near King's Buildings would venture up Blackford Glen to try the *Best of Blackford* which surmounted the roof of the cave on the historic Agassiz Boulder. Higher up on the loose basalt of Corbies Crag the *Bathgate VS* was always good value, with its in-situ peg. George Gibson's speciality was traversing the skyline girders of the Forth Railway Bridge which he repeated several times while his most audacious stunt was hanging a huge **For Sale** banner across the Forth Road Bridge during charities week, to the consternation of the authorities. The less bold among us stuck to climbing along Princes Street with a collecting can, eliciting the memorable suggestion from one local worthy to 'Eff off student bastards!'

George also had a persuasive charm which helped extend our climbing contacts beyond the confines of the EUMC. Through our perusal of guide-books we were aware of many talented climbers on the University staff such as Colin Stead at the Dick Vet, Arthur Ewing in Zoology, Derek Leaver in Chemistry, Andrew Fraser in Bacteriology and newly appointed Professor of Geology Mike O'Hara, but most of these kept a safe distance from us student climbers. Ian Rowe was our energetic Honorary President but other Squirrels were now less active or gradually migrating across the Atlantic. George and David Geddes became friendly with Geoff Cohen, a new lecturer in the Statistics Department. Geoff had a knack of finding out where the most promising climbing possibilities lay and in due course David became Geoff's lodger in St Bernard's Row down in Stockbridge while George moved in with Gordon Macnair, a Cambridge friend of Geoff's working at the Scottish Office.

While our predecessors Haston and Smith were still revered, we tended to look further back for our heroes and role models, to the likes of Bill Murray and Jock Nimlin. Delighted when the latter agreed to come and give a slide-show, we were a bit disappointed at the choice of either St Kilda or Gemstones as his subject. Previous generations of Yummicks such as Iain Smart, Malcolm Slesser, Donald Bennet, Paul Bryan, Robin Campbell and Peter Macdonald were now SMC stalwarts and most were happy to give slide-shows or speak at our Annual Dinner and their involvement was always much appreciated. I do not recall any contact with the JMCS or the Edinburgh Mountaineering Club but a new club, the Jacobites suddenly appeared, instigated by the late Martin Plant, an authority on alcohol and drug addiction. He attracted a bunch of keen young climbers including Noel Williams, Douglas Anderson, Anthony Walker and Willie Jeffrey and had no qualms about allowing women to

Des Rubens and Ken Macdonald frying trout in Carnmore Barn, 1976. Photo:author.

join too. There were plenty of females in the EUMC but few serious climbers, apart from Sheila Kirkwood.

    With the support of the Jacobites, we were able to extend our informal EUMC slide shows and invite big names like Doug Scott and Joe Tasker to give public lectures in the city. At the other end of the spectrum were the Urchins, who I remember as a scruffy bunch of youths sometimes encountered on Salisbury Crags. Bob Duncan was the only one I got to know, after a very unpromising introduction. One Saturday morning, as I lay soaking in my weekly bath, the door burst open and David Geddes gleefully emptied a bucket of cold water over me. Once they had stopped laughing, I was introduced to Bob who was hoping to get a cheap rope through the expedition we were organising.

Seeds for the expedition had been sown a few years earlier when Dave Page joined the EUMC. A native of Oban with dozens of ascents of Ben Cruachan under his belt, he quickly became a strong and enthusiastic climber and joined Adam Harris and me on our first trip to the Alps, traveling out to Switzerland by train. After indifferent weather in Arolla, Adam headed home while Dave and I hitched to the Dolomites for more climbing adventures and a visit to Venice. We were back in the Alps the following summer, along with Errol Meidinger, an American exchange student. Many of these trans-Atlantic visitors made a valuable contribution to the EUMC during their year with us. Jane Sokolic is probably the best known, soon becoming Mrs Rubens.

In that same year Des also climbed with Greg Shannan. A wild looking character with long hair and a bushy beard, permanently clad in a tatty, tartan lumberjack shirt and distinctive Robbins boots, he was a seasoned big wall climber and muttered 'shennard' whenever winter climbing was mentioned. He introduced us to front pointing and soon we were all scrimping and saving to buy Chouinard axes and curved hammers. Together with another American, Barney Ng, Errol Meidinger finally persuaded Graham Tiso to accept a club order to enable members to buy gear more cheaply. In his shop, now relocated to larger premises in Leith, mention of the word 'discount' would transform Graham's normally smiling visage to an icy sneer. Later when we were organising our expeditions, he showed his kinder side and even gave us some free gear 'for testing'. Alison Clough was a superb cartoonist whose drawings featured in the EUMC Journal and later in the Sierra Club's fabulous periodical *Ascent*. (Sadly, just a few weeks before writing this, David Geddes e-mailed to say that Alison had recently died in a multi-vehicle pile-up in Utah).

The University also had an Expeditionary Society which organised occasional guest speakers. I remember seeing Eric Shipton and Sir Vivian Fuchs but the one who made the most impression was Geoff Cohen, talking about his trip to the Pin Parbati mountains of Kullu, in the Indian Himalaya, with friends from Cambridge. This was probably the first time I met Geoff and when Dave Page and I decided to organise our own Himalayan expedition, Geoff was the obvious choice to invite as leader and we started climbing together.

Ours was the first such EUMC expedition and plenty of other Yummicks were keen to join us but insistence on glacier experience whittled it down to Des Rubens and George Gibson to make up the team

Gear:Tiso Sac, canvas gaiters, patched breeks, wooden ice axe, Salewa Crampons and Arran sweater knitted by Mum. Ben Nevis 1974. Photo:Broadhead collection.

of five. The Edinburgh University Hindu Raj Expedition 1975 achieved a few modest mountaineering successes but we all returned safely, even closer friends than before and many more expeditions followed. We were the first recipients of the University's Livingstone Trophy *for the most outstanding expeditionary activity during the previous year* and hired dinner suits to attend the Sport's Union Ball for the official presentation. Dave and I immediately started planning another trip but he dropped out and the Edinburgh University East Greenland Expedition 1976 was made up of myself and fellow Moray House student Mungo Ross along with Anthony Walker and Andrea Mountain from the Jacobites.

On my return I moved west to take up my first teaching post in Renfrewshire, gradually cutting my ties with the EUMC but not with Edinburgh where a new group started meeting on a Wednesday evening in the Raeburn Bar in Stockbridge. Working in or around the city new faces like Stan Pearson, Grahame Nicoll, John Hutchinson, John Hall and many others revitalised our climbing ambitions and became good friends, but that is another story for someone else to tell.

AMONG MAD PEOPLE

By Ian Crofton

'But I don't want to go among mad people,' Alice remarked.
'Oh, you can't help that,' said the Cat: 'we're all mad here. I'm mad.
You're mad.'
'How do you know I'm mad?' said Alice.
'You must be,' said the Cat, 'or you wouldn't have come here.'
(Lewis Carroll, *Alice's Adventures in Wonderland*, chapter vi)

ON 15 APRIL 2015, the week before the SMC's first Peak District meet, I fell thirty feet off Froggatt Edge while leading. My gear pulled, and I landed on my head. I was unconscious for ten minutes, and don't remember anything of the first twenty-four hours. Edale Mountain Rescue were on the scene very quickly, and I was airlifted to Sheffield Northern General Hospital, where I spent ten days. I had chipped a number of vertebra, and broken three ribs and a shoulder blade. I had also suffered three brain bleeds, resulting in persistent double vision, confusion, anxiety and fatigue. The doctors in Sheffield said I should see a brain-injury specialist as soon as possible after I returned home to London. It took over three months to get an appointment. I wrote this account some months later.[1]

---

[1] All photographs by the author. Illustrations by Tenniel from *Alice's Adventures in Wonderland*; captions unnecessary. (Ed.)

There was no whiteout, no nightfall, not even a veil of mist. But I was lost – not in the hills, but in London, in a maze my brain could not map.

Things had been confusing for some time now. Someone said, when I emerged blinking from the dark of the Tube, I should turn down an alley at the back of a grandiose late-Victorian hotel. I did, and soon entered a world where nothing was as it seemed, or should be.

There was a more modest, older brick building in front of me. Across its frontage, in large letters, was painted a sign that said 'Horse Hospital'. I knew I was looking for a hospital. But I knew I wasn't a horse, so concluded I should be somewhere else.

I continued, my wife Sally at my side. We turned left along a wider street. Here I spotted the White Rabbit. He was not running down the road, not muttering 'Oh dear! Oh dear!' It was I, after all, who feared I would be too late. This White Rabbit was printed on a blue plaque on a stuccoed building, and had adopted an alias, that of Wing Commander F.F.E. Yeo-Thomas. The wing commander had lived in this house, the plaque said, and during the Second World War had been codenamed the White Rabbit. Yeo-Thomas had worked for the Special Operations Executive in occupied France.

I was getting in more of a muddle. Hospitals for horses. Rabbits who were secret agents. I knew I'd fallen, but I'd not fallen down a rabbit-hole. 'Down, down, down. Would the fall never come to an end?' Alice had wondered. My fall had certainly come to an end, on the hard ground at the foot of Froggatt Edge, which was why – three and a half months later – I was trying to get to the hospital. The hospital for people who had fallen onto their heads from a height of thirty feet.

We entered a square full of ambulances, parked and parking. No lights flashed. Sometimes a crew would disembark a person onto the pavement in a wheelchair. There was a grand entrance with a sign that suggested this might be the hospital I was looking for. So we went in, entering a hallway full of plasterwork and wood panelling, framed paintings and memories of Empire.

I offered my appointment letter to the smartly dressed woman behind the large oak reception desk. She stared at the letter, then took it from me reluctantly. 'I have an appointment at the Brain Injury Clinic at ten o'clock,' I said. She looked at the letter, as if it had been specifically created to make her life difficult. She avoided my eye. Instead she grabbed a bunch of stapled papers, which seemed to contain lists of appointments. She ran her fingernail extension down the list, turned a page, started at the top again and worked her way down. Eventually she'd gone through several pages, until there were no pages left. She sighed, flicked the pile of papers in irritation, and started on the first page again. About half way through her second review she stopped and looked up at me. 'Through there,' she pointed over my shoulder with her fingernail extension. 'Take the lift to the second floor. Turn right, then left.'

We obeyed orders. Emerging from the lift on the second floor there were no signs, but we turned right, then left, as instructed. The corridors grew darker. No one was about. I turned a corner and there was a cleaner. I asked him about the Clinic. He didn't know. We wandered on, asked another cleaner. She pointed straight ahead. The corridor opened out into a larger, darker room. There was a big table in the middle, round which a number of people were milling. Some were in wheelchairs, others wore helmets, most were in their nightwear, none looked well. The light had left their eyes.

'This is a ward,' said Sally. 'I don't think we're in the right place.'

Out of the gloom I spied a nurse. I asked her.

'You're in the wrong building,' she said. 'You should be next door.'

We retraced our steps, all the way back out of the entrance hall, out again onto the pavement. The door next door, a more modern building, had a sign that said 'Outpatients'. I was one of those, so I went in. A different receptionist looked at my letter, looked at her screen, tapped a few keys, and returned the letter. 'Take a seat please,' she said. We did.

In a while I heard my name called. I looked up. A young man in pink shirt and tie and carrying a clipboard stood some distance away, down a corridor into the interior. Oh no, I thought, three and half months waiting for an appointment and I get to see a junior doctor aged about twelve. I followed him to a door, and was relieved to see the consultant's name on it.

'This is Mr Agam's room,' the young man didn't say. 'I'm just a student.'

'Agam?' I might have said.

'Yes,' the young man didn't say. 'Agam. A God Among Mortals.'

'Oh,' I said.

The door opened and we were swept into the presence.

'Hello Mr Crofton,' said a thin smiling man of at least sixty. He had twinkling, disdainful eyes and an impish grin. 'Agam,' he didn't say. 'Take a seat. There.'

I did.

'You don't mind?' He gestured at the young man. 'This is one of my students, Mr … Mr … Aaah.'

'No, of course not.'

Agam sat down and peered at me over his spectacles. Then he looked down at the open file on his desk. He flicked over a page or two. 'Hmm,' he said. 'You had a fall? Ah. Yes.'

He peered up at me again, as if I was something quite extraordinary. 'Could you sit there?' He gestured towards the examination couch. 'Good. We'll take a look.'

'I've got a list here,' I said, 'of all the things I've noticed. Can I tell you? They may not be important, but there's lots of things that are different.'

'Hmm. Not surprising really, falling on your head like that,' Agam said. 'Go on. Meanwhile I'll just test some reactions. Just sit there with your legs hanging over the edge. Good.' He tapped my knees with a little hammer. I dutifully kicked. He did some more tapping, here and there. Then he got me to push against his arms, and follow a pen with my eyes.

'Shall I tell you?' I asked.

'Tell me what?'

'I've got a list here. First of all there's the mental things. I'm a writer, but I can't concentrate enough to write. I can't work. Too much fatigue.'

'Also he gets confused,' Sally added. 'And anxious.'

'I don't like having to organize things. It gives me stress. I haven't got the confidence I had.'

'Mmm,' said Agam.

'He's much more negative about things,' Sally said.

'I'm depressed a lot of the time,' I said. 'Thinking about what I used to be able to do and what I can do now. There's a big before and after. And there's funny stuff. Wooziness in the back of my head. And time's slowed right down. It feels like hours have passed but it turns out it's just been a few minutes.'

'Hmm,' said Agam. He turned to Sally. 'Was he talking nonsense when he was in hospital in … aah …' he turned to the file, 'In Sheffield?'

'He was rather,' said Sally.

'Was I?' I said, 'I didn't think I was.'

'You were,' Sally said. 'You didn't even know who the prime minister is. You said Margaret Thatcher.'

'I didn't?'

'You did.'

'That's one of our tricks,' said Agam. 'How did you know to ask that?'

'Everybody knows that's what doctors ask someone who's banged their head,' I said.

'Do they?' asked Agam. 'Everybody knows that, do they?'

'It's an old chestnut,' I said.

'Hmm. Bet my student here, Mr … Aaah, I bet he doesn't know that.' The student looked down at his clipboard. Agam paused, turned to Sally again. 'How long was he talking nonsense? More than a day?'

'Yes, several days.'

'Was I really?'

'More than a day or two?' Agam inquired. 'I'll classify it as severe traumatic brain injury.'

'Anyway,' I said. 'One of the worst things is the double vision.'

'The diplopia, yes. Are you seeing someone about that?'

'Yes. The Eye Hospital,' I said. 'I had lots of tests. They said I probably banged the back of my head. They call it Fourth Nerve Palsy.'

'Oh, now that's spoilt it. I was going to ask,' he turned to the student. 'I was going to ask him that. Never mind.'

'There's some other physical things,' I said. 'My right leg. The hamstring's tight and when I really stretch it I feel this sharp electric shock in the heel. There's also a slight tingling on the top of my right forearm.' Agam let me talk. He scribbled down notes, but I wasn't sure he was writing down what I was telling him. 'And I feel the cold more.'

'He does,' said Sally. 'He always had hot sweaty hands. Now they're cold and dry. And he's wearing a fleece when everybody else is just wearing a t-shirt.'

'My mouth is swollen and sensitive inside. Like someone's scraped the sides of my tongue with sandpaper. I don't enjoy food like I used to'.

'Except biscuits,' Sally said. 'You never used to eat biscuits. Now you can't get enough.'

'I'm off cheese though,' I said. 'I love cheese. Now cheese doesn't feel right. It doesn't taste as good as it used to. Smells the same though, which is strange.'

Agam let me ramble. 'The important thing,' he said, 'is not to try to do too much too soon. Don't start something and then find you're so fatigued you fail. You'll only go downhill if that happens.' He turned to look at me, and seemed to penetrate me with his sharp eyes. 'Yes?'

'Er, yes,' I said, though without any clear idea what I was agreeing with.

'Good. I'll see you in three months time in the Brain Injury Clinic.'

'I thought this was the Brain Injury Clinic,' I said, surprised.

'No, this is Neurology. I do both. But I wear a different jacket for the Brain Injury Clinic.'

I laughed. He liked that. 'We do neuropsychological assessments and an MRI on the second Thursday of each month,' he told me, warming to his theme. 'Then we chat about the results on the fourth Thursday. You'll have to wait three months, though.' He paused. 'It takes time. Recovery from serious brain injury. You have a chance of improving a lot. But you're never going to be quite the same. Not one hundred per cent.'

He shook my hand, smiled, then shook Sally's. The student opened the door for us.

" 'All right,' said the Cat; and this time it vanished quite slowly, beginning with the end of the tail, and ending with the grin, which remained some time after the rest of it had gone."

WELSH 3000´ PEAKS RECORD

By Finlay Wild

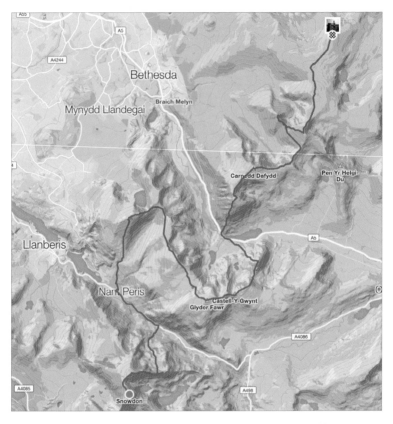

The route across all the three thousand feet Welsh peaks. Photo:Finlay Wild.

FOR ME A GOOD challenge involves pushing myself in the mountains. For it to be really engaging it would need to involve at least some technical ground – rough tracks, scree runs, a wee bit of scrambling. It would be about speed but also stamina, a route that would push me hard. Racing is good, but an 'against the clock' solo adventure is often better. You're still racing your biggest rival and harshest critic. As an example, when I first started reccying the Cuillin Ridge Traverse in 2012 I had no idea if the record was even possible for me. I'd have guessed my chances were below fifty-fifty. The unknown factor is key to the allure: daring to try, trying in the face of possible failure. Records have a magic about them too – a lifetime of experience, often days of planning, hours of exact physical and mental execution summarised to just a time. A time to strive

The descent from Crib Goch to Llanberis valley. Photo: Finlay Wild.
(The photos by Finlay were not taken on the run but during reconnaissance trips. Ed.)

for, to beat. And of course, the older the record the bigger the draw. With time grows a mystique: both enticing and cautionary. Colin Donnelly's 1988 Welsh 3000ft Mountains record had all of these qualities.[1]

I must have been aware of the '3000ers' record for over ten years. I didn't know the specifics, other than it would be tough if not impossible, but it remained on some subconscious dream list. I only knew one person who had attempted the record, and couldn't understand why I had not heard of more attempts on such a great line. Maybe getting older and looking for different projects was a catalyst of sorts for my own attempt – I would miss some races but make a late spring trip to Wales a priority.

Between its start atop Britain's highest mountain south of the Scottish Highlands and its end, touching the trigpoint on Foel-fras, the route covers over 35km and around 3000m of ascent. The unusual summit to summit course conjured images of a 'line in the sky', which was augmented by watching the very 1980s video reconstruction of Colin's record breaking run. The route splits logically into three sections: the rough and technical descent from Snowdon to Nant Peris via Crib Goch; the increasingly rocky peaks of the Glyderau skyline and down to Llyn Ogwen; and the big steep climb up Pen yr Ole Wen, crossing the Carneddau to the final lonely wall on Foel-fras.

---

[1] Colin Donnelly's record, set in 1988, of 4 hrs 19 mins, was 28 mins faster than Joss Naylor's record in 1973. (Ed.)

The brief road section at the west end of Llyn Ogwen. Photo:Roger Wild.

Logistically at least, these two big valley crossings were useful as it meant I could carefully recce each section on its own, and more importantly I could get support at the two road crossings. My parents usefully decided to come to North Wales on holiday and so were able to meet me at these points with food supplies and water during my record attempt. This meant I didn't have to carry much at all while running, and the need for support runners to carry sustenance was removed.

Learning the route I did slowly and carefully, with reference to Roy Clayton and Ronald Turnbull's book The Welsh Three Thousand Foot Challenges. It took quite a degree of discipline to turn around frequently and go back, checking out every small trod and alternative line as I went. I made sure to memorise my best lines before I moved on to a new section. I didn't spend too much time looking at Colin's split times – they worried me and made me feel tired! Running the 2.3km road section slightly downhill to Nant Peris at the fastest pace that seemed reasonably possible I was somewhat heartened to find I was bang on record pace of 3:14 minutes/km for that short but rapid part of the route.

I had timed my trip perfectly to coincide with a long dry spell in Wales but the window was forecast to close. I had a day of complete rest then set off to walk up Snowdon for my first attempt. Often apprehensiveness can present itself as feeling physically suboptimal, slightly fatigued, and this was the case as I slowly made my way to the summit. I was intimidated but yet bursting to have a shot. At the least, I consoled myself,

Starting up Pen Yr Ole Wen; Tryfan, Mrs Wild and Ogwen Cottage in the background.
Photo: Roger Wild.

this would be a stunningly varied journey through the best mountains of Snowdonia done in a way that was bound to push me. The weather was ideal too – clear but with a little high cloud and wind to avoid unpleasant valley inferno conditions.

The watch hit 9 a.m. and I hit the descent. Crib y Ddysgl arrived in a little over five minutes but already I was behind on Colin's time. I had prepared myself for this likelihood, but I knew he felt he had lost some time later in the Carneddau, so perhaps things could change. The ridge to Crib Goch was fast but again I lagged slightly behind. I attacked the rough descent from Bwlch Goch hard on my optimal line. Arriving at the road at Blaen-y-nant I couldn't believe it – I was ahead of the split! This spurred me into a fast road section and solid ascent of Elidir Fawr, getting there a minute faster than the record. This was the first point where I dared to imagine actually breaking it, though there was still a long way to go. Being so close to the split times kept the fire lit and I pushed hard to stay ahead through the runnable terrain to Y Garn and the Glyders. As the ground got rougher I summited Tryfan over two minutes ahead and jumped between Adam and Eve to gain 'the freedom of Tryfan' – it would've been rude not to enjoy it.

From Llyn Ogwen I had decided on the shorter but steeper south ridge up Pen yr Ole Wen instead of Colin's east ridge route. My reasoning was that at this point in the run a rough power hike might suit my legs better than the more runnable but marginally longer variation. I pushed upwards

The ascent of Pen Yr Ole Wen; Y Garn, Cwm Idwal and Snowdon behind.
Photo: Finlay Wild.

as hard as I could, trying to remain strong where I knew Colin had confessed to feeling weakest. Touching the cairn I was ecstatic to find the tactic had worked - I was now over seven minutes ahead of his schedule.

The Carneddau now stretched out before me, runnable and broad but still rocky and interesting. Heading directly along the traverse trod to Yr Elen was a joy after faffing about reccying the best line here earlier, although I can't explain why I was ten percent slower than both Colin and Joss Naylor on this short leg – stopping to refill water only explaining a small part of this. From Carnedd Llewelyn the Irish Sea to the north gave a backdrop to the final summits. I knew the splits and I knew the record was within my grasp. But it was a mental battle to keep pushing on, breathing hard and holding psychological tyranny over my body's physical protestations. Continuing up the final gradual climb and round the corner of the wall the lone trigpoint came into view. Slamming into it with both hands I had done it. Legs that had felt so focussed a moment earlier were now unsteady and I slumped to the ground amongst the boulders, a delicious desistance. 4hrs 10mins 48secs was my new benchmark: I made the slow journey down in elated astonishment.

Foel-fras: Finlay at the end of a remarkable journey. Photo: Joe Hester.

Split times:

```
Snowdon 0
Carnedd Ugain 05.20                          ( 5.20)
Crib Goch 09.44                              (15.04)
Blaen-y-nant 14.01                           (29.05)
Nant Peris PO 07.19                          (36.24)
Elidir Fawr 35.33                            (1.11.57)
Y Garn 22.21                                 (1.34.17)
Glyder Fawr 18.39                            (1.52.56)
Glyder Fach 09.09                            (2.02.05)
Tryfan 15.29                                 (2.17.33)
Llyn Ogwen west end bridge 14.39             (2.32.12)
Pen yr Ole Wen 31.18                         (3.03.30)
Carnedd Dafydd 10.42                         (3.14.12)
Yr Elen 22.09                                (3.36.20)
Carnedd Llewelyn 11.42                       (3.48.02)
Foel Grach 08.59                             (3.57.01)
Carnedd Uchaf 05.26                          (4.02.27)
Foel-fras 08.19                              (4.10.48)
```

THAT FASCIST GROOVE THANG
12 February 1983 Indicator Wall

By Roger Webb

I PULLED ONTO THE slab, made two moves and was committed. I suppose I could have jumped, fear, a jangle of gear, a moment of panic and then relief as the ropes came tight. But maybe they wouldn't come tight? Maybe there would be the fear and the jangle then awful acceleration as Chris joined me in fatal flight hurtling over Observatory Buttress to the gully beneath.

Indicator Wall and the line of Fascist Groove. Photo: Murdoch Jamieson.

Chris had assured me that the belay was good but I hadn't seen much except his axe and hammer whacked into ice. Runners weren't an option. The slab had perhaps an inch of ice. It was excellent ice as far as it went. The issue was I didn't know how far 'as far as it went' was. I knew the thickness where I teetered, I didn't know the thickness where I was going which, given the size of the capping overhang above and the steep wall to the left, was clearly up and right. Up and right the slab kicked up steeply. It looked grey. Not a good look. However three quarters of the way across or more there was grass showing through the ice, below was a runnel of whiteness. Maybe I could get there? Maybe where there is grass there's a crack? Maybe the ice is thick enough for a warthog or even a screw? Though quite how I would get both hands off for that procedure

The author's Curver (R) and a Vulture axe; the head fell off the hammer a year later on Point 5, curiously in the same place as the pick fell off his previous Curver in 1981.
Photo: Roger Webb.

(this was 1983 and screws were slightly less sharp and less one-handed then) was unclear.

With a trembling heart I headed up and right toward the turf. This wasn't so easy; I had a Curver in my right hand and a Vulture hammer in the left. The Curver might have 'given better penetration' as the advert said but it didn't really do thin ice. The Vulture faired a little better. I battled on, my world closed in. I watched the words 'Curver Snowdon Mouldings' which were engraved in the pick of my axe. I hoped they would disappear into the ice, they never did. They never got closer than two inches. Less than an inch in the ice then, fine these days with reverse curve picks not wonderful with positive ones.

In frozen time, as Chris receded, I stepped through fear and into cold calculation. Do the moves or die. That was fine for me but my calf muscles were beginning to disagree. To them oblivion was starting to seem a better option. Hurry didn't work. The Curver had a tendency to shatter the ice unless placed perpendicular to it. Salewa strap-on crampons didn't neatly slice into ice but needed kicked and kicked again to obtain almost literal toeholds. The grass and the whiteness below it crept closer. Tension streamed up the ropes as Chris, aware that his life was mine to lose, watched my progress. Three feet, two feet, one foot then, finally, I sank the Curver into the turf. It didn't go far, perhaps two inches, 'Snowdon Mouldings' didn't get in, but it was solid. Respite.

The tongue of whiteness proved to be an illusory temptation caused by a slight change of angle but with the solid placement I was able to ease my protesting calves while I contemplated the situation. There was no crack. There wasn't going to be any protection. A little above and right I could see white ice at the junction of the slab and the capping overhang. That junction was maybe two or three metres away. Between me and it the slab steepened and the ice greyed out and thinned. I couldn't see beyond that because of a slight concavity. I decided to assume that the ice I could see above me was solid. The good news was, at foot level at the base of the concavity, the ice appeared to retain its thickness. In theory as long as I could maintain my balance, I ought to be able to traverse rightwards.

There being no other course to the right I had to go. To do this I needed my left hand where my right hand was. Achieving this involved a problem that those brought up on leashed straight shafted handleless axes will remember without regret. If your right axe is in the last good placement how do you get the left one there?

There are two realistic options. The first is to extract your hands from the wrist loops, which, while wearing dachsteins with homemade loops is a hard trick, then, without dropping an axe, get your hands into the other loops. At some point in this process, one of your axes won't be in a placement, won't be attached to you and you will be trying to fit your mittened hand into a loop specifically tied to stop that hand easily coming out of and hence into it.

The second is to accept the at least temporary loss of your good placement. Remove the good axe, find something else adequate and then place the other in the vacated space. Easily said but it may result in the destruction of that good placement. On the basis that blowing the second option still left you with two axes and hence possibilities I went for that.

Hanging off the Curver I made my feet as solid as possible, stood up, stopped breathing, gently eased the axe out and scratched it into the ice at the edge of the vegetation. Still not breathing I lifted the Vulture from its placement, worried it into the turf, seated it with a strong pull and relaxed. So far so good. Now with a solid left hand I tried an experimental swing out right with the Curver, it penetrated the ice no more than two teeth before hitting rock. When pulled on, it pulled out. While I am sure that there are climbers who could have oozed across without handholds. I was not and am not one of them. It was time to go back a decade.

With my left hand on the Vulture I reversed the Curver and, using the adze, chipped away the ice at shoulder height to create a long nick stretching as far right as I could reach. Trying not to contemplate the 20m of gearless rope sweeping down to Chris and his dubious belay I felt rightwards, let the Curver dangle from my wrist and gripped my newly cut finger ledge as best I could. The mitten didn't help. Still grasping the

Vulture with my left I brought my right foot across and kicked it in below my right hand until the foot was solid. I repeated the process with my left. It was time to leave turf haven. Bracing feet and right hand I eased the Vulture out, let it dangle and brought my left hand to match my right, slid my right hand further across the nick to its end and repeated the shuffle. It was tempting to grab the Curver and swing wildly for the edge, It might have worked, it might not, so screwing my nerve down to the sticking point I chipped away rightwards once more. I shuffled further right. I was getting good at this, my brain was drifting away, 'Heaven 17' started playing in my head 'Brothers, sisters, we don't need this Fascist Groove Thang'. I moved right again, calf muscles beginning to scream, 'History will repeat itself', further right, calf muscles at full volume, I could see ice beyond the slab edge, good ice? bad ice? further right, 'Crisis Point We're on the Hour'. The ice was in range, time to swing. I swung. The happy thwunk of an axe in the good stuff, the world turned from grey to colour, 'Heaven 17' went full volume 'We don't need that Fascist Groove Thang', I wellied the Vulture next to the Curver and pulled into an icy groove, whacking my feet into glorious snow ice. Colour turned Technicolor and Chris's heartfelt 'well done' floated up from below. Now he could contemplate the future.

The groove offered relief but little protection, (some years later in 2007, *Arctic Tern* went this way with a healthy VII,5). The ice screw I tried lifted out. I carried on upwards on more satisfying ice but aware now that with, the then standard, 45m of rope I needed to belay at the first available place. I hugged the rock on the left until, stopped by a steepening, a decision was forced on me. By now I was hard against the bounding rib subsequently taken by *Riders on the Storm*, a steep icy line led to its crest. I considered it briefly; it was too steep and gearless for me. I dug for a belay in the hope of passing the problem to Chris, my digging was unsuccessful. Onward it would have to be. To my right the edge of my groove had become less defined and, although the steepening also extended rightwards it looked possible to pull out that way and traverse beneath it toward what looked to be a further icy groove. With a 'I really hope these tools don't pull' feeling I did the pull out. Somehow a renewed sensation of tension transmitted up the rope possibly in response to the 'I am seriously frightened' sensation transmitting down it. Either way the combination of the two was not healthy. I needed to derelax and get back in the groove both metaphorically and literally, although literally it was into a new groove just to my right. The music in my head started again 'Brothers sisters we don't need this Fascist Groove Thang' my conscious mind snapped back 'actually I really do need this f*cking Fascist Groove or I'm f*cking dead'. I gingered rightwards, I swung the Curver. If the first groove had been Relief and Technicolor this was Righteous Plastic Psychedelia. No need to whack an axe, just tap, no kicking feet, just place them. Worst case scenario, a decent two axe belay.

Above, my new groove again ran out into the left wall, but again I could see a step further right to a further groove. Buoyed by plastic ice, dragged back by the absence of gear, presence of fear and complaining calves, I made it to the move right. This really would have to be the last time, I could sense the increased stress as Chris watched the ropes come to their end. I stepped right. The new new groove, defined on the left, more open to the right ran out at a corner in a rock barrier a few metres above. Out right, a few moves away there was the promise of thicker ice, between me and that looked decidedly thin. I had done enough thin for one day so chose to hope that in the rock on my left or above there would be one piece of decent gear. The left wall was blank or so plated with ice as to be useless but, to my joy it quickly became apparent as I climbed toward it that the corner wasn't just a corner but a corner with enough depth at is base to kick out a ledge. Not a huge ledge but big enough for two feet. On cue the calf muscles picked up their complaints as the prospect of relief approached, I gave vent to those complaints, cursing both them and my general stupidity until, with a sensation that only those who've spent too long on front points know, I reached both rock and the space to kick out a foot ledge. Standing flatfooted and in balance I enjoyed the lack of pain and immediate threat, less so the lack of obvious belay.

I hunted high, I hunted low, there were no nice clean cracks, there were no bosses of ice, what cracks there were were blind or verglassed, what ice too thin or too far. I scraped and scratched and prodded with adze and pick. Time passed, stress travelled up the rope from my unseen and unknowing belayer. I chopped and chipped finally uncovering a short iced up crack. Too icy for a nut, too choked for my pegs, perfect for a warthog if you didn't care about getting it back, I didn't care. I took one of my two warthogs and hammered it in as far as its eye, looped a sling through it and hammered it some more. I hammered it so much it is probably still there. I clipped myself in, placed axe and hammer as best I could and clipped them too.

Turning to face down and right I shouted 'Belayed!' and started to take in. I stopped almost immediately, the rope had come tight, I shouted 'Climb when you're ready' and was surprised how quickly the instruction was obeyed. Fearful of dragging Chris off the delicate rising traverse I could only keep a light strain on the rope. A modicum of the helpless fear he must have felt eroded my new found calm. Unhelpful thought flooded my brain 'Suppose he falls off and takes a swing? Maybe the warthog's rubbish? Maybe it will come straight out? He weighs more than me. If he comes off we are seriously screwed'– pointless useless stuff. I needed distraction, I started humming to myself 'Brothers sisters we don't need that Fascist Groove Thang' just the chorus, over and over and over again. The world slowed down. The ropes crept in. The song in my head kept up its now monotonous chant. My feet froze, from tense and nervous I turned to cold and shivery.

Then I could see an axe, then a helmet, then another axe, then a face looking up, then I heard a stream of unprintable cursing, the face looked down again, the axes kept swinging, the ropes speeded up, the odd curse continued to join me. Closer he came, then he pulled into the bottom of my groove, paused and spoke, 'Good lead, glad you didn't fall off', 'Why's that?' I asked with a horrible feeling I knew the answer. 'No belay' came the expected unexpected punchline. 'I couldn't see any point in making it worse by telling you'. A further pause, 'What's that one like?' Dismissing my earlier panicky doubts I assured him that the hammered in warthog was good. He joined me on the foot ledge.

We were in a roofless sentry box, steep walls on both sides, steep above. The right wall had the most ice, two inches or so. It also had the added advantage of a distinct skyline and the suggestion of an easing angle. Right it was then, back in the fascist groove. This bit wasn't going to be easy either. A slightly impending short wall of two or three moves might promise brief difficulty but it also advertised steep toughness. No balance mind game this. Just bash, smash, lean out and pull. Chris stepped right and, with decisive determination, did just that but, as he reached over the top, his feet skated, I braced for impact but with muttered curse and mighty kick he recovered his position, grunted and disappeared out of sight. I was alone again. The ropes crept out with satisfying consistency but a disappointing lack of stopping and pulling indicated a lack of gear. After 15m or so a halt gave me hope, tentative movement and retreat destroyed it. I eyed my warthog with a lack of faith. Cold crept into my body, morale was low. I waited, nothing happened. The ropes remained static. I waited, then a slight slackening, a burst of movement, I struggled to pay out until, as rapidly as it started, movement ceased. All was static. I waited and then waited some more. My mind wandered; maybe I should take up squash? The now annoying Heaven 17 started up again with their interminable moan about fascists and grooves. I looked out at blue sky and sunshine that I was not in, I considered golf. The noise in my head was just hitting a crescendo, 'Let's cruise out of the dance war'. 'What does that line even mean?' my conscious mind complained, when it's gurning was interrupted by what is, if you happen to be on the side of a cold shadowy cliff, balanced on a foot ledge, attached to a dubious belay, shivering uncontrollably and generally frightened, the most beautiful noise in the world, the clear ring of a piton being driven into a crack. Not wishy washy tapping but full on ringing belting. Then silence, a sudden pull on one rope, then slack again, maybe a runner, maybe a belay who knows? Then joy of joys another episode of clear ringing piton driving, safety beckoning sound. A pull on the rope, a slackening and the one noise that could outdo a ringing piton, the deep loud booming shout, that only Chris could do, 'Belayed! Climb when you're ready!'

I unclipped and, after making a token effort to retrieve the warthog, anxious to escape my lonely box, moved to the suddenly much steeper than it had looked right wall. I repeated Chris's bash, smash and pull, I even repeated the skating feet at which panic flowed, only partially calmed by the quick response to my pathetic cry for tight rope. With grunt

The author and partner are in the lower part of the picture, Roger, belayed, contemplating the sunlight he is not in and Chris Rice digging unsuccessfully for protection above. Photo: Alan Shand.

and heave I pulled on to the more open world of a commodious snow bay.

Above me I could see a wide corner system that ran to the cornice, its base barred by a short steep wall. Over to my right, maintaining the rightward theme, Chris was perched on a ledge above that wall, below him the evidence of disappointed excavation. The still gearless rope extended down as did Chris's confident grin. Happy is the man with a ledge and two pegs. I wasn't that man. I was the fearful man traversing above a big drop. Despite being on the blunt end and easier ground doubt gnawed and nibbled, no one was singing in my head anymore. My movement became stilted, it was a sorry man who reached the scene of Chris's fruitless digging. There the cracks were filled with black glassy verglas, the rock plated with too little ice. Contemplating the scene, and its disappointment, I dallied lacking the drive to power the remaining steeper moves.

A sharp tug reminded me that others were involved so, with weary limbs and tired mind, I thrutched up to Chris's eyrie. Not giving me a choice Chris handed over the gear, a warthog, three ice screws, a few pegs and some nuts. Not having been given a choice I got on with the task in ahead. For the first time we were to move left, an awkward little downward traverse into what looked to be a straight forward couloir. The traverse,

Yellow: Fascist Groove (Webb and Rice 1983); Red: Arctic Tern (S. Richardson and I. Small 2007); Blue: Albatross (M.Geddes and C.Higgins 1978). Photo: Murdoch Jamieson.

with rope above, was an issue of moments, the couloir a haven of chewy ice. Confidence and energy restored both by the ice and sight of the cornice above I trundled upwards.

The ice was so good it would require an effort to fall off. Happily I sped on, the now not so annoying tune returned, 'Brothers sisters…' A steep bulge appeared, I considered stopping to put in a screw, but, the ice was so good I didn't bother, too much effort. I pulled over. The ice stopped. So did I.

Once again the rope draped gearless back to my belayer while I scratched for placements. To come this far and die from laziness seemed a hard fate. I tried left, I tried right, placements improved but not to the standard of before. Heaven 17 went silent, Chris, who couldn't see me asked how it was going, my lack of reply would have had him eyeing his pegs. I limped upward, things improved, right up to the moment I ran out of rope.

I stopped, I called for rope. None came. I waited, my calves got annoyed. I waited. The rope went slack. Cold mind came back, 'the belay's off'. Cold mind said 'remember the descending traverse' the rope got tighter, Cold mind said 'too late to move' the rope got tighter still. I pushed my weight through my feet and prayed to any available God. The rope got slacker, I thanked whichever God it had been and set off for the cornice.

New calculation, 'is that cornice closer to me than that bulge to Chris?' It wasn't, I felt him reach it, felt the hesitation and the slowdown. The cornice was feet away, better still it was insignificant. I could touch it, I could reach over, my hand was in sunshine. Chris couldn't move as fast. He stopped, I stopped. Stuck in limbo, eyeing my sunlit hand, remembering the crud over the bulge, I awaited my fate, 'Will he fall?' Seconds extended to minutes. Chris moved, I got more rope, I could see onto the plateau. I could see a man dangerously near the cornice edge and wondered at his foolhardiness. Chris moved again, I got more rope; my shoulders were above the edge, then my waist. The mysterious man leaned forward and clipped my harness 'I thought you might like this' I noticed that 'this' connected to a belay.

We were safe.

That kind and generous Irishman had been watching from the top of Gardyloo Buttress. He had realised we would run out of rope and ran around to give the assistance that he could. As it happened Chris didn't fall but that gesture remains one of the most treasured of my life. I never knew his name. It was a fitting end to an epic.

Author's Note:

This epic took place on 12 February 1983. At the time the best available guide book was Ed Grindley's 1981 update of the 1969 Ian Clough guide. It mentioned routes on Indicator Wall: Psychedelic Wall and Albatross but little in the way of description. Chris and I had decided to investigate and made the long slog up Observatory Gully. There was a party ensconced on what they claimed to be Psychedelic Wall so we wandered along until we spotted a likely looking groove. Chris climbed the groove, I then moved right onto a slab and this story began.

After we got back to Fort William we looked at the guidebook. There was no matching route. Not knowing what else to do we wrote it up in the Nevisport new routes book. Unfortunately the name picked itself.

As far as I know the line we climbed is unrepeated. Although described as a start to Albatross, it does not join that route until the easier top pitches. It is a good line. Modern kit may make it less intense but it is worth repeating.

ALEISTER CROWLEY

Part1: Early Adventures and Antagonisms (1890–1894)

By Michael Cocker

(When researching this article the writer got rather carried away with his subject and ended up with a paper just short of 5,000 words. The editor wisely declined to inflict such a long-winded piece on a discerning readership and instead suggested that it might be split over two journals. The content of the article remains unchanged. Part 1 stops just short of the point when Crowley joined the SMC in December 1894. Part 2 covers the latter years of Crowley's climbing career and his connection with the origins of bouldering. Relevant references are included at the end of each section).

EGOTISTICAL, POLYMATHIC, COMPLEX AND controversial, Aleister Crowley is one of the more memorable characters to have passed through the pages of British mountaineering history. He was an early member of the Scottish Mountaineering Club and in his youth a mountaineer of some note; in later life he became infamous for his hedonistic lifestyle and interest in the occult. He wrote a thousand page autobiography, *The Confessions of Aleister Crowley*, and is the subject of at least five biographies, numerous articles and websites and appears on the cover of one of the most influential and iconic rock albums of all time – the Beatles' *Sergeant Pepper's Lonely Hearts Club Band*. With such notoriety and wealth of material available one might wonder if there is any need for another article on Crowley, and there probably isn't, but some material from the Wastwater Hotel Climbing Book that has not been previously published lends a faint justification.

The sport of rock climbing, as distinct from Alpine climbing, began at Wasdale Head, in the Lake District, in the early 1880s, and the Wastwater Hotel, known today as the Wasdale[1] Head Inn, soon became a focal point for climbers. In the final decade of the nineteenth century their numbers were still small, no more than a couple of hundred, many of whom would have known each other, at least by reputation, if not personally. Crowley was one of the regular visitors to the hotel during this heyday. A book specifically for recording climbs was donated to the hotel in 1890 which, in this article, is referred to as the Climbing Book. During the period Crowley was active this was kept in the Smoking Room and freely available to all the residents. Similar books were kept at the Sligachan Hotel on Skye and the Pen-y-Gwryd Hotel in Snowdonia.

Crowley dictated his autobiography, *Confessions*, in the early 1920s, largely from memory, and many years after he had stopped climbing. His recollections of events are always interesting, original and entertaining,

---

[1] Wastdale is the old spelling of Wasdale. Both versions are used in this article depending on the context.

Wastwater Hotel in the 1890s. Photo: Cocker collection.

although, at times, somewhat rambling and disconnected making it difficult to assemble a clear chronology. They are also coloured with his own prejudice and perceptions and cannot always be relied upon. Using the information Crowley recorded in the Climbing Book, his SMC application, autobiography and other writing, this article attempts to provide a record of Crowley's climbing in Britain, primarily the Lake District, with brief reference to other areas.

Crowley was fourteen years old when he climbed his first mountain, Ben Venue, in the Trossachs, on a wet day in August 1890. Shortly after this he made ascents of Ben Cruachan and Ben Nevis in similar conditions. Two years later he returned to the Southern Highlands and made some further ascents, which included Ben Vorlich (Loch Earn), Ben More and Ben Lawers before moving on to Skye. He checked into the Sligachan Hotel on 23 August 1892 and that evening met Sir Joseph Lister, the founder of anaesthetic surgery, and talked about his hill walking experiences. It seems that Lister was impressed for he persuaded three climbers to take Crowley with them on an ascent of Pinnacle Ridge, on Sgùrr nan Gillean, the following day. Crowley's entry in the hotel climbing book reads:

E A Crowley climbed Sgurr nan Gillean by the Pinnacle route in thick mist. Rocks very slippery, rope was needed in places.

He followed this introduction with solo ascents of Bruach na Frithe, the Basteir Tooth (to within 5 metres of the summit) and the four peaks on Sgùrr a' Mhadaidh.

In April 1893 Crowley went to Snowdonia and climbed Tryfan, the Glyders and several peaks in the Carneddau. He claimed, controversially, that in early May he made the first ascent, solo, of Twll-Du or Devil's

Kitchen, in Cwm Idwal. Crowley recorded this in his SMC application but his claim has never been accepted. It is, however, not inconceivable that he made the ascent for it was an unusually dry spring and the line he professed to have taken, the left or SE face, was the same as that followed by W.R. Reade and W.P. McCulloch when they made the first acknowledged ascent in May 1898.

In his autobiography Crowley said:

It came natural to me to find ways up mountains which looked to me interesting and difficult. But it never occurred to me to match myself against other people. It was from purely aesthetic considerations that I climbed the gullies of Tryfan and Twll Du.

These are the only climbs Crowley is known to have made in Snowdonia. For the next six years his mountain adventures, in Britain, were mainly focused on the Lake District, where he made nine visits, his length of stay varying from a few days to a month or more.

Crowley's first visit to the Lake District was in June 1893 when he stayed at a farmhouse in Langdale with his tutor and his tutor's sister. He heard that the great challenge of the district was to climb the four highest mountains, Helvellyn, Scafell Pike, Scafell and Skiddaw in twenty four hours. Fired with enthusiasm Crowley set out on a training walk which took in the Langdale Pikes, Scafell Pike, Scafell via Broad Stand, solo ascents of Scafell Pinnacle, Napes Needle (Original Route) and Needle Ridge on Great Gable. It was a hot day and he had taken no water with him so by the time he reached the summit of Great Gable he was suffering from severe dehydration and heat exhaustion. In *Confessions*, Crowley says he 'crawled on hands and knees down to Sty Head Tarn', where he was able to refresh himself, and 'struggled on' to Rossett Gill, which he reached 'shortly after nightfall'. Back in the valley he encountered a small search party that had set out to look for him.

On another occasion he took his tutor's sister scrambling on the Langdale Pikes. At one point the girl, who seems to have been older than Crowley, was frozen with fear and broke into what Crowley described as an emotional monologue of prayer, screams and demands that Crowley, who was supporting her from below, stop looking at her legs.

Crowley returned to the Lake District in August 1893. There is no record of where he stayed but the climbs noted in his SMC application suggested that he probably went to Langdale initially and then walked over to Wasdale Head. It was during this holiday that he soloed a new route on Napes Needle that is still known as The Crowley Route (Hard Severe), although the line taken today is more direct. It was also the occasion when he first met John Robinson and Owen Glynne Jones, two of the leading climbers of the district. Crowley and Jones did not take to each other. In Confessions Crowley recalls:

I had a taste of the malice of people's envy in my first week [at Wasdale]. *A personal issue arose from the very start. Robinson happened to ask me if I had climbed in Wales. I told him yes, and mentioned one particular*

Entry by Crowley in the Wastwater Hotel Climbing Book documenting one of his routes on Napes Needle and his exploits on Kern Knotts. Photo:Cocker collection.

place, the Devil's Kitchen or Twll Du, which I had climbed by taking off my boots. I had no idea that the place was famous, but it was. It was reputedly unclimbable. Almighty Jones himself had failed. I found myself, to my astonishment, the storm centre. Jones, behind my back, accused me flatly of lying.

In fact it was two years after this meeting that Jones made his first attempt on the Devil's Kitchen. However, and for what it's worth, it is the opinion of the writer that Crowley probably did climb the Devil's Kitchen, a route that is currently graded Very Difficult.

Crowley's SMC application records a number of other climbs and hill walks made during this autumn visit, all of which, it appears, were undertaken alone. These include: Jack's Rake (Easy) on Pavey Ark, Great Gully (Moderate) on Gable Crag and the Old West (Moderate) on Pillar Rock.

Crowley was back in the Lake District again in April 1894 and, as before, he stayed a couple of nights in Langdale before walking to the hotel at Wasdale Head, where the visitors' book records he arrived on 23 April and departed on 12 May. On 25 April he made a solo ascent of Steep Gill, on Scafell Crag, with a new variation, which he recorded in the Climbing Book, his first entry. The following day he did North Climb, on Pillar Rock, with C.W. Patchell and H.V. Reade, which, at the time, was considered one of the hardest routes in the district. This is one of the few occasions when Crowley teamed up with other climbers, most of the time he climbed alone. This may have been his preference but equally his prickly personality is likely to have made him unpopular.

Crowley returned to Pillar Rock on 27 April and made solo ascents of several short routes from the Jordan Gap to the High Man and then a new route on the east face of Pisgah. The exact line of the Pisgah route has not been established. The weather deteriorated shortly after he completed the last climb and he was soon engulfed in a terrific thunder storm:

The storm increasing in violence, my attention was attracted by the little flames of lightning that played upon the iron uprights. I forgot about my axe. The next thing I knew was that I had been knocked down. I can hardly say that I felt any definite electrical shock: but I knew what must have happened. I was seized by a curious mixture of exhilaration and terror; and dashed down the face of the mountain at its steepest point, leaping from rock to rock like a goat. I easily beat the record from the summit to the hotel! Despite the intense concentration necessary to jump down the dangerous crags, my conscious attention was absorbed by the magnificent spectacle of the cliffs of Scafell, framed in lurid purple storm clouds and literally ablaze with lightning; continuous and vivid to a degree that I have never seen since except on one occasion near Madrid, when the entire sky was a kaleidoscopic network of flames for nearly two hours.

Kern Knotts Chimney, on Great Gable, was first climbed by O.G. Jones, John Robinson and W.H. Fowler on a cold, showery day, in December 1893, and a difficult step at the start of the second pitch required the aid of a shoulder. Crowley made the third ascent, alone, on 30 April 1894. In *Confessions* he wrote:

Now as it happened, Jones had been blowing his trumpet about the first ascent of Kern Knotts Chimney; the top pitch, however, he had failed to do unaided. He had been hoisted on the shoulders of the second man. I went to have a look at it and found that by wedging a stone into a convenient crack, and thus starting a foot higher up, I could get to the top, and did so. I recorded this in the Climbers' Book; and the following day a man named H.V. Reade, possibly in a sceptical mood, followed in my footsteps. He found my wedged stone, contemptuously threw it away, climbed the pitch without it, and recorded the feat. This was a double blow to Mr Jones. It was no longer a convincing argument that if he couldn't do a thing it couldn't be done.

Actually Reade dispensed with Crowley's stone six months later and not the following day as recollected by Crowley. Due to wear and the polished nature of the rock Kern Knotts Chimney is now graded Hard Severe, but in the 1890s would have been more like Very Difficult.

During this holiday Crowley made a number of further entries in the Climbing Book, including a variation finish to Mickledore Chimney, on Scafell Crag, and a descent of North Climb on Pillar Rock. On 8 May he went up to the Napes crags, on Great Gable, and made a solo ascent of a new route which he referred to as the 'Ridge to the West of Arrowhead Ridge'. He filled an entire page when writing this up in the Climbing Book, but the route was later forgotten and, until 2007, not included in the *Gable and Pillar* guidebook. It is now called Crowley's Chimney Route with a tentative grade of Very Difficult. When the guidebook was published the route was not known to have had a second ascent and this may still be the case.

The narrow ridge that separates Scafell from Scafell Pike is called Mickledore. At the point where the ridge joins the crags, on the Scafell side, there is a short steep wall with a crack running down it. Crowley made a solo ascent of this wall, on 9 May, using an ice axe wedged in the crack as a foothold. On returning to the hotel he recorded this in the Climbing Book and in his autobiography recalled:

It had always been the ambition of every climber to start at the exact top of the ridge. This was called the direct climb of Mickledoor [sic]; and nobody had done it. That seemed a shame, so I did it. This time the fat was in the fire. My good faith was openly challenged in the smoking–room. I shrugged my shoulder, but offered to repeat the climb the following day before witnesses – which I accordingly did. I suppose I am a very innocent ass, but I could not understand why anyone calling himself human should start a series of malicious intrigues on such a cause of a quarrel. I must admit my methods were sometimes calculated to annoy; but I had no patience with the idiotic vanity of mediocrities.

Climbers had probably attempted the 'direct climb of Mickledoor' before but with only one vague reference to it in the Climbing Book Crowley is probably overstating the case when he says: 'it had always been the ambition of every climber.' The climb is now called Crowley's Direct and graded Severe. The first unaided ascent was made by H.B. Gibson in 1907.

Crowley moved to Eastbourne, to live with his tutor, and spent the early summer of 1894 exploring the chalk cliffs of Beachy Head with his cousin Gregor Grant. They made a number of technically difficult and dangerous ascents where an ice axe was often required to clear away rubble or to cut steps. The unusual nature of the chalk led them to acquire considerable expertise in dealing with loose rock and in developing the art of balance climbing; skills which Crowley would later put to good use on the crags around Wasdale and elsewhere. Crowley wrote an account of these adventures and sent it to the local press. The editor was not impressed and took the opportunity to publish a stern rebuke beginning with the words 'Insensate folly takes various forms'. William Douglas, the editor of the *SMC Journal*, was more understanding and an entertaining article on chalk climbing by Crowley, was included in the 1895 issue. The following extract gives a flavour of the article and the style of climbing appropriate to these crags:

Five times I tried to cross the Gash but with no decent handhold it is hardly to be expected that one can pull one's self up to a vertical wall. One chance, however, remained. I scooped a hole out in the E. face, inserted my chin, and hauled. I had not shaved for a day or two, so was practically enjoying the advantages of Mummery spikes! The extra steadiness proved sufficient, and I came up into a position of the most ticklish balance conceivable.

Of the prominent tower, known locally as the Devil's Chimney, Crowley commented that no one who had been twice on the summit, as he had, would 'entertain the smallest doubt as to its ownership'. When the tower fell down in 2001 it was reported on the national news along with a story that Crowley had predicted that if the tower ever collapsed so would the fortunes of the people of Eastbourne. Although there is no record that Crowley ever actually suggested this, the news report went on to say that there was no cause for concern as a 'white witch' had volunteered to perform a purification ceremony!

References and Sources:

Booth, M., *A Magick Life, A Biography of Aleister Crowley* (Hodder & Stoughton, 2000).

Cocker, M., *Wasdale Climbing Book* (Glasgow: Ernest Press, 2006). (Facsimile and commentary on the climbing book kept at the Wastwater Hotel 1890–1919).

Crowley A.E. Application for membership of Scottish Mountaineering Club (1894).

Crowley A.E., 'Chalk Climbing on Beachy Head', *Scottish Mountaineering Club Journal*, 111/17 (1895), pp. 288–94.

Jones, O.G., *Rock Climbing in the English Lake District* (London: Longmans, Green & Co, 1897).

Rigby, P.C. Reid, S.J.H., *Gable & Pillar* (Fell and Rock Climbing Club, 2007).

Symonds J. and Grant K. (Editors), *The Confessions of Aleister Crowley* (London: Routledge & Kegan Paul, 1979).

Wastwater Hotel Climbing Book 1890–1919.

Wastwater Hotel Visitors' Books 1891–1894 & 1894–1901.

THE RUNNEL

A strip of neon white,
fixed as a frozen light
forking down a quiet face
below a chaliced curve of ice,
under winter's altared glaze.
A route we hoped to raise
to a climb, demanding celebration.
Axe and hammer lifted in adoration,
ritualised movements of the lead
climber, probing up ahead,
scanning the way prematurely,
checking the line carefully
for difficulty or reprieve
as the wind whispered, 'Believe.'

DESCENT

In the end I will know nothing
of climbing, will have missed
the cracks and holds of schist,
the rugosities of rhyolite,
now random as the wind
by the Allt a' Mhuilinn.

I will be nothing but limbs.
A body falling into fears.
The friable grasp of years,
the friction of memory
as smooth as the water
skirting Achtriochtan.

My lonely impulse
will delight no more
high above Arrochar,
where the burns will run,
through summer ferns
and the wind will still be blowing.

Donald Orr

DEVIL TAKE THE HINDMOST

By Iain Young

THIS IS A WINTER'S TALE that starts in summer. The summer of a Deeside August evening. It's late enough in the year to be dark outside, there's a gentle rain falling and, if you're a climber, you might wish you were somewhere else entirely. Riglos say, or Kalymnos, or maybe even Valtos. But I'm lounging about, idle-handedly surfing the net looking for photographs of, of all hills, Beinn Bhrotain and Monadh Mor as input to an idea I have in mind for the autumn. Then, an image appears on screen that makes me sit up. It's an early morning photograph of the south side of the Devil's Point, a featureless, grassy, slabby hillside in my memory, but in this shot there's a continuous shadow running diagonally left to right up the mountainside from where the grass and heather thin, interfinger and give out onto steepening rock of the crags all the way to the summit. Now, a shadow needs something to cast it. Could this mean that there's an unclimbed ridge or buttress or series of linked ribs that make up a thousand feet of elevation gain high above Glen Geusachan? A thousand feet of vertical would make for more than twelve hundred feet as the rope travels. I reckon I know the Cairngorms pretty well and such a thing doesn't exist. But maybe it's all an illusion, or more than likely it's described in the small print of the Cairngorms climbers' guide. I nip to the bookshelf and check. No mention of any ridge and a pretty dismissive description of the cliffs of the mountain. In fact, it's all really quite off-putting, *In spite of its fierce appearance, it (The Devil's Point) is most disappointing to the climber.* More surfing provides further glimmers of encouragement. But if such a ridge exists, then the lack of a mention in the guide, and any other old guide I have, means that it's been missed or dismissed, ignored or planned for, but never climbed, by the likes of Mac Smith, Bill Brooker, Tom Patey, Greg Strange, Andy Nisbet and Simon Richardson. Hard to believe. The first recorded climb on the Devil's Point was in 1908 and it's now 2019. And one of the longest ridges in the Cairngorms is unclimbed? I had to see for myself.

Autumn, and one of those mornings when the world emerges crisp and clean, wall to wall blue sky and every detail is pin sharp. Perfect for a wee look. I take my bike to White Bridge and up the west side of the Dee to check out the possible target. My moving time is quick, my elapsed time is slow. The day demands time for photograph after photograph. My originally estimated two hours to the base of the cliff still leave me an hour short and, with a deadline to meet, needs must, and I turn for home. I haven't seen nearly enough to be sure, but I've seen just enough to tempt me back with a rope and a rack and a friend or two.

Of course, I now get increasingly worried that someone else might have the same idea. With all the recent attention to Lurcher's Crag, surely someone might decide to take a look at the other end of the Lairig Ghru?

John Higham well up on the ridge. Photo: Iain Young.

And, having come across one photograph unexpectedly, it seems I now start to see images of the ridge everywhere. Gloriously displayed in Anke Addy's recent book dedicated to Nan Shepherd's Cairngorms, standing proud in a photo on the web from Beinn Bhrotain, lurking in someone's website trip report. Even more worryingly, one is posted on a popular climbing website looking down the uppermost part of the ridge from the summit. Just for the hell of it, I also check Google earth, and sure enough you can see the ridge from space. While these images convince me more and more that the effort to get in there in the winter will be worthwhile, they ramp up the concern that someone else might get there first.

Winter comes in November. A month of short days, little built-up snow, but frost. Promising. For a south-facing, rocky line a long way from the road you need snow, but not so much you can't get there and not so little that there's no sign of winter. To go exploring, you need sun, not so little that you can't see where you're headed, but not so much that the crag is stripped bare. A sort of Scottish winter Goldilocks zone. Such a window of opportunity appears to approach on all the weather forecasts around the middle of the month, so for a change I don't need to choose only the one I most like. There's snow on the hills of mid-Deeside, but not to too low a level, and everything's white higher up. Now John Higham is always keen for something new, Kenny Brookman has boundless energy, both have been in touch and both are easily roped into a mystery foray into the hills. Linn of Dee, 5.00 a.m. and a 5.30 start. First light at the

Kenny Brookman at the top of the climb. Photo: Iain Young.

Robber's Copse, the sun turning the tops red then pink then gold as we crest the rise and turn into the Lairig. The bogs are frozen, and snow is everywhere, everywhere that is except on the line of our intended route. That looks as black as the Earl of Hell's waistcoat. There's plenty of snow low down higher up Glen Geusachan, which doesn't seem to make sense, but nothing where we want to go. Frozen turf and rock might be an option for some routes, but not today. We turn right and choose the alternative of a romp up a broad rocky rib that takes us up and over Càrn a' Mhaim and on to long flat whites, a kind of demon drink for millennials, in Braemar. Over coffee and cake, we make a pact of secrecy and start thinking about a return.

Nature had other plans. Winter disappears in December as quickly as a snowball in hell. An unusually mild spell lasts through January, until the series of storms that rescues the winter deposits snow all across the highlands. Another day of a fine forecast and all three of us keen. We ponder options. It's a long way in and the road to Derry Lodge has snow, never mind the track to Corrour. Overnight in the bothy, or a camp in Glen Geusachan are options, but better the devil you know, so it's another one-day foray from the car. Maybe we're now not quite so keen, but we will simply have to suck up the inevitable suffering. Go light is the mantra, three of us to share the one proper rope (a whole eight millimetres thick), John's sixty metre fluorescent string and a minimalist rack. Linn of Dee, 5.30 a.m. again and a sinking sense of déjà vu. But this time the track is rutted with that hell on wheels combination of icy snow and iced over puddles and the cycle is hard going. This time we see first light at Derry Lodge where we swap wheels for boots. Pleasant going along the track in Glen Luibeg and then the really hard graft starts when we cross the burn at the Robber's Copse where most of the previous footfall has headed rightwards for one munro or the other. But needs must and John drives us onward, up and over the bealach again and round and down into the Lairig and sights of snow-plastered mountains. We meet a lone walker coming out of Corrour bothy as we cross the Dee. The usual pleasantries pass, *Fabulous morning... the bothy busy?...* a couple of skiers about, but then he asks, *Where are you guys headed...?* Kenny is closest, always friendly, always chatty and I wonder what he will say, it will surely be very non-committal, but then I hear a very cheerful *Oh, we're off to do a new route round the back of the Devil's Point*. Instantly the walker doesn't look like a walker to me, his boots are too technical, his clothing too colour coordinated, and he looks too fit and too relaxed. He must be a climber out for a stroll and now that the cat's out of the bag we really do need to keep postholing through the snow. Head down, I lead us into temptation, up and around, spiralling towards our goal. We get there, the ridge looks great, it's certainly a significant feature, but maybe a bit black. It's been five hours since we left the car, we need to look even more closely.

Kicking cramponless steps in icy snow on the outrun from Geusachan Gully, the sunshine means there's a kind of devil may care attitude about the party. Or there is at least till Kenny slips or trips but doesn't fall, just avoiding a long slide towards the Geusachan Burn. Crampons on, and after around a hundred metres of more steep névé, we're setting up a belay beneath twin, turfy, icy grooves just past the initial nose of the ridge. The route's on and looks fun without being onerous. Four long pitches of relaxed, enjoyable climbing follow on a natural line; first leftwards, then rightwards, then right on the ridge crest. Sometimes good, sometimes heathery, but always frozen. Runners just when we need them, then Kenny falls off clutching a loose block while seconding. Even that is more humorous than frightening. From the top of the fourth pitch, two hundred more metres of easy ground takes us in two huge 'pitches' to a finish right on the summit cairn. The sun's shining, there's no wind, everyone is smiling and for a change the ambiance is more alpine than arctic. The only signs of anyone else are a set of ski tracks stitching curves down the side of the Tailor's Burn. But we can't stay forever as the idea of the four hours to go back to the car intrudes. So down, down and back into the deep and not so steep. Some brief respite and food in Corrour then off again until the effort eases back at the Robber's Copse. The last of the light sees the bikes at Derry Lodge. Just the rutted, icy cycle now, so it's every man for himself and...

REST AND BE THANKFUL

By John Allen

ON 1 JANUARY 2016 I did Beinn Luibhean above the Rest and be Thankful road from Arrochar to Inverary. Solo. Wintry. Snow on the ground, poor visibility, short daylight; a mountain day conjured out of nothing. Wonderful. I even took photos on the clouded summit as proof. It could have been anywhere. Would I need photographs to prove solo ascents? Could I make a new year resolution to do another hundred and complete my list of Corbetts?

Fortunately no-one else rally cares. As with Munros, a completion of the Corbetts is a matter of personal adventure and absolute integrity: a self-certified boast, a private matter of personal honesty, empty of meaning to sea-level mortals, an ultimate selfie for hill-walkers. When I got home I filled two sides of A4 paper with my to-do list, and then ran out of space on the paper, with unclimbed peaks in Sections 14–17 still not noted down. There were still about a hundred to do to meet the 221 target of the 1990 SMC guidebook, so long as they didn't find any more (they did, just one, later in 2016 – Cnoc Còinnich above Lochgoilhead at just over 762m). I had better get a move on.

As a solo walker, there is the extra dimension – immersion of self into nature. There is also the need for complete self-reliance – forget some item of equipment and take the consequences; or as Whymper put it: *Look well to each step; do nothing in haste; and from the beginning think what may be the end.*

The end nearly came on the next trip to one of the Argyll peaks – Beinn Bheula, 779m. By a strange coincidence I had just been listening to the BBC World Service 'From our own Correspondent', that described how families of war-torn, immigrant Syrians were being welcomed to live in Scotland and re-located to Rothesay, a bit further down the road from Beinn Bheula. My OS map and road signs to Rothesay seemed like a good omen for my day too. Unlike refugees in flight from war, I had the privilege of choice on my day – early alarm clock at some ungodly hour of the January night in order to breakfast in the dark, drive for an hour and a half, and start walking at 10.00 up a snow covered hill. Daylight would end at 16.30, so I would need to keep to a schedule to avoid clashing with the next night, out on my feet, weary, ready to drive home to my possibly anxious partner – not very anxious actually, since I keep quiet about my mountaineering antics, leave a detailed note of my route under the car windscreen and mobile phone her when I am safely off the hill.

As soon as I got out of the car, snow began to fall. Cloud on the hill. The earlier MWIS forecast had snow arriving later in the day, not now, but the 07.00 BBC forecast predicted snow more or less all day. This turned out to be correct. I hurried with the booting up and general faffing around in order to persuade myself that I was not on a futile mission. The forestry track had been hard frozen for days, so that a light covering meant that I was making new prints. This being 2016, twenty six years since the guidebook's publication, the forestry saplings had grown up. The starter path was overgrown, resulting in a confusing route choice, and being slowed down by casting around for better options.

I was wading my own furrow through the hinterland, when two other guys appeared in my wake. These could be bloody fools, I thought; fanciful Saturday walkers who thought the guy ahead was 'going the right way' somewhere. I felt like fending them off, but they caught me up, as I was ploughing the trail. 'Confusing, isn't it?' said one, as an opener. No destination mentioned. Somewhat irritated, I came clean, 'Where are you going? I intend to climb Beinn Bheula today,' just to put them off from following me, and pointed into the cloud. They conferred, and each produced a magic weapon – a GPS, and told me exactly where we were in the forest, and that our intended objectives coincided, through the tussocks, tangles, broken crags and steepnesses to by-pass a waterfall. As for me and GPS, I am a bit behind with technology and only carry photocopied guidebook pages.

Thoroughly taken aback by their expertise, I let them get on with it up front. They were fast. The deep soft going was ameliorated for me by their tracks and rapid coverage of steep ground, so that they almost disappeared ahead. I quickly realised that it would benefit me to keep up. Thus they might be deceived about my antiquity and slowness, but when they stopped to consult their instruments and quarrel about the right answers, I said that I was probably older than them, would probably be slower, and that they should leave me out of their arrangements. No, no, they reassured me. Stay with us. Their routes via dog-legs from the gizmos seemed eccentric to me, who just pointed uphill, following the compass needle and made deviations as visibility and common sense required.

Then came the need to snack. They had found a boulder as windbreak, no good for three, so between getting cold and maybe dispirited, we speeded up the coffee or soup or snack bars or yesterday's Greggs' made-to-measure filled rolls (me). They continued ahead until this dog-legging got steep with new snow over old snow, and I was at the front, ploughing the knee-deep furrow with a feeling that I was continually climbing out of a crevasse and slithering back in. Another dog-leg and I got confused whether I might not be able to find my own way back down by myself unless I turned around now in order to follow footprints that would soon be obliterated by spindrift; and said so openly. 'No don't do that, follow us,' came the reply. 'We are so close to the summit.'

Uneasy in myself, this could be why people die in mountains, I thought – solo climber, out on the hill beyond his years or ability, unable to get back down safely. I mumbled aloud about responsibilities, but felt welcomed, included now. They insisted that I should be with them; so I followed. Another dog-leg, a ridge reached, and within ten minutes we shook hands on the summit. It was 14.00 – four hours taken for my guidebook time of two hours twenty minutes (summer). A photo was taken. Robin and Andy introduced themselves and we shook hands. I became one of them.

Descent by the ascent route followed all the dog-legs, with controlled falls and slides down the steeper, spindrifty bits over old snow, hesitantly, and we got out of the cloud but into the gloom of dusk. Snow still fell. My phone gizmo pinged in my pocket, a text message to say that snow was settling at sea-level at home in Stirling, but by the time I could relax my concentration to reply, I had passed out of network contact again. More walking, now along the level tracks of the glen, and the car, where also the other guys had parked. We threw off ice-rimed gear, said our good-byes and thanks, and motored off. I told them I would not have made the summit without their guidance by way of their GPS.

It was only a matter of minutes before we met again, in our respective cars, attempting to slither uphill to the Rest and be Thankful pass. Ahead, our road had become impassable, so that a careful reversing slither became necessary from a high point. We needed to take the alternative road; my OS sheet 56 showed that Rothesay was only 21 miles off the edge. Such irony, I thought as I remembered that Syrian family. More nightmare driving ensued; the map said the B839 Hell's Glen was now my route home and heaven. It was a single track road with powder snow, and no doubt soft edges, I thought. Not the place to meet oncoming vehicles.

I had met snow ploughs before, coming towards me, but that was on two-way roads, and the looming monster had trundled past. This was single track. In the deepening gloom of this January afternoon, I had a decision to make and about a second in which to make it; much quicker than the writing about it here; either expect him to stop in front of my on-coming headlights, likewise myself to stop; or swerve to the left onto the open moor. In the same second, in a kind of subliminal terror, I feared my partner's wrath, for it was her car. I swerved brazenly onto the open moor, thinking that a non-crash with only breakdown rescue consequences was preferable to a head-on write-off of her beautiful, bright green, difficult to replace, music box on wheels.

He swept by without as much as a scratch, and didn't stop. I could not believe that he had not ripped off the right side of the car, and my right arm too. I was now sitting in serene silence, engine gone, headlights staring vacantly into black space, the wheels on soft ground, chassis on a bedding of open heather moorland, a frozen surface surrounded by silent blanket of snow. The snowplough had vanished; it might even have been an apparition, but my raised heartbeat registered cold-blooded shock, as if a ghost had materialised and then de-materialised. I sat up straight in this roadside nightmare, and began to grovel for the RAC breakdown rescue phone number.

There was no need. Robin and Andy appeared from behind me and noticed that I was off-road. Thankfully they had avoided the snow plough and now really came to my rescue. With my wheels bogged in snow and mire, my new hill-friends offered a push and a shove. An old rug from the boot persuaded a driving wheel to grip and pop back onto the single track road, now perfectly swept and gritted. How utterly bizarre! I had not been dreaming. Real people had materialised, real mountaineers! And I was suffering only from shock, and shaking still, unscathed, in complete bemusement at my good fortune, when I could have been bull-dozed off the planet.

Only now the long, eye-watering stare into a black and white world of headlights and darkness. Late for dinner, but in safe contact by texting and mobile phoning from laybies. A home-made pizza and baked potato with red wine welcome! Had I enjoyed a good day? she asked. She will never know how good.

I fell to thinking about the Syrian families. Were they prospering? My latest news from Rothesay (December 2019) indicated that they were settling well, had opened businesses, with children going to school, and had started up a much needed and by now well-patronised café.

Rest and be thankful…

TAKING ON THE GRADIENT

By Ian Simpson

A STORY FROM MY Munro round: the first twenty in The National Park. My life had contained marriage, a son and a career in construction as a retail site fixer, but in that time I would still go hill walking with my wife and son. Then came the difficulties of divorce and, having more time on my hands afterwards, I decided to get more serious about my hill walking and take on Britain's hardest land challenge: a round of Munros.

In starting this round I would do the first twenty as a solo charity traverse of Lomond and Trossachs National Park Munros by climbing all the summits within its boundary in five consecutive days: a distance of 91ml or 145km with 13,000m of ascent. There are nineteen Munro summits within the boundary with one summit added just outside its boundary. To do this would create a National Park record for consecutive days, even bettering the mighty Stephen Pyke's visit to the Park. This was not my intention, but it just turned out that way after the event.

I chose Glasgow Hospitals' Children's Charity in order to give something back: they had saved my life after my near fatal road accident.[1] *Good things together will get to an end* was my motto for this challenge.

Looking at what I had to achieve it was not going to be easy, but by summiting all the Park's Munros in this time-frame I would grab people's attention; I wanted to do something special for my charity. So began my training for the event. I had three months to get on the pace and have the strength and stamina to endure what these Munros would throw at me. I had scheduled in 2 July to start this challenge. I had to prepare the best and quickest way to navigate on foot from public roads to the park's twenty Munro summits with an OS Ranger Map and a compass: old school navigation. I set to work getting OS sheets on my dining table and working my eye over this large area of high ground which makes up the Park's Munros – an area of 720 sq miles with a boundary of 220 miles. At first it seemed impossible to do it in five days. I realised I would have to break it down to four Munros a day over the five days.

The training began: off I went from my home, looking at Ben Lomond as I left my apartment, and into my van. I could reach the National park in fifteen minutes. I ascended Cruach Ardrain to blow the cobwebs off, the weather was fair and I was able to get visuals on almost the whole park and its Munros. Over the next three months I tried to summit as many as I could weekly, eventually doing twelve Munros a week in training for the last few weeks leading up to the challenge itself. I worked out and navigated different routes and variations of Munros before finally choosing my event routes. I became mentally stronger weekly and so did

---

[1] As a boy Ian was injured as a result of falling under the wheels of a lorry on which he was hitching an illegal ride: part of a dangerous schoolboy game. He sustained life-threatening injuries and was in hospital for three months. (Ed.)

The Allt Coire Laoigh below a rainbow from Ben Oss. Photo: Ian Simpson.

my cardio. The key to success would be my recovery times and nutrition: could I maintain this programme on consecutive days? I must also mention the weather: even though it was British summertime it could still become extreme with wind and rain in July, and low visibility too could create serious problems.

Once my preparation was complete and training done, I had to promote the event itself and get the support of friends, family and members of the public by running a Facebook 'Just Giving' page, and also putting up some flyers with ways to give. I was not disappointed with the kindness of the people and managed to raise a good amount of money. This acted as a great boost to my morale.

My final preparation was to decide what kit to take. Fast and light was my method: a small pack with packable waterproofs, energy bars, water and sports drinks, small first aid kit, map and compass, ten metres of cord, whistle and head torch. I would be wearing shorts with base layer and mid layer with packable Polartec fleece and Salomon 4d hiking boots.

On 2 July 2016 at 5 a.m. day one had arrived. I could feel the battle fever coming on as I headed to Tyndrum and on to my start point, a crossing on the river Lochy. The weather was poor with rain persisting all morning, but looking at the forecast for the week that's what I would be facing. I adopted a carry on regardless approach. I crossed the river Lochy with my boots off. Then I started up the Fionn Chorein onto Beinn a' Chleibh. Pushing it on the ascent I hit the summit in less than an hour,

*The ascent from Loch
Sloy to Ben Vorlich.
Photo: Ian Simpson.*

then came back to the bealach and ascended Ben Lui: at the summit I encountered summer hail stones; the temperature was only around five to seven degrees. I knew then that this was no ordinary walk in the park. I continued day one's Munros by adding the summits of Ben Oss and Beinn Dubhcraig.

My recovery was good and I was feeling strong thanks to my training. I took on day two with changeable weather, navigating my way round these four Munros in the rain on ground that saps your energy quicker. My route to Sgiath Chùill and Meall Glas consisted of sections of moorland and peatbog similar to Rannoch Moor. It was hard graft in the conditions, but I got the job done and went on to complete the Earn Munros, Ben Vorlich and Stùc a'Chroin: day two's twenty miles completed. I was now getting into my stride and my anxious anticipation of the event itself was receding.

On day three I went through Rob Roy territory passing his farmhouse at Inverlochlarig and up the glen to a burn taking me on the path to Beinn

Tulaichean and then the summit of Cruach Ardrain. From there I descended steep ground then over to the foot of Stob Garbh where I picked up a burn and followed it. I could see the way up Ben More after the early morning mist had lifted. I descended this burn then ascended to the bealach between Ben More and Stob Binnein. The only person I saw that day was the hill farmer from Ben More Farm gathering his flock at the bealach. As I gained the final two summits it was a great feeling knowing I had these four Munros in the bag, and I headed back to Inverlochlarig. With a route time of six hours I was up to speed.

Looking at the way the first three days had gone I was pleased with my performance on the first twelve Munros but realised I must not get complacent, for the Arrochar Alps in one day is no easy feat. Starting from Ben Vorlich it comprises three Munros with full ascents and descents, the last being a full 800 ft. I was feeling a wee bit of fatigue but this was normal on a trip of this magnitude on consecutive days. Fortunately I had more recovery time going into day four.

At 6 a.m. I started out from Inveruglas up the hydro road to the dam. I went with Vorlich and Vane either side of the dam wall, Ben Vorlich was first. I ascended steep ground on grass ledges and rock with some scrambling, gaining the summit in under an hour. I descended the same way to the dam wall, crossed the dam and ascended Beinn Vane on a burn past the wee lochans in changeable weather. There followed a full descent and re-ascent to Beinn Ime's summit, navigating in thick cloud, but reaching it was worth the effort, knowing I was on course for all twenty

A blink of sunlight on the ascent of Ben Vane. Photo: Ian Simpson.

summits. Over onto Beinn Narnain and, day four's summits all reached, I was in high spirits.

On descending I had to go over some farm fencing when my foot slipped and I ran my shin right over the wire with weight on it just before I reached the bealach. This would be my first injury of this challenge but it wasn't a show stopper, although it was something that would give me a lot of discomfort for the four summits I had left; there was blood under the skin, bruising and pain.

I got back to my van in good time to recover for the following day, feeling relieved my injury was not more serious. I went through my usual evening routine, but then started to feel sick. Then I started to be sick and couldn't keep anything down. Feeling ill, on the pan all night, can't move, nothing could stop me being sick, I felt like death and thought this was the end of my challenge. Even after I had slept, nothing could stop me being sick. Getting up and trying to get organized was a nightmare. I looked at the clock: it was 12.30 p.m. on my last day. One last chance of a cure: I pulled a can of Diet Coke from the fridge and drank it as quick as I could, three minutes passed and I had to run to the bathroom again and empty my stomach's contents. Amazingly I instantly felt better and everything was back to normal. I couldn't believe it.

I gathered myself together and out the door I went with the massive task of completing the last four Munros in the little that was left of the fifth day. To add to my problems it was raining, a heavy, low, misty murk, and I didn't get to my start point until 3 p.m. I would just have to go for

A contrasting view from the lochan on Ben Vane. Photo: Ian Simpson.

it. This final route was broken into two sections: three Munros in the Crianlarich group, then drive round Loch Lomond to Rowardennan and climb Ben Lomond.

I started over the river Falloch by Derrydaroch farm on route to An Casteil in the mist. Navigating by the burns onto a bealach between An Casteil and Beinn a' Chroin, I put a large piece of quartz down as a marker then scrambled in the rain to Beinn a' Chroin's summit. I came back and over to An Casteil only stopping to take summit photos with my charity t-shirt on. I then descended steep, slippery ground down the burn keeping to one side of its gorge, exposed greasy areas made for cautious work.

I was now at the foot of the misty hill, Beinn Chabhair, its summit always difficult to locate. I navigated by another burn which on the map was around 400 ft just east of the summit. The whole hill was now in spate and I climbed up the side of this burn gaining height quickly, summer warm, but soaking wet in the persistent rain. I hit the summit with a spate burn right to the cairn: success. I descended as fast as I could in the conditions back to my van. With little time to waste I put some dry kit on and with the heater going full blast drove round Loch Lomond to Rowardennan for my last summit, Ben Lomond.

It was now just before 10.30 p.m. The very last of the summer light was fading. The Beacon Hill I knew very well and even with most of the ascent in the dark I was sure I could do it. I put pace on, pumping my knees and running on some sections of Sròn Aonaich with a limp from the day before. I gained my last summit in the wind and rain minutes before midnight to complete the challenge. *Good things together will get to an end.*

JOINING THE CLUB
A Tale of Winter Belays

By Adam Kassyk

WHEN I MOVED BACK to Edinburgh in the early1990s, after nearly ten years south of the Border, I soon fell in with familiar faces from my University Mountaineering Club days. Then they had been fresh faced undergraduates, now it seemed they had all already become Members of the Club. Soon, it was suggested that I too should join – all that was required for my application form seemed to be a few more winter climbs in the company of Club Members.

So it was that a Friday evening in March found me at Linn of Dee with Derek Bearhop and Alec Keith, intending to walk in to Derry Lodge. Due to my lengthy sojourn in the south, my rucksack was more suited to a day's cragging in Derbyshire than a winter camping trip in Scotland, and I didn't have much space to carry camping gear. Not that I felt at all guilty, I thought my main role on the trip was to perform at the sharp end of the rope, and if my companions, stalwart as they were, carried a bigger share of the load, then that would even up the balance. After all, Alec and Derek were marathon men both, quite accustomed to dashing across the Scottish mountains in a few strides of their seven league boots (plastic in those days). A little extra weight would surely not inconvenience them. However I kept these rather selfish thoughts to myself; we shared out the

Derek Bearhop walking in up Glen Derry. Photo: Alec Keith.

The wisely pitched tent in the pines near Derry Lodge. Photo: Alec Keith.

gear as far as possible and soon we were off up the track.

It was a fine evening, and the walk didn't seem to take long. The stand of pine trees at Derry Lodge brought a flood of memories. I hadn't been there since my student days, and I remembered coming up to camp among the trees, full of excitement and ambitions – an optimism that was rarely fulfilled. Meanwhile for some reason Derek and Alec were spending what seemed to me an unnecessarily long time debating the precise location of the tent. I was reminded of Bill Murray's comment, in a different mountaineering context, of mediaeval theologians debating the number of angels who could balance on the point of a needle. Eventually the precise disposition of tent, poles and guy-lines was agreed and we settled in.

Next morning was still fine. The air had that slightly fuzzy atmosphere of deep winter. The distant skylines softened against the horizon. Snow lay thickly over the hills as we walked up Glen Derry to Coire Etchachan. The southern flank of Beinn Mheadhoin appeared almost alpine in these conditions, white ridge lines converging towards the summit. At the bend in the glen the crag came into view. Derek stopped and exclaimed 'We've got to climb That!'

'That' was a gleam of blue, standing out prominently on the otherwise white plastered Creagan a' Choire Etchachan. We consulted guidebooks. It seemed to be Square Cut Gully, and my ancient guide, dating back some twenty years, suggested it was a grade IV with three points of aid. The party speculated on whether it might still await a free ascent, but it did seem unlikely that passing Aberdonians would have ignored it over such a long period of time.

I have to admit, my heart sank a little. After all, I was going to have to lead. I'd had in mind a less exciting grade four mixed climb on the left of the crag, which would certainly have a much lower grip factor than the blue ice feature. My companions however were not to be deterred.

At the foot of the crag the feature stood out as a huge blue ice pillar. At least it seemed huge to my nervous eyes. There was a shallow basin at its foot a short way up the crag, and a white patch near the top of the pillar, which might offer a momentary respite. I must have felt that I stood a chance of success, for I didn't start to invent excuses. Or maybe I didn't dare. Alec climbed up into the basin and spent a while looking for a belay, to be frustrated by deep crust. Once up there, I didn't investigate his anchor too closely. There was after all a pretty soft landing.

The lower part of the pillar was shrouded by an apron of ever steepening snow which eventually ran out against the blue ice. I could punch steps in this for a while, until it became too steep, but the ice was still buried. There was a slight rock rib marking the edge of the ice wall to the left, and it was possible to bridge off this to gain some more height. To my great delight, a narrow crack appeared in the rib. I clipped in to a wire nut and felt much better. At least the party was now secure. From a higher bridging position I even managed to place an ice screw where the ice came within reach. Doubly secure, the next problem was to transfer out of a bridging position onto the ice wall. This felt daunting, moving from weight on legs to weight on arms.

The swing was made, and I still remember clearly the two things that flashed into my mind in the instant. I realised that I'd never been on ice this steep before. This was not Point Five style 'vertical'. The rope fell from my waist, well clear from the ice, and didn't touch anything until the snow apron now far below. The second thing that flashed into my mind was that if I didn't move quickly, I would be going nowhere but down.

I set off thrashing upwards. The bluntness of my axes was compensated by great effort and determination. The ice pillar passed in a blur, thankfully upwards. After a while the left-hand rock rib made a faint reappearance, but wasn't much help, and I pressed on to the white patch. This turned out to be a shallow depression filled with powder snow, and saw me flailing madly until I'd excavated enough ice to gain a standing position. Still too steep to rest, but I'd uncovered an organ pipe icicle frieze, and my recent gritstone experience kicked in. I stuffed a Dachsteined mitt between two icicles and locked off a perfect hand jam. I could now stop and contemplate the situation.

This was rather dramatic. There was still another bulge above, and I felt too extended to rest properly. The runners were a long way below, and pressing on without protection would unduly tempt the fates. Unfortunately none of my meagre stock of ice screws could easily be placed one handed. Eventually I cut a nick in the ice, precariously balanced a drive in, tapped it gently until it bit, and then pounded it in. With this in place I was invincible, at least for the next few moves, and with burning arms and heaving lungs I arrived in the 45 degree upper gully, to more flailing in deep soft snow.

The climb now lived up to its name, short vertical rock walls making a square cut chute in the upper crag. In the right wall I found a horizontal crack, into which I hammered two belay pegs. On closer inspection the crack was formed by a rectangular undercut block, with cracks all round it. I eyed it warily, but there was nothing else.

Physicists and psychologists have expounded the relative nature of time. While the pitch had passed in a rush of frantic action on my part, for my companions below there had been an interminable wait, when very little seemed to be happening. So they must have been greatly relieved when the time came to follow.

After taking in for a while, the rope suddenly went taut as a bowstring, the belay's knots locked and my snow stance disintegrated. One of my companions had clearly decided to test the belay, in a most unsettling fashion. There was a certain amount of dangling on both our parts before equilibrium was restored. I mused on whether this might be an unwritten qualification for entry to the Club – 'ensure the prospective Member's belays are sound and effective'.

Eventually the party was reunited without further incident. Derek was despatched upwards to deal with the next obstacle, a short vertical wall. Alec and I passed the time of day at the belay, one of the pleasures of climbing as a rope of three. I felt justified in relaxing. After all, I'd done my fair share of the hard work out in front, and we had a tried and tested belay. Surely the climb was in the bag.

Except that progress seemed very slow above, and eventually Derek announced 'I'm coming down. There's no protection'. So Alec went up instead, but despite his redoubtable efforts, after a while he too retreated. I was dismayed. Both my companions were very capable, and I set off resignedly 'to have a look'.

The wall was steep and caked in deep soft snow which was definitely not weight bearing. I did some serious digging, and eventually excavated a cave of sorts at the base of the wall. This enabled some uncertain nuts to be placed at the back of the cave among some loose looking blocks. Unfortunately in my quest for protection I had inadvertently undercut the wall, and now there was a bulge to cross as well.

After some consideration it appeared to be possible, though unlikely, to move up the right-angled corner, with my back on the rock wall and my boots punching footholds in the cake-like snow. Having gained some height, a few tentative sweeps of my axes discovered rare patches of slightly firmer snow hidden in the crust. Perhaps a few icicles had previously formed under the snow cover. I gently weighted my picks on two such invisible placements and stood up. Everything stayed in place,

Derek Bearhop seconding the crux. Photo: Alec Keith.

so I held my breath and repeated the moves until the upper slope arrived. This was less of a rectilinear feature than below, merely a shallow runnel outlined by low ribs. There was no rock visible to offer the prospect of an anchor.

Being in one hundred percent creative mode now, I came up with a novel solution. I climbed onto the flanking rib and a little way down the far side. Thus the rope could run up and over the heathery ledge above me and there would be enough friction to hold a fall below. Thus secured the rest of the party arrived in due course, this time without putting the mechanics of my Heath Robinson belay to the test.

Above lay a steep convex snow slope, disappearing into a rather gloomy sky. This did not appear particularly safe, but it was our only way out. Derek bravely volunteered to go first. The ropes ran out before he had crossed the bulge at the top of the convexity, and we both followed with some trepidation. The plateau was not a welcoming place, despite our relief at escaping from the snow burdened crag. The sky was grey and glowering, and we plunged quickly down into the corrie. Despite our combined navigational abilities, we floundered in deeply snow covered heather in upper Glen Derry, and it was with some relief we finally found the path. Flakes of snow were swirling around in the rising wind. The gloom of a highland afternoon merged into twilight then darkness. At the tent we were all equally unwilling to pack up and walk out, and equally keen to climb into sleeping bags. We had no food, but were soon asleep. A couple of hours later we were woken by the sound of heavy rain, and later again by the sounds of storm and blizzard.

No-one was in a hurry to emerge the following morning, to uncover boots and rucksacks from the overnight drifts. The snow blew horizontally through the trees, and my companions' prescience in siting the tent was vindicated. The glen was shrouded by blizzard, and when we eventually reached Braemar we heard, not surprisingly, that the road over the Cairnwell was closed, so we had a lengthy drive back to Edinburgh via the north east. I returned home at around the same time as I'd left two days earlier, and reflected that it had taken nearly forty eight hours to achieve three pitches of Cairngorm climbing. Welcome back to Scotland, I thought.

NOT A NICE VIEW

By Phil Gribbon

WE LAY STRETCHED OUT on the tin beds with the bare linked-iron diamond grid pressed into our backs. We didn't mind the incongruity of our *schlafplatz*. It was so peaceful just dozing softly in the wilderness while the friendly sun crept over the upward sweep of the fringe of the icecap and toasted us in our snug bags. The grazing caribou and its calf just gave us a brief look and continued snuffling tasty bits out of the dried lichen crisps that blanketed the tundra. We had so blended with the land that we were unworthy of a second glance.

The expedition[1] members were ensconced on the ledges above a thin lochan scooped out when the icesheet was pushing its way towards the sea. We had toiled uphill after the bus from the boat had dumped us at the airfield. Our search had been for a peaceful bivouac site well away from the mournful abandoned huts of the air force base. By good fortune we had found an ideal place with water for cooking, drinking and frantic swimming. A token fire provided a sociable circle round which to spin a few tales and relive our past mountain days before slinking off to a bed under the stars.

Next morning no one showed much enthusiasm to do anything. Lethargy reigned: contentment and indolence were winning the day. The sun was shining, the wind was somewhere else, the mosquitoes had vanished.

'How about a dander up to see the icesheet close up? It can't be more than ten miles, probably less. Take our bags and bivouac en route.'

'One piece of ice is like any other. We'll just stay here. Feel free, go if you like, you'll have a good trip.'

'Okay, it will while away a day before we have to leave. Anyone else interested?'

Thus Roger Nisbet and I found ourselves promenading through the arctic landscape as it drifted from summer to autumn, wandering over little hills and along shallow hollows, skirting minute lochans on slabby cliffs perched above rafts of fading bogbean, trapping ourselves in sandy scoops, and getting waylaid by thicketed mazes of scraggy scrub. Slowly we were heading eastward and imagining the fabled realm of a monster ice dragon where we would come up against her melting dripping snout as she gnawed imperceptibly into the border of endless heaths and heathers, bear berries and succulent fungi, all the poor wee plants so unaware of the looming threat from the chill mass encamping overhead on their border.

We rounded a tiny pond. Snow buntings flitted away to a more restful place. At the water's edge in the grass the glass glinted green, a beer bottle,

[1] The University of St. Andrews Expedition to Sukkertoppen (now Maniitsoq), 1967.

empty, of course, with a pair of scrunched-up dark sun specs. Humanity had been here.

Ahead we saw the angular silhouette of a pair of beds standing out against the deepening blue of the evening sky. Rose blushes stained the remote cirrus streaks high in the atmosphere. A solitary planet was pricking through the deep dome of the gathering night.

What was all this domestic junk doing here in the back of beyond? We shed our packs and twanged down on the bed springs. Blest with inquisitiveness we scoured the ground for souvenirs and came up with the strange collection of one Tilley paraffin lamp sans mantle or fuel, two fire extinguishers, some highly inefficient crude US army knives, forks and a spoon to take home for my kids, an unopened tin of grape jam and a single sturdy crampon. It was darkening rapidly so with no time to waste we gathered twigs for the fire, and soon there was a crackling flickering ring of flames and we knew our unappetizing precooked meal could be warmed, if nothing else. Shake the plastic bag and out came the blackened mess tins to be held over the fire. The water-filled kettle, a used pear tin, was balanced in the embers, once we made sure that any innocuous water beetles were removed. Endless cups of coffee would help to pass the evening.

Let's not just sit here all evening looking at the twinkling stars, let's have a debate, a discussion, even an argument.

'You know about my brush, in a manner of speaking, with Christine Keeler some years ago? '

'Well, it all began like this. Once upon a time, and are you sitting comfortably? In an earlier expedition[2] we had to make sure that the assorted contents of our eight-man-day food boxes did not rattle about in their cardboard homes by stuffing any excess space with wads of old newspaper...'

Toiling in a commandeered living room the food box packers were using a job lot of unsold surplus *Daily Records* that had been printed in excess to appeal to the lascivious instincts of a scandal-loving populace. Yes, every box we opened for breakfast cereal had within an identical newspaper given over in imaginative detail to lurid sexy columns about the innocent teenage good-time girls beguiled in their massively important intimate friendships with both a high government war minister and, at the other end of their liaison business, a ranked naval officer drafted into the consular service of the Soviet State. Yes, we could be titillated, but the daily dose of these feminine exposures bred familiarity, and we soon got bored by the same intrusive photos of the delectable Christine scampering along the narrow streets of swinging London with the press in hot pursuit. Every morning she and her friend Mandy Rice-Davies greeted us when we sat down to chew into our breakfast muesli. We ate in silence the only sound the scrape of spoon on mess tin or the slither of a little pebble slipping down a sandy slope nearby.

[2] The Scottish East Greenland Expedition to the 'Caledonian Alps', 1963.

What was it like in those former days when there were no smart phones for those who could read the small print without glasses, no social media in which to homogenise yourself with what your 'friends' think and then to promulgate your own thoughts and second hand opinions to all your other 'friends', and no twenty-four-hour news outlets of radio, computer, tablet, iPad, laptop and dear knows what else?

Years ago the daily papers had dominated the news world. They were printed in multitudinous columns and were spiced with articles by reliable journalists, designed to be read thoroughly or browsed at leisure. They helped to pass the time and finally could be used to light the sticks to boost the fire lighter to get the coal fire going. A quick skim through allowed the factual truth to be digested with no suspicion of fake news. Just an ideal situation to set up the reader with the where-with-all to regurgitate its opinions as if they had been freshly minted in his own mind. All this worked so well if your antagonist had no access to the same opinions that you had absorbed a few minutes before. You could hold forth until the cows came home.

We began to bat some questions back and forth. My adversary Roger had a sharp mind and could be induced to argue black was white. He may have doubted my adherence to my principles and was finding it difficult to provide a contradictory answer. One topic that formed in the darkening tundra night was querying how far the political slant of the paper would force the reader into a chosen direction to adopt the attitudes consistent with the aim of the owners and its editorial board. Are you reading only those pieces whose slant agrees with your own views? The unanswerable answer was how do you know if your views agree with what you read unless you have read the article? Slow indoctrination was insidiously rebuilding your personal political belief. However the most significant question to consider was why should you bother reading newspapers at all? How do you benefit from absorbing a litany of stories many of which are so trivial that they are forgotten by the time you read next morning's edition? Maybe you think that you absorb everything but in reality take in nothing. Why is so much time used up in pursuit of fleeting inconsequential knowledge? Why couldn't you be doing something more worthwhile?

Delving deep into the pit of philosophy: 'Facts hardly matter, only moral concepts are vital. Morality should govern what we should do. We may subvert our principles and do so all the time, but that does not detract from their moral importance.'

'How were you brought up? Sunday School? It's politics not morality that matter. Newspapers have nothing to do with morality. They want to make money or win elections. It is you that take either good or bad decisions. Listen, the water is boiling. How about a final cup of tea?'

'Take a look around, there is not another person about for miles and miles. Look up, millions of galaxies, infinite space, no one else in the universe except us. Just amazing! God is great!'

A crescent moon hung over the icecap and ribbons of glitter marked the reflections from the water trickling down its distant surface. The moon tried its best to impress but it was outshone by the shimmering green streamers of aurora as they skipped around the heavens, waltzing off to the horizon before sprinting back to the zenith.

'Bags the north facing bed so that I can go to sleep in the glow of the curtains overhead shining at me.'

With a clang we got up and kicked our unseen mess tins.

Squeak, squeak went the bed springs.

We brewed up in the pear tin, then warmed and ate unadulterated porridge oats. Stuffed our bags in our sacks and wandered off to look at the significant stone cairn perched nearby on a roche moutonnée shaped by the relentless flow of the icesheet. Its rough stones were colonised by a jigsaw of yellow and black lichens. A narrow neat entrance passage ran in at the base: perhaps it had been an animal trap to ensnare an arctic fox clad in its valuable white winter fur coat. Best to get down on my knees and peer inside. It was not a trap; it was a grave occupied by a long-bleached Inuit skull beside a single limb clothed in faded animal skins. Where were the rest? Well, well!

Let's go. We knew that we had to get as close as we could get to the very edge of the ice cap. We tramped off, following old vehicle tracks cut through the sand. Painted on a smooth boulder was a request to STOP, DO NOT PROCEED, the airbase authorities must have relished curtailing their bored personnel coming out on their little adventures. Perhaps the height of their enjoyment had been camping out in the wilderness on the beds we had sampled the night before. We came to an abandoned caboose that according to the lettering on its side had been a Frankfurter hot dog stall. Inside the walls had become the spread sheet for innumerable signatures, often dated and geographically listing their home towns from across the USA, and moaning about their incarceration in the tedium of the arctic. Some had even noted the number of days, like 210 days that still remained before they would escape their sentence.

We made it, but the ice front was a sore disappointment even if it was just as we had expected. Dirty grey ice everywhere, rarely split by a crevasse of glacial blue deep inside its depth, a soggy outwash plain of lurking quicksand, a rare clutter of assorted boulders, and a repulsive cavern out of which poured a bubbling brown torrent of churning meltwater, but then for our benefit an unstable serac shed a sizeable ice chunk directly into a convenient pool raising a cloud of spray to create a spectral rainbow of flashing dazzle in the low sun. Bright purple flowers of willowherb waved gently in the breeze spilling down the ice surface.

We lunched on scraps, marmalade on rye, and managed to drink our overboiled baby food milk substitute, free gifted and unappetizing, weakly stained with the remaining coffee grains and still tasting of chicken soup. We had travelled to see the icecap and were unimpressed.

We sensed a distant roar from the direction of the airfield, and an ancient

DC4 slowly rose into the sky streaming warm, shimmering paraffin fumes into the clear air. Our time to go back. We stepped out vigorously as we wanted to beat darkness and so we chose the gouged tire tracks that just had to lead towards the airfield.

We wandered off course. Track plodding was not inspiring. Let's walk a bit of that flat plain for a change. Yes, it is a boring sandy waste, but look at the footprints everywhere, there must have been ten thousand reindeer on the move, their hoof marks and hairy pad pits, scuffs, grooves and scrapes, and little dainty shoe prints from the elves and a wisp of white whiskers off Santa's beard, some lost Viking berserker amulets and ancient wheel splinters from Assyrian chariots and scrimshaw slivers made by Dundee whalers whittling away at walrus tusks….

'Do you believe what I am saying. Roger?'

'No, of course not. Stop it.'

Footnote

This trip is a minor extension beyond the current commercial Arctic Circle Trail, a four day trek from Sisimiut (previously Holsteinborg) on the west Greenland coast, to Kangerlussuaq at the head of the long inlet of what was Sondre Stromfjord. In those long gone days the Danish names were used and access to west Greenland was by its sole airfield at the end of the fjord. Recently Horatio Clare made this trek and recorded its vagaries in a BBC3 Slow Radio Sound Walk broadcast over three programmes at Christmas 2019.

Of more interesting relevance, the ups and downs of those swinging Sixties days and the escapades of the young ladies in question got a six part dramatization in The Trial of Christine Keeler shown on BBC1 in January 2020.

THE LAGANGARBH PAINTING

By Colwyn Jones

Every picture tells a story. But sometimes it's hard to know what story is actually being told. Anastasia Hollings.

OBSERVANT AND ACTIVE CLUB MEMBERS may have noticed that an oil painting now hangs in the sitting room of our fine club hut, Lagangarbh Cottage in Glen Coe. It was on 9 December 2016 that I first saw the painting, instantly recognisable as featuring Buachaille Etive Mòr, from north east of The (old) Kingshouse Hotel. For those who have not seen the painting, it is 45 by 35cm rendered on canvas with a noticeable weave. The ceiling lamp shade in the sitting room casts a fabric shadow across the painting but the shade can be tipped forwards to give a clearer view.

There is a notice accompanying the painting which reads: *Bequeathed to the SMC by Mr Stuart A. Booth MBE who was a resident of the Falkland Islands and a mountaineer.*

Booth's will stated *I give my oil painting of Buchaille Etive Mhor[1] to the secretary at the date of my death (4th February 2015) then serving of the Scottish Mountaineering Club to be displayed in such public location in Scotland as the secretary may decide. The cost of packing, transporting and insuring the painting is to be paid from my Estate.* Arrangements to transport the painting from Stanley, to the UK were made by his executor Mrs Rosemarie King during the summer of 2015.

For professional reasons, I had enjoyed visits to the Falkland Islands in both 2012 and again in 2017, therefore my interest was stimulated. Who was Stuart A. Booth MBE, this mountaineering benefactor and what had caused him to arrange for the oil painting to be sent over 8,000 miles to the secretary of the SMC after his death? I simply had to find out the story behind the bequest. Indeed, I would still welcome any information about Stuart Booth and D McLaren (the painter) should any reader be able to provide any.

Our Club Secretary provided the recent history of the painting. John Fowler was able to provide me with Mrs Rosemarie King's e-mail address and thus I was able to make contact in 2016, and we later met when I visited the islands in 2017. Without the help Rosemarie has given to me over recent years, this article could not have been written.

Further research produced an obituary published in the Falkland Islands Newsletter in October 2015. There was also a delightful article written by Danielle Harris, a pupil at Stanley Community School. The article is a history of her family home, Racecourse Cottage, where Stuart Booth and his wife Jessie lived from 1974 until 2014.

---

[1] The spelling of the name of the peak Buachaille Etive Mòr has changed over the years.

McLaren's painting hanging on the wall of the sitting room in Lagangarbh.
Photo: Colwyn Jones.

Stuart Booth died aged 94 in the capital of the Falkland Islands on 4 February 2015. (His wife died sixteen days later on the 20 February, after 69 years of marriage at the age of 99 years). His funeral was held on the 13 February 2015 at the King Edward VII Memorial Hospital day centre in Stanley. This venue was chosen to allow his wife to attend. He is buried in Stanley cemetery and his wife is buried next to him. The obituary in the Falkland Islands Newsletter supplemented by an entry in *The Dictionary of Falklands Biography*[2] provided the following information:

Stuart Alfred Booth, 12/08/1920 to 4/2/2015, *was born on 12 August 1920 in Widnes, Lancashire, the only child of Alfred Booth, a cooperative grocery manager and Alice May Booth (née Parker), a milliner. He was educated locally in Widnes elementary school, the Wade Deacon Grammar School and he then trained as a teacher at Chester College. By that time World War two had broken out and he served his country as a chemist in The Chemical Defence Research Establishment in Sutton Oak until July 1945.*

On release from the military he taught in various schools for Liverpool Education Authority. He met and married Jessie Kay; their wedding was in 1946. Jessie was a Hollerith machine operator (an early form of mechanical computing system). He was reported to have had great interest in the natural sciences, flowers, birds and wildlife, interests shared by his wife.

---

[2] <https://www.falklandsbiographies.org/biographies/65> retrieved 2/09/2020.

He was also a mountaineer. I was told by his unofficially adopted daughter, Joan Talbot (née Halliday), that he was a member of a mountain rescue team. Which team I have not been able to ascertain, but you can imagine my surprise when I was told, during a phone conversation, by the author of the early history of mountain rescue in England and Wales, that the first civilian MRT in North Wales was not established until the 1950s, some years after Stuart Booth had left the UK. Notwithstanding that voluntary precursors existed before the first civilian team formed, the prosaic explanation is that he was in fact a member of one of the first RAF teams, perhaps RAF Valley. His work at the chemical defence research facility in the North West of England would have brought him into contact with all of the armed forces.

In 1951 he replied to an advertisement by the Foreign and Commonwealth Office for a teaching post in the Falklands and was accepted as a teacher in the Stanley Senior School. At that time the minimum school leaving age on the Falkland Islands was fourteen, although there was a continuation class for those pupils who wished to remain for a further year. Many children went overseas to finish their education.

In the following years Mr Booth developed a science course and in time a science laboratory was built and equipped. In 1964 he was appointed headmaster of the Stanley Schools. In 1968 the minimum school leaving age limit was raised to fifteen. With few job opportunities available for girls on the islands, Mr Booth used the extra year to start a commercial course: book keeping, shorthand and typing to The Royal Society of Arts standard. He taught bookkeeping and his wife taught shorthand and typing. The course proved very successful and many pupils passed the RSA examinations and subsequently found careers in various business offices. This useful course explains much of the subsequent business success of the thriving Falkland Islands.

In 1970 the school was badly damaged by fire, which meant that for several months some classes had to be held at 44 Davis Street while the main building was repaired. Visitors to Stanley will know about the steep streets of the town and the frequent climbs up and down Davis Street and John Street each day, headmaster Booth felt, were good for the wind if not for the limbs.

Mr Booth retired in 1976 after 12 years (a total of 25 years teaching on The Falklands), but then had a busy, varied life acting as a locum for teachers on leave, and, among other positions he served as harbour master, customs officer and central store officer. When the vacancy appeared, he took over the position of librarian and also found himself almost overwhelmed with requests from a number of farms and small businesses in Stanley to meet their bookkeeping and accountancy needs.

It was not until he was 80 years old in 2000 that he retired for the second time from all of the further work he had taken on. In addition to other responsibilities, he and his wife Jessie were both active as Justices of the

Peace. His contribution to the Community in The Falkland Islands had already been celebrated when he was 63 years of age in the 1983 New Years Honours list when he was made an OBE. 1983 was the 150th Anniversary of British administration of the Falkland Islands (1833–1983). He also received the Queen's Silver Jubilee Medal in 1977. His wife Jessie also received an MBE in 1989 for services to the community. The couple spent their latter days at Racecourse Cottage in Stanley, or birdwatching, walking and gardening. They also made regular visits to Australia to the family of their unofficially adopted daughter, Joan Talbot.

At the outbreak of the Falklands War in 1982 the Booths were at home, Mr Booth being 62 years of age. Despite the Argentine occupation they stayed in their home for the first 71 days of the Falklands conflict. However, the adjacent flat racecourse was used as a command centre by Argentine forces and a helicopter base. Stanley suffered considerable damage during the war, a result of both the Argentine occupation and the British naval shelling of the town, which killed three civilians. After the British secured the high ground around the town the Argentines surrendered with no fighting in the town itself. However, the final three days of the conflict were very dangerous, and the Booths had to move to safer accommodation in the town centre. Mr Booth would walk to check his home every morning and this was why on 14 June he was one of the first Stanley residents to meet the victorious British Forces.

Stuart Booth was indeed a mountaineer and was reported by many people to have climbed in Scotland and Wales before 1951, and later continued visiting Scotland when back in the UK on leave. He is mentioned in the book *Penguin Summer* by Eleanor Rice Pettingill (1962). He accompanied the author and her husband Sewall, to film penguins on a trip to Sparrow Cove on board The Stockfish, one of the few boats able to leave the relative shelter of Stanley Harbour. 'Mr Booth was an accomplished hiker and mountaineer he always walked in the lead with his long strides.' Joan Talbot (and others) told me he had climbed on the 'mountain in the painting' but had experienced, 'a particularly hairy experience' to quote him. I gather the weather had turned to their disadvantage during the climb, but I have been unable to pinpoint the date or the route on which they found themselves. It seems that it was in memory of this adventure that he purchased the oil painting.

Stuart Booth may have had the painting hanging in his various houses on the Falklands for perhaps 64 years. The painting hung on their sitting room wall at 3 Ross Road and then their home at Racecourse Cottage. Mr Booth was reported to be very fond of it and the inclusion of its disposal in his will shows it meant a great deal to him.

When the Booths moved into sheltered hospital accommodation in December 2014, he made sure the painting went with him carried in the basket of his mobility scooter. He left the picture at the reception desk of the hospital, wrapped in an old orange towel, and asked the receptionist to pass it to Rosemarie King when he was admitted to hospital. He wanted it to be safe and knew that Rosemarie would be at the hospital as she visited daily. It seems he wanted to repatriate part of himself or his memory, pleasure or longing, through the oil painting, to his original country, while he himself remained to be buried at his home in the Falkland Islands. Perhaps he wanted people to know that for all of the years he lived in The Falklands he thought of climbing in Glen Coe.

I believe that I may even have seen Stuart Booth in Stanley in 2012, as by this stage in his life, he moved around the town on a maroon coloured electric buggy. I do recall seeing such a vehicle, and I understand that in 2012 few islanders had a mobility scooter.

Mr Booth and his wife once walked along the Wickham Heights to Ajax Bay, reportedly living mostly on pemmican and porridge. Ajax Bay is a settlement on East Falkland, on the shore of San Carlos Water, a few miles from Port San Carlos. During the Falklands War, the first British bridgehead was established on San Carlos Water. Ajax Bay was one of three landing points, and codenamed Red Beach as part of Operation Sutton and was the site of a military hospital during the war. The Booths' walk along the Wickham Heights would have overlooked the yomping route taken by the British Army from San Carlos Water to Stanley, but in the opposite direction. At the time of the Booth's marathon walk, Ajax Bay was simply an abandoned settlement. The Wickham Heights are a glaciated chain of mountains in the northern area of East Falkland, running east to west. They form the spine of East Falkland and include the highest point on the islands, Mount Usborne (705m) which I climbed with my wife Ann on 22 November 2017. The peak is named after Alexander Burns Usborne, Master's Assistant on HMS Beagle, the ship that took Charles Darwin on his famous voyage. I estimate that their walk along The Wickham Heights would have been close to 100 miles, against the prevailing wind, over very rough, steep and wild terrain, with nights under canvas at altitude.

Two other climbing artefacts survive the Booths and are on display at the Falkland Islands Museum and National Trust in the Historic Dockyard Museum, Ross Road in Stanley. They are two ice axes confirming that the couple were mountaineers, and indeed winter mountaineers. One is a Marke Mischabel ice (on right) axe and the second axe was made by François Simond et Fils, Chamonix Mont Blanc. Both axes have wooden shafts of about 80 cm in length.

Mischabel ice axes were made by the Andermatten brothers who were based in Saas Almagel, Central Switzerland. The Andermattens were one of the old mountain guiding families of that popular Alpine region and making ice axes was, in days gone by, the job of the blacksmith's side of the family. Mischabel axes (named for the mountain range above Saas Almagel) were produced in large numbers with the Swiss Army being a big customer. I believe that this axe dates from the late 1940s. The name Albert is stamped on the ice axe pick, then some symbol I can't identify, then the number 7. Below is the name 'Teufen.' This is a town in the

Appenzell Ausserrhoden Canton in central Switzerland. One similar artefact in the SMC collection is exactly the same type of axe once owned by Robin Smith. The second, a Simond axe has a number 1 (or perhaps 7) and a manufacturer's crest stamped on the pick.

Sadly there were no climbing logbooks or guidebooks donated to the Falkland Islands Museum and National Trust after his death so, to date, details of his climbing achievements remain unrecorded, but this article may prompt someone and details could still appear.

'The Booths were lovely people; they made the world a better place' (Stuart Wallace: a Booth era school pupil and Falkland's businessman). Stuart Booth was also described as a genuine polymath. They were the oldest residents on the Falkland Islands when they died.

Forensic examination of the painting:
I sought permission from the SMC secretary, and the Lagangarbh hut custodian to take down the painting temporarily, and have it assessed and

Stuart Booth as a young man. Photo: courtesy of Rosemarie King.

examined by art experts. The painting is signed D. McLaren. I have been singularly unsuccessful in identifying the artist. External examination showed there was a faded sticker on the back of the painting from Dunn's Art Stores, 35 Scott Street, Perth. The establishment still exists, but the current proprietor was unable to provide me with any history of the painting.

SMC member Helen Forde confirmed that it was ... *an oil on canvas, the fabric having a fairly open weave probably not hand stretched but bought ready-made. The paint is rather tentatively applied to the canvas, lacking any strong bold strokes but more gentle dabs in an impressionistic manner.* Helen suggests that: *the style shows that it was worked from a secondary source either a photograph or illustration not from real life and certainly not en plein air. The paint is all applied by brush with no evidence of palette knife work and is very sparse in some areas. This may have been due to not having much paint to spare (post wartime rationing?) or the artist's decision to keep it fresh and not over worked. This is all assumption but neither the composition nor paint work make me think the Artist was professionally trained to any degree. Obviously, its value lies in the subject matter and many miles away in the Falklands a painting of a mountain in Scotland was seen through rose-tinted spectacles and valued as an image of a remembered memory.*

Later the painting and frame were dismantled and examined by Fiona McCrindle, owner and director of the Edinburgh Drawing School. This confirmed that the canvas was a commercial product called Daler Board. The Daler Board Company was established in 1946 by Terry Daler on his return from a German prisoner of war camp. His brother Ken created a surface for oil painting that pulled the oil colour off the brush. Cardboard was sealed and primed through a mesh (originally a net curtain) which became the commercial product called Daler Board. Thus, we can date the start of the painting to between 1946 and 1960.

No other signatures, labels, notes or identifying features were found perhaps confirming the painting had been the work of an amateur artist. Fiona kindly professionally restored the painting and frame, which hangs once again in the sitting room of Lagangarbh.

Location:

Artistic licence typical of mountain landscapes uses vertical exaggeration and McLaren was similarly accomplished in this respect. Despite this variance from reality, on several occasions I have attempted to find out the exact position the painting represented. The original painting had the old Kingshouse Hotel, which has since been rebuilt and enlarged, and the surrounding area has also changed as the evergreen trees planted for shelter nearby have thrived. The line of the A82 trunk road through Glen Coe has also changed from the road shown on the oil painting. The relevant section of the road was completed in 1933, but this does not help to date the painting. If the painting was secondary to a photograph, or other illustration, the production date of the original may have been before 1933.

So far, my meanderings on the moorland accessed from the Black Corries Lodge track below Meall Bhalach, an eastern outlier of Beinn a' Chrulaiste, have failed to identify the exact position of either the likely photographer of Buachaille Etive Mòr, or where the artist might have set up her or his easel. The search has highlighted just how varied I found this bland looking piece of moorland. I even found a small number of cairns which might have been used by an artist to return with his easel to the same spot to give the same perspective of the mountain. Alas, none of these have proved to coincide with the many boulders shown in the foreground of the landscape or of the topography of the painted moorland.

If future visits coincide with suitable weather, never a certainty in Glen Coe, the search for the original site of the landscape may continue, but at least I now know part of the life story of Mr Stuart A. Booth MBE, and some of the history behind why his oil painting is hanging in the sitting room of Lagangarbh.

(With thanks to Helen Forde, John Fowler, Joan Talbot, Rosemarie King, Fiona McCrindle, Ann MacDonald, Stan Pearson, Bernard Swan and Teena Ormond, Records and Research Assistant, F.I. Museum & National Trust, Historic Dockyard Museum, Ross Road, Stanley, Falkland Islands, for their help with this article).

GLASCHOILLE

Too long confined we scented sea and pressed
Through bosky twilight dunes to Morar's strand,
To tread like moonlit snow the silver sand,
With Rum a cave against the golden west;
Then rose at dawn to air already warm
And skimmed impatiently across the sound,
Climbed Ladharbheinn in the searing sun and found
Half Scotland's hills stretched out past Coire Gorm.

Bless clouds that smoor the bens and shade the shore
And justify repose! All ardour spent,
Along the rose-hedged road next day we went,
And round a bend drew into memory's store
A summer scene to gladden winter toil:
The lassie with her dog beside Glaschoille.*

Graeme Morrison

* The folk at Inverie baffled us by pronouncing this '-coil' rather than '-collie'. It is a delightful spot.

THE LAST MEET

By Stan Pearson

FRIDAY WAS A BEAUTIFUL winter day, cold and clear, with a bright blue sky and little wind. It was so welcome after a winter of mild, wet, grey weather and limited climbing. Fresh snow lined the roads in the east on the way north and all the hills had at last donned a winter mantle of white. The snow line was a little higher in the west.

The classic shot of the CIC and NE Buttress: much snow. Photo: Stan Pearson.

For me there was the novelty of walking up to the CIC in late afternoon by daylight rather than the usual grind starting at 8 p.m. in the dark. It was a fine walk. The Ben was white, covered in fresh snow from the last two days. As we walked up, we could watch past excursions and future prospects unfold as we debated what did or did not hold ice beneath the fresh white cover; a distraction from the weight of the weekend's rucksack.

Various parties paused for a chat on their way down and attested to the volume of new snow but suggested the Minus face held good conditions underneath the white blanket. As ever in Scotland conditions would be good if… if we just had a little wind to blow the worst of the powder away, if that wind turned to be from the North and froze the snow after a brief spell in the sun and if that cold spell held for a just a while we could salvage the season and have a great few weeks climbing conditions. 'If,' the Scottish 'if.' As we walked, we filled in a schedule for all the little gaps in our climbing CVs, some classic lines some obscure little projects as we mentally cleared the diary for the coming weeks.

If, if it just...now, climbing would be great. How often have we thought that, climbing in Scotland? Years of experience of reality can still be overwhelmed by the optimism of one bright day to induce hope, plans and aspirations. Even if the forecast for the weekend was not promising there was the prospect of the following weeks with longer days. Now, having retired at the start of the year, the coming good conditions could be fully exploited. We salivated at the prospect. The immediate forecast was not promising. Saturday was to be windy, mild and wet with the freezing level above the tops. Sunday was to be little better with the freezing level above the tops, not ideal and potentially dangerous. Often this sort of forecast would have encouraged cancellation, but the wind was to be below gale force, and this winter had so far offered so little that a weekend at the hut assessing conditions up close had attractions. Once the Good Friday weather was added, plans were set and found Dave Broadhead and me on the path around 5p.m. just below the hut.

Here we met Robin Clothier on his way down after a few days in residence. We stopped for a chat: conditions, what had been getting done, the functioning of the cooker, the planned May gas lift, which weekend was preferred, respective domestic limitations, the success of the international meet and then the conversation turned to international climbers and more specifically Italian visitors, visitors from Northern Italy.

Since the start of the year there had been bits in the news about some virus in China. This had stayed fairly peripheral in the news what with Christmas, the election, finally getting Brexit off the front pages and was there not always some pending virus from China? We had the threat of SARS a few years back. It did not disrupt day-to-day life much. Gradually, news had started to spread of some deaths on the continent, a cruise ship somewhere. By late February things seemed to be getting serious in Italy. There had been some deaths, travel restrictions had been introduced in the north and movement outside the home in some areas had been restricted because of a Coronavirus, Covid-19. There had been some reported news items of panic buying here in the UK. There had apparently been a run on loo roles and dried foods. So northern Italians staying in the CIC, when there were now travel restrictions, raised a few questions. Robin's focus in the last few days had not been so much on climbing as on cleaning the hut and seeking advice from the authorities. This advice was confused so the hut had had a good clean and the Italians had returned home after their stay. Now a casual comment from someone else we had met on the path about how clean the hut was, took on some new significance. Still, through previous foresight and innovations there was plenty of hand sanitiser and loo roll in the hut. Italy was big place and if they had shown no symptoms probably there was not too much risk of catching any bugs. With that we parted. Robin said the hut was now empty but the meet was full and he expected to be back up on Saturday night. We carried on for a welcome brew.

The hut was not empty. Brian Shackleton and Helen had the kettle on having just come off The Curtain, taking advantage of the fine weather to catch a route before heading off to Switzerland for some ski touring. Conditions were a bit mushy, fresh snow on top of crud, not good for ice screws but if we had a few overnight frosts conditions would be good with plenty of lines complete.

We settled in. Gradually over the course of the evening the hut filled with some familiar faces some new, not crowded but cosy as all adopted the hut routine in their own preferred order: disrobing, brew, finding a bed, making introductions, something to eat, sorting kit, making plans for tomorrow. Here there was more divergence. Some had clear objectives in mind: kit sorting was purposeful, not much chat and early to bed. Others were ambitious, checking the books, what had recently been done? And as the drink flowed the shackles of the weather forecast and actual conditions were dropped in preference for more rosy, ambitious prospects. There were many other versions of preparation in each team's own style: quick guidebook flicking, overly influenced by the last route mentioned; discussion of the merits of different parts of the mountain. Had anyone ever done so and so? the merits of hardware, ice screws, a huddled review of the hit-list, whispered to avoid competition for the plumb choice to suit conditions, and, inevitably, the sloth approach. After a week at work merely getting here escaping work and domestic commitments was enough of an achievement. For now, a bit of banter and a few drams was sufficient preparation. Tomorrow would take care of itself. Anticipation worked its magic and triumphed over realism and the damp wind bring rain outside. Realism could be suspended until the morning. Everyone gradually drifted off to bed for the snoring and the wheezing on the shared bunks, having done their own preparation, before the final late arrival of some bod banging around searching, incredulous with himself, for the forgotten sleeping bag – thank goodness for friends and belay jackets. Embarrassment will keep him warm for years to come.

The morning started early, for some. Away after a quick brew while others slumbered to emerge gradually with varying degrees of enthusiasm tempered by the morning visitors, club members, already wet, who had popped in for a cuppa after their walk up. All were pulled by the inexorable force of the hut faff. From muesli to full fry up hours could easily drift away as last night's considered ambitions succumbed to the dampness outside and the general lack of urgency inside. No one was immune. Breakfast became the singular focus of the day for one party. Who was to say theirs was not the best mountaineering choice?

Dave Broadhead leading on the SW Ridge of the Douglas Boulder as the weather worsens.
Photo: Stan Pearson.

Slowly almost imperceptibly the hut emptied. Fully kitted and hooded figures bent into the warm wind and headed up toward the cliffs. Various parties headed towards the Minus face, some for the Douglas Boulder, others into the mist. It was not cold. Spindrift was adding to the already loaded slopes. Trial stabs at ice had it laminating off the rock. Once established after negotiating the doubtful slopes would there be sufficient ice? A ridge? A walk? What about descent later in the day? Retreat?

Our hopes for the Minus face receded the closer we approached. We worked up through heavy, wet snow with a base of who knows what. Despite the early hour a return to the hut was the most realistic option. We turned and headed down. Various other parties were heading down, some up, a few lingered below The Curtain; a few milled around the hut but mostly the hill was fairly quiet. The forecast had taken its toll on the usual numbers.

We were passing the Boulder. It loomed out of the mist still white, still close. Could it perhaps yet again be a way to salvage something from the day? A little recompense in this so far sparse winter? Amazingly there was only one party investigating its snow-covered flanks and even they seemed to be drifting towards an objective on the right. A few absorbing hours wandering upward in soft, increasingly wet snow, no ice, justified donning the rope before an ab back down from the Boulder summit. By then there was persistent rain. Various other parties were also abseiling from their forays: the mixed fortunes and consolations of a day on the Ben. You take what you can get.

The hut was nearly full again. A few pitches broke the ice between parties as endeavours and commiserations were shared. Who was that guy without the sleeping bag? Were we expecting anyone new tonight? No secret projects today. The all-day breakfast team were applauded for their good mountaineering judgement. Tentative suggestions to abandon the meet and head down to the valley were quashed by more optimistic partners who could find a mobile signal and an optimistic weather forecast for tomorrow. Competing weather forecasts were traded. But the mobile signal brought more than weather forecasts.

Gradually news drifted in of Coronavirus. Ski resorts in Switzerland were to close. Italy and France had moved to full lock-down. Hoarding of supplies in anticipation of what was to come was gripping the UK. The conversation turned to disruption of holiday plans, our previous week's Italian visitors, various emergency plans at peoples' work now being implemented. How severe would the situation become? What would it do for outdoor access? How bad would it be compared to foot and mouth? Some wag suggested conditions and weather were bound to get good now just as access to the hills was prohibited. There was a lively exchange of views but little did we appreciate how prescient the joke was. The tone turned more serious, less about climbing. Hand sanitiser was being rigorously applied by all.

The next day the weather was still mild and poor. The activity followed the same range and pattern as yesterday with the additional option of heading down to the valley. By Sunday night the news was warning that people over seventy and other vulnerable groups might have to self-isolate for thirteen weeks, for their own good. I got several ranting and incredulous calls from those bracketed as vulnerable. It turned cold over Sunday night with a frost. Conditions would be improving with a cold spell of settled weather in prospect. The clocks would be changing soon. A full moon was due. There would be long climbing days. Ski touring would be an option.

By Monday night restrictions were introduced to deal with the pandemic. These restrictions have gradually been tightened and advice has morphed to guidance, to rules and special powers, all with one message: stay at home. Do not go to the hills. Do not go out. Only essential travel is permitted. Mountain huts don't do social distancing. All the huts have been closed. Suddenly the climbing season is over. More important things have taken over. Already after only a few weeks into the new world the simple pleasures, once taken for granted: a chat, a walk, a little climbing, seem luxuries that we don't know when we will get back. My e-mail informs me: There will be no club meets for the foreseeable future.

NEW ROUTES

New Route descriptions can be sent directly to the New Routes Editor at newroutes@smc.org.uk Please ensure the description includes information in the following order – area, crag, route name, length, grade, suggested stars, first ascensionist(s), date, route description. Alternatively, descriptions can be submitted to the SMC website (which automatically formats them correctly) <https://www.smc.org.uk/climbs/report>

Submission of diagrams and topos is strongly encouraged. These are kept on file for future guidebook authors.

The deadline for sending route descriptions for the 2021 Journal is 31 May 2021.

OUTER HEBRIDES

LEWIS, Mullach an Taroin, Geòdha an Taroin:
Thirty-Two   30m   E2 5c **.   Gary & Karen Latter, Ewan Lyons. 10 Aug 2018.
The Direct Start to *Twelve Years On*. Start at the back of the recess. Climb the crack round the roof on good jams.

Gary Latter suggests that *Copper Koala* is E2 5b. Although the initial groove is about VS, the route is neither E1 nor "possibly easy for the grade."

LEWIS, Aird Mhor Mhangarstaidh South, Screaming Geòdha:
Gary Latter notes that *Singapore Sling* (E2 5c) has suffered a rockfall, with a large section missing at the base, and is no longer climbable at the grade.

LEWIS, Uig Sea Cliffs, Crowlista, Fiabhaig Geòdha, Landward Side:
Time and Tide   25m   E3 5c **.   Rab Anderson, Chris Anderson. 19 Sep 2019.
The line *Kitty Wake* should have taken. Climb the right-hand crack as for *Kitty Wake*, up and around the edge, then step left to climb the edge to gain and finish up a crack on the left side of the arete.

LEWIS, Druim a' Bheannaich, Boardwalk Central:
Gary Latter notes that *Magic Dragon* has suffered a rockfall and looks much harder than when originally climbed. A huge block has gone and the crack is no longer 'gained by a hand traverse rightwards from the corner.'

Boardwalk Right:
Underwhelming Corner   10m   H.Severe 4b *.   Ewan Lyons. 12 Aug 2018.
The left-facing corner right of *Twostep Crack*.

Mind the Gap   10m   H.Severe 4c *.   Ewan Lyons (solo). 12 Aug 2018.
The ramp line just right of *Underwhelming Corner*, starting with a high step.

Overjoyed   10m   Severe 4a *.   Karen & Gary Latter, Ewan Lyons. 12 Aug 2018.
The obvious large crack-line further right, going through two steps.

A pair of short steep cracks towards the right end, (a few metres left of the Difficult descent) are both Severe 4a.

LEWIS, Druim Mor, Crulabhig:
Burqa 15m HVS 5a *. Gary Latter (solo). 15 Aug 2018.
Climb a direct line up the wall right of *Letterbox Wall*, finishing on the right.

LEWIS, Creagan Ben Guidamol:
The Outer Hebrides guidebook mentions a right-hand buttress directly above a fence line. It also mentions a 'far left section of cliff' that contains three Severes. The following route lies on a crag just right of the 'far left' buttress. It has an open-book corner with an old metal fence post sticking out at the top of the corner. No routes have previously been recorded on this section of the cliff.

Flintstones 10m E4 6b *. Kevin Woods, David Macmorris. 12 Jul 2019.
The left wall of the prominent corner has a crack running through an obvious overlap at two-thirds height. Easier moves through the lower half lead to a long move past the overlap and the top out.

LEWIS, Stornoway, Creag nan Ghroida:
This cliff us located on the north side of the river Ghroida (TL 420 319) on the peninsula looking out to sea, in Lews Castle grounds, Stornoway.

Tragedy of the Commons 8m E1 5b *. Dan Fitzsimmons. 17 Jun 2017.
The obvious crack starting from the right side of the ramp. The top of which can be seen from above. Roped solo ascent ground up, using ground anchors and placing leader protection.

LEWIS, The Uig Hills, Creagan Tealasdale:
Gary Latter notes that *Caledonian McBrain Justice* was thought to be E2 5c. A further 30m VS 4c pitch was added above the large terrace, taking the rightmost of twin cracks, then left up a ramp and finishing easily rightwards. Gary & Karen Latter. 15 Jul 2019.

Gary Latter also notes that a rope sling and maillon was left on block 1m down from the top of *Grime of the Century* (25m to terrace). A further sling and maillon was also left on large block near the centre of the terrace beneath the Upper Tier (60m to base).

HARRIS, Tiorga Beag, Creagan Leathan:
The correct map reference for this crag is NB 070 135 (typo in Outer Hebrides).

Giolabhal Glas, Lochan Crag:
Deep Play 75m HVS **. John Mackenzie, Charles White. 8 Jul 2019.
A direct line up the highest part of the crag. An excellent initial pitch, bold and with spaced protection but on wonderful rock.
1. 40m 4c The climb starts below the concave slab left of *Stonechat Corner* and just right of the groove of that route. Gain the slab base by awkward moves, then climb the slabs right side to step left above it and climb the steep rib to the grass terrace. Climb the steepening rib right of the deep V-groove of *Lochan Crag*

Climb, aiming for a niche high up below a cracked headwall. Move into this 'sentry box'. Good cam belays above; a very scenic stance.
2. 35m 4a Climb the cracked headwall on good holds to exit on easy ground. Continue up to a short juggy wall on the left, climb this and finish by scrambling.

Tiorga Mor (NB 060 104):

Slabs and shorter steep walls lie on the southern flanks of Tiorga Mor between 350 and 400m altitude. These are best approached from the track off the B887 Huisinis road, limited parking 300m along this. Follow the track to a just beyond the power station and up a rocky ridge which has a good section of scrambling up red feldspar slabs to a hollow where the crags lie above.

Roughly right of centre is a narrow grass gully and a double-tiered slab tilted to the right, which appears to be the longest route here. A steep heathery scramble leads to a stance and a good belay crack. Descent lies above the route below a steeper cracked wall and down a grass ramp and then a short grassy gully on the left.

Lag MacCodrium's Dainty Gambol   70m   Severe. John Mackenzie, Charles White. 6 Jul 2019.
1. 40m 4b Move right from the stance to below the slab and climb this, a little mossy, to a glacis. Cross this to a red feldspar wall split by twin cracks. Climb the right-hand one and then move right on a slab to good belays below a short wall. Wet when climbed so hard to grade and protection a little lacking on the initial slab.
2. Move right around the wall to a rough slab and up this and the little overlaps above to an easing and the top. To reach the descent ramp the short wall above makes a good juggy finish.

SOUTH HARRIS, Ceann Reamhar, Uamascleit:

Approximately 300m south-east of the main crag lies a line of shorter crags of good brown gneiss at NB 131 997. The following route lies on the right side of these crags, prominently marked by a left-facing corner.

Joint Effort   40m   HVS 6a **. John Mackenzie, Stephen Venables. 2 Jul 2019.
The slab left of the corner has a sizeable overhang at the base. One and a half metres left of the corner is a way through via a nut-protected finger-lock crack. A predictably strenuous pull leads to a pleasant slab left of the corner which is climbed to where the corner ends. Step right onto the upper slab via some blocks and finish up the good slab.

BARRA, Feudail, Upper Tier:

Thistle Be Easy   12m   V.Diff 4a. Fenella Corrick, Tom Mallinson. 11 Aug 2019.
Start at the left most end of the Upper Tier, and make blocky moves with good protection just right of a chest-height ceiling. A few metres up, a large platform provides reassurance followed by the crux finish up a bold unprotected bulge.

Party Thyme   12m   H.Severe 4a. Tom Mallinson, Fenella Corrick. 11 Aug 2019.
Start one metre left of *Ivy Groove* and climb the prominent slightly right-leaning crack-line. An obvious horizontal rectangular recess marks the line. There is some loose rock on the route.

Fennel I See You Again? 12m Severe 4a. Tom Mallinson, Fenella Corrick. 11 Aug 2019.
Climb slightly left of the plant-filled crack that lies approximately in the centre of the Upper Tier.

PABBAY, Rubha Greotach, Banded Geo:
Oban Jellyfish Apocalypse 30m HVS 5a **. Andrew Marshall, Matthew Crawford. 23 Jun 2019.
Start as for *Tide Race*, but exit directly though the unlikely looking gap in the roof on huge holds.

MINGULAY, Rubha Liath, The Point:
Fulmars Fly For Fun 35m VS 4c **. Scott Herrett, Franklin Jacoby. 30 Jul 2019.
A well protected route of varied character. Start as for *Eaglesea*, but climb the wall rightward to a short crack. Go up this to a small ledge and climb the excellent steep corner to another ledge, from which a broken arete can be climbed to easier ground. (Topo provided.)

Franklin Loves The Big Juicy 30m VS 4c *. Nathan Adam, Matthew Rowbottom. 30 Jul 2019.
Climbs the arete right of *Crack nan Euan*, easy escape possible at the harder sections but clean climbing. From a semi-hanging stance at the base of *Crack nan Euan*, follow the clean-cut arete mostly on its right side to a prominent ledge about half way up the crag and below a steep wall. Climb the wall trending left on good horizontal breaks (maybe 5a), step right and continue up a yellowish ramp and finish by a short steep corner above.

Nathan Adam notes that *Crack nan Euan* felt about H.Severe and deserves two stars. *Eaglesea* was excellent at the grade and worth two stars.

MINGULAY, Sloc Chiasigeo:
The following two lines are on the huge black NW-facing south side of the geo. Viewing the face from the promontory opposite one sees the middle of the face cleft by a stepped crack with a prominent square birdy ledge half way up. To its right is a discontinuous crack that forks and arches rightwards at the top; right again is a deep chimney crack-line which must be *Pot of Gold*.

Amber through Obsidian 55m E3 5c **. Rick Campbell, Iain Small. 18 Jun 2008.
Abseil from the second small bluff right on the edge some 40m south of a Thrift bollard down to a long ledge above overhangs and birdy ledges. Prominent high up is an S-shaped pink quartz band. Start up a short crack midway between two larger crack systems and continue up until forced into the right-hand fault-line. Move straight back left up into steeper rock which is followed into the pink quartz band and a steep juggy flake crack. Continue up the line of the abseil over slabbier rock to finish.

Tinkling the Ebonies 55m E3 5c *. Rick Campbell, Iain Small. 22 Jun 2008.
Right of the chimney crack of *Pot of Gold* and just before the face turns a slight corner is a curious puffy double crack low down between two large pink quartz

splodges. Abseil down the line of *Pot of Gold* some 15m south of the previous route and belay on a ledge, below which the rock is greener and less pleasant. Start up *Pot of Gold* for 8m to where the lower quartz splodge leads out right onto the face. Move up a recess and pull steeply out right onto a ledge. The curious bulging double crack is up right and it is followed with difficulty to large ledges above. Finish up the first crack right of the large chimney-crack to finish. A better finish would be to break right above the bulging crux to finish up the bulging prow on the right.

MINGULAY, Guarsay Mor, The Arena:
Eye of the Storm, Variation Start 25m E2 5b ***. Michael Barnard, Lucy Spark. 3 Aug 2019.
Belay as for the normal route. Traverse out left, move up then step back right below where the wall steepens. Climb via cracks up steep rock to regain the normal route after its left traverse.

Lower Cobweb Wall:
Michael Barnard notes that *The Adventures of Ray Chup, the Brummie Midget* was thought to be E2 (5b, 5b). Pitch 1 is 15m, pitch 2 is 45m. *Cuan a Bochan* was thought to be 5b, 5a (not the other way round).

INNER HEBRIDES & ARRAN

MULL, Ulva, Basalt Columns:
Unnamed (New Routes Supplement 2018) is called *Blackboard*.

Aird Dearg:
Another One 7m H.Severe. Colin Moody (with backrope). 20 Aug 2019.
Start left of Red Oak behind the left side of the oak tree. Gain the shelf then climb the corner-crack.

The Lie 10m VS 4c. Colin Moody (with Soloist device). 20 Aug 2019.
There are two lines between *In Stalin's Steps* and *Lenin*; a chimney on the left and twin cracks on the right. Climb the twin cracks.

Missing Ladder 8m Severe. Colin Moody, Cynthia Grindley. 20 Mar 2020.
Start just left of *Collie Dug*. Go up the rib then the crack. *Blood Money* was climbed directly to make the two routes independent.

Colin Moody notes that the detached flakes at the start of *Ginger Rodent* (SMCJ 2014) are now on the ground but the route can be climbed on the left to get past the rock scar.

ERRAID, Karen's Slab:
Erica 14m HVS 4c *. Steve Kennedy, Cynthia Grindley, Colin Moody. 20 Oct 2019.
Start just left of *Emma Rose* and climb up to the wide crack. Follow the wide crack left across the face then up to finish.

Two short routes (VS and Severe) were climbed by the same party near *Ria*.

LISMORE, Drum Mor:
This NW-facing cliff can be approached either by boat into Bàgh Clach an Dobhrain bay then make your way under cliffs along shoreline, or from the end of the B8045 beyond Kilcheran followed by an abseil. Stakes would be needed as there are no belays at top.

Restricted Vocabulary 55m XS 5b **. Chris Moore, Jenny Mather. 23 Jul 2017.
The obvious prow, up the centre of the crag. Climb up the right side of the arete for 5m, then move right of the arete and climb delicately up the wall until a step left around the arete and into a scoop can be made at around 15m. Follow the scoop up (good wire) then make a bold step left and swing around onto the left wall. Move directly up through the overhang and finish up the easier ground above. The rock is incredibly loose and friable, and most gear is behind visibly moving flakes. Despite this – great adventure climbing!

KERRERA, Catnip Crag (Cladh A Bearnaig) (NM 844 310):
A small, sunbathed wall of basalt at the north end of Kerrera. The leaning wall offers steep jamming cracks and smooth technical problems on slopers, all in a delightful Hebridean setting. The crag and boulders nearby also offer a good bouldering circuit for those without ropes. A miniature Bowden-by-the-Sea.

Approach: The crag can be reached via the Kerrera Marina ferry from Oban, or by canoe or kayak from the mainland. From the marina, head up towards the monument then continue on a further 100m past it to come into sight of the crag. A 10-minute walk from the marina. The crag dries relatively quickly with sun and a good breeze, though cracks may seep. Belays can be tricky, however two small birches towards the seaward end of the fin provide good anchors for most climbs, better still with an extra rope to extend them. A large protruding block on the north side provides a solid anchor at the eastern end (best to lasso this prior to climbing a route!)

History: The crag has possibly been climbed on in the past by the local outdoor instructor groups, and was originally known as Cladh a' Bearnaig after the ruined enclosure nearby. Adrian Macleod, Tom and Rob Adams were the first to discover its full potential in 2016 climbing the obvious crack lines *Monty*, *Treacle*, *Rooey* and the prize line *Smithy*. Alex Thomson visited Catnip in Spring 2019 and came racing back with pads the next week after seeing visions of the grit crags of home. Various trips with Nick Turner, Rich Abell, Michi Arn, Fatima Gianelli and Chris Murphy uncovered the remaining routes.

Climbs are described from left to right facing the crag. At the far left of the fin, facing Lismore, is a short overhanging cave. *Gustav Meowler* climbs the cave from sitting at Font 6a. Eliminating the aretes gives *Gustav Direct* (Font 6a+).

On the main wall starting in the overgrown alcove on the left:

Doollie 5m Severe. Alex Thomson. Sep 2019.
The small capped corner to the left of *Monty*.

Monty   8m   VS 4c *. Tom Adams, Adrian Macleod. Jun 2016.
The leftmost crackline on good jams and holds.

Treacle   10m   E1 5b. Tom Adams, Adrian Macleod. Jun 2016.
The crackline to the right of *Monty* on loose jams and rounded breaks to an engaging top out.

Clawed DePussy   10m   E3 6a **. Alex Thomson. Sep 2019
Claudes out! The flared crack to the left of *Rooey* topping out through the small roof. A good Font 5+ problem to the horn.

Rooey   12m   E3 5c *. Rob Adams, Tom Adams. Jun 2016.
The central crackline leading in to the large niche. Top out steeply towards the left-hand end of the alcove taking care of loose blocks.

Claws Kinsky   12m   E4 6a **. Alex Thomson. Nov 2019.
A difficult cat. The flared crack and breaks right of *Rooey*. Follow the line to the niche and finish up good cracks to the right. Font 5+ to the break. (Climbed with preplaced gear at the crux after various failed attempts – a paw performance…)

Smithy   12m   E2 5c ***. Rob Adams, Tom Adams. Jun 2016.
The Top Cat of Catnip cracks. Fight your way up the obvious right hand crackline on delicious jams. Finish direct or trend slightly right at the top.

Perryn's Paws   10m   VS 4c *. Alex Thomson, Rich Abell. Aug 2019.
The right-hand arete of the fin, finishing up the groove.

Felines On A Shirt   20m   E2 5b ***. First ascent unknown.
The obvious traverse of the crag. From right to left or left to right.

Daphne Du Meowrier   15m   VS 4c **. Alex Thomson, Fatima Gianelli. Sep 2019.
The slab to the right of the fin. Climb the starting slab to the alcove, place your largest cam in the crack over the top, then pad your way up the well positioned top half.

Uilleam Dona   15m   VS 4c **. Alex Thomson, Michi Arn. Sep 2019.
On the north facing wall 50m back towards the monument. Trend left up positive cracks to a final rightwards traverse at the top. Belay from the heathery niche off anchors further back.

Back up towards the monument there lies a small ivy-covered wall just before the descent to the main crag. The clean monolithic face offers a great fridge-hugging exercise – *Parsley* (Font 6a+).

ISLAY:
The following new routes have been climbed since the publication of Islay Rock (Graham Little, published privately, 2019).

Sanaigmore Area, Candle Buttress:

Candle in the Wind 25m HVS 4c. Graham Little, Lucy Spark, Catherine Hobaiter. 7 Oct 2019.
Start on the right side of the grassy bay that foots the gully of *Peaches en Regalia*, about 5m right of *Steve's Saunter*, below a big spike. Although a good line there is some dubious rock. Climb over flakes to pass left of a big embedded square block. Step left onto a big shaky flake then climb the steep, left facing groove until a pull out right can be made onto the front face. Climb the face and vegetated ground above to an optional belay. A much better belay is available another 15m up the steep, heathery slope.

Smaull Walls, The Light Side:

Smaull World 9m E1 5b **. Graham Little (solo). 3 May 2019.
Start a couple of metres up the steepening footing slab to the right of *The Right Edge*, below a clump of sea pink. Climb the centre of the wall.

Smaull Walls, The West Side:

Westward Ho 8m Severe 4b *. Graham Little (solo). 3 May 2019.
Start just right of *West Side Story*. Gain and climb the wall on the left side of the low roof and then climb the corner above.

North of Portnahaven, Eilean Cam, Island Defile Wall:

Aphrodite's Eyes 15m E2 5b Graham Little (unseconded). 6 May 2019.
Start about 6m to the right of the corner taken by *Darth Maureen*. Climb over big flakes then move up left to a bay. Above is a band of flakey, overhanging, rock. Move up and slightly right, then cross it using an 'eye socket' foothold (the bold crux) to improving rock quality and better protection and thence the top.

Mrs Bridge 20m Severe **. Mark Hudson, Nic Bassnett. 23 Aug 2019.
A fun and spectacular route that gains and climbs the big scoop left of the *Mr Bridge* corner. Start up that route and swing round left onto the front face on massive flakes. Move up and left to climb the left edge of the scoop on huge honeycombs.

Just So 22m H.Severe 4b. Nic Bassnett, Mark Hudson. 23 Aug 2019.
A rising diagonal line of flakes across the wall between *Mr Bridge* and *Darth Maureen*. Start above a turgid pool just L of *Mr B* and climb easy flakes up and left to reach the corner of *Darth Maureen*. Bridge up that route and step back right to finish up a pleasant short wall.

Handle With Care 12m HVS 4c. Graham Little (unseconded). 6 May 2019.
Near the northern end of Eilean Cam is a big chossy corner. Climb the steep wall (on big but brittle holds) a couple of metres right of the corner. The start is tidal.

Result 15m V.Diff. Mark Hudson, Nic Bassnett 23 Aug 2019
A vertical crack system on the north end of the landward face, opposite a huge chossy corner on the northern end of the Eilean. A good way to finish the day. Start above a slim brown pool and climb the crack direct, passing a steeper section holding a small pod.

South of Portnahaven, The Fan:

And He Sang The Wild Rover   25m   V.Diff *. Mark Hudson, Nic Bassnett. 19 Aug 2019.
A high level traverse of the Fan, fantastically positioned but on huge flakes, and unaffected by the tide. Downclimb the final moves of *Pretty In Pink* (or start up that route) and traverse right on an obvious line of monster holds, passing below the cream roof and finishing up the arete of *Graphite Edge*. Belay well back.

Ferg   15m   H.Severe 4b. Mark Hudson, Andrew Holden. 19 Aug 2019.
The vertical crack system opposite the landward end of the Fan, on the south wall of the inlet, holding a huge wedge low down. Downclimb and step over a rift to belay level with the wedge.
   Stride across a bottomless gap to climb the right-hand side of the wedge (crux) then follow the leaning left-facing corner above. Pleasantly V.Diff if you start up the left-hand side of the wedge.

Am Burg Defile, Slate Slab (NR 192 648):

The Am Burgh Defile is an impressive connection between two tidal inlets that separate the headland of Am Burg from the mainland, creating a semi-island. There is easy access into the defile from its bend. Slate Slab lies on the mainland side of the long arm of the defile and is the slabby right flank of a prominent corner (a weep-line). The foot of the slab is above all but the highest tides. From the top of both these routes 14m of steep grass must be ascended to reach a steel stake belay. Dry conditions are essential.

A Date With Slate   16m   VS 4c **. Graham Little, Christina Woodrow. 15 May 2019.
Start at the foot of the thin crack that runs the full height of the slab. Climb the line of the crack, with one short deviation to the right, to just above half height (bold – scant protection) then take an easier blocky fault line running up and right to finish.

Slate Accompli   15m   VS 5a **. Graham Little (unseconded). 15 May 2019.
Start 3m right of the thin crack – at the right edge of the slab. Take a direct line up the right side of the slab to finish up a steepening slabby wall (crux), using a turf-embedded rock tablet for the final (careful) pull over.

ARRAN, Creag na Davie (NR 955 452):

This is the west-facing crag situated at 500m on the west flank of Carn Mor above Loch na Davie, accessed from Gleann Easan Biorach. (Photo of cliff provided).

Davie's Anvil   60m   Severe 4a. Andrew Fraser, Ian Magill. 7 Jun 2019.
Good clean rock and an unusual outlook. At the bottom of the steepest, most continuous section of crag is a small bay, with cracks above.
1. 25m Climb up and right to gain and climb a shallow groove. A further wall, then a foot traverse left gains a crack and belay below a small overhang – a nice pitch.
2. 35m Turn the overhang on the right, traverse the ledge above the overhang then climb walls to the top.

SKYE THE CUILLIN

SGÙRR NAN GILLEAN, High Crag:
Christmas Comes but Once a Year 175m IV,4 ***. Mike Lates, Lucy Spark. 13 Feb 2020.
Takes the line of least resistance in the left-hand half of the crag.
1. 15m Start up ice in the corner fault, from the lowest point of the crag.
2. 30m Easy ground leads to a choice of parallel ice lines. Climb the right hand option for 6m and belay.
3. 50m Climb the icy corner ramp for 35m then easy ground to good spike belay beside a red wall.
4. 30m Step left to re-join the central line past an awkward bulge at 5m. Avoid rightward escape by an icy corner to gain a chimney running behind a pinnacle. Cave belay above this.
5. 50m Easy ground leads to block belays on top of the crag.

Pinnacle Ridge:
In March 2020, Lucy Spark and Ian Hall repeated *West Ridge* of Knights Peak and provided the following revised description:

West Ridge of Knights Peak 180m IV,4.
The route gains the ridge from the obvious ramp trending up right from the foot of Third-Fourth Gully. From the top of the ramp climb it takes grooves left of the crest until the crest becomes unavoidable. From here, the route continues up the crest and then finishes up a steep chimney
1. 50m. Ramp pitch: Climb up to the base of grooves. Poor belay.
2 and 3. 70m. Grooves: Climb the grooves. Variation possible. Good belays.
4. 30m. Crest pitch: Turn the first steepening on the right then follow the crest to an airy shoulder and ledge before the final tower. Good belay.
5. 30m. Chimney pitch (crux): Climb the steep mixed chimney 1m right of crest with poor runners. Good belay immediately above the chimney.
From here, finish up the summit arete of Knight's Peak (Grade II).

INNACCESSIBLE PINNACLE, Coire Lagan:
In Pinn I.F.L. (Icefall Lite) III,5 * 120m. Mike lates and Lucy Spark. 6 Mar 2020.
Start immediately right of *In Pinn Fall*.
1. 30m Climb the snow bib that leads to a narrow slot. Exit onto the slopes that extend to the In Pinn high above.
2. 25m A prominent sheet of ice lies 20m right. Take the narrowing fault before this is reached. The crux cave is short with steep and well protected moves to huge spike belay.
3 and 4. 65m Easier terrain leads up and right to the An Stac bypass.

SGÙRR THEÀRLAICH, North-East Face:
The following route lies to the right of Raeburn's Route (1913).

Cliff and the Shadows 120m II. Noel & Lucy Williams. 19 Mar 2009.
Start to the right of the lowest rocks of the north-east face. Ascend an easy snow slope, then climb diagonally leftwards to reach the start of a prominent sloping terrace. Head straight up to a left-facing corner-groove in the wall above. Climb

the groove, moving right near the top and ascend to a good stance. Climb a groove to gain an obvious rightward diagonal traverse line. Continue easily to finish at a prominent notch on the north ridge. (Topo provided)

SRÒN NA CÌCHE, Eastern Buttress:
The Daleks 25m E1 5b *. Michael Barnard, Doug Bartholomew. 14 Jul 2019. This pitch is well seen from the top of Vulcan Wall, and can be taken in after a route on that buttress. Above the descent rake, gained by a scramble up and left, is a vertical crack just right of an arete and leading to a right-slanting dyke. Gain and climb the crack (crux) to reach the arete. Continue up rightwards, then back left to finish up a groove.

COIRE A' GHRUNNDA, Sròn na Cìche, North Crag:
Jupiter 40m E1 5b **
Steve Kennedy, Cynthia Grindley & Colin Moody. 14th July 2019
The prominent crack running up the left side of the roof right of the slab containing *Zeus* (SMCJ 2012). This is the buttress just right of *North Crag Gully*. Start 5m right of *Zeus* at a short left facing corner. Climb leftwards into a corner/crack at the left end of the roof. Climb the crack (crux) to the girdle ledge and belay below a dirty corner (25m). From the ledge finish up the slabby wall on the left (joining *Zeus*) (4b) (15m).

GREATER CUILLIN:
Will Rowland notes that he completed the Greater Cuillin Traverse (starting up *Pinnacle Ridge*) followed by the Red Cuillin 20–21 Mar 2020. He left Slichagan at 3a.m. and reached Camasunary at 9p.m. that evening. He started at 7a.m. next morning and reached Slichagan at 7p.m.

SKYE SEA CLIFFS & OUTCROPS

TROTTERNISH, Coire Scamadal:
Correction: *Tom's Gully* (SMCJ 2019) should be named *Consolation Gully*.

STAFFIN, Southern Cliffs, Little Kilt:
Gary & Karen Latter made a free ascent of *Run of the Tide* at E2 5c ** on 2 May 2017. The route has suffered a couple of rockfalls; one at the base, and a more substantial one affecting the final section. The route was climbed as far as good ledge at half-height, then descent by abseil. The upper section looks like it could be bypassed fairly readily.

Tempest Buttress Area:
Andy Moles notes that he abseiled the line of *Blood of an Englishman* in Jun 2019 not knowing it had been climbed in 2017. He removed a fair amount of loose rock in its upper half, and at one-third height he found an alarmingly semi-detached massive flake of rock (still in place).

Northern Cliffs, Staffin Slip South:
Windom Earle 40m E2 5c **. James Sutton, Douglas Sutton. May 2019. The twin white cracks in the wall right of *Sasha* lead to a spacious ledge near the top.

Fire Walk with Me   45m   E3 5c ***. James Sutton, Douglas Sutton, M.Barratt.
29 Jun 2019.
A perfect sustained finger crack 8m right of *Silly Pollack*, finishing at the highest
part of the crag.

BORNESKETAIG, Gully Walls, East Face:

Stac Polly   16m   E2 5b ***. Colin Moody, Steve Kennedy, Cynthia Grindley. 13
Jul 2019.
The twin cracks just right of *Polysexual*. Bridge up the corner on the left then
move right using a foothold on the arete between the twin cracks. At the end move
left to the belay on *Polysexual*. A more direct start can be taken up the left-hand
crack for 2m moving right using a handhold on the arete that is a foothold above.
This start is harder but makes the route independent.

Gallipoli   16m   HVS 5a *. Steve Kennedy, Cynthia Grindley, Colin Moody. 25
Jul 2019.
The twin cracks 3m right of *Polystyrene*, moving rightwards at two-thirds height
to gain and finish up a crack in a rib just right of a corner.

Glue Cuts   16m   E1 5b ***. Colin Moody, Steve Kennedy, Cynthia Grindley. 8
Sep 2019.
At the right-hand side of Poly Wall is a slight bay. Climb twin cracks just left of
the bay, in the upper part keep to the right-hand crack.

NA HURANAN, Arrival Cliff, Lower Left Sector:

Towards the left end of the lower crag is a short, semi-detached stocky pinnacle,
right of which is a wall of ribs and cracks. At the base is the Milestone that locates
the route *Milestone, Ribs n Cracks*.

Rubber Duck   18m   VS 5a *. Nicola Bassnett, Roger Brown. 7 Jun 2019.
Immediately left of *Milestone, Ribs n Cracks* is a stout pinnacle. To the right and
level with its top is a triangular gently-inclined overhang, with ragged vertical
cracks sprouting from its top corners. Gain and climb the cracks, which soon
converge. Climb the right-facing corner and associated raggedy cracks. Move
right onto the arete to a fine finish.

Red Balloons   15m   VS 4c. Nicola Bassnett, Roger Brown (with rests), Kat
Lenz. 10 Jun 2019.
Three metres left of the pinnacle and just to the right of *Cuckoo* is a crack with a
protruding jammed flake near its start. Climb the crack and, at the heather ledge,
take the central crack with help from its right-hand neighbour, to a blocky exit.

Medium Oatmeal Slab   10m   VS 4b. Andrew Holden, Mark Hudson. 29 May
2019.
Climb the slab in the recess midway between its right-facing corner and *Crunchy
Nut Corner* (SMCJ 2019). The top out is deceptively steep.

Room 101   10m   VS 5a. Nicola Bassnett, Roger Brown, Kat Lenz. 10 Jun 2019.
The zigzaggy crack immediately right of *Crunchy Nut Corner*, although short, is
worthwhile.

Seven Plus Two   15m   VS 4b *. N Bassnett, R Brown. 29 May 2019.
Three metres right of arete, which is right of *Crunchy Nut Corner*, is a left-facing concave corner below a crack. Climb this and the crack above, with interest, and finish up another left-facing corner system.

NEIST POINT, Upper Cliffs, The Green Lady Area:

Green Flash   35m   E4 6a **. Masa Sakano, Edward Nind (Headpoint). 20 Sep 2019.
The route climbs the groove system and through the roof at three-quarters of the height in the centre-left of the northwest face of Green Lady and then the left arete to top out. Start at the very bottom and left side of north-west face. Climb an easy (right-facing) groove, then the steeper right-facing corner of the prow. Step left at the top of the prow to rest. Arrange good gear, step right, and blast through the bottomless steep groove (technical crux). Step left and up to the cracked roof and climb it and the hanging groove above (power crux). Step left to the sloping wide ledge. Finally, climb the poorly-protected overhanging arete above to spectacular airy finish (psychological crux). Belay anchors are found 5m back. (Topo provided)

Destitution Point:

Squeenius, Right Finish   20m   HVS 5a *. Gary & Karen Latter. 6 May 2019.
Instead of swinging left onto the front face of the pillar, climb direct up the tight right-facing groove, finishing with care up the right side of detached pinnacle.

Gary Latter notes that the upper section of *Squeenius* has been affected by the Spring 2009 rockfall that removed several routes on the right side of the Prow Area – looks very loose towards the top.

The Ramps:

Andy Moles notes that *Sore Phalanges* fully deserves its ***.

Yellow Walls:
Hokusai   25m   HVS 5b **. Andy Moles, Mike Lates. 4 Oct 2019.
The obvious vertical groove to the right of *Cornflake Wall*, just left of a wide stepped corner. A tricky entry from the right leads into the groove, which gives good sustained climbing. At the top either finish direct or step left onto a shelf and finish from here. Block thread belay well back. (Topo provided).

Andy Moles notes that *Barabbas* and *1 and 1 Groove* are situated 5m to the left of *Cornflake Wall*, not right, as stated in Skye Sea Cliffs & Outcrops.

ELGOL, Suidhe Biorach:

DIY Direct   25m   E1 5c **. Michael Barnard, Doug Bartholomew. 13 Jul 2019.
Start as for *DIY Arete*, but step right at first opportunity and move up (crux) to the halfway ledge. Continue as for the normal route.

Prince of Whales   25m   E2 5c *. Michael Barnard, Doug Bartholomew. 13 Jul 2019.
Between *Rum Doodle* and *Angel of Sharkness*. Move up to an obvious break immediately right of the overhangs. Reach up for a good hold, then make tricky

moves up and left. Go up the crack on the left (*Rum Doodle*?), then continue directly past another interesting section and on to the top.

Mary Hinge 25m E2 5c **. Gary & Karen Latter. 10 Apr 2018.
A spectacular direct start to *Hairy Mary*, with good holds and protection. Climb directly up to the roof, cross it (good cam on right over lip), then move leftwards to finish up the upper section of *Hairy Mary*.

NORTHERN HIGHLANDS NORTH

CUL MOR, South-West Flank:
Table Rib 400m III,4. Iain Young, John Higham. 28 Jan 2020.
Follow the summer route throughout (see p82 Highland Scrambles North) starting via the 'slimy slabs' of summer.

CUL BEAG, Lurgainn Slabs, Top Tier:
This lies above and left of Middle Tier and is the biggest and steepest of the tiers containing the longest and best routes here. The tier is in fact a big higher one (that contains *Breakthrough* (SMCJ 2018) and *Breakout* (SMCJ 2019)) and a smaller lower one, which is described below. Both tiers are reached by the same access, done in two ways. Either follow the base of the Middle Tier leftwards along the deer trod, exposed in places, or else from the top of the grassy gully, move up left to cairns and descend down broken rock to the deer trod. All descents are to the right, looking up. Moving left along the deer trod a short distance is a two-tiered slab and to the left a steeper slab with a jutting block. Routes are described right to left.

Rippling Delight 27m Mild Severe *. Andrew James, John Mackenzie. 26 Aug 2019.
The pleasant open slab with lots of horizontal holds leads to a ledge and a short upper continuation and a scramble to excellent belays in a slanting crack.

Rogue Ripple 23m E1 5b *. John Mackenzie, Andrew James. 26 Aug 2019.
The steeper slab to the left with a jutting block. A partly cleaned crack on its right provides good small wires and the occasional cam, but the climbing is all on the slab to the left. Start at the lowest point on pebbles and move up right towards the crack. Continue delicately to the top exiting just right of the jutting block. Scramble to the same belays as the previous route.

Friends Alone 20m Severe **. Andrew James, John Mackenzie. 26 Aug 2019.
This takes the slender pillar left of a steeper one at a higher level than the previous two routes. A lovely amble, well protected by cams, starting and following the arete all the way to the top.

STAC POLLAIDH, No.2 Buttress:
Bats in the Belfry, Blind as a Bat Start 150m VS 4b *. John Higham, Iain Young, Siobhan Young. 19 Apr 2019.
Between and immediately right of the scree gully below West Buttress and the true No.2 Buttress is a subsidiary, broken, rocky rib that terminates at the base of

the Upper No.2 Buttress. This pleasant, but easily escapable route follows the rib, and is an excellent approach to *Bats in the Belfry* or other routes on the Upper Buttress. The route is mainly V.Diff and scrambling apart from the 25m arete on pitch 4 which is VS 4b.

1. 50m Start from a large ledge above the broken rocks at the base of the ridge. Follow the crest via a series of short walls to belay on broad ledge below a steep wall.

2. 20m Climb this wall via crack, and a squeeze chimney above onto narrow arete.

3. 30m Cross arete and short wall above to easier ground.

4. 50m An escape left here is possible, but it is better to continue up the wall above, climb its right-hand arete (25m) followed by a short scramble (25m) to reach the base of the Upper No.2 Buttress and *Bats in the Belfry*. (Topo provided)

John Higham notes that *Bats in the Belfry* was thought to be VS 5a. The relationship of *Bats in the Belfry* to *Going Batty* (SMCJ 2018) seems uncertain – they may share the same crux moves.

REIFF, Stone Pig Cliffs:
Double Leaning Joweler   15m   VS 5a *. Dominic Oughton and Helen Oughton. 17 May 2019.
The rightmost of two new routes that takes the undercut slab between *Slabby Corner Crack* and *Daunts Arete*. Tricky moves up the right-hand overhanging slot to get established on the upper slab, which is followed more easily direct to the top. (Topo provided)

Makin' Bacon   15m   Severe 4a *. Dominic Oughton and Helen Oughton. 17 May 2019.
The leftmost of two new routes that takes the undercut slab between *Slabby Corner Crack* and *Daunts Arete*. Take the crack right of the foot of *Slabby Corner Crack* (and 2m left of *Double Leaning Joweler*) to gain an easier entry onto the slab, and follow a parallel line direct to the top. (Topo provided)

Rubha Coigeach, Black Magic Bay:
Chocolate Girl   15m   E1 5a *. Gary & Karen Latter. 26 Aug 2014.
Line up left edge, left of *Milk Tray*.

Rubha Coigeach, Slab Inlet:
The Millionaire's Club   10m   E2 5c **. Ian Taylor, Tess Fryer. 15 Jul 2019.
The wall left of *Eag Dubh* climbed direct.

Rubha Coigeach, Platform Walls:
Minch View   15m   VS 4c *. Gary & Karen Latter. 26 Aug 2014.
Line up wall right of *Minch Crack*.

Rubha Coigeach, Amphitheatre Bay:
Nought to Sixty   20m   E5 6a ***. Ian Taylor, Tess Fryer. 2 August 2019.
Start just left of *Roaring Forties* below a short hanging corner. Climb the corner, step left then follow thin cracks over bulges to a good break at 10m. Move right and make a long move to a big jug on the arete and a junction with *Roaring Forties*. Go up the *Roaring Forties* groove for 5m to a good Friend 2 placement

then down climb and make tricky moves left to gain the bottom of a small hanging groove. Finish up this.

Rubha Coigeach, Leaning Block Cliffs:
A Part Heid 15m HVS 5a *. Gary & Karen Latter. 27 Aug 2014.
Line up wall left of *The Africaan Problem*.

SUMMER ISLES, Tanera Beg, Sròn Slugain Uaine (NB 958 077):
The cliff comprises twin pillars with a long 6m wide roof in between, above a sloping shelf. The first four routes are on the highest NW-facing wall. The best descent is to scramble down shelves (low-mid tide) at south end of crag, or easiest by 10m abseil from two large blocks 5m back from edge near north end.

Transitions 18m E2 5c **. Gary & Karen Latter. 9 Sep 2015.
Climb the left-slanting corner at the left end of the wall up into the easy-angled final corner. Step down onto small square block and traverse the lip of the roof, stepping out left to finish at a short black crack/groove.

Large cams (3" to 5") are particularly useful for the breaks on the following three routes:

Segue 12m E1 5b *. Gary & Karen Latter. 9 Sep 2015.
The most continuous, leftmost of the trio of left-slanting crack-lines.

Timbre 12m E1 5b *. Gary & Karen Latter. 9 Sep 2015.
The hanging central crack, pulling slightly left onto the easy ramp. Finish directly up wall, just left of the next route.

Liminal 12m E2 5c **. Gary & Karen Latter. 9 Sep 2015.
The hanging rightmost crack. Start up the easy right side of the arete, then climb the wall on superb incut holds and the crack to ledge near top. Finish up short wall above.

Clapotis 10m Severe 4a *. Gary Latter (solo). 9 Sep 2015.
The prominent corner at the left end, gained direct over small roof on good holds.

LOCHINVER CRAGS, Creag Rodha Mor (Super Crag), The Burnished Walls:
Gem 30m HVS 5a *. Gary & Karen Latter. 17 Apr 2019.
The vertical crack above the triangular block in the low roof at the right end of the crag (right of *Midget*).

BREABAG, West Face, Breabag North Slabs (NC 2819 1648):
This is the lower and left-hand slab seen from the approach situated at an altitude of 570m. It is most easily reached by the 'Bone Caves' path then up the short glen to the south past the cave track before heading up the hillside. Descent is best to the right (looking down) over blocks before heading down a narrow grassy ramp that curves leftwards back to a grass ledge near the slabs base. Allow 1hr to 1hr 15mins hours from the car park to the slabs. The rock is quartzite pipe rock with great friction, even in the wet. The slabs are convex, steepest at the base and the left side is marked by a curving wall and there is a prominent square-cut recessed

slab bounded by overlaps in the centre. The rock is very clean apart from occasional grass tufts in the corners or on ledges. (Topo provided)

Lucy's Slab   65m   Grade 2/3. Eve Mackenzie, Lucy (Cocker Spaniel). 3 Jun 2018.
Follow the cleanest slab to the right of the bounding corner, taking a line of choice, but avoiding a wet black area near the top on the right. Easy apart from the start.

Corvid's Corner   65m   V.Diff ** John Mackenzie, Colin Tarbat. 20 Jul 2019.
Left of the square-cut recess is a clean curving corner. Start at a lower level than the recess at a smooth and quite steep slab on the left and below the start of the corner.
1. 20m Climb the centre of the slab on friction to broken ledges.
2. 45m Step down and right to enter the corner and follow the slab on its right, over small overlaps and up easy slabs to the top. A good natural line with little protection.

Recess Direct   55m   VS 4c *. John Mackenzie, Colin Tarbat. 20 Jul 2019.
Start left of centre in the recess and climb slabs near the left corner to a narrow ramp that leads to the centre of the overlap; Friend 1 below the overlap on the right. Climb the overlap, crux, and then head up the slabs above taking the best line to the block field at the top, thread belay around the biggest.

Investigation Corner   70m   Diff *. John Mackenzie. 3 Jun 2018.
To the right of the square-cut recess is a corner higher up. Climb a series of quite steep slabs to the overlap and move right into the corner. Follow the best line up the slabs just right of the corner. Some pleasant non-taxing climbing.

FAR NORTH-WEST CRAGS, Tarbet Sea-Cliffs, Brown Crag:
Farewell Mrs May! 20m VS 4c. Ron Kenyon, Phil Blanshard. 19 Jun 2019.
Start as for *Raw Sienna*, then take an ascending line leftwards, crossing *Distinctly Ochreish*, to gain sloping ledges and finish as for *Brown*.

Oh No! It Could Be Boris! 12m HVS 5a. Ron Kenyon, Phil Blanshard, Hilary Robertson. 19 Jun 2019.
Start just left of *Raw Sienna* and ascend leftwards to the diagonal line of *Distinctly Ochreish*. Continue up leftwards to finish up the headwall, just right of *Dun*.

Ridgway View Crag:
Gary Latter notes that this is the correct spelling of the crag – named after John Ridgway, whose School of Adventure is located nearby at Ardmore. Many of the climbs at this crag were in use by instructors at the adventure school by at least 1977.

Tormentil Arete 20m MVS 4b. Ron Kenyon, Hilary Robertson, Phil Blanshard. 22 Jun 2019.
Takes the triangular arete right of *Oars Aft*. Start up vegetated rock to below the arete and gain the arete from the left and continue up and leftwards to the top.

Doddle 14m Easy *. Gary Latter (solo). 25 Apr 2019.
The blocky heathery crack just left of *Michael*.

Plonker's Start * 10m HVS 5a *. Gary Latter (solo). 25 Apr 2019.
A direct start to *Rodney's Gneiss Route* up the blunt arete. Unprotected.

Ardmore View Crag, Four Lochans View Crag (NC 2299 5191):
The large easy-angled north-west facing slab 50m down left of The Balcony, with lots of pegmatite. Protection is almost exclusively from cams, as many of the cracks are flared. The descent is easiest down the left end.

Do You Expect Me to Talk? 30m Severe 4a *. Karen & Gary Latter. 29 Apr 2019.
Intermittent cracks up the left side, finishing rightwards.

No Mr Tick, I Expect You to Die 40m Severe 4a **. Gary & Karen Latter. 29 Apr 2019.
Climb the left-slanting crack, then the central cracks. Continue easily above the terrace to belay further back.

Stoneflow 30m Severe 4a *. Karen & Gary Latter. 29 Apr 2019.
Cracks up the right edge, moving rightwards to ascend slim groove. Finish leftwards to pull through on heather.

Creag an Fhithich, Grey Wall:
The following route shares some common ground with the unrecorded route *Giff*, but the diagonal traverse and upper wall is new (briefly cleaned on abseil).

The Sound of One Tick Popping 30m HVS 5a **. Gary & Karen Latter. 28 Apr 2019.
The vertical crack just left of *Gaff*. Start a few metres left of that route. Climb the crack to prominent horizontal, move rightwards along this then direct up the wall. Belay on wall 8m back from top.

Creag an Fhithich, Russett Wall:
Iridescence 35m E3 **. Gary & Karen Latter. 28 Apr 2019.
The left-slanting diagonal crack.
1. 20m 5c Climb the crack with increasing difficulty to its end. Pull through the roof with a long reach to gain a superb pegmatite jug and belay just above.
2. 15m 4a Move left 3m and climb the rib left of the gully, crossing the top of the gully rightwards.

Cladonia Dreaming 25m E1 5b **. Gary & Karen Latter. 28 Apr 2019.
A direct line up the wall and hanging crack right of *Horseshit Direct*. Start directly beneath the crack, climb the wall, first leftwards, then rightwards to gain the crack. Climb this, then direct, finishing up the fine pocketed wall left of the niche of *Dung Beetle*.

FOINAVEN, Creag Urbhard:
Fiscal Gruel 150m Severe. Daniel Moore. 28 Jun 2019.
Start up *Pantagruel* but where it traverses right move up and left to a distinctive water-worn concave slab. Climb up this then traverse back right over the overlap then work your way up slabs to a prominent deep crack behind a block. Climb this (or avoid it by going left then back right) to a grassy ledge. Climb delicately

up rightwards before heading straight up to join the fantastic upper slabs of Creag Urbhard. The route may coincide with *Fiscal's Rib* and *Pantagruel* but the former has scant info and the latter I think is further right.

SARCLET, Big Buttress:
Shakedown Street 35m E1 5a **. Michael Barnard, Alan Hill. 25 Aug 2019.
Good climbing between *The Orchid Hunter* and *Baron von Midgehousen*. Belay as for the latter. Move out left to climb a much shallower line of flakes, sometimes quite near the *Baron*, to a good ledge. Step left and go up to good holds near *The Orchid Hunter*, then step right and continue boldly to gain the groove above. Go up to the top of the pillar and finish up the short wall as for *The Orchid Hunter*.

Wee Buttress, Right Section:
The Chains Are On 30m E1 5a **. Michael Barnard, Alan Hill. 26 Aug 2019.
A flake-crack up the front face of the buttress is the line of the crag and can be seen from the top of Big Buttress. Abseil down the line of the route to a good barnacled ledge which is only covered at high tide (as for *Eat Your Greens*). Climb the flake-crack, quite bold in places, until forced to step left into the roofed corner of *Unnecessary Egyptian*. Continue as for that route.

Michael Barnard notes that *Eat Your Greens* (SMCJ 2012) is also 30m. For that route a short crack just right of the arete gave a good finish, no change in grade. From the same belay at the base, the main crack system right of the arete was also climbed at Severe and thought worth a star. This may be the same as *Moonstone*.

Captain's Buttress:
Partially Tidal South to East facing
The following routes lie on the next small promontory north of Wee Buttress. The fine steep south-facing wall (*Captain Sarclet* to *Hidden Pleasure*) can be seen from the top of both Wee Buttress and Big Buttress. Best gained by abseil.

Captain Sarclet 20m HVS 5a **. Michael Barnard, Alan Hill. 26 Aug 2019.
The slanting flake-crack on the left. Continue directly to the top.

Diamond Dust 20m E1 5c ***. Michael Barnard, Alan Hill 26 Aug 2019
The vertical crack in the centre of the wall. Continue to the upper ledge, then step right to finish up a short corner.

Hidden Pleasure 20m HVS 5c *. Michael Barnard, Alan Hill. 20 Sep 2019.
The right-hand crack in the wall has a short fingery section.

Breakfast Means Breakfast 20m H.Severe 4b *. Alan Hill, Michael Barnard. 20 Sep 2019.
Around the corner from the above. Climb thin cracks just right of the arete.

Twister 20m V.Diff *. Alan Hill, Michael Barnard. 20 Sep 2019.
The corner just right of *Breakfast Means Breakfast*.

Next is a shorter section of wall; right of this is an easy groove and a fine cracked face.

Should Have Gone to Specsavers   15m   Moderate. Alan Hill, Michael Barnard.
20 Sep 2019.
The easy groove.

Crackatoa   15m   Severe *. Alan Hill, Michael Barnard. 20 Sep 2019.
Climbs the most prominent crack on the wall.

Always a Mysteron   20m   Severe *. Michael Barnard, Alan Hill. 20 Sep 2019.
The twin cracks to the right, starting up the right-hand one.

The Last in Line   20m   VS 4b *. Michael Barnard, Alan Hill. 20 Sep 2019.
The arete, unfortunately escapable. Try to stay on the left side!

Occam's Buttress:
Immediately right of *Just Visiting* is a steep buttress with a few crack-lines. The
rock looks worrying to the uninitiated, but was found to be perfectly reliable.

Shadow Captain   20m   HVS 5b **. Michael Barnard, Alan Hill. 20 Sep 2019.
Roughly in the centre of the buttress lies a bottomless crack with a steep groove
immediately on its right. Move up into the base of the steep groove then pull out
left into the crack (crux). Climb the crack to a ledge, step right onto a rib and
finish directly.

Treacherous Tattiebogles   20m   E1 5b *. Michael Barnard, Alan Hill. 20 Sep
2019.
Start as for the above, but continue up the steep groove to ledges. Go up more
easily to finish as for *Shadow Captain*.

Rogue Wave   20m   HVS 5a *. Michael Barnard, Alan Hill. 20 Sep 2019.
In the right arete of the buttress, climb a groove leading to a ledge below a short
roofed corner. Move up past the guano to the roof and pull left into a steep groove
to finish.

Around the arete is a fine wall with a crack up its front face. Further right is a
vertical crack going up past roofs and lying just left of a two-stepped corner (the
lines of *Roof and Ready* and *Sparklet*, SMCJ 2008).

Sea Major   25m   E1 5a ***. Michael Barnard, Alan Hill. 21 Sep 2019.
The obvious line up the front face; a pumpy lower crack followed by a bold finish.
Start up a short slabby groove on the left to gain the crack and follow this to a
ledge below a final groove/crack. Pull left into a much shallower groove and finish
up this.

The next route starts from a higher ledge and as with *Roof and Ready* and *Sparklet*,
can be climbed during rough seas.

Sarclet Fever   15m   HVS 5a ***. Michael Barnard, Alan Hill. 21 Sep 2019.
Climb the shallow groove between *Sea Major* and *Roof and Ready* to reach the
ledge shared with *Sea Major*. Continue up the groove/crack above. RPs and
Friends 3.5 & 4 useful.

Roof and Ready was thought worth **.

Pudding Stone Buttress:
Billericay Dickie   15m   E2 5b *. Michael Barnard, Alan Hill. 21 Sep 2019.
Go up to the first ledge on *Cross Waves*. Place gear in the thin crack above, then pull right into the short groove in the arete. Make tricky moves up this to gain a hold on the right edge, then continue more easily.

Oily Buttress (SMCJ 2006):
There are two obvious non-tidal ledges; looking down, *That Petrel Emotion* etc. start from the right-hand one. This 'small' wall is actually quite impressive and the routes are more like 25m than 15m.

Stiff Little Fingers   25m   E1 5b ***. Michael Barnard, Alan Hill. 13 Oct 2019.
Shares some ground with *That Petrel Emotion*, but is essentially the line of the crag. Climb the main groove immediately left of that route to the roof. Pull through this and up the headwall via the obvious hanging crack.

Inflammable Material   25m   E2 5b ***. Michael Barnard, Alan Hill. 13 Oct 2019.
The fine wall right of *That Petrel Emotion*. Start on the right, moving back left towards the first break. Continue up the obvious line and past small overlaps to join *That Petrel Emotion* near the top.

Abominable Overtrousers   25m   E2 5b. Michael Barnard, Alan Hill. 26 Oct 2019.
A line just right of *Inflammable Material*. A serious start on potentially snappy holds.

The next four routes start from the other, slightly higher, non-tidal ledge Abseil the groove of *Marginal Futility* which lies above the top left end of the ledge (looking down).

Syncopating Sandy   25m   H.Severe 4b *. Alan Hill, Michael Barnard. 26 Oct 2019.
From the bottom end of the ledge, move up and left to climb the easier groove right of the previous routes.

Salopette Sabotage   25m   VS 4c *. Michael Barnard, Alan Hill. 26 Oct 2019.
Starting just right of the above, climb via thin cracks, finishing directly up the top wall.

Haar Like a Pirate   20m   H.Severe 4b *. Alan Hill, Michael Barnard. 26 Oct 2019.
Start at the top end of the ledge, below the *Marginal Futility* groove. Move left up a shallow groove for a couple of metres, before stepping right to climb thin cracks.

Marginal Futility   20m   Moderate. Alan Hill, Michael Barnard. 26 Oct 2019.
The easy groove above the top end of the ledge.

Coast Line   25m   Severe *. Alan Hill, Michael Barnard. 26 Oct 2019.

Right of *Marginal Futility* is a smaller groove; this route climbs the next groove right of this, gained by abseiling the line of the route

The next two routes are tidal. The following route lies directly below the small square boulder on the gearing up ledge. Abseil the line of the route.

I Saw it on the Radio   25m   VS 4b *. Michael Barnard, Alan Hill. 13 Oct 2019. Climb the wall via thin vertical cracks.

I Ate it off the Grapevine   25m   Severe *. Michael Barnard, Alan Hill. 13 Oct 2019
From a semi-hanging belay, a choice of lines lead up the blank-looking slabby wall left of *I Heard it Down the Pub* (SMCJ 2006).

Animal Wall:
Non-tidal South facing
A fine trio of routes lie on this steep wall on the next promontory north of Oily Buttress, well seen from the top of that crag. Abseil to a slab below the wall and move left to good belay ledges.

The Hare Who Lost His Spectacles   30m   VS 4c **. Michael Barnard, Alan Hill. 13 Oct 2019.
The left-hand line – a shallow right-facing groove.

The Bear was Bulgy   20m   E1 5b **. Michael Barnard, Alan Hill 13 Oct 2019
Slightly eliminate but very good climbing up the crack system between *The Hare…* and *Tigger Happy*.

Tigger Happy   20m   HVS 5a **. Michael Barnard, Alan Hill 13 Oct 2019
The steep crack 5m right of *The Hare Who Lost His Spectacles*. A quality line and would be *** were it not for the rattly top groove.

Ellen's Geo:
Cat Burglar   35m   E2 5c **. Michael Barnard, Alan Hill. 14 Oct 2019.
Follow *The Cat's Outta the Bag* up the sandstone and a couple of metres up the conglomerate, then move left via a line of knobbly holds towards a short slanting undercut crack. Use this to gain the steep groove out left and climb this to ledges. Continue as for *Guest Pass Violation*.

The Cat's Outta the Bag   35m   E3 5c ***. Michael Barnard, Alan Hill. 24 Aug 2019.
A line just left of the yellow crack left of *Stratagem*. Climb directly up the sandstone wall to reach a crack in the conglomerate and continue up this to ledges (optional belay, moving left from here to finish up *Guest Pass Violation* would give an excellent HVS 5a). Move up rightwards into the *Breaking the Rules* groove, traverse left on pockets to gain the crack to its left and continue to a ledge. Finish up the steep crack above (bold).

Breaking the Rules   35m   E3 5c **. Michael Barnard, Alan Hill. 14 Oct 2019.
The yellow crack left of *Stratagem*. Climb directly up to the lower yellow crack and up this to ledges (optional belay; if a fulmar present then start as for *The Cat's*

Outta the Bag). Climb up into the groove above, through the roof and up the yellow crack (crux) to the top.

Michael Barnard notes a good link-up at E3 5c is to start as for *Brains As Well As Brawn*, pull right into the hanging corner as for *Third Degree*, but then go all the way up to the roof before hand traversing right to finish as for *Hundreds and Thousands*.

Toad in the Shoe   35m   E2 5b **. Michael Barnard, Alan Hill. 20 Jul 2019.
Move up to climb the crack in the right wall of *Where the Taught Wave Hangs* to reach the conglomerate. Step left into that route, move up then take the obvious traverse line left above the roof. Move up to another roof and traverse left beneath it via perfect two-finger pockets to gain the big hanging groove above. Finish up this.

Squeal Like a Pig   65m   E2 ***. Michael Barnard, Alan Hill. 21 Jul 2019.
An excellent left-right rising traverse along a continuous crack starting near the base of *Where the Taught Wave Hangs*.
1. 15m 5a Follow the crack to belay on *Kathleen*.
2. 25m 5c Continue along the crack, moving up/down as necessary, to reach good ledges around the arete.
3. 25m 5b Move up the corner above, then hand traverse right below the roof (as for *Oliver's Travels*) to join *Layer Cake*. Finish up this.

Pork Scratchings   35m   E3 5c ***. Michael Barnard, Alan Hill. 22 Sep 2019.
Another brilliant pitch. Climb the initial cracks and shallow corner of *Non Stop Nitty Gritty* to the first smaller line of roofs. Step left and pull through these, then continue directly to the horizontal break below the conglomerate (junction with *Kathleen*). Hand traverse right with feet on the lip of the big roof to reach a fine steep crack. Climb this to the top.

Michael Barnard notes that most of the existing routes are over 30m long despite *Stratagem* etc. being listed as 26m! *So This is Summer* was thought to be E1.

MID CLYTH, Lighthouse Wall:
Mick Tighe notes that the description of this wall in Northern Highlands North is a little confusing as it is not 'directly below the lighthouse', rather a little to the north, and adjoining the wall that is directly below the lighthouse. Finding the existing routes can be quite tricky too with the best reference probably *Rapture of the Deep* which is at the southern end of the large, sea-level platform above a small triangular pool, the apex of which points to the start of the route. The following routes use *Rapture of the Deep* as a reference point, and whilst most of them can be accessed below, it's easier to abseil from a good ledge immediately below the lighthouse wall.

Test Match Special   30m   HVS 5b **. Mick & Kathy Tighe. 27 Aug 2019.
Start 3m left of *Rapture of the Deep* below a crack-line. Follow the crack to a short, smooth wall and exit left onto a good ledge. Go up the steep wall to exit right of a small triangular overhang. Climb the short little arete above – hard to start. Alternatively finish up *Rapture* or the following route.

Surge of the Sea   30m   HVS 5a **. Mick & Kathy Tighe. 17 Aug 2018.
Just around the corner on the front face there is a shallow, right-leaning, crack-line. Follow this and the horizontal holds above to pass a small triangular overhang on the right and reach a good ledge. Climb the excellent steep wall above, passing another overhang on the left.

Bay Owl   30m   HVS 5b **. Mick & Kathy Tighe. 17 Aug 2018.
Approximately 5m left of *An Ataireachd Ard* is a fine triangular niche about 8m high. Bridge up this to a short steep section, which is climbed to a good ledge. The fine steep headwall has excellent horizontal holds and runners.

Eiderwand   30m   E1 5b. Mick & Kathy Tighe. 18 Aug 2018.
Left again there is a big ledge at 8m with a short diagonal crack leading up to it from the right. Climb the diagonal crack and the continuation to a tricky move to the left of a small overhang. Climb the fine wall above to finish up a left-facing corner.

White Wall   30m   E1 5b. Mick & Kathy Tighe.19 Aug 2019.
Climb the diagonal crack, as for *Eiderwand*, to the big ledge. Halfway along the ledge take a diagonal crack just left of the white wall. Go up and left through two small overhangs to a ledge. Climb the steep corner and wall above.

The Beacon   30m   HVS ***. Mick & Kathy Tighe. 18 Aug 2018.
There is an excellent little crack in the arete below the left end of the 8m ledge. Balance up the crack to the ledge. Tiptoe up the wall above to the mid-way ledge. Go a couple of metres left, up a short steep wall and the fabulous crack up the headwall.

Beyond there is a small inverted triangular recess topped with a mossy green groove. Access along the tidal ledge to the following routes can only be done at low tide, so it maybe best to abseil to ledges on the high tide line.

Lightning Conductor   30m   HVS 5a. Mick & Kathy Tighe. Date unknown.
A fun route following the copper-bronze bolts that once held the lightning conductor for the lighthouse. Start at the remains of the conductor and shimmy up the grooves and the upper wall, which is rather tricky.

Black Jack   30m   HVS 5a **. Mick & Kathy Tighe, Morten Hansen. 25 Aug 2019.
There is a fine crack 10m left of the conductor. Climb this to the mid-way ledge. Go left along this for a couple of metres to climb a steep little wall and the excellent crack in the headwall.

Carbide Corner   30m   H.Severe **. Mick & Kathy Tighe, Morten Hansen, John Fraser, Harvey Kirkhope. 20 Jul 2019.
There is an area of white rock at the southern end of both top and bottom ledges, the result of carbide discarded from the lighthouse. The fine corner groove-line gives an excellent outing with a fine ledge above the sea if the tide is in.

NORTHERN HIGHLANDS CENTRAL

AN TEALLACH, Glas Tholl, Hayfork Wall:
Local Hero   105m   VIII,9 ***. Greg Boswell, Guy Robertson. 18 Nov 2019.
Outstanding climbing up the left-hand corner system on the main wall to the left of the Wailing Wall Area.
1. 45m Climb steep turfy ground to gain a small corner and climb this. At its top take the rightwards-trending line to gain a ledge at the bottom of the clean-cut hanging corner.
2. 30m Climb the corner stepping left at the top to gain the big ledge and belay on the wall at the back of this.
3. 30m Step right to gain the groove system and climb up to the left of the pointy tooth-like rock feature. Climb up and direct through the bulge to eventually gain easier ground about. Meander to the top.

FANNAICHS, Meall a' Chrasgaidh, East Face (NH 187 731):
On the east face, south of the summit and north of the col between Meall a' Chrasgaidh and Carn na Criche, are broken cliffs. The most prominent and continuous buttress being toward the southern end. This buttress forms a corner with the more northerly cliffs. The following route climbs that corner and is a sporting way to the summit of Meall a' Chrasgaidh.

Dundonnell Donalds's Couloir   120m   I/II. Donald MacRae and DMRT party. 21 Apr 2013.
Climb the attractive gully in the corner between the southern buttress and east face cliffs.

SGÙRR NAN CLACHAN GEALA, Creag a' Chaorainn:
Escape Gully   120m   II. Roger Webb, Neil Wilson. 19 Jan 2020.
Approximately 50 to 100m right of *The Last Lap* (SMCJ 2012) is a prominent gully. It is the only gully on the face so cannot be missed.
Climb the gully, which is surprisingly entertaining in its upper third.

STRATHCONON, Creag Ruadh, North-East Face:
Unnamed   90m   III,4. John Mackenzie. 20 Mar 2020.
This climb lies to the right of the existing routes, and like all else here it consists of a series of tiers separated by easier ground. To the right of *The Backstop Option* is a shallow curving gully, and to the right again is a prominent block buttress. A flat rock with a small boulder below this feature provides a good starting spot. Climb easily to the block buttress, turn this on the left via an icy scoop, then continue more easily up and right to a prominent long buttress with a central groove (clearly seen from below). The groove is steep, but short with a bulge. (Thicker ice and less snow might make it a bit easier). Above, move left and follow mixed ground to where the angle falls back. If all difficulties are avoided, the route will be Grade II.

BEN WYVIS, Creag Coire Na Feola:
Little Sister   25m   V,5. Simon Tickle. 11 Feb 2019.
Climb the broad, steep icefall which forms mid-way between *True Blue* on the left, and *Rapunzel* on the right. To descend to the corrie floor, traverse slightly

right and descend an icy ramp (Grade III) to the right of *Rapunzel*, or continue further right, for an easier descent.

Sideshow 180m V,6. Steven Andrews, Alex Reid. 14 Feb 2020.
The icefall of *Little Sister* continuing to the coire rim by the low-angled buttress above buttress. (Topo provided)
1. 25m Climb the icefall of *Little Sister*.
2. 35m Continue up easier mixed ground on the crest of the buttress.
3 and 4. 120m Snow slopes lead to the top (beware large cornices).

NORTHERN HIGHLANDS SOUTH

GLEOURAICH, Sròn na Breun Leitir:
Feadan Breun 250m II. Jamie Hageman. 22 Mar 2020.
The gully cutting the north-east face of this peak, which is the outlying shoulder projecting north from the western end of Gleouriach. (Topo provided.)

THE SADDLE, Coire Caol:
The ridge that runs north from The Saddle is named Sgùrr na Creige. The following route climbs from Coire Caol on the east side of this ridge to finish on a 930m-high sub-summit about 600m north from the summit of The Saddle. Approach by the main path from Glen Shiel to the Bealach na Chraoibhe (NG 952 142). Leave the path here and descend 100m into Coire Caol, cross the river and traverse round the corrie below the cliffs to reach the foot of the route, which now appears as a prominent gully (NG 940 137).

Caol Couloir 500m I/II *. Chris Dickinson. 11 Nov 2019.
A fine mountaineering route in a remote setting. The route lies north of and parallel to the Forcan Ridge. An unusual gully feature runs the full height of what is actually a ridge. The entry gully is linked to the final gully by an exposed and narrowing shelf with surprisingly big drop offs to the right. Descend by first ascending south to the summit of The Saddle and then following the path down. (Topo provided)

Coire Uaine:
Early Bird 50m III **. Oonagh Thin, James Milton. 16 Nov 2019.
On the North-West face of The Saddle is a buttress in the centre of the face at half height at NG 929 131. A number of ice routes form here. *Early Bird* takes the central feature of this buttress. (Topo provided.)
1. 30m Follow the stepped ice corner for 15m to easier ground. Continue for 10m to reach a large ledge below a large wall of ice.
2. 20m Climb the steep wall gently trending right with interest for 15m until the wall eases, from here continue over the top to belay.
    Descend either by a narrow gully 10m to climber's right, or traverse left round the whole buttress.

CREAG LUNDIE (New Routes Supplement 2018):
Antisocial Media 15m Severe 4a. Ewan Lyons (solo). 20 Sep 2019.
This route is situated on Slab Three in the Belvedere Zone. Start 10m left of *Instagram* and climb vague cracks that lead to a flake in a shallow groove.

GLEN PEAN, Splitter Crag (SMCJ 2018):

Pean Padding   20m   Difficult. Caelan Barnes, Joe Barlow. 6 Jul 2019.
Follow the rightmost obvious crack on the buttress visible from outside Oban bothy above and to the left of the buttress containing The Crossing. (Topo provided)

Morar Flake   20m   Severe *. Joe Barlow, Caelan Barnes. 6 Jul 2019.
On a buttress about 100m behind *Pean Padding* is another buttress with an obvious detached flake. Climb directly up to this flake and climb diagonally rightwards across the top of it and then finish directly. (Topo provided)

AN RUADH-STAC:

End Of Days   300m   VI,6. Mark Robson, Simon Richardson. 13 Mar 2020.
An independent line taking in all three tiers to the left of *North Face*. Start approximately 100m left of *North Face*, 20m left of the foot of a prominent right-to-left ramp cutting through the first tier.
1 and 2. 80m Climb a steep corner-slot to gain the ramp and follow it to the terrace at the top of the first tier.
2. 50m The second tier is cut by a prominent square-cut chimney above and to the right. Left of this is a steep left-trending ramp that leads into a square-cut gully (visible from the foot of the route). Climb the ramp and gully to the terrace below the steep third tier.
3. 40m Traverse left along the terrace to a left-slanting slab feature that provides a likely line of weakness through the third tier.
4. 50m Make difficult moves to gain the slab (crux) then follow this (thin) to a good ledge at its top. Continue directly upwards via steep cracks and corners to a ledge.
5. 50m Move 5m right to an exposed crest and zigzag up short corners and groves to a ledge where the angle eases.
6. 30m Move right and take the diagonal line of weakness to the top of the third tier. Walk off left. (Topo provided)

TORRIDON SANDSTONE CRAGS, Creag nan Leumnach – Upper Upper Tier (NG 898 571):

Up and left of the upper tier is another tier of rock which is mainly short or broken, but does have a fine longer wall on the right.

Planes Crashing Into Birds   20m   HVS 5a *. Michael Barnard, Alan Hill. 23 Jun 2019.
A wide right-slanting flake-crack is prominent on the slabbier upper wall of the crag. Start directly below this and go up a short thin crack to stand up on the arete. Reach right to gain and climb another thin crack which leads through a bulge to join the upper flake-crack.

State of Grace   15m   E3 6a **. Michael Barnard, Alan Hill. 23 Jun 2019.
An excellent well protected pitch up the overhung right-slanting corner-groove. Two crucial blocky holds low in the corner would not budge on abseil.

Fragile World   12m   HVS 5a *. Michael Barnard, Alan Hill. 23 Jun 2019.
Good climbing up cracks on the right side of the buttress.

Creag nan Muile-mhag (NG 896 571):

This smaller South-South-West facing wall lies roughly halfway between Creag nan Leumnach and Creag nan Uiamh. The following routes are on the far left end of the crag.

Jailhouse Toad   15m   VS 4c *. Michael Barnard, Alan Hill. 23 Jun 2019.
Start 2m right of the left end of the crag. Move up to a left-slanting flake-crack and climb this (large cam useful) to a ledge. Continue via flake-cracks up the left edge of the wall, exiting left to finish (or directly at 5a).

Birthday Wall   15m   E1 5b *. Michael Barnard, Alan Hill. 23 Jun 2019.
Right of Jailhouse Toad is a steeper line through a bulge and leading to a short V-groove at the top. Climb up to and through the bulge (crux) and continue to below the V-groove. This looks hard, so escape out right.

When I'm Sixty-Six   15m   VS 5a. Michael Barnard, Alan Hill. 23 Jun 2019.
Start as for the above. Go up an easy corner, step right and move back up leftwards via a large flake-edge to gain a ledge awkwardly. Climb the steep corner above to finish as for Birthday Wall.

Creag nan Uaimh:

The following routes lie on the large buttress at the far left end of the crag (NG 893 572). Go up the gully on the right side of the crag to below a fine side wall.

Comes a Time   20m   E2 5b *. Michael Barnard (unseconded). 11 May 2019.
Climb cracks up the left side of the wall, passing left of a green area of rock, to reach the break under the top arete. Move boldly up a slanting feature to reach a good cam slot high on the arete, then continue with further interest to the top.

Wharf Rat   20m   HVS 5a *. Michael Barnard, Alan Hill. 22 Jun 2019.
Right of the above are two cracks. Climb the left-hand crack then continue to finish up a short corner left of a wide crack.

Cuckoo Cocoon   20m   E1 5b *. Michael Barnard, Alan Hill. 22 Jun 2019.
The steeper right-hand crack, finishing up the short wide crack.

The following two routes take counter-diagonal lines in the Reach the Road buttress.

Ride the Scree   30m   HVS 5a *. Michael Barnard, Alan Hill. 22 Jun 2019.
Start 12m left of Reach the Road, below a short corner above a small holly and rowan. Go up the corner, then traverse right above the roofs to gain a short hanging groove. Go up this to gain and move rightwards up the slab above, finishing up the top crack of *Reach the Road*.

Evil Knievel   30m   E3 5c *. Michael Barnard, Alan Hill. 22 Jun 2019.
Start up the Reach the Road corner, then move left to hand traverse the break to gain the arete. Continue left, crossing *Ride the Scree*. Step up left to the next arete (good cams), and continue left to a good undercling. Now climb the wall above (crux), finishing back out right. Good rope work required to avoid drag.

Motorhome Madness   20m   E1 5a. Michael Barnard, Alan Hill. 22 Jun 2019.
The steep corner up and right from the Reach the Road buttress.

Creag Niamh (NG 891 573):
A more broken South-South-East facing crag further left of Creag nan Uiamh. A
clean wall is prominent up on the right; the crack up the left side of the wall is
taken by *Gabriel.*

Stella Blue   12m   HVS 5a *. Michael Barnard, Jeannie Sherwood. 11 May 2019.
The wall right of *Gabriel* is climbed via a flake-edge and a series of small edges.
Better protected than it looks. Finish up a thin slanting crack.

Gabriel   12m   Severe *. Michael Barnard, Jeannie Sherwood. 11 May 2019.
The crack and the ramp/corner above.

Lilywhite Lilleth   15m   VS 5a *. Michael Barnard (unseconded). 11 May 2019.
Around the corner left of the above, an awkward wide crack (crux) leads to a
corner-crack.

The following route lies further down and left, on a black wall right of a larger
steeper area of crag.

Black Peter   12m   HVS 5a. Michael Barnard, Jeannie Sherwood. 11 May 2019.
Climb the wall just left of a dead holly tree and right of a (usually) wet streak.

BEINN ALLIGIN, Horns of Alligin:
Dundonnell Face   290m   IV,4. Neil Wilson, Simon Richardson, Roger Webb. 19
Nov 2019.
The line of least resistance up the previously unclimbed 200m-high face to the
left of *Diamond Fire*. Start approximately 60m left of Diamond Fire where a
horizontal ledge provides easy access to a wide right-to-left turfy ramp cutting
through the lower tier.
1 and 2. 100m Climb the ramp easily and continue in a similar diagonal line
across the wide second terrace. Belay below a line of weakness below the second
tier.
3. 50m Climb diagonally left for 20m to reach a small terrace then continue up
two steep corners to a good ledge below a steep wall near the left edge of the face.
4. 30m Traverse right beneath the wall into a bay with a turfy weakness leading
up from the back of the bay.
5. 30m Climb the weakness over two steep steps and then continue more easily
to the top of the second tier.
6. 50m Move easily up the foot of the triangular headwall and climb a left slanting
corner-ramp to a ledge. Move right to belay below a vertical groove cutting up to
the apex of the headwall.
7. 30m Climb the groove, which gradually eases to reach the top of the wall.
From here it is straightforward to traverse left across easy ground to the notch
between the second and third Horns. (Topo provided)

Na Fasreidhnean , South Face:
Saltire Gully Right to Left   200m   II *. Adrian Gaughan, Jo Polak. 4 Mar 2020.
Two intersecting gully lines (NG 859 591) form a saltire-shape when viewed from

Torridon House. The route takes the right to left gully line and its continuation to the left. Two easy Grade I pitches lead to a short narrow steepening and the junction of the gully lines. Continue by a short steeper Grade II pitch followed by easier slopes leading to the ridge crest. SE facing and rarely in condition for long. (Topo provided).

DIABAIG, Rolling Wall:
Michael Barnard notes that *Aquamarine* was thought E3 5c ***.

Rubha na h-Airde, Witches' Wall:
This impressive overhanging wall is the 'even steeper base wall' (p263 Northern Highlands South), well seen from the pier. The route *Bitch Witch* climbs a smaller wall just to its left. There is potential for harder lines.

Enchantment 20m E4 6a **. Michael Barnard, Alan Hill. 15 Jul 2019.
The easiest line on the wall, climbing the obvious crack right of centre. Climb through the initial bulge (first crux) and continue more easily up the crack. Where the holds run out, move out right and up to keyed-in blocks (second crux). Go up left to a rest, then finish out right. Continue up heather to a tree belay. Pre-practiced.

Witches' Rave 20m E2 5b *. Michael Barnard, Alan Hill. 7 May 2017.
On the left wall of the gully immediately right of *Witches' Wall* is a fine vertical crack capped by a roof. Traverse left across a slab, then move up and step left again to reach the crack (bold). Follow the crack to its top, gain a horizontal break above the roof and use this to finish out left.

The Condome:
The following two routes are on the small dome of rock at the left end of the wall, just down and right of *The Con Dome*. Descend by abseiling (18m) from sling and maillon on birch tree back from top, or easily down gully on left, immediately underneath right side of *The Con Dome*.

Eeny 10m VS 4c. Gary & Karen Latter. 21 Jun 2019.
Direct line up the twin tramline cracks up left side of the wall. Not easy to protect, with easy though unprotected rock out to the left.

Meeny 10m Severe 4a. Karen & Gary Latter. 21 Jun 2019.
The easier line a few metres right, finishing up short crack.

A top pitch has been added to the following route:

Help ma Boab 90m E3 6a **. Gary & Karen Latter. 9 Apr 2019 (Pitch 1). 21 Jun 2019 (Pitch 2).
Good climbing up the thin hanging crack right of *Boab's Corner*. Start 4m right of that route.
1. 30m 6a Pull left along thin horizontal to good flake hold, then move up rightwards to gain the base of the crack. Climb this with difficult moves where it fades to good finishing hold. Belay at vertical crack at base of short steep wall.
2. 60m 6a Climb up through short diagonal cracks on left, then the black streak,

as for *Oor Willie*. Follow the lower right-slanting crack to a flake at its end, then the easier continuation flake/ramp up rightwards, continuing up rightwards.

BEINN EIGHE, Eastern Ramparts:

The Modern Idiot   105m   VIII,8. Tim Miller, Jamie Skelton. 19 Mar 2020.
Climb the summer route throughout in two pitches followed by 50m easy climbing to the top. Steep climbing on pitch two with great positions.

The Irony   80m   IX,9. Dave Almond, Jamie Skelton. 11 Mar 2020.
A direct version of *Claustrophobic Corner*. It follows the groove and cracks direct rather than stepping left into the summer groove.
1. 10m Climb easy ground up to ledge 5m and then move 5m left to belay by pedestal block.
2. 35m Climb onto the pedestal in the corner. Climb the corner and continue direct on small features and poor protection through the overhang onto the headwall and the belay ledge of the summer route.
3. 35m Follow the summer line diagonally right to break through the overhangs at a jutting block, then climb the headwall moving diagonally left to easy ground.

Scotophobia   125m   VII,7. Dave Almond, Jamie Skelton. 12 Mar 2020.
Starts at the same point as *Fear of the Dark*.
1. 45m Climb the right-hand side of the big chimney and the wide crack on the right hand side of the chimney/cave up to the Upper Girdle. Move to the right hand side of the huge standing pillar (long sling required) to a peg 1.5m right of the big right-facing corner formed by the right side of the standing pillar.
2. 40m Climb the corner for 6m moving right at the overhangs into a V-groove, through the small overhang and into the open book corner. Continue directly up to huge belay ledge.
3. 40m Follow the chimney line directly above the right hand edge of the belay ledge to easier ground and trend left to finish up the gully of Shang-High.

THE CAIRNGORMS

COIRE AN T-SNEACHDA, Mess of Pottage:

Wachacha Direct   90m   HVS *. Jamie Graham, Grant Shorten. 26 Aug 2019.
1. 50m 4c Start directly below the right hand side of the roof 5m right of *Wachacha*. Climb to the roof then traverse out right to join the obvious crack line. Bold start with limited gear and potential ground fall. In a direct line, follow the weakness to an obvious small belay ledge.
2. 40m 4b Continue up to join *Wachacha* and up the shallow left-facing corner to top out.

Crescent Crags:

These are the line of high crags just under the crest of Stob Choire an-Sneachda, between Jacob's Ladder and Aladdin's Couloir. To the right of Jacob's Ladder a broken area of rock runs the full height of the cliff and gives a few lines at Grade II. The next crags right start much higher up and vary between 50 to 70m in height. The approach can feel quite serious, and the upper slope is a regular starting zone for large avalanches. Large build up of snow means that some of the gully lines vary greatly in grade through the season. People have winter climbed in this area for years but nothing has been recorded, so first ascents are not included. The cliff is infrequently visited in summer, so first ascent details are included for those routes. (Topo provided)

Left Buttress:
This protruding buttress has a broad front face.

Left Off Gully   70m   II.
Curves up the left side of the buttress.

Stormbringer   70m   IV,6 *.
The left edge of the front face of the buttress.
1. 25m Surmount a bulge, climb up to a roof, move left and continue up a shallow left-facing corner on the buttress edge. Step right and climb the edge.
2. 45m Blocky ground leads to the top.

Folklore   70m   III.
Start at the mid-line of the buttress, go up to a recess, move out right and then back left to climb a wide, blocky fault. Finish up easy ground to top.

Boutros Buttress-Ghali   70m   IV,5 *.
1. 30m Just left of the right edge is a short, shallow chimney. Go up this and continue up a crack straight above, then slant leftwards to finish.
2. 40m Blocky ground leads to the top.

An area of more broken ground now lies a little higher up before the next prominent buttress.

Slimline Gully   60m   II.
A narrow fault running straight up the middle of the broken ground between the two buttresses.

Cinnamon Buttress:
The next prominent buttress with a steep right-facing corner.

Dark Days   60m   V.Diff. Sarah Atkinson, John Lyall, Jonathan Preston. 28 Jun 2019.
Start at the lowest rocks of the front face and move up to climb the most prominent crack near the right edge, then follow scrappy ground to the top.

Dark Days   60m   IV,4. John Lyall, Scott Frazer, Mick Twomey. 28 Jan 2020.
Follow the summer line.

Cinnamon Corner   50m   VS *. Jonathan Preston, Sarah Atkinson, John Lyall. 28 Jun 2019.
1. 20m 5a The prominent right-facing corner gives good well protected climbing.
2. 30m Walls and blocky ground lead to the top.

Sinnerman   50m   VS. John Lyall, Sarah Atkinson, Jonathan Preston. 28 Jun 2019.
1. 25m 4c Start 5m right of *Cinnamon Corner* at the edge of a chimney. Go up to a shallow right facing corner, then follow right slanting cracks to a big ledge.

2. 25m Walls and blocks lead to the top.

Crescent Groove   50m   III *.
A wide chimney followed by a curving groove. Finish by an awkward slanting slot on the right.

Another section of cliff with a few lines leads right to the highest point, where there are two right-slanting ramps cutting across the face.

Stiff Upper Lip   60m   II.
Go right along the upper ramp, then a few steep moves up left lead to snow slopes finishing just left of summit cairn.

Pouting Lip   75m   III
Climb the lower ramp followed right to a crest overlooking *Tractor Gully*, then go sharp left up a slanting groove to a steep finish.

Tractor Gully   60m   II
The deep right-slanting gully with a large chokestone that takes a while to bank out.

Hiemal Crack   70m   IV,4.
Start on the right wall of a snow bay right of the start of *Tractor Gully*. Follow a right-slanting crack then easier slopes to the top.

Manila Pillar   75m   V.Diff. Jonathan Preston, John Lyall. 8 Jul 2019.
The front face of the buttress left of the obvious wide chimney. Bold, delicate moves lead to a steep crack exit, then easier ground to top.

Kudos Corner   75m   III.
The right corner of the wide chimney, then easier slopes. Harder early in the season.

Vanilla Pillar   75m   Severe. John Lyall, Jonathan Preston. 8 Jul 2019.
The left edge of the pale pillar to the right of *Kudos Corner* is followed up an incipient crack to more helpful cracks to reach easier ground. Loose ground above was avoided by traversing left and up, as for *Manila Pillar*.

Detractor Gully   75m   II.
The left-leaning gully to the right of the pale pillar takes a while to fill up but is then straightforward.

Passmark   75m   IV,4.
The broken buttress right of *Detractor Gully*. Slant up left to a short corner and climb the crack up the slab above, then continue by the fault and finish by upper buttress.

SHELTER STONE CRAG:
Michael Barnard notes that the long first pitch of *The Heel Stone* (SMCJ 2019) incorporates all the good climbing on *Spire Independent Start* (SMCJ 2014), making that variation redundant.

STAC AN FHARAIDH, West Flank:
Onlooker 60m IV,5. Jonathan Preston, Mungo Ross. 20 Mar 2020.
Start at the bottom right-hand corner of the furthest left of the three buttresses (i.e. at the base of the deep Grade I gully that separates the left and central buttresses) – this would appear to be well to the right of *Lookout Buttress* (SMCJ 2014).
1. 30m Climb either of two steep turfy grooves to where they join and follow the continuation groove to a big ledge with block and thread belays.
2. 30m Easy ground up the broad crest of the buttress, overlooking the deep gully on the right, leads to the top.

Looking Up 30m III. Jonathan Preston, Mungo Ross. 20th Mar 2020.
Several Grade III grooves lead out left from part way up the deep Grade I gully, gaining the crest of the left buttress at various points. This route takes the best and longest of these. When facing the left wall of the gully follow a well-defined slanting turfy groove system rightwards to a steep finish through a slot to the crest. Easy ground leads to the top, as above.

CAIRN GORM, Cnap Coire na Spreidhe:
Nethy Crack 30m V,6. Roger Webb, Gary Kinsey, Simon Richardson. 9 Jan 2020.
A winter version of the summer line. Start more directly and climb the initial turfy groove and step around a small roof to enter the crack. Instead of finishing direct, traverse right below the final roof to a good ledge and finish up the steep turfy wall above. A double rack of large cams (3.5 particularly useful) and medium to large hexes were used.

Brain Melt 30m V,7. Simon Richardson, Gary Kinsey, Roger Webb. 9 Jan 2020.
The prominent chimney left of *The Late Show*. Start immediately below the chimney and climb easily up to a smooth right-facing corner (crux) that leads to a ledge. Struggle up the chimney above to the top.

CREAGAN COIRE A' CHA-NO, Left-Hand Buttress:
Dave Brookes and Jules Harris made a free ascent of *The Edge of Profanity* on 30 Nov 2019.

The Arc of Profanity 30m VI,8. Dave Brookes, Jules Harris. 18 Jan 2020.
The arcing crack on the right side of the *Edge of Profanity* buttress. Start at the base of a recess to the right of a large block that forms the foot of the right flank. Climb the vertical crack at the back of the recess on good hooks. Continue climbing the crack as it becomes overhanging, and follow it right as it widens and exits onto the buttress above. Finish by climbing up and rightwards to easier ground and the top. A technical and strenuous route. Two falls taken. (Topo provided)

International Rib:
Crack On 20m IV,4. Simon Richardson, Mark Robson. 14 Dec 2019.
The prominent chimney to the left of *Continental Chimney* provides a fun pitch.

The Chimney Sweeper 40m IV,5. Mark Robson, Simon Richardson. 14 Dec 2019.
Climb the left-slanting chimney that joins *Continental Chimney* at its top below

a steep tower. Finish as for *Continental Chimney* by stepping right and finishing up *International Rib*.

Nimbus 2000   50m   II or III. Simon Richardson, Mark Robson. 17 Nov 2019.
A line between *Lowbrow Corner* and *Broomstick Buttress*. Climb directly up to the start of the ramp of *Broomstick Buttress* and continue straight up a short steep corner to the right side of the hanging bay of *Lowbrow Corner*. The snow build up in the bay will determine the difficulty of the exit that will vary from a straightforward step to a strenuous climb up a 3m-high impending crack.

Blood Buttress:
Snape   50m   IV,6. Roger Webb, Simon Richardson. 28 Jan 2020.
The direct line of grooves bisecting *Half Blood*.
1. 25m   Start just right of *Half Blood* below a right-angled corner. Climb the awkward fault one metre right of the corner and move up to a ledge. Climb a short corner above (common with *Half Blood*) and belay on a chockstone on the right.
2. 25m   Move left across the amphitheatre of *Half Blood* until below an open shallow groove. Climb steeply up into the groove and follow steep steps to below a prominent fault in the final vertical wall. This can be avoided on the left, but for maximum fun climb it (crux) to enter a short wide square-cut gully to finish.

Heart is Highland   50m   IV,5. Simon Richardson, Mark Robson. 17 Nov 2019.
The line of square-cut corners between *Half Blood* and *The Blood is Strong*.
1. 25m   Climb easily up to the foot of the first corner and belay by a 2m-high pinnacle-flake.
2. 25m   Climb the first corner using a hidden flake and continue up the second corner with interest. Finish up a third and final corner to the top. A good route.

A Special Sort of Idiot   50m   IV,4. Simon Richardson, Roger Webb. 30 Nov 2019.
The grooves, wall and arete between *Captain Fairweather* and *Flood Warning*.
1. 25m Start just right of *Captain Fairweather* and take the zigzag line of grooves linking diagonal turf ledges to gain the large depression of *Flood Warning*.
2. 25m Climb a steep crack to a small col formed by a tower and continue up the arete right of the final groove of *The Blood is Strong/Captain Fairweather* in a fine position to the top.

Grooved Pinnacle Buttress:
Cub Corner   40m   IV,6. Roger Webb, Simon Richardson. 28 Jan 2020.
The book-shaped corner between *Slyboots* and *Vixen*. Climb easily up to the foot of the corner and climb it using good holds on the left wall. Ice may ease the technical difficulty but will make finding protection harder.

Vandal's Arete   40m   III,5. Simon Richardson, Mark Robson. 17 Nov 2019.
Climb the grooved arete between *Fox Gully* and *Ghost*, step left at its top below a jammed block and finish behind the pinnacle tower via a short wide gully as for *Dingo Grooves*.

White   30m   V,6. Mark Robson, Simon Richardson. 14 Dec 2019.
The vertical line of cracks between *Ghoul* and *White Walker*. Start below a short crack and climb up to a ledge. Continue up the left-facing corner and the steep

crack above to a niche. Move awkwardly left around a protruding block and finish up the final depression of *Ghoul*.

White Walker 30m V,6. Mark Robson, Simon Richardson. 17 Nov 2019.
The superbly featured wall of flakes and cracks to the right of *Ghoul*. Start just right of *White* and climb thin cracks in the wall before stepping left on to the ledge of *White*. Gain the line of steep cracks and flakes leading to a break below an impending offwidth flake-crack (crux) using a good hidden hold to gain easier ground and the top. An excellent pitch.

Wildling 30m V,6. Simon Richardson, Mark Robson. 14 Dec 2019.
Climb the crack right of *White Walker* to a ledge. From the right end of the ledge climb a left-facing corner to the top. Another good pitch.

Mainmast Area:
Chocks Away 30m V,7. Steve Elliott, Graeme Gatherer. 29 Jan 2020.
A direct line 5m right of *Auld Reekie, Direct Start*. Pull through the initial steep niche on positive hooks to gain two parallel cracks. Climb these to reach the ledge where *Auld Reekie* ordinary comes in from the right. Climb the overhanging groove above, immediately right of the deep chimney of *Auld Reekie* using a number of chockstones to finish. (Topo provided)

LURCHER'S CRAG:
Berserker 115m VI,8 *. Dave Almond, Jamie Skelton. 21 Nov 2019.
The series of steep stepped cracks just to the left of *Shapeshifter* offer a good number of powerful moves between good rests.
1. 25m For those looking for a challenge start at the V-groove below and left of the main buttress, or easier, start by moving through a turfy ledge system to gain the large ledge.
2. 40 m Climb the wall above the belay ledge on the left hand side and follow crack systems keeping left of the arete by climbing the shallow/flared left facing corner via a stiff pull and then step right join *Shapeshifter* for the final few moves.
3. 50m Finish by blocky scrambling to gain the plateau. (Topo provided)

BRAERIACH, Coire Beanaidh:
Pong 50m III. Mark Robson, Simon Richardson. 19 Jan 2020.
The icy gully defining the left side of *Rum Doodle Rib*.

Rum Doodle Rib 90m III,4. Simon Richardson, Sophie Grace Chappell. 12 Jan 2020.
The rib left of *Rumbling Ridge* divides into two ribs separated by a depression in its upper half. This route takes the upper left-hand rib.
1. 30m Climb the lower central rib to its top.
2. 30m Step left onto the left-hand rib and climb steeply just right of the crest to where the angle eases.
3. 30m Easy ground leads to the top.

Half Rations 50m II. Mark Robson, Simon Richardson. 19 Jan 2020.
The icy gully defining the right side of the upper section of *Rum Doodle Rib*. Start 20m up *Snow Devil Gully* (the Grade I gully between *Rum Doodle Rib* and

Rumbling Ridge) and climb an icy depression on the left wall to gain the upper gully.

Rum Corner   100m   III. Simon Richardson. 1 Dec 2019.
The second rib right of *Rumbling Ridge*. Start up a prominent left-facing corner to gain a depression. Exit via a short wall on the right and continue up the crest to where it merges with easier ground leading to the top.

Coire an Lochain:
Skeleton Creek   100m   IV,5. Mark Robson, Simon Richardson. 19 Jan 2020.
A good line up the centre of the buttress to the left of *Ice Elation*.
1. 60m Start just left of *Sinister Dredge* and exit a snow depression via narrow slot in its top left corner. Continue up grooves and shallow corners to a belay below the steep headwall.
2. 25m Climb the steep slabby right-facing corner for 15m then step right (crux) to cracks leading to a good ledge below a cracked tower.
3. 15m Easy ground left of the tower leads to the top.

Coire nan Clach:
Guiding Spirit   100m   III. Simon Richardson. 30 Oct 2019.
A line of least resistance up the slabby buttress left of *Schoolmaster's Gully*. Under heavy snow some parts of the route will bank out. Start 20m below and left of the foot of *Schoolmaster's Gully* and climb a left slanting break towards a short steep tower. Zigzag right then left up short grooves to gain easier ground in an upper bay. A short left-trending gully leads to the top.

Mixed Blessings   100m   III,5. Simon Richardson, Mark Robson. 10 Nov 2019.
Start at the foot of *Schoolmaster's Gully* (above and right of *Guiding Spirit*).
1. 30m Climb a short groove and continue in the same line, parallel with *Schoolmaster's Gully*, to belay below a huge block overlooking the gully.
2. 30m Step left onto the wall and trend up and left via a turfy weakness to easier ground.
3. 40m Continue up via a zigzag line of short grooves and corners to the top.

Coire Dondhail:
Lightning Runnel   70m   II. Simon Richardson. 30 Oct 2019.
The turfy runnel just left of *Thunder Groove*. Low in the grade.

THE DEVIL'S POINT:
Hindmost Ridge   400m   IV,4. Kenny Brookman, John Higham, Iain Young. 4 Mar 2020.
This route takes the right bounding (looking up) ridge of *Geusachan Gully* and provides one of the longest ridge climbs in the Cairngorms. Being south facing and remote it needs careful consideration of conditions for both the climbing and the approach. The ridge starts with a steep nose and slabs on the right of the gully (NN 9750 9479). On this ascent the nose was snow-free and a start was made up a turfy / icy corner just inside the gully. (Topo provided)
1. 60m Climb the corner and pass to the left of a prow leading to easy ground on the ridge crest.
2. 60m Follow snow and turf up a prominent line of weakness parallel to the crest.

3. 35m Move up and left and make tricky moves over slabs to belay below a steeper, blocky wall.
4. 45m Climb the wall on good hooks and flakes and follow the narrow crest to belay on blocks.
5. 200m Easy Grade I/II ground leads to the summit cairn.

CÀRN A' MHAIM:
Mixed Media 130m II,3. Kenny Brookman, John Higham, Iain Young. 18 Nov 2019.
This route takes the broad, slabby buttress on the west flank of Càrn a' Mhaim that terminates on the summit ridge just below its final steepening. It is defined by two long, straight, shallow gullies. Avoid the lower most isolated rock band. Start up turfy grooves just left of centre and climb to final slabs and a broad snow arete in three pitches. (Topo provided)

BEN AVON, East Muir Gorm Craig:
Dinner Gully 100m I. John Higham, Iain Young. 1 Dec 2012.
The straightforward central gully on the crag.

LOCHNAGAR, Southern Sector, The Cathedral:
Hocus Pocus 80m V,5. Simon Richardson, Sophie Grace Chappell. 17 Dec 2019.
 The furthest right groove system on the buttress taken by *Magic Pillar*. Start by climbing easy mixed ground and belay just right of the square-cut corner of *The Sorcerer*. Climbed under very heavy snow conditions so the grade may be easier when not buried.
1. 40m Enter the grove on the right on its right side (awkward) and continue up the groove above with interest to a good ledge.
2. 40m Move right along the ledge and climb easier ground to the steep headwall left of *Forsaken Gully*. Climb a short wall to gain a right-trending ramp. Step left at its top and finish up steep snow to the plateau.

Tough Brown Face:
Tough Brown Ridge Superdirect 55m V,6 **. Douglas Bartholomew, Graham Wyllie. 11 Mar 2020.
Climbed in good icy mixed conditions. Both pitches may have been climbed before but first ascent details have not been recorded. The second pitch approximates to the summer line.
1. 30m Start 5m further up *Raeburn's Gully* than *Tough Brown Ridge Direct* at the foot of a corner leading straight up to grooves that continue directly upwards. Follow these until a snow bay at the base of a large triangular vertical wall is reached and belay at a flake on the wall to the left. (*Tough Brown Ridge Direct* joins here from the left, likely same belay).
2. 25m An ice smear forms where the left wall of the bay meets with the triangular vertical wall. Climb this onto turfy slabs and continue upwards until easy ground and *Tough Brown Ridge Direct* joins from the right. (Topo provided)

Coire Loch Nan Eun, The Stuic:
Erick Baillot and Dave Kerr made a possible second ascent of *The Stooee Chimney* on November 10 Nov 2019. They were able to climb under the crux chockstone reducing the grade to IV,6.

CREAG AN DUBH LOCH, Central Gully Wall:
The Israelite   125m   VIII,8. Greg Boswell, Guy Robertson. 4 Mar 2020.
Follows the summer line all the way taking the line of ice direct into the top corner. Gaining the ice at the start was thin, but the *Goliath Icicle* was in pretty good shape. Above this, a beautiful weep formed on the slab just right of the thin crack, which led to the big upper corner. This sported a few ice streaks, but unfortunately these were of the eggshell variety, so little use. This mixed pitch was probably the crux, giving sustained teetering on reasonable hooks but very poor feet. The final pitch up the plateau was a romp up thick Grade IV ice.

GLEN CLOVA, Cairn Broadlands, East Face:
Broadlands Rib   150m   II. Simon Richardson. 4 Mar 2020.
Climb the right bounding ridge of the corrie over several short steps.

NORTH-EAST OUTCROPS

COVESEA, Honeycomb Wall:
Look to Windward   25m   E5 6b **. Ted Collins, Graham Tyldesley. 26 Aug 2019.
The wall round the arete left of *Hacuna Matatta* joining the arete higher up. Start by abseiling down the corner left of *Hacuna Matatta* then follow down the face left of the arete. Take a hanging belay above the poor sandstone layer below a crack-flake that moves through a bulge a few metres left of the arete. Climb this line to move right to the arete when onto the wall after the bulge, then continue up the arete mainly on the left side to join *Hacuna Matatta* at the top. The crux start is well protected but the gear is strenuous to place. The rest of the route is run out but safe.

GLEN CLOVA, Elf Hillock (NO 348 703):
This small slabby crag was exposed following forestry felling operations, and the following routes were climbed by Ged Reilly and Forrest Templeton during summer of 2018. The crag was dirty and mossy prior to cleaning, and if not climbed on, may readily revert back to nature. Eight lines were climbed ranging from V.Diff to VS. Although short, the climbing is pleasant, protection reasonable, and abseil trees plentiful. A fairly accurate assessment of the route grade and available protection can be made from below. With a south-easterly aspect and fine open views, the crag lends itself to morning/early afternoon climbing, and may 'save the day' if it is looking dreich further up the Glen.
   Approach is by the forestry track starting at a layby on the left (NO 357 697) approximately 500m before the cottage named Wester Eggie. Follow the wide forestry track in a westerly direction and just before it opens out on to open (de-forested) hillside, take another track to the right. The crag is visible from this point on. Follow a fenced off plantation on the left with mature woodland on the right. After 200m a gate allows access to a forestry break heading uphill in the direction of the crag. The break becomes a bit overgrown and rough at the top, but eventually a deer fence can be crossed to reach the crag.

Line 1   10m   VS.
Starts left of a prominent vegetated crack and has an obvious horizontal friend placement about one-third of the way up.

Line 2 10m MVS.
Start at the break right of Line 1and climb up just right of it.

Line 3 10m MVS.
The line just right of Line 2. The first route climbed on the cliff.

Line 4 10m MVS.
The line right again and that keeps left of the remnants of the black moss which
decorated this area before cleaning. It aims for a small down-pointing triangular
cream-coloured overlapping feature.

Line 5 10m MVS.
The cleaned line further right.

Three more routes were climbed further right (V.Diff to Severe) but they are more
broken than the climbs above. There is scope for scrappier easier routes.

HIGHLAND OUTCROPS SOUTH

GLEN GOUR, Indian Slab:
Mullenium, Right-Hand Finish 200m VS 5a. Will Rowland. Jun 2019.
From below the last pitch of *Mullenium*, move further right and climb a lovely
smooth square-cut slab for around 40m and continue up on the next terrace via a
ramp. The ramp narrows to form a blunt arete capped by an overlap. Pass the
overlap on the left then traverse right (bold) and continue up the face. The angle
soon eases but the climbing remains enjoyable to the top of the cliff.

ARDNAMURCHAN, Meall an Fhir-eoin Beag:
Up Pompei, Direct Start 5b *. Steve Kennedy, Cynthia Grindley. 5 Sep 1998.
From the starting ledge, instead of climbing the crack left of the rib, climb a crack
on the right wall which develops into a Y-shaped crack. Follow the left arm leading
to the ledge below the main slab. The overall grade (E1) is unchanged.

Dome Buttress:
Mr Lavaman 25m HVS 5a **. Dave Brookes, Jules Harris. 6 Jul 2019.
Start 3m left of *Claude* on the left side of the block that forms the right side of the
obvious large overhang. Climb easily up to the base of a fine finger flake that
curves up and left. Climb the flake directly to its top then make some delicate
moves to mantel onto the shelf above. Climb the triangular block from the shelf
then move left and underneath the final overhanging block at the top of the route.
Turn this block on its left-hand side.

GLEN NEVIS, Polldubh Upper Tier, Secretaries' Buttress:
Ian Taylor and Neil Brodie made the first ascent of *Just Passing* on 22 Jun 1989.

Crown Buttress:
The Truants Arete 18m E1/2 5b **. Iain Howie, David Lamond, Nathan Adam.
19 Sep 2017.
Start up the obvious undercut, triangular wall between *Fibrillation* and *Jewels*.

Climb the wall with bouldery moves off the ground via a quartz crack to a better hold just on the left, move right slightly and then follow the arete (without straying onto Jewels) to below the upper corner of *Fibrillation*. Swing wildly out left and follow the obvious hanging crack with better protection to the top.

LOCHAILORT CRAGS, Quadruple Crack Buttress (NM 799 831):

Township Rebellion 12m E2 5b. Nathan Adam, Raiyah Strachan. 8 Jul 2019.
Slightly contrived but enjoyable climbing. Start at the base of *Line Dance* and climb the thin crack on the right before laybacking to below a long narrow roof with a good cluster of protection. Make a long reach left above the roof (without using the block behind!) for a small quartz bannister rail and rock over to a junction with *Line Dance*. Place a blind cam in a crack below and left before following the thin crack directly with steep heather to finish on the final short slab just right of the other routes. Low in the grade but there is ground-fall potential from near the top.

LOCHAILORT CRAGS, Druim Fiaclach, Gleann Mama Slabs:

The following two routes start 20m up and left of *Scooby Dubh* on short walls of immaculate and good quality rock and lie directly below the descent from the main crag. They are described right to left leading on from *Scooby Dubh* in Highland Outcrops South.

Dubh it at the Disco 12m H.Severe 4b *. Nathan Adam, Garry Campbell. 28 Sep 2019.
Start up small right-trending steps to reach an overlap and crack. Climb these into a right-facing corner groove which leads pleasantly to a steep final move onto the heather.

Out of Touch 12m Severe 4a *. Garry Campbell, Nathan Adam. 28 Sep 2019.
Two metres left again is a left-slanting crack-line. Climb this to a small ledge and follow the continuation crack and rib above.

Nathan Adams notes that *Underneath the Arches* can be climbed in a single pitch with 60m ropes and may be worth HVS 4c. *Scooby Dubh* is a good route and best done as two pitches as per the guide. The approach described in Highland Outcrops South involves head high bracken in summer and is best avoided by following the approach notes to Glac Ruadh instead and following the ridge until an easy descent on the right can be made to the crag. The farmer is friendly although his barking dog may cause concern when approaching and descending!

Druim Fiaclach West:

Orange Blank 45m VS 4c* Nathan Adam, Raiyah Strachan, Garry Campbell. 7 Jul 2019.
Eighty metres east of *Arisaig Arete* is the next defined buttress, this climb follows its left edge. Start below a left-facing corner topped by a rectangular roof. Climb the corner and bridge strenuously over the roof with good handholds to reach the slab on the left. Follow the very edge with excellent exposure and good holds but no protection to reach a heather ledge at about 20m (possible belay). Continue on slabs with intermittent protection before a step back right onto a small rib leads to another heather ledge below a large embedded block and belay. Walk off up and right then descend grassy slopes and gullies back to the base.

Corrected line of Ardanfreaky.
See Highland Outcrops South p. 322.

THE FORTRESS, BINNEIN SHUAS

1. Mind Riot E10 7a
2. Siege Engine E7 6b
3. Stronghold E8 6c
4. Greatness and Perfection . . E7 6c
5. Isinglass E7 6b
6. Braes of Balquither E7/8 6c
7. Horrible Histories E8 7a

Nathan Adam notes that he (and others) consider pitch 1 of *Arisaig Arete* to be E1 5b. It involves a committing move out right with poor gear that is low down, but the climbing is still good and the route in general is worth doing. The upper pitch is not particularly bold as described in the guidebook and the technical grade is 4b.

BINNEIN SHUAS, The Fortress:

Mind Riot   45m   E10 7a ***. Dave MacLeod. 30 Sep 2019.
A desperate line cutting through the diagonal flake of *Siege Engine*, with ground fall potential on the crux. Start at the same point as *Siege Engine* but where that traverses left across the wall, continue up the steep flake rightwards and arrange crucial gear at its termination. Launch up the overhanging groove above with a sustained bouldery sequence to reach the flake of *Siege Engine*. The remainder of the route is common to *Dun Briste* (E8 6c). Follow this to below the roof and arrange good cams in the roof. Span across the roof to reach the flake on the lip and continue with another hard boulder problem to reach the lip. Finish easily up the slab above. F8c climbing. (Topo provided)

Horrible Histories   35m   E8 7a ***. Dave MacLeod. 25 Jun 2019.
This route cuts through the diagonal crack of *Wild Mountain Thyme* via the steep lower wall, passing an obvious triangular undercut feature. Start a few metres right of *Wild Mountain Thyme*, directly below the undercut feature. Climb up an orange groove on the right to its termination and arrange runners in some quartz, then step back down to the slab. Climb up and left on the slab until it is possible to gain the large undercuts leading rightwards across the overhanging wall. Step up to the triangular undercut feature and fill this with crucial shallow cam placements. Pass this with difficulty and continue on small crimps to gain jugs and a small ledge on *Wild Mountain Thyme*. Climb the wall above the edge to a roof, turning this on the left, and continue to another small overlap near the top. Step left and make a few technical moves onto the slab above to finish. F8a+ climbing. (Topo provided)

STRATH NAIRN, Creag Bhuidhe:

Creag Bhuidhe (NH663312) lies on the south side of the hill of the same name. Park on the road north-east of the crag. Approach by walking south-west keeping the lochan on the left. (5 mins).

Cold Dark Matter   10m   E1 5a **. Dan Fitzsimmons, Ed Runnalls. 28 Jan 2020.
From the middle of the lower left to right diagonal break. Pull onto the heathery ledge to a thread. Climb slightly rightwards and straight up from here to bomber gear, then a semi-exciting finish. Tree belays. Partially cleaned by abseil, and more on lead.

BEN NEVIS, AONACHS, CREAG MEAGAIDH

BEN NEVIS, Minus Face:

Calculus   270m   VIII,8 **. Maarten van Haeren, Andy Inglis. 24 Feb 2020.
A direct line up Minus Two Buttress with very physical crux pitch through the overhanging barrier wall.

1. 55m From the toe of the buttress, climb the shallow right facing corner (between *Central Route* and *Right-Hand Route*) feature leading to the right side of the bay and a belay at the base of the steep rock.

2. 35m Step left and climb low angle snow and ice for approximately 10m to the second of three overhanging left-facing corner features. Climb the sustained and strenuous corner via poor rest positions to exit onto ice and a belay 5m up the face.

3 to 5. 180m Continue directly up the easier angled buttress to the top via a series of chimneys staying to the left of *Minus Two Gully* (common with *Right-Hand Route*). (Topo provided)

Tower Ridge, East Flank:
Wonderwoman 120m V,6. Stuart MacFarlane, Simon Richardson, Ian Dempster. 27 Feb 2020.
The groove system just right of the blunt crest to the right of *Alaskan Highway*.
1. 20m Start just right of the crest and climb a two-stepped icefall to the right end of a terrace.
2. 40m Move right behind a large block and climb diagonally right across a steep snowfield aiming for a short gully-groove at its apex. Climb this for 10m to belay on large block on the right.
3. 40m Move right around the block and climb the stepped corner system above (crux) to reach a belay below a small alcove.
4. 20m Step down and traverse 3m right to gain a right-facing corner leading to easier ground and the crest of *Tower Ridge*.

Secondary Tower Ridge:
Dry Birds 100m V,6 *. Will Rowland, Nathan Adam. 11 Mar 2020.
This route follows the left facing corner just left of the steep cracked wall of *Watery Fowls* and gives good technical mixed climbing. Start 10m up *West Gully*, at the same place as *Watery Fowls*. The second pitch is very close to Inception (SMCJ 2015).
1. 40m Climb the corner until it blanks out, step slightly left and follow the continuation above to reach the large spike belay of *Inception*. A good pitch.
2. 60m Directly above is a turfy groove, climb this and move left on snow and ice before traversing rightwards to reach an icy groove. Climb a widening crack immediately left of the groove and then easier ground to reach a belay just below *Tower Ridge*. (Topo provided)

Creag Coire na Ciste:
The Sorcerer, Variation Finish 50m VI,7. Dave Almond, Jack Brooks. 18 Nov 2019.
From the big bay belay, after the crux crack-line of pitch 2, trend right up the ramp, to pass a large boulder balanced on a horizontal ledge at the foot of a vertical wall. Foot traverse right on a narrowing ledge to turn the corner, and finish up the gully line of *Cloudwalker*. Good balance required! (Topo provided)

Piccadilly Circus 110m V,6. Simon Richardson, Mark Robson. 5 Feb 2020.
The well-defined rib between *Central Gully* and *Central Gully Right-Hand*. Start midway between *Central Gully* and *Central Gully Right-Hand* at the foot of a mixed triangle directly below the rib.

1. 20m Gain the triangle from the left and climb two short left-facing corners to reach a good belay at the base of the rib.
2. 40m The front face of the rib overhangs, so climb its right side for 3m then take the first groove on the left to gain the crest. Trend right up easier ground to a short wall. Surmount this directly and continue up to the base of the final tower.
3. 20m Start up short groove on the right to gain a left-slanting crack (crux) that leads to the top of the tower.
4. 30m Finish easily up the snow scoop above.

Jive Turkey   120m   V,6 *. Jonathan Livesey, Connor Henley. 14 Dec 2019. Start up a small corner groove 10m downhill from the prominent chocked chimney in the left wall of *Number Four Gully*. Climbed in lean conditions. Topo supplied.
1. 40m Climb the corner groove for 5m to a good runner then take a leftward rising traverse on thin hooks to a horizontal turfy break. Follow this round the arete (spike runner) into a chimney groove. Follow the groove into a snow bay and belay.
2. 50m Easily gain a rightward ramp and follow to the bottom of a short right-facing corner. Climb this on good hooks to easier ground.
3. 30m Continue up easy ground to the top. (Topo provided)

North Face of Castle Ridge:
Red Edge   120m   II. Simon Richardson. 26 Feb 2020.
The narrow buttress to the right of *Red Gully*. Climb an easy angled rib followed by a right-facing corner formed by a fin of rock on the left to gain the platform on top of the fin. Move steeply through a mixed wall on the right to gain a broken gully system leading to the top.

MAMORES, Mullach nan Coirean, Coire Dearg:
New Kids on the Block   80m   V,6 *. Suzana El Massri, Nathan Adam. 23 Feb 2020.
Ten metres left of *Captain Caveman*, and just left of the obvious snow streak in the centre of the crag, are three parallel left facing corners. This route takes the central steep and most obvious corner, which gives a good sustained pitch. Graded for useful ice, likely to be harder without.
1. 40m Climb easy snow to just below the base of the corner and make difficult moves to enter it. Climb the iced corner (crux) and exit right over a steep step before traversing left across a snowy bay to belay.
2. 40m Traverse up and right across the bay to reach a short corner. Climb this and the easier snow slope above to the top. (Topo provided)

Turf Factory   70m   VI,6 *. Nathan Adam, Suzana El Massri. 23 Feb 2020.
This route is on the crag left of *Gendarme Buttress*, and below and left of the other route here, *Mistaken Identity* (SMCJ 2018). Start below a large snow slope at the right side of this part of the cliff. A technical and poorly protected first pitch gives way to enjoyable steep climbing on the second. Frozen turf is essential. Descent can be made down an easy snow gully to the right, or continue up *Mistaken Identity*.
1. 45m Go up the initial slope easily, aiming for a right-facing corner-ramp. Climb this with increasing difficulty and poor gear over several small steps and ledges until forced right to a large ledge. Move right again, and climb a steep step to a

MULLACH NAN COIREAN

Coire Dearg - North Face

1. Turf Factory VI,6
2. Mistaken Identity III,4
3. Gendarme Ridge . . . . III *

d. Descent

4. New Kids on the Block . . . V,6 *
5. Disco Corner IV,4
6. Captain Caveman III,4
7. Not Bad for a Dad VI,7
8. Himalayan Shuffle VII/VIII,8
9. Yo Bro VIII,9
10. Kid Gloves IV,4

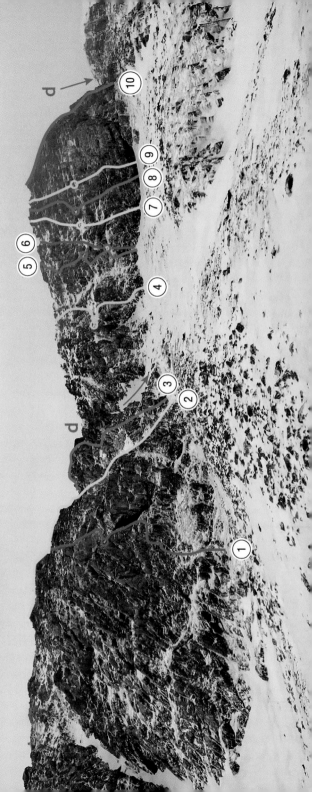

MULLACH NAN COIREAN

Black Buttress - Central Sector

1. Boab's Buttress V,6
2. A Roll and Hot Boaby VI,7
3. No! IV,5
4. Ramp Route II
5. The Shuffler VI,6
6. Descent Gully II

left-slanting flake-crack with some welcome protection, and climb this to a good ledge and belay.
2. 25m Step right from the belay and climb onto a higher ledge with difficulty to reach a wide left-leaning crack which gives excellent climbing on good chockstones to reach easier ground leading to the top. (Topo provided)

Black Buttress:
Boab's Buttress 150m V,6. Simon Teitjen, Will Rowland. Dec 2015.
Follows the crest of the buttress via the obvious weakness starting at its toe.
1. 30m Start up a corner leading to an overhang. Climb the overhang on ice and continue up mixed ground. Belay below a short wall.
2. 40m Climb the short wall and steep corner to the left. A great pitch!
3. 50m Follow ramps left then right to avoid the steep wall above.
4. 30m Continue up the ramp to gain the crest. (Topo provided)

Boab's Burnt Head Gasket 70m V,6. Simon Teitjen, Will Rowland. Dec 2016.
1. 50m Around the corner from the toe of the buttress (left-hand side) follow an easy-angled slab using frozen turf (bold) to belay below the big corner.
2. 20m Climb the fine steep and technical corner. (Topo provided)

I'll Decide 40m IV,4. Will Rowland. Mar 2020.
The corner-ramp down and left from *Boab's Burnt Head Gasket*.

The Polish Variation 50m VI,7 *. Suzana El Massri, Nathan Adam. 12 Feb 2020.
Start in the same bay as *Boab's Burnt Head Gasket*, 5m to the right and below a wide right-facing corner crack. Good sustained climbing, no verglas and dry cracks recommended.
1. 30m Climb the wide crack strenuously to a small roof which is surmounted to reach twin cracks above. Continue up these steeply on good hooks to reach the terrace above.
2. 20m Surmount the block of *Ramp Route* and climb the impending groove above (crux) which is steep and well protected (shared pitch with *A Roll and Hot Boaby*). (Topo provided)

It's Not A Jeep! 70m IV,5. Simon Teitjen, Will Rowland. Dec 2016.
Gained from the descent gully right-hand side of the buttress there is a left-facing corner leading to a broken wall. Climb the corner, step left and climb a short steep wall. Branch out left then back right to continue up the wall. (Topo provided)

A Roll and Hot Boaby 95m VI,7. Fran Thompson, Will Rowland, Dec 2017.
The third pitch is the crux and can be linked with *Boab's Buttress*.
Start just right of the toe of the buttress.
1. 25m Climb the corner.
2. 40m Branch left and climb a series of short walls to belay below the steep wall.
3. 20m Climb the pedestal and commit to the groove. Belay above. (Topo provided)

No! 60m IV,5. Fran Thompson, Will Rowland. Dec 2017.
Just right of the toe of the buttress and to the right of *A Roll and Hot Boaby* there is an obvious ledge. The route starts on the right side of ledge.

Climb a steep cracked wall and join *Ramp Route* above. (Topo provided)

The Shuffler   60m   VI,6 *. Will Rowland, Suzana El Massri, Nathan Adam. 13 Feb 2020.
Start left of *Could Be Worse*, a few metres up *Ramp Route*.
1. 30m Climb the left-hand of two wide icy gullies and continue on easier ground to below a short steep crack, up this to a good platform and block belay.
2. 30m Above is a cracked arete. Strenuously climb the crack (thin and poorly protected) until level with a ledge on the right. Awkwardly pull up onto this and climb a series of short difficult corners before moving left to a turfy groove which is followed to the top. (Topo provided)

Not Paid To Rush   50m   IV,4. Will Rowland. 13 Feb 2020.
Above *Ramp Route* is another parallel ramp system (Grade II). Start halfway along this and climb a turfy line directly up the wall above.

Could Be Worse   70m   V,4. Iain Howie, Nathan Adam. 15 Jan 2020.
Start at the toe of the buttress where *Ramp Route* goes left and just before the crag turns to face the easy gully on the right. A serious second pitch, although not technically difficult.
1. 40m Climb the groove in the crest to a block, move right and climb up and follow several short tricky steps to a right trending snowy ramp. Climb this until a grooved rib is reached with a gully on the left and a right facing corner groove on the right, poor belay.
2. 30m Climb the corner groove on good hooks but with poor protection and continue up snow to reach a good thread in a pinnacle. Continue trending right along short steps to a shallow left facing corner, climb this (serious) to below a large block and exit right to a huge terrace. (Topo provided)

Cooking the Books   60m   V Diff. Will Rowland. July 2015.
Arete and wall gained from the descent gully on the right-hand side of the buttress at the start of the second ramp.

In winter, the rib right of the descent gully on the right side of the buttress can also be descended – *Descent Rib* (II).

SGÙRR A' BHUICH, Spider Crag (NN 196 696):
This fine summit is dwarfed by the bulk of Aonach Beag but offers excellent views down into Glen Nevis and Steall Meadow. The routes on the south-west facing slab all share a useful large boulder belay at the top, and a few metres back, with 60m ropes being useful to reach it. Approach through Steall Gorge and along to the ruin from where the crag is obvious on the hillside above (the big silvery grey sweep of slabs and ribs), follow the broad ridge to the right of the Allt Coire nan Laogh before striking up steep slopes to the crag (around 1 hour 30 minutes). Descent is easiest by traversing right (looking up; left from the top of *The Big Ribeye*) into a narrow heather filled gully and carefully descending this back to the base. Alternatively head left to reach the hillside and easily down.
     The crag offers slabby and bold climbing but the angle is never too steep and the friction is good with a mix of quartzite and schist, although the routes are fairly high up and a bit dirty in places. The climbs are interesting and open, if escapable, but it is a fairly long walk past many good crags in the glen!

Schist Happens   55m   VS 4b. Cameron McIlvar, Nathan Adam. 19 Sep 2015.
Technically easy, but bold with almost no worthwhile runners for the whole pitch,
start at the left side of the crag. Climb up a short slab and follow blank crack lines
and more slabs to reach a left facing corner. Climb this and exit right onto more
slabs and trend rightwards to reach the belay.

The Amazing Adventures of the Land Octopus   55m   H.Severe 4b. Cameron
McIlvar, Nathan Adam. 19 Sep 2015.
Climb the central section of the slabs just right of a heather patch. The line trends
left before climbing straight up to reach the boulder, another bold line.

Go the Distance   55m   VS 4b. Cameron McIlvar, Nathan Adam. 19 Sep 2015.
Just left of the heather filled gully is a long, narrow roof. Climb to the roof and
place a reasonable small cam at the back of this. Pull over at the left hand side
and go right to a short crack which is followed straight up. Cross a heather step
and climb the gritty rib above with a good wire on the right. Trend left up the slab
beyond to the boulder.

The Big Ribeye   60m   VS 4c *. Cameron McIlvar, Nathan Adam. 19 Sep 2015.
The obvious wide rib right of the heather filled gully. It gives a series of technical
steps which are easily escapable on either side but the rock is clean and the
positions are pleasant with an optional 40m of easier ground above.

AONACH BEAG, An Aghaidh Gharbh:
Old Folks Boogie   110m   II *. Steve Kennedy, Andy MacDonald. 18 Jan 2020.
The ridge which falls into the corrie from the rocky outcrop on the summit ridge
(NN 200 712), close to the descent normally used to access the routes in the east
corrie (i.e. routes south of the *North-East Ridge*). Climb the ridge fairly directly
until close to the top where a leftwards traverse onto a narrow ridge was taken to
avoid a steep wall. Finish on top of the outcrop.

Lower West Face:
Hamster's Paradise   140m   IV,5. Will Rowland. Jan 2019.
This route lies right of *Dasher* on the buttress containing *Prominent Chimney*.
Start just right of *Dasher* at the bottom right of the lower tier and climb the right
wall of a prominent corner to the terrace. Gain the upper buttress and follow the
crest to a large detached block. Back and foot up between the block and steep
wall to gain the top. (Topo provided)

Hold Tight   80m   V,6. Will Rowland. Jan 2019.
A direct line up the buttress between *Pugilist* and *North Gully*. Go up a broken
slabby wall to a steep wall, climb the wall direct via a steep corner-crack to gain
a ledge. From the ledge, traverse left onto a slab and move up and into a groove,
which eases to a steady ridge and the top section of *Pugilist*. Two nuts were placed
to protect moves through the steep corner. (Topo provided)

STOB COIRE SGRIODAIN, Creag Mholach (NN 35168 74631):
This buttress lies on east side of Loch Treig directly above the West Highland line
and is well seen from the Laggan Road. The base is quite low so it needs a good
dump of snow and cold weather, which means that the approach for vehicles to
Fersit may not be possible.

Hairy Maclarey 170m III. Alan Halewood, Dave Anderson. 13 Feb 2020.
Start just right of the lowest rocks.
1. 25m Follow a rising traverse up and right past an ice bulge.
2. 35m Keep left of the bulk of the buttress following a heather strip cutting through a long thinly iced pair of slabs.
3. 60m Take a ramp up the right side of a steep buttress before stepping to a continuation ramp-line up the left side of the upper buttress until it is possible to head back right up the first of two short steep icy grooves.
4. 50m Move left from the belay up a short chimney before following heathery terraces and ramps back up right to easy ground on the crest of the ridge. (Topo provided)

CREAG MEAGAIDH, Stob Poite Coire Ardair, South-East Face:
The following two routes lie on the fourth and smallest of the upper buttresses, left of *Eyecatcher* (SMCJ 2019), and can be gained by the gully and ramp from the right, or by climbing the lower tier. Many ice pitches have been climbed on this lower tier at Grade III to IV. (Topo provided)

Wandering Charlie 280m III. John Lyall. 16 Nov 2019.
Start on the lower tier by a left-slanting ramp and a short ice pitch, then a long section of easy ground leads to the upper buttress. Follow a left slanting slab and a prominent short crack to gain the left edge. Continue up the edge, avoiding the steep tower on the left. A poor, escapable line.

Young Pretender 100m III,4. John Lyall. 16 Nov 2019.
Climb the right edge of the buttress overlooking the gully on the right and move into the top of the obvious corner on the left to gain the crest. Finish direct up the bulging crack in the tower.

MONADHLIATH, Stac Buidhe, South-East Face (NN630962):
Cabin Fever 70m IV,6. Al Todd, Simon Richardson. 28 Feb 2020.
A line of weakness on the right side of the cliff. Start below a vegetated gully directly below an icicle frieze at two-thirds height.
1. 30m Pull over a steep step to gain the gully and follow it to a prominent right-slanting ramp under a steep wall. Climb the ramp and make a steep exit to a narrow ledge below the icicle frieze.
2. 20m Move right along the ledge below the icicle frieze and climb a steep wall (crux) immediately right of a deep corner (with a large tree at its top) to gain a large terrace.
3. 20m Finish up the snow gully left of a blunt rib to the top.

GLEN GLOY, Coire Ceirsle Hill:
In very cold conditions a number of easily accessible icefalls form on the north side of Coire Ceirsle Hill above Glen Gloy. The easiest approach is to cross the river via the bridge at NN 248 877.

Duane Dibbley 300m IV,4. Will Rowland, James Cooper. Feb 2018.
The main central icefall. It gave around 300m of cascade climbing, starting in the trees. Nice, non serious climbing similar to *Smoking the White Owl* on Sgùrr Finniosgaig on Aonach Mòr.

Friday Night Frolic 150m III,4. Will Rowland. Feb 2018.
An icefall to the right of the main falls giving three or four pitches, the last cascade being around III,4 and finishing near the top of the moor.

GLEN COE

BUACHAILLE ETIVE MOR, Crowberry Ridge North-East Face:
Fracture Route 65m VI,6. Neil Adams, Gordon Lacey. 11 Feb 2017.
Climbed as two independent pitches before continuing up *Crowberry Ridge* to the summit.

Rannoch Wall:
Grooved Arete, Variation Start 25m HVS 5a **. Michael Barnard, Ewan Lyons. 7 Jul 2019.
Climbs shallower grooves immediately right of the normal way. Start by bridging up the 6m chimney-crack on the right for a few moves, then step onto the wall and move up (bold) towards two short grooves which go up past a small overlap. Climb the clean left-hand groove past the overlap, then step left to join the normal way.

Broad Buttress, West Face:
The following two routes lie either side of *Ephemeron Gully* and require a good freeze and low lying snow. (Topo provided)

Broad Buttress 325m III,3 *. John Higham, John Hutchinson. 11 Dec 2011.
The left-hand buttress (NN 22507 54833). Avoid the steep foot of the buttress by starting 10m to the left and following a right-trending ramp to regain the centre of the buttress (25m). Continue up straightforward mixed ground for approximately 100m to reach steeper rocky ground. (It is possible to avoid this lower section and traverse in directly from the base of *Ephemeron Buttress*). Ascend the upper section directly for 200m keeping to the centre of the buttress finishing at the top of Great Gully upper Buttress. Steep snow leads to the summit slopes of Coire na Tualaich. Possibly climbed before.

Ephemeron Buttress 300m IV,4 **. John Higham, John Hutchinson. 26 Feb 2020.
The narrow buttress to the right of *Broad Buttress* and immediately right of *Ephemeron Gully*. Start on the right-hand side of the buttress at NN22413 54851. Runners and belays are difficult to find.
1. 50m After a steep start follow snowy grooves until a rock barrier, traverse 5m left to belay below a left-slanting wide crack.
2. 50m Ascend the crack and move directly up steep ground to a leftwards trending snowy ramp ascend this and move up onto a large ledge below an impending wall move to right end of ledge and ascend with difficulty the narrow groove and cracks above to a large ledge.
3. 50m Avoid the steep wall above on the right following mixed ground to belay on large spike on left wall.
4. 60m Traverse left for 5m to the centre of the buttress ascend a steep groove and then easier mixed ground to a belay ledge.

5. 50m   Continue up a bulging corner and enter a snowy gully and belay on the left.

6. 40m   Follow a snow gully with a minor rock bulge to a good belay.

Finish by following easier ground to a fine snow arete interrupted by a short tricky step to the final snow slope.

Lagangarbh Buttress:

The following route approximates to the line of *Lagangarbh Buttress* in Highland Scrambles South (p292) which lies lower down and right of the feature Lagangarbh Buttress described on p104 Glen Coe Rock and Ice Climbs. (Topo provided)

Lower Lagangarbh Buttress   200m   II,3 *. John Higham, Chris Gilmore. 6 Dec 2008.

Follow the right crest of the buttress starting at NN 22310 54991 for approximately 150m via short walls, tricky slabs, ledges and turfy ramps. Above, 50m of easier ground leads to a finish at the foot of the upper buttress. Escape can be made to the left and down snow slopes or continue up the following route. Possibly climbed before.

Last Outing   60m   IV,4. John Higham, Chris Gilmore. 6 Dec 2008.

Start at the highest point of the *Lower Lagangarbh Buttress* where it abuts the upper buttress (the upper right flank of the feature *Lagangarh Buttress* described in Glen Coe Rock and Ice Climbs p104). Ascend a leftwards trending icy corner at this point and finish to the right via a steep step onto the eastern slopes of Coire na Tulaich.

Coire na Tulaich:

Foolish Notion   250m   II. John Higham. 12 Feb 2012.

This route winds it way up the area of indistinct slabby buttresses (NN 21875 54587) that dominate the central area of the east side of Coire na Tulaich to the right of the Blotch Buttresses. This area is highly avalanche prone and needs stable snow conditions. In thin snow cover, but icy conditions, a prominent low-angle gully provides Grade II ice as a pleasant approach to the base of the lower buttress. At the lowest buttress take a left leaning ramp for 50m. Easy ground follows to the foot of the next buttress. This was ascended by a series of rightwards trending ramps and short walls leading to a steep wall on the next buttress barring access to slabs above (100m). This was ascended by moving right for 20m to find and ascend a short steep chimney and then ascending thin ice runnels on the insecure slabs above (100m). Easy ground continues for a considerable way to the summit ridge of the Buachaille Etive Mor or a long escape to the right can be made onto the normal descent route. (Topo provided)

BIDEAN NAM BIAN, Lost Valley Buttress:

Sapiens   85m   VIII,7. Tim Miller, Jamie Skelton. 18 Feb 2020.

A serious route based on the direct finish to the *Neanderthal* corner.

1. 35m   Start 10m up and right of *Neanderthal*. Climb a corner for 20m to below a steep wall with an obvious crack. Initially climb the crack then move up and left, on good hooks, to belay at a large ledge.

2. 15m   From the left of the ledge climb steep turf then traverse left to the *Neanderthal* belay.

3. 35m From the belay climb directly up the corner to a ledge. Climb thin ice in the corner (peg on right) to an icicle. Follow a chimney to below a roof and turn this on the right. (Topo provided)

Stob Coire nan Lochan, Summit Buttress:

Spectre, Far Right Start   60m   VI,5 *. Ken Applegate, Neil Matthews. 16 Feb 2020.
Climbed in icy conditions, otherwise probably V,5.
1. 50m This pitch takes a steep corner a few metres to the right of the Alternative Start to Spectre, just beyond where the crag turns a corner. It is in line with the 60m abseil from the top of the difficulties of *Scabbard Chimney* and *Spectre*. Climb the steep, shallow corner, before the angle eases. Continue up a series of shallow grooves to reach an in-situ peg belay, overlooking *The Tempest*.
2. 10m From the belay, traverse left and join *Spectre* a couple of metres above where the *Alternative Start* comes in. (Topo provided)

GARBH BHEINN, South Wall:

Gralloch 45m IX,10. Peter Hoang, Neil Adams, Lukas Klingora. 28 Feb 2020.
A more direct version of the summer line. Instead of traversing out right to bypass the initial roof, the winter route goes through the left-hand side of the roof and straight up into the obvious crack-ramp system. Start in the same snowy bay as *Scimitar*. Climb straight up to the left-hand side of the roof above on easy ice and turf. Turn the roof on the left to enter a crack/ramp system which runs up to the base of the open groove of the summer route. Stein pull wildly up these cracks to gain the relative respite of the icy groove, and climb this with difficulty to a ledge at 40m. Continue more easily to the top.

Scimitar 115m VII,8. Tim Miller, Damian Granowski, Callum Johnson. 28 Feb 2020.
A winter ascent of the summer line.
1. 10m Climb a a rightwards ramp to spike belay below the obvious crack.
2. 20m Climb the steep well protected crack on good hooks to a short corner. Belay up and left of the corner.
3. 25m Climb the chimney above to the terrace.
4. 20m Climb the short corner directly in front, then traverse right into another slabby corner and climb this on thin hooks to belay in a recess.
5. 40m Climb the short steep wall above the belay and continue easily to the top.

Butterknife 105m VI,6. Tim Miller, Jamie Skelton. 20 Feb 2020.
The summer route was followed throughout. The lower two pitches provided some very enjoyable climbing. The crux second pitch in particular had fantastic steep pulls on solid hooks, however as the angle eased off on the second half of the route so too did the quality of the climbing. One could be forgiven for walking off along the terrace.

MAOL ODHAR, Coire nam Frithallt:

Papa Shango, Right-Hand Finish   145m   I *. Andy MacDonald. 15 Nov 2019.
Climb *Papa Shango* (SMCJ 2010) until the gully splits at three-quarters height below a triangular buttress. Follow the right-hand branch to an abrupt finish close to the summit cairn.

CREACH BHEINN, An Coire Dhuibh, The Zeppelin Face:
D'yer Mak'er   140m (excluding the approach)   II *. Steve Kennedy, Andy MacDonald. 20 Feb 2020.
The left-slanting groove about 12m left of *Celebration Day* (SMCJ 2019). Climb the groove to a snow bay (50m). Follow the continuation of the groove up and rightwards (45m). Finish by aiming for a prominent notch on the left which forms a short squeeze chimney leading to the top (30m).

Moby Dick 145m (excluding the approach) I/II. Andy MacDonald. 30 Nov 2017. The vague right trending snowy rampline situated on the extreme right side of the face just before it merges into more open slopes. Follow the ramp towards a notch formed by a large rock. Climb this step to a broad shelf, move right then finish up the same general line with a couple of steeper steps.

SOUTHERN HIGHLANDS

THE COBBLER, South Peak:
Southern Freeze 60m   IX,9.Dave MacLeod, Helen Rennard. Jan 2016
By the summer route.

BEINN NARNAIN, Yawning Crag:
Second Time Lucky 25m   IV,5. Gavin McColl, Jon Wylie. 25 Feb 2020.
A line right of the cave of *Muckle Mou'*. The top section may coincide with the summer route *Cicatrice*.
1. 15m Traverse 5m right from the base of the cave of *Muckle Mou'* then follow the crack and squeeze chimney to another cave visible from below. Traverse right under the overhang to belay below the prominent chimney.
2. 10m Climb the chimney to the top (crux).

BEN CRUACHAN, Coire Chat, Noe Buttress:
Double OO 70m   IV,4. Stuart McFarlane, Robin Clothier. 10 Jan 2020.
An alternative start to *Noe Buttress* starting up the parallel corner to its left.
1. 40m. Climb the corner crossing *One of Nine* to join *Noe Buttress*.
2. 30m. Continue up *Noe Buttress* to the top.

One Of Nine 105m   IV,5. Robin Clothier, Stuart McFarlane. 13 Dec 2019.
Start as for *Hats Off* on the left flank of *Noe Buttress*.
1. 35m. Climb snow ledges and and initial ice smear (*Hats Off* steps right above to gain a second ice smear). Instead, pull left onto a ledge to gain the crest, and follow the groove above leading to deep corner. Belay on the right.
2. 25m. Step left on to a flake and again on to a triangular wall and surmount this. Move left, and continue up short corners to beneath a huge recess and belay.
3. 45m. Walk right to gain snowy grooves leading to easier ground above.

STOB GHABHAR, North-East Corrie:
Last Call 130m   III,4 *. Steve Kennedy, Andy MacDonald. 20 Mar 2020.
The two-tiered buttress about 50m right of *Upper Couloir Keyhole*, beyond a recessed area. Start just left of the lowest point and move up left to reach a shallow groove. Follow the groove then move leftwards towards a short rock wall. Mixed ground leads a belay on the snow shelf near the top of the initial buttress (50m).

Finish in two pitches up straightforward snow slopes immediately right of the upper buttress via a small cornice (80m).

BEINN DORAIN, Creag an Socach:

A Very Naughty Boy 100m VII,8/9 **. Tim Miller, Damian Granowski. 27 Feb 2020.
The route takes a left-trending line across the steep wall to the right of *False Rumour Gully* and climbs a series of short steep steps. Start at the right-facing groove on the right-hand side of the wall.
1. 30m Climb up and left easily to below a steep roof (overhead protection). Pull steeply over the roof and belay at a big ledge up and left.
2. 20m Climb the steep corner above and continue to below a large flat roof where the route joins *The Enemy Within*.
3. 50m Step left and follow *The Enemy Within* to the top via a steep corner. (Topo provided)

MEALL A' CHOIRE LEITH, Coire Ban:

Ace In The Hole 80m III,4. Simon Richardson, Sophie Grace Chappell. 14 Nov 2019.
To the left of the gully running up the centre of the crag is a broken buttress. This route takes a line of grooves up the centre of the buttress, with an unlikely finish.
1. 50m Start below the centre of the buttress below a V-groove between two steep walls. Climb the groove passing a bulge after 10m then continue up easier mixed ground to a large platform with boulders below the headwall.
2. 30m Trend right and climb a steep wall of overlapping shelves near the right edge of the buttress. Exit via a short gully that curls left to an unexpected exit via a hole. Easy angled terrain now leads to the top.

Wild Card 70m IV,5. Simon Richardson, Sophie Grace Chappell. 14 Nov 2019.
Right of the central gully is an area of steep walls. The steepest of these lies at the right end and has an icy left to right ramp running up from its foot.
1. 50m Climb the ramp for 40m to where it finishes at a narrow ledge girdling the wall. Step left and climb a steep vegetated groove and exit right onto a ledge with a 20m-high flake.
2. 70m Step off the top of the flake and climb a series of steep walls above until a low angled ramp leads right to easy ground. Easy angled terrain leads to the top.

BEN VORLICH, South Face:

Door Step Route 120m III,4 **. James Seaman, Peter Nellist. 28 Feb 2020.
A winter ascent based on *Central Rib* – see p359 Highland Scrambles South. Approach via the regular walking route to Ben Vorlich. Descend east of the summit then contour west first passing a major rib. Start at a flat ledge on the second rib with a short overhanging wall.
1. 40m Climb a turfy groove on left of the overhang to gain the crest of the rib. Step right then move up the rib as it rises to the left side of the steepening buttress to reach a spike belay.
2. 40m Climb a short groove on left side of the buttress and traverse until a groove that leads to the flat crest of buttress below a steep wall. Climb the steep wall with good gear and excellent hooks and belay below the next wall.

3. 40m Climb directly up this second shorter wall. The ridge now eases off and difficulties quickly abate.

Note: An ascent of *South Face, Right-Hand Rib* – see p361 Highland Scrambles South – was made in Feb 2020, but precise details are unknown.

MEALL DUBH, Coire Cruinn (NN 865 308):

This interesting and readily accessible north-east facing buttress lies below the summit of Meall Dubh (698m), in Coire Cruinn overlooking Glen Almond. The cliff base sits at about 500m and from the entrance to the corrie it looks a little similar to Stob Coire nam Beith in Glen Coe, albeit on a smaller, easier and less grand scale. Members of the Perth JMCS climbed here in the 1930s but it appears nothing was ever recorded. In 1941, M.B.Nettleton noted a few summer and winter ascents during his period teaching at nearby Glen Almond School; see article in 1943 SMCJ, p90.

The cliff was rediscovered by Rab Anderson whilst checking out a route on the opposite side of the glen for an SMC's Hillwalkers' guide and on his subsequent investigation in Feb 2015 he climbed the major gully systems. The cliff provides a useful winter venue within a short distance of the Central Belt.

Approach from the Newton Bridge parking area in the Sma Glen. Go through a gate on the south side of the bridge and follow a rough track though the trees alongside the River Almond. Step over a wall and under an electric fence to gain the flat pasture then cross this to reach some large boulders at an area known as Alpinshields. Go through a gate and ascend the hillside to gain the flat corrie floor, out of which tumbles the Allt a' Choire Chruinn (3km; 300m; 1h).

Given the cliff's altitude and its easy-angled nature, conditions do vary, although it does hold more snow than might be expected. It is possible to have a virtually snow-free walk-in and find that the cliff is holding a fair amount. The cliff is covered in copious amount of heather, which whilst not of much use does make the climbing a bit more insecure and exciting!

There are three main buttresses; Pinnacle Buttress on the left, the recessed Central Buttress, then North Buttress on the right, which is the main mass of rock rising full height from the centre of the flat corrie floor. These buttresses are defined by the principal gully systems.

Climbs pretty much finish on the summit of Meall Dubh. Descent is best achieved via the north ridge which runs down the right side (facing) of the corrie. Head north-west to pick-up a fence and follow this down the ridge to a step, from where easy ground leads back to the base of the buttress. The head of *Allt Gully* is crossed, which can also be descended but will require more care, especially if the snow is hard. (Topo provided)

Pinnacle Gully Buttress 120m II. C.McNee, D.Kirk. 31 Jan 1999.
Climbs the buttress immediately left of *Pinnacle Gully*, keeping generally to the crest.

Pinnacle Gully 250m II *
The left-hand gully; there is a chockstone and cave pitch high on the left which is normally covered. From below it a short summer route goes out onto a flake-pinnacle on the left wall; *The Pinnacle* (V.Diff) recorded by M.B. Nettleton & C.V.B. Marquand, M.E.D. Poore & Spence but thought to be the same as a climb made in October 1930 by J.H.B. Bell.

Rowantree Buttress 300m IV,4. Tom Prentice, Rab Anderson. 23 Feb 2016.
The edge of *Central Buttress* to the right of *Pinnacle Gully*. Go easily up and left past the entrance to Central Gully then zigzag to a tiny rowan. Climb up and left to a more substantial rowan. Step left and climb directly above by heathery ledges; stepping right then back left and up via grooves to reach easy ground. Belay up on the right at a small plaque near the edge. Climb grooves and cross a narrow neck to below the upper buttress. A short steep section gains easier ground at the top of the buttress.

Central Groove 250m III *. Tom Prentice, Rab Anderson. 7 Mar 2016.
The groove-line up the middle of *Central Buttress*. Go easily up and left past the entrance to Central Gully then climb up and step left to belay on the tiny rowan as for *Rowantree Buttress*. Continue up the groove. In the wide upper funnel, a groove on the left provides a finish.

Central Gully 250m II **
The gully just right of centre; initially hidden from the approach. A large chockstone near the start can present some difficulty and there can be a few short steps elsewhere. Take the left fork up the side of a small buttress near the top; the right is easy. This is thought to be the same as a winter ascent made by M.B. Nettleton, Poore & Spence in the early 1940s.

Crest Route 300m III *. Rab Anderson, Tom Prentice. 4 Mar 2015.
The line of grooves up the crest of *North Buttress*, overlooking *Central Gully*; climbed in six pitches of 50m or more. Start at the toe of the buttress and climb to a small rowan tree then go up right into a groove and continue in the same line to finish up easy ground around the head of *Central Gully*. This probably takes a similar line to *North Buttress* (Diff) by Nettleton, who along with others also made some scrambling routes on this buttress.

Twisting Grooves 300m III *. Rab Anderson, Tom Prentice. 7 Mar 2016.
The line of grooves up the centre of *North Buttress*. Start at the foot of *Shallow Gully* and go easily up left beneath a wall which can hold some ice. Climb the groove in the corner to its top and traverse right to a block belay. Ignore the open groove on the left and climb up and right into the main groove-line which leads to a cave. Continue up the groove to the buttress crest. Traverse across Central Gully and climb the groove up the centre of the upper buttress.

Shallow Gully 250m I/II
The gully which curves up around the right side of North Buttress. To the left of its foot two icefalls can form. The easier right-hand one has a bush to its right and gives a short but more interesting start to the gully.

Allt Gully 200m I
The gully on the far right, down which the Allt a' Choire Chruinn flows from just beneath the summit of Meall Dubh.

A route recorded in SMCJ 1986 (p342) on Meall Dubh has a grid reference NN845305, which places it in the next corrie to the west; Coire na Còinnich. The approach distance given of 3 miles (5km) would be correct for this corrie.

Central Buttress   200m   II. A.Fraser, G.Leslie. 18 Feb 1985.
Climb an icefall, then easy ground to the gully. Climb the gully to a large ledge beneath the upper buttress. This is also split by a narrow gully, which is reached by a traverse from the right, then climbed directly. The climbing in this corrie is disappointing.

LOWLAND OUTCROPS & GALLOWAY HILLS

THE TROSSACHS, An Garadh, Meall na Boineide (NN 408 126):
The following two routes lie on the clean, vaguely-square buttress at the bottom of the Meall na Boineide crags complex, on An Garadh on the north side of Loch Katrine in the Trossachs. There is potential for (slightly adventurous) new routes in this area. Approach is a half hour cycle from Stronachlachar then a half hour walk uphill from the burial ground at Portnellan. (Topo provided)

The Factor   20m   HVS 5a. Danny Carden, Tim Reid. 3 Aug 2019.
Follow the vertical crack that starts to the left of the roofed toe of the buttress, past a small tree, then up a slightly slabbier headwall. Good well-protected climbing but care with the rock is required, particularly at the start. (The first ascensionists wondered if this route had been done, or attempted, years ago as a small holly bush on it showed marks that were potentially very old secateur clippings).

The Lady   15m   VS 4c. Danny Carden, Tim Reid. 3 Aug 2019.
Start at a shallow scoop near the right end of buttress, directly beneath the right end of the large flake at four metres. After a bold start, pass the right end of the flake then climb direct to the top.

GALLOWAY HILLS, Craigdews, Billy Goat Bluff:
To the left of the Ramp is a short, very steep wall (Billy Goat Bluff). Immediately left of this is a rib, which gives the following two routes:

Guerdon Hooves   40m   VS *. Andrew Fraser, Ian Magill. 8 Aug 2019.
A pleasant climb on good rock that is very quick to dry. Start at a short cracked pinnacle just down and left of the roof under the rib.
1. 20m 4b Climb the pinnacle to a ledge. Pull up awkwardly onto the left side of the rib and take a leftward rising line to belay on a slab just left of a pinnacle block.
2. 20m 4b Step up right, then take the lower left slanting groove with a tricky pull out left at the top.

A Goatly Apparition   40m   VS 4c *. Andrew Fraser, Ian Magill. 28 Aug 2019.
The slab on the right side of the rib to a shared belay with *Guerdon Hooves*, then the second bottom leftward trending ramp on the upper wall.

THE BORDERS & DUMFRIES, Clifton:
Shooting Gallery   12m   E2 5c **. James Milton, Oonagh Thin. 2 Nov 2019.
An eliminate line up the fine arete between *Sidekick* and *Aqualine Direct*.
Climb the wall below the arete. Arrange protection then climb the arete on its right hand side using side pulls and culminating in a slap for a sloper. Finish easily, directly as for *Sidekick Variations*. (Topo provided)

GALLOWAY SEA CLIFFS, Larbrax:
On the north side of Pinnacle Bay are some slabs.

Seal Slab 25m V Diff. Ian Magill, Andrew Fraser. 8 Aug 2019.
The left slab, starting immediately left of the recessed bay and finishing to the right.

Seal of Approval 25m Severe 4a * Andrew Fraser, Ian Magill. 7 Jun 2019.
The right slab, to the right of the corner. Pleasant.

STIRLING AREA, Cambusbarron, Fourth Quarry:
Ethanol 12m E3 5c **. Nicholas Wylie, Ryan McKenzie. 19 Mar 2020.
Start up *Malky The Alky* to the triangular block just before the good ledge. Hand traverse rightwards on small crimps and climb the wall above using face holds (small cams useful) to the cracks above. Finish direct. A bit of an eliminate, and only E2 if the crack of *Doobie Brothers* is used for protection.

BERWICKSHIRE COAST, St Abbs Head, Pettico Wick Bay (NT 907 691):
Teflon Terrier 45m VS 4b *. Robert Middleton, Terry Middleton. 19 Sep 2019.
The impressive clean hanging slab at the western tip of the bay. Accessible three hours either side of low tide. An awkward start gains the greasy hanging slab which is followed leftwards pleasantly to its conclusion (some poor rock, but decent cam runners). A step left leads to steep grass and disposable rock holds, until a move right reaches an old fence post of use as dubious protection. Yet more steep grass climbing leads to the fence line proper and belays. In hindsight, the steep grassy exit would benefit from an escape rope pre-rigged to the fence, and the grade and stars suggested assume this. (Topo provided)

Note: the bay also contains three small sea stacks accessible at low tide, which look good sport for a short day, and a couple of other lesser lines look possible on the western cliffs.

SPORT CLIMBS

MULL, Balmeanach:
Light Rain 15m F5+ **. Colin Moody, Cynthia Grindley. 8 Jul 2019.
Start right of *Glueless Groove* (SMCJ 2017). Move up left and climb the bulge then continue up right.

Loch Buie, Grey Cave (Uamh Liath):
Large Boy Stops for No One 22m F7a ***. Cal Bentley-Abbot, Jane Bentley. 20 Jul 2019.
The line left of *Drop Jaw Crack* sharing the same start, bolted by Andy Hyslop in 2013. There is an alternative start to the right.

APPIN, Dallen's Rock (SMCJ 2018 p172–3):
Cassandra 13m 6a *. Steve Kennedy, Cynthia Grindley. 27 May 2019.
The line of bolts left of *Philomena*, following a rightwards trending line to a bulge. Surmount the bulge, pull strenuously up a right facing corner and finish with a reachy move up right. No grabbing the lower off to finish!

MISCELLANEOUS NOTES

THE W.H. MURRAY LITERARY PRIZE

As a tribute to the late Bill Murray, whose mountain and environment writings have been an inspiration to many a budding mountaineer, the SMC have set up a modest writing prize, to be run through the pages of the Journal. The basic rules are set out below, and will be reprinted each year. The prize is run with a deadline of midnight on the last day of April each year.

The Rules:
1. There shall be a competition for the best entry on Scottish Mountaineering published in the *Scottish Mountaineering Club Journal*. The competition shall be called the 'W.H. Murray Literary Prize', hereafter called the 'Prize'.
2. The judging panel shall consist of, in the first instance, the following: The current Editor of the *SMC Journal*; The current President of the SMC; and two or three lay members, who may be drawn from the membership of the SMC. The lay members of the panel will sit for three years after which they will be replaced.
3. If, in the view of the panel, there is in any year no entry suitable for the Prize, then there shall be no award that year.
4. Entries shall be writing on the general theme of 'Scottish Mountaineering', and may be prose articles of up to approximately 3000 words in length, or shorter verse. Entries may be fictional.
5. Panel members may not enter for the competition during the period of their membership.
6. Entries must be of original, previously unpublished material. Entries should be submitted to the Editor of the *SMC Journal* by the end of April for consideration that year. Electronic contributions are preferred and should be submitted via e-mail, although double-spaced typewritten hard copies will also be accepted by post. (See Office Bearers page at end of this Journal for address etc.) Any contributor to the *SMC Journal* is entitled to exclude their material from consideration for the Prize and should so notify the Editor of this wish in advance.
7. The Prize will be a cheque for the amount £250.
8. Contributors may make different submissions in different years.
9. The decision of the panel is final.
10. Any winning entry will be announced in the *SMC Journal*, and will be published in the *SMC Journal* and on the SMC Website. Thereafter, authors retain copyright.

THE WH MURRAY LITERARY PRIZE 2020

THIS YEAR'S PRIZE GOES to Mike Jacob who chose the difficult topic of depression. He gives the reader an insight into his dark mental state but provides illuminating contrasts in the vivid description of a wild day and a perfect sunny day in the mountains. In the conclusion his own dejection is put into perspective by a tragedy involving someone else. To achieve this resolution in a brief article takes no little skill.

The judges admired Sophie-Grace Chappell's poetry which had *good imagery* and *a strong doze of English Mountain Romanticism*. Also in romantic vein was the speech-become-article by Murdo MacLeod: *lyrical, like a pibroch, ...endlessly weaving variations on a theme*. Another lyricist was Helen Forde who visited the Long Island for the first time to follow in the steps of her Grandfather while at the same time providing *a wonderful evocation of the Outer Hebrides*. There was nothing romantic in the mountaineering situations described by Geoff Cohen, but his modest self-deprecation and his examination of his various partners' unsung heroism were exemplary. Geoff also featured in the piece by Graham Little describing a lifelong love affair with a certain Arran rock climb and the music of Jimmy Hendrix: a strange conjunction but handled well in characteristic voice.

Adam Kassyk's description of his initiation into the Club displayed that *rare skill to bring a move-by-move account to life*. In a completely different sphere, John Allen provided a deceptively simple account of a day's hill walking which *had more thought and depth to it*, involving trust between young and old.

The sardonic humour of Tim Pettifer was much admired in his evocation of the Arctic. Tim is a writer with a distinctive voice. Let's hope we hear more of him. Scrambling aficionado Noel Williams almost came to grief on a buttress seen from his living room: a cautionary tale this, told with a mixture of chagrin and humour.

The young (or younger) contributors were represented by Finlay Wild and Will Rowland, both of whom had truly remarkable achievements to relate and, with a little breathlessness at times, managed to involve the reader in their exploits. One hopes they'll continue to reflect on what they do in the Journal. First time contributor Iain Young was amazed to find an unclimbed ridge in the Cairngorms and wrote a good piece about it.

Among those not dealing directly with mountaineering, Bob Reid's examination of the role played by our National Scenic Areas in the conservation of wild land was a timely reminder of the work of Bill Murray in this sphere: endless vigilance is the key. Amazing was the zeal of Colwyn Jones in unravelling the history behind a certain painting in the Club's possession. Mike Cocker also expanded our understanding of the spiky but fascinating personality and exploits of Aleister Crowley, to be concluded in next year's edition.

Work must reach the Editor by 30 April to be considered for the Prize.

Hon. Ed.

SCOTTISH WINTER NOTES 2019–20

THE 2020 SEASON will be remembered as a challenging and frustrating one. It started reasonably enough, with good early season climbing on the high cliffs of the Cairngorms, but a devastating Christmas thaw stripped the mountains bare and it was not until the end of January that significant snow cover returned. February was a story of gales and never-ending storms, although this did have a significant upside of plastering north-west facing cliffs with snow-ice. The International Winter Meet at the end of February was the undoubted highlight of the season. Its timing was something of a miracle, squeezed in between poor mid-season conditions and the onset of Covid-19 Virus international travel restrictions.

Dave Almond on the second ascent of Satyr (IX, 9) Stob Coire nan Lochain.
Photo: James Skelton.

Finally, in the third week of March, a long awaited high-pressure system arrived and winter climbing conditions were outstanding. Unfortunately this coincided with the rapidly escalating Covid-19 Virus situation and eventual lockdown on 23 March. Scottish winter climbers were left frustrated staring at long distance webcam shots of the Ben in perfect condition, wondering what might have been.

As a silver lining, we can take heart that despite the warming climate, the great Scottish ice routes can still form given the right combination of snowfall, wind direction and temperature fluctuations. With luck the stars will align again soon – perfect weather, immaculate conditions, and no access restrictions – we can but dream!

Early Season

Winter arrived in late October when a cold north-westerly deposited a layer of snow over the high tops. The best climbing was found in the colder and less snowy Cairngorms with routes climbed in the Northern Corries, Creagan Cha-no and Braeriach.

Mark Robson and I made an early start on the new routing front with the first ascent of Mixed Blessings (III,5), the buttress left of Schoolmaster's Gully on Braeriach's Coire nan Clach. The following week we added several new routes to Creagan Cha-no including the excellent White Walker (V,6) on Grooved Pinnacle Wall. On the same cliff, Dave Brookes and Jules Harris put to bed an outstanding problem when they made the first free ascent of The Edge of Profanity (V,7). Erick Baillot and Dave Kerr made another notable Cairngorms second ascent when they climbed The Stooee Chimney on The Stuic on Lochnagar. They

Guy Robertson on FA of Local Hero (VIII,9), An Teallach. Photo: Greg Boswell.

found a through-route under the crux chockstone reducing the grade to IV,6.

Jamie Skelton and Dave Almond had two excellent days climbing in Northern Cairngorms in the middle of November that resulted in an early repeat of The Snowpimp (VIII,9) in Coire an Lochain and Berserker (VI,8), an excellent addition to Lurcher's Crag. The route takes a parallel line left of Shapeshifter (VIII,8), and was repeated a few weeks later by Ross Cowie and Steve Elliot who confirmed its quality. The Almond-Skelton team maintained an excellent run of routes early in December with the second ascent of Dark Angel (VII,8) in Glen Coe, and an early repeat of Brass Monkey (VII,8) on Ben Nevis. Also on the Ben, Jonathan Livesey and Connor Henley found Jive Turkey (V,6) on the left wall of Number Four Gully. In the Southern Highlands, Sophie-Grace Chappell and I made an exploratory visit to Coire Ban on Meall a' Choire Leith and came up trumps with Ace In The Hole (III,4) and Wild Card (IV,5).

The big early season event took place in mid November when Greg Boswell and Guy Robertson climbed Local Hero (VIII,9) on An Teallach. This spectacular route lies on the Hayfork Gully wall and was named in memory of Martin Moran. Roger Webb, Neil Wilson and I took advantage of the same cold weather window to climb Dundonnell Face (IV,4) on Beinn Alligin. This is the first route to tackle the 200m-high triangular face framed by Backfire Ridge and the cleft of Diamond Fire.

Mid Season
January and the first half of February were characterised by deep thaws and generally thin conditions. Roger Webb, Gary Kinsey and I took advantage of an early January snowfall to make the first winter ascent of Nethy Crack (V,6) on Cnap Coire na Spreidhe on Cairn Gorm. Although only a single pitch, the route is good quality and hoars readily. Nearby on the Left-Hand Buttress of Creagan Cha-no, Dave Brookes and Jules Harris made the first ascent of a difficult test-piece called The Arc of Profanity (VI,8).

Conditions were lean in the West too, and a well timed early repeat of Archangel (VII,7) on Ben Nevis by Malcolm Bass and Nick Clement was possibly the finest technical winter climb in January. Rather surprisingly, a very thin Point Five Gully

Roger Webb on FA of Nethy Crack (V,6) Cnap Coire na Spreidhe, Cairngorm.
Photo: Simon Richardson.

was climbed during this period too. On Ben Cruachan, Robin Clothier and Stuart McFarlane added Double OO (IV,4) on Noe Buttress.

Things began to pick up at the end of January with more snow and cooler temperatures. Iain Young and John Higham pulled off a superbly-timed piece of exploratory winter mountaineering when they made the first winter ascent of Table Rib (III,4) on Cul Mòr. Mike Lates and Lucy Spark climbed the finest new route of the winter on Skye on 13 February when they made the first ascent of Christmas Comes but Once a Year (IV,4) on Sgùrr nan Gillean. This follows a beautiful icy groove on the left side of High Crag. The same day Callum Johnson and Andy MacKinnon pulled off a major repeat when they made the second ascent of Crack of Dawn (VII,8) on Sgùrr MhicCoinnich.

In mid February Tim Miller and Jamie Skelton made the first ascent of the serious Sapiens (VIII,9) on Lost Valley Buttress in Glen Coe. This outstanding route climbs the upper Neanderthal corner with a new start. Two days later, the same team made the first winter ascent of Butterknife (VI,6) on the South Wall of Garbh Bheinn.

Nathan Adam made several visits to Black Buttress on Mullach nan Coirean. In January he climbed Could be Worse (V,4) on the right flank of the cliff with Iain Howie, and later he returned with Suzana El Massri and Will Rowland to

Robin Clothier FA One of Nine (IV,5) Ben Cruachan. Photo: Stuart McFarlane.

Tim Miller FA of Sapiens (VIII,7), Lost Valley Buttress. Photo: James Skelton.

climb The Polish Variation (VI,7) to Boab's Burn Head Gasket and The Shuffler (VI,6). Nathan and Suzana continued their exploration of Mullach nan Coirean in February with two routes in Coire Dearg. New Kids on the Block (V,6) takes a line left of Captain Caveman, and Turf Factory (VI,6) lies on the crag left of Gendarme Ridge.

Winter Meet
The Scottish International Winter Meet has been a key event on the world mountaineering stage for over 20 years. The meet had been held on a two-year basis by the BMC since 1997, but had not run since 2016. This year, the Alpine Club and BMC provided funding, the SMC provided hut accommodation, Salewa kitted out the hosts, and the event was hosted by Mountaineering Scotland. On the evening of Saturday 22 February, 28 guest climbers from 22 countries and 28 British hosts met up in Aviemore. They went on to enjoy six non-stop days of winter climbing notching up ascents of 150 climbs including seven new routes.

DAY 1: 23 February
The psyche was high as teams dispersed to Mill Cottage, Lagangarbh, Raeburn and the CIC Hut early on Sunday morning before hitting the cliffs. In the Cairngorms, the first pair down was Nicolas Dieu and Michael Poulsen from Denmark who climbed the classic Pot of Gold in Coire an t-Sneachda. Other routes climbed in the corrie included Fingers Ridge, Fluted Ridge Direct, Doctor's Choice, The Lamp, Vortex, Original Summer Route, Yukon Jack, The Slant Direct and Aladdin's Mirror Direct. Jamie Skelton and Damian Granowski from Poland had an impressive day with No Blue Skies, The Message and Pot of Gold.

Stuart McFarlane on FA of Wonderwoman (V,6), Ben Nevis. Photo: Simon Richardson.

A couple of pairs ventured north to Torridon and found excellent conditions on Beinn Eighe. On the Far East Wall, Neil Adams and Peter Hoang (Canada) made an ascent of the modern classic Sundance (VIII,8), and on the Eastern Ramparts, Callum Johnson and Lukas Klingora (Czech Republic) came away with the fourth ascent of Boggle (VIII,8). In Glen Coe, Paul Ramsden and Wadim Jablonski (Poland) climbed the superlative Central Grooves (VII,7) in Stob Coire nan Lochan.

On Ben Nevis, ascents were made of Waterfall Gully, The Curtain, 1931 Route, Italian Climb, Route II/Route I Combination and Orion Direct. Dave Almond and Trym Saeland (Norway) climbed Darth Vader (VII,7) and Rich Bentley and Seokju Woo (South Korea) made an ascent of Tower Face of The Comb (VI,6).

DAY 2: 24 February
The weather forecast predicted Scotland would be in the eye of a storm providing a break in the wind, but the exact timing of the anticipated heavy snowfall varied from forecast to forecast. Unfortunately, after a calm start it soon started to snow and blizzards persisted all day.

Four pairs visited Creag Meagaidh, but were turned back by dangerous avalanche conditions on the approach slopes and routes buried in snow. The weather was wild in the Northern Corries, but Murray Cutforth, Tom Phillips (Netherlands), Nicolas Dieu and Michael Poulsen succeeded on Auricle in Coire an Lochain – a good effort in the conditions as this route is no push over at VI,7. A couple of teams visited Ciste Crag on Cairn Gorm (also known as Cranberry Rocks) and climbed a pair of routes apiece in relative shelter on this low-lying cliff.

Across in Glen Coe, two teams climbed North Buttress on Buachaille Etive Mor, and up in Stob Coire nan Lochan, Scabbard Chimney and Spectre saw ascents. Four teams made the long haul up to Church Door Buttress. Willis Morris and Steve Towne (USA) were particularly impressive making a possible second ascent of Greg Boswell and Uisdean Hawthorn's 2016 route Hoargasm (VII,8), followed by Crypt Route (IV,6). Paul Ramsden and Wadim Jablonski chose a lower level option and made a rare ascent of Antichrist (VI,7) on Creag an Socach above Bridge of Orchy.

Big news from Ben Nevis was a new route on Minus Two Buttress by Maarten Van Haeren (Canada) and Andy Inglis. Calculus (VIII,8) takes a line directly through the overhangs that girdle the buttress at one-third height. Andy led the

Luca Celano and Carl Nystedt on Minus One Gully, Ben Nevis. Photo Hamish Frost.

Grade VI entry pitch up icy grooves and Maarten pulled out the stops with a superb lead up a stepped corner through the overhang on tenuous hooks. Easier ground shared with Central Route led to the crest of North-East Buttress. Also of note was Rich Bentley and Seokju Woo's (South Korea) enchainment of Turf War (V,6) and East Ridge (IV,5) on the Douglas Boulder.

DAY 3: 25 February
Excellent ice conditions focused the climbing on Ben Nevis. Minus One Gully (VI,6) had three ascents, and Callum Johnson and Lukas Klingora climbed the route so quickly that they also had time for Minus Two Gully (V,5). Fresh from his success on Minus Two Buttress the day before, Maarten Van Haeren soloed

Rene Lisac (Croatia) on Gully of the Gods, Beinn Bhan. Photo: Scott Grosdanoff.

Orion Direct in a two-hour round trip from the hut. Other ice routes climbed include Left-Hand Route, Waterfall Gully, Vanishing Gully, Thompson's Route and Tower Ridge which was plated in ice from bottom to top.

The mixed routes in Coire na Ciste were very icy and in challenging condition. Dave Almond and Trym Saeland (Norway) made an ascent of Sioux Wall (VIII,8), and Rich Bentley and Seokju Woo climbed a very bold and icy Gargoyle Wall (VI,6), finding only seven pieces of protection in five pitches! Mixed conditions were more amenable lower down the mountain and Neil Adams and Peter Hoang made an ascent of the rarely climbed Kellett's North Wall Route (VII,7).

In Glen Coe, North Buttress on the Buachaille saw an ascent, and in Stob Coire nan Lochan, Scabbard Chimney, Crest Route and Chimney Route were climbed. Further south on Creag an Socach, Kick Start and The Glass Bead Game had a couple of ascents apiece, and on Beinn Eighe, Central Buttress Direct received an ascent.

DAY 4: 26 February

The wind finally dropped and all eyes turned to Ben Nevis with close to 40 climbers from the meet active on the mountain. The standout performance came from Peter Hoang and Neil Adams who made an ascent of The Shroud (VI,6) followed by Mega Route X (VI,6). Peter was keen to reach the summit of the Ben, so they continued up Jubilee Climb and circumnavigated Coire na Ciste to tag the summit before descending Coire Leis. The Shroud had not touched down and was climbed as a hanging ice fang. Peter used his extensive Canadian icefall experience to judge that this potentially very risky ascent was in safe condition. Even so, he rated the climb at WI6/WI6+ on the Canadian scale and commented that he had never climbed an icicle that did not hang vertically before – it had been blown sideways by the wind.

Mega Route X was also climbed by Murray Cutforth and Tom Phillips, and Gemini (VI,6), another highly sought after Ben Nevis classic, was climbed by Alex Mathie and Franz Friebel (Switzerland). Other routes climbed on the Ben include Boomer's Requiem, Minus Two Gully, Minus Three Gully, The Curtain, Orion Direct, Platforms Rib and Route II/Route I combination. CIC hut host Robin Clothier made a rare ascent of Right-Hand Route (VI,6) on Minus Two Buttress with Nicholas Wylie. This route also saw an ascent by Masa Sakano and Frano Udovic (Croatia).

Meet Coordinator Al Todd, found time in his busy schedule to climb the classic Vanishing Gully with Meet Photographer Hamish Frost. Wadim Jablonski, Emily Ward and Alfie Maun abseiled off their route on the Douglas Boulder to assist a climber (not on the meet) who had been avalanched in Number Five Gully.

Further north, Scott Grosdanoff and Rene Lisac (Croatia) climbed Gully of the Gods (VI,6) on Beinn Bhan and Dave Almond and Trym Saeland (Norway) made the third ascent of Feast of the East (VIII,9) on the Eastern Ramparts of Beinn Eighe. Dave said that Trym, who is best known for the first ascent of The Corkscrew Route on Cerro Torre, was absolutely buzzing after the ascent.

In Stob Coire nan Lochan in Glen Coe, Dorsal Arete, Raeburn's Route and Twisting Grooves saw ascents, and on the Buachaille, North Buttress was climbed. Also in Glen Coe, meet volunteer John Higham took a break from resupplying the huts with food to make the first ascent of the 350m-high Ephemeron Buttress (IV,4) to the right of Ephemeron Gully, with John Hutchinson.

International Meet group photo in Aviemore. Photo: Hamish Frost.

DAY 5: 27 February

Heavy snowfall overnight on strong westerly winds resulted in dangerous windslab conditions on the fifth day of the meet. On Ben Nevis this confined teams to wind scoured cliffs such as the Minus Face, where the three Minus gullies saw multiple ascents. I took time out of my Meet Coordinator role to team up with volunteers Stuart MacFarlane and Ian Dempster (who had carried supplies of fresh food up to the hut) to make the first ascent of Wonderwoman (V,6). This takes a line of icy grooves up the lower east flank of Tower Ridge, and even though the route lies low in the mountain, we had to tread very carefully to avoid setting off windslab that was lying precariously over smooth névé. The route was named after Carole Hawthorn who kept everyone superbly fed and watered in the CIC Hut throughout the meet.

In Glen Coe, Andy Inglis and Maarten Van Haaren made an ascent of Central Grooves (VII,7) in Stob Coire nan Lochan, and Luca Celano, Carl Nystedt (Sweden), Nicolas Dieu, Michael Poulsen ploughed through deep snow along the Aonach Eagach traverse. Other Glen Coe based teams, headed to Creag an Socach above Bridge of Orchy, in search of less snowy conditions. Messiah (VI,7) had ascents from at least three teams, but the most notable climb was the third ascent of Defenders of the Faith (IX,9) by Peter Hoang and Neil Adams. This very steep mixed route was first climbed by Dave MacLeod and Fiona Murray in 2006, and was the first Scottish Grade IX to receive an on sight first ascent. Also of note was the first ascent of A Very Naughty Boy (VII,8/9) by Tim Miller and Damian Granowski from Poland. The route takes a left-trending line across the steep wall to the right of False Rumour Gully finishing up The Enemy Within.

A little to the south, Paul Headland, Kirsty Pallas and Neil Byrne (Ireland) made a ski ascent into Beinn Udlaidh and climbed the classic Quartzvein Scoop (IV,4).

Further north, Rich Bentley, Seokju Woo and Neil Silver picked their way through a difficult avalanche-prone approach to make an ascent of Trespasser

Dave Almond FA of The Irony (IX,9) E .Ramparts, Beinn Eighe. Photo: Jamie Skelton.

Buttress (IV,5) on Creag Meagaidh. Seokju, who had a superb meet climbing several challenging routes, enjoyed the wild setting, and rated this climb his finest experience of the week. In the Cairngorms, The Message and Honeypot were climbed in Coire an t-Sneachda, and Andrew Marshall, Jakub Cejpek (Czech Republic) and Gwilym Lynn visited Hell's Lum and ascended a very snowy Deep Cut Chimney.

DAY 6: 28 February
Two new routes on Garbh Bheinn were the big news from the last day of the meet. The South Wall is very rarely in winter condition, but continuous storms had plastered it in snow making it a very wintry proposition. Tim Miller, Callum Johnson and Damian Granowski made the first winter ascent of Scimitar (VII,8) and Neil Adams, Peter Hoang and Lukas Klingora made the first winter ascent of Gralloch (IX,10). Damian led the crux of Scimitar, and Peter made an outstanding lead of Gralloch, which is E2 in summer.

At a more modest level, Al Todd and I took a few hours away from our meet coordination duties to make the first ascent of Cabin Fever (IV,6) in the Monadhliath. This two-pitch route lies on the south-east facing Stac Buidhe and was the first route on the cliff. Situated less than an hour's walk from the Meet HQ in Laggan it was ideal for a quick morning dash.

The weather deteriorated quickly through the day and the avalanche danger was very high. Teams on Ben Nevis wisely restricted themselves to the Douglas Boulder and Vanishing Gully areas. Of note was the possible second ascent of Right-Hand Chimney (VI,7) by Alfie Maun, Emily Ward and Wadim Jablonski from Poland.

Greg Boswell FA of Israelite (VIII,8) Creag an Dubh Loch. Photo: Guy Robertson.

The weather was wild in the Northern Corries, but ascents were made of Honeypot and Wachacha on the Mess of Pottage, and Jamie Skelton and Tyrm Saeland climbed Big Daddy (VII,7) in Coire an Lochain. Everyone was back in good time for the final event at Tisos store in Aviemore where Guy Robertson made an outstanding presentation that captured the essence of pioneering new routes across the Highlands in both winter and summer.

The 2020 Scottish International Winter Meet was a major success. Great routes had been climbed, ideas shared, friendships made and new partnerships formed.

Our international guests had been given a magnificent taste of Scottish winter climbing and left with huge smiles on their faces.

Late Season

Guy Robertson and Greg Boswell pulled off a long sought after first ascent on 4 March when they made the first winter ascent of The Israelite (VIII,8) on Creag an Dubh Loch. This summer E4 provides superlative rock climbing but is often wet, so it was a logical winter target. The same day, the first ascent of Hindmost Ridge (IV,4) on The Devil's Point, demonstrated that there are still major unclimbed features even in well-known parts of the Highlands. Iain Young, John Higham and Kenny Brookman's ascent of the 400m-long ridge bounding the right side of Geusachan Gully on the south side of the mountain was a significant coup and one of the finest exploratory ascents of the season.

Good conditions extended to the Northern Highlands. Dave Almond and Jamie Skelton visited the Eastern Ramparts on Beinn Eighe and climbed a more direct version of the summer line of Claustrophobic Corner. They called their route The Irony and after some careful pondering graded it IX,9. The following day they returned to add Scotophobia (VII,8), which is based on the summer E1 Fear of the Dark on the Eastern Ramparts. Mark Robson and I had a fine adventure on End of Days (VI,6) on An Ruadh-Stac. This takes an unlikely six-pitch line taking in all three tiers to the left of Patey-Bonington summer line North Face. Finally, just before lockdown, Tim Miller and Jamie Skelton made the first winter ascent of The Modern Idiot (VIII,8) on Beinn Eighe's Eastern Ramparts.

In the days leading up to the enforced close of play on 23 March, many teams enjoyed superb conditions on Ben Nevis and multiple ascents were made of the Minus gullies and Orion Direct. The most significant took place on Skye however, when Will Rowland completed the Greater Cuillin Traverse followed by the Red Cuillin. This is thought to be the first time this link up has been achieved in winter, and Will follows in his father Clive's footsteps, who was first to complete the feat in the summer of 1982.

Simon Richardson

SCOTTISH INTERNATIONAL WINTER MEET 2020

The 2020 International Winter Climbing – Streap Alba Geamhradh – kicked off in Aviemore on 22 February. It was hosted by Mountaineering Scotland and supported by the Scottish Mountaineering Club, The Alpine Club, British Mountaineering Council and Salewa. It attracted 56 climbers from 23 countries.

Introduction – Simon Richardson

One evening in the autumn of 2018, I sat down with the President of the Alpine Club over a bottle of whisky and we drank late into the night. Although John Porter is a modest man, he is a mountaineer of considerable repute. Back in the 1970s he partnered Alex MacIntyre on cutting edge first ascents in the Hindu Kush and on Changabang, and it was fascinating to hear these stories first hand. John was keen to encourage younger climbers in the Alpine Club to pursue similar adventures and was looking for ways to promote mountaineering within the Alpine Club. We lamented the demise of the Scottish International Winter Meet, and then we had a president-to-president moment. If the Alpine Club came up with some funding, and the SMC provided accommodation in our huts, perhaps we could relaunch the meet?

At the SMC Committee meeting a few weeks later I broached the idea and it was enthusiastically supported. The hut custodians graciously agreed to make space in the huts and David Myatt, our energetic Meets Secretary, leapt into action and booked Lagangarbh, Raeburn and the CIC for the last week of February 2020, together with a night at Aviemore Youth Hostel at either end. The BMC then stepped in with more financial support so with the accommodation and money in place we had all the key ingredients to hold the meet. Job done!

Well not quite… we still needed an organisation to host the meet. Several months later, I was delighted (and somewhat relieved) when Mountaineering Scotland agreed to take on this crucial role. The meet tied in with their 50th anniversary celebrations and Mountaineering Scotland embraced the project with great enthusiasm and professionalism.

Now the hard work began. Previous meets had been hosted by the BMC and held at Glenmore Lodge. The new model of rotating climbers between four different locations was considerably more complicated and would involve careful planning and choreography. Here the SMC really came into its own. Robin Clothier, who had been dreaming of an international meet on Ben Nevis for many years, took on the responsibility of the CIC Hut logistics – no easy task. Chris Huntley and Dave Broadhead stepped forward to act as hut hosts for Raeburn and Lagangarbh and John Higham offered to act in a resupply role. The mathematics of the hut rotations meant we needed more capacity than Raeburn could take, so we split groups into two when they came east and used Mill Cottage with Heather Morning acting as hut host and providing delicious home cooking.

Meanwhile, Helen Gestwicki at Mountaineering Scotland wrote to the 64 UIAA mountaineering associations inviting them to send a pair of climbers to the meet. Here in Scotland we widely advertised for hosts with the result that we had nearly double the number of applicants. SMC members Andy Inglis, Neil Adams and Tim Elson diligently worked through the applications aiming for a cross-section of climbers and pairing up guests and hosts with equal ability. It was sad to turn so many people down, but the end result was 28 visitors from 22 different countries and 30 hosts equally representing the four supporting organisations of the BMC, Alpine Club, Mountaineering Scotland and the SMC.

As the planning progressed, the activity ramped up. Every guest was asked to bring a presentation about climbing in their country and we set up projection facilities in the huts. Salewa offered to kit out all the host climbers. Catering was arranged from the Clachaig and Laggan Shop. Raeburn and Lagangarbh have poor mobile coverage so paper copies of the weather forecast and avalanche reports were delivered by Glenmore Lodge. As the event drew closer, the tasks multiplied, but it was like pushing on an open door. If anything needed doing someone immediately volunteered. Social media was ramped up. T-shirts were printed. Press releases were issued. Lochaber Mountain Rescue Team ferried supplies up to the CIC. Tim Elson took on the critical job of ensuring the guests were collected from multiple different airports.

The only thing left to do was to pray to the gods for some winter weather. Fortunately they were on side, and after a dismal early winter, February storms plastered Ben Nevis and the Glen Coe mountains with copious amounts of snow, and the ensuing frequent freeze thaws produced some of the best ice conditions for several years. Although the climbing conditions were good, the weather was wild, and the avalanche danger ramped up through the week. This caused Event Coordinators Al Todd and myself some concern, but everyone returned safe and sound for a final celebration in Aviemore on 28 February.

Up at the CIC Hut, Robin Clothier, with assistance from Doug Hawthorn (together with his mother Carole and son and daughter Echan and Marie) kept everyone fed and watered. Stuart MacFarlane and Ian Dempster arrived mid week with fresh supplies. For many, their stay at the CIC was the highlight of the meet. The food was both excellent and plentiful, and being handed a glass of gluhwein from a beaming hut custodian after completing a route on the Ben was a novel and very welcome experience. Staying at the CIC Hut will never be quite the same again!

The meet enjoyed six non-stop days of winter climbing notching up ascents of 150 climbs including seven new routes. The Minus Face was in excellent condition, and routes were climbed from the North-West to the Southern Highlands. The SMC representatives on the meet, including climbing hosts Masa Sakano, Neil Adams, Andy Inglis, Tim Miller, Callum Johnson, Scott Grosdanoff, Tim Elson and Emily Ward, were at the forefront of this activity and involved in all the new routes. For a detailed account of the routes climbed during the week see Scottish Winter Notes 2019–20 in this edition. The most significant additions were Calculus (VIII,8), a direct route on Minus Two Buttress that breaches the band of overhangs at one-third height, A Very Naughty Boy (VII,8) on Creag an Socach, and first winter ascents of Gralloch (IX,10) and Scimitar (VII,8) on Garbh Bheinn.

Chris Huntley, who made everyone so welcome at the Raeburn Hut, and Neil Adams, who had an outstanding week climbing notable routes on all six days, give a flavour of their experiences below.

Hut Host – Chris Huntley

I came to the party late and it was thanks to chatting to Paul Ramsden in the pub after his talk to the Eastern Section in December that I realised I'd be missing a great opportunity if I didn't offer my services to the meet. Paul was already signed up as a host Climber and this reflected the calibre of host and visiting climbers expected. A message came back that my services could be used at the club's

Lagangarbh group, anti-clockwise: Seokju Woo (Korea), Charles Hutchinson, Andrew Marshall, Paul Winder, Ido Gayer (Israel), Neil Silver, Mark Chambers, Jacob Cejpek (Czech Republic), Csanad Boros (Hungary) and Luis Silva (Portugal). Photo: Broadhead Collection.

Raeburn hut. One friend immediately suggested I needed a cookery book on Alpine Hut Cookery. He even sent me the online purchase link! Fortunately the evening catering came from the Laggan Coffee Bothy who provided excellent meals each evening. These I just had to heat up as the climbing groups arrived back at the hut.

Day One for me meant I just had to get the huge stock of food into the hut and somewhat sorted out, while the Raeburn's climbing teams were split as far afield as the Northern Corries and Beinn Eighe. I can see that the climbing culture is clearly much more thoughtful than a few years ago; you study the weather and preceding days conditions, consider the aspect of cliffs and then make your route selection. A longer drive combined with good cliff selection makes for a memorable day. The host climbers certainly did this to perfection and I could tell the visitors were impressed as each evening the teams came back buzzing after some splendid route had been completed. The good first day inspired plans for some of the pairs to take the shorter drive but longer walk-in option and head into Creag Meagaidh. The weather and avalanche reports indicated some caution was necessary but I was really hoping that at least the visiting climbers would get the classic view of the cliffs opening up as you complete the steeper uphill section from Aberarder Farm. Unfortunately the mist was down and light snow was falling throughout the walk in and the view never materialised.

My own plan for that day was to follow the groups into the corrie and attempt to get photos once they were dispersed over the routes. As I plodded I knew this would be impractical and the only sign that I was near the slopes of Pinnacle Face was that the ground got steeper. Time to turn around. The climbing pairs ventured a little further but snow conditions dictated it was not a day for any routes.

Back at the hut, the evening routine got underway; I prepared the food, and the climbers sorted gear, sharpened the ice tools and made good use of the hut drying facilities to get all prepared for the next day. During the fairly short evenings I was impressed at how the host climbers shared many of the unwritten ethics of winter climbing in Scotland and then went on to justify their route choices for the next day. The hosts also seemed to manage to exude the sheer adventure of Scottish winter climbing. The guests had all prepared short presentations about their home climbing but unfortunately there was never enough time to share these. In reality these would have been perfect for a really bad weather day.

The next few days saw a rotation of the climbers come and go, during which I managed between my hut duties an interesting day with ridge scramble in the northern corries and a visit to the Dirc Mhor. This narrow gorge almost resembled an Alpine Gorge in winter with lots of opportunities for low grade gullies and open faces using trees as belays. After some of the climbers moved across to take up their nights at the CIC Hut on Ben Nevis, I also fitted in a walk up to the CIC and was made most welcome by the three generations of the Hawthorn family as they prepared the evening meal for the residents that night. With time short, I was at least able to walk into Observatory Gully and met a few of the teams descending after successful ascent of the ice routes on the Minus Face. More happy climbers: although one Polish visitor was going to report to the manufacturer of his prototype ice axe that the shaft was not up to Scottish ice; the shaft and pick were no longer connected.

The final climbing day for the Meet meant the climbers were away early to maximise their time for just one more route before an end of Meet party and talk at Tiso's in Aviemore. I cleared the hut and hoped for one last jaunt into the corries. However by the time I arrived at the Corrie Cas car park the wind was howling and I was likely to lose the car door. All credit to those who still managed a route before joining the convoy of cars escaping the wild weather back down to Loch Morlich.

For me this was a totally inspiring week, meeting some of the most adventurous UK climbers around and seeing them sharing their expertise with the visiting climbers. Finally, thanks to Vicky Smith from Glenmore Lodge who every evening delivered the weather and avalanche reports to the hut. These were invaluable as conditions were changing each day and much attention was paid to the aspects of the approach to technical routes and consideration given to suitable ground for descent.

Climbing Host – Neil Adams

I don't know which deity Simon Richardson prayed to, or whose soul he had to sell, but it worked. Somehow in the days before the meet, the warm wet weather that had plagued Scotland all year gave way to snow and ice. Fifty-six hosts and guests breathed a collective sigh of relief – the 2020 Scottish Winter Meet was on!

Having not had a chance to pull hard on axes for a few weeks, I was looking forward to a gentle warm-up in the Northern Corries. That all changed when I met my partner for the week, Pete Hoang. Canada has a history of sending very strong climbers to the meets – previous attendees include Jon Walsh and Rafael Slawinsky – and while Pete isn't as well-known, it quickly became clear that he's

Pete Hoang on the classic Sundance, Far East Wall, Beinn Eighe. Photo: Neil Adams.

very handy indeed. He and his compatriot Maarten had already climbed Big Daddy (VII,8) under their own steam, so any thoughts of an easy start were put aside.

The logistics of the event dictated that if we were going to try to visit the North West, it would be best to do it on day one, so Pete and I squeezed into my car with Callum Johnson and his partner Lucáš Klingora (Czech Republic) and set off for Beinn Eighe. Callum had been there a few days previously and reported good conditions, and I thought the modern classic Sundance (VIII,8)[1] would be a good way of showcasing the best that Scotland had to offer. Pete loved it, but seemed worryingly unfazed by the difficulty. Callum and Lucáš also seemed remarkably chirpy after their ascent of Boggle, another VIII on the Eastern Ramparts. I was going to have to put in some serious effort to keep up.

On the drive south to the Raeburn hut, we debated numerous options for the next day. The forecast was uncertain and different forecasters predicted a front to arrive at different times. In the end, eight of us headed for Creag Meagaidh, with Luca Celano, Tim Miller and their partners as the advance party. However, the weather arrived early and the snowpack was much less stable than expected. We met Luca and partner beginning their retreat as we approached the corrie, then as we were debating our options, Tim and his partner appeared saying they'd just triggered an avalanche. Decision made – we turned round and joined Simon and Al for tea in their Laggan basecamp.

The third night was our turn to be in the CIC hut, so we made an early start (again) to get two full days' climbing on the Ben. Pete was keen for more mixed climbing but I thought the better-known mixed routes on the high crags would be

---

[1] For an account of the FWA of Sundance see *SMCJ*, 43/206 (2015), pp 405–9. (Ed.)

Hoang on The Shroud, North Wall of Càrn Dearg, Ben Nevis. Photo: Neil Adams.

in poor condition, so we stayed relatively low on the mountain. Rather than join the crowds on the Douglas Boulder, Pete and I went round to the north face of Càrn Dearg and climbed Kellett's North Wall Route (VII,7), which involved a more serious and draining lead on the third pitch than I expected. Still, nobody fell off so we were in good spirits when we arrived back at the hut. And what a welcome we got – Robin had drafted in three generations of the Hawthorn clan to cater in the hut. We were greeted with soup and mulled wine to keep us going until a wonderful dinner of roast beef and veggies followed by port, cheese and a

Hoang on the FWA of Gralloch, South Wall, Garbh Bheinn. Photo: Callum Johnson.

dram. Possibly the best meal I've ever had in a mountain hut! It was only appropriate that another party named a new route Wonderwoman in honour of Carole (Hawthorn Senior), head chef and matriarch of the whole enterprise.

While we were descending, we had passed the classic ice line of The Shroud. By any sensible Scottish standards, it wasn't formed yet – the icicle was miles off touching down. However, such details don't seem to matter to hotshot Canadians, so the following morning we set off for a look at it. After soloing up the approach pitch, Pete declared that it would definitely go but (much to my relief) he'd rather do it as a single big pitch. I didn't argue. I held my breath as he bridged out onto the icicle, swung an axe and committed his weight to it. Somehow the icicle held and he ran up the next few metres until he found ice solid enough for a screw. I started breathing again and prepared to follow.

After a quick descent on Abalakov threads (another novelty in Scotland), we returned to the hut for a cup of tea while we pondered what to do with the rest of the day. Someone had mentioned that Mega Route X looked climbable, but Pete wanted to go to the summit of the Ben at some point. Could we combine the two? Well, I suppose we could. So, off we went, with Pete making the crux pitch look trivial and me making the easier pitch look much more of a struggle. Above the difficulties, we continued up Jubilee Climb, diverting onto the rib higher up to avoid a deteriorating snowpack, and then up to the plateau. By now, the weather had gone 'full Scottish' so Pete got the traditional Ben Nevis summit vista before we set of on a bearing towards the CMD arête and the Coire Leis descent. Yet more fine Hawthorn soup set us up for the descent and the journey to Lagangarbh.

The strong westerly winds and persistent snow made venue choice critical for the latter stages of the meet. Pete was keen to try something hard (!) and I was keen not to get avalanched, so we headed south to Beinn Dòrain. The crag was in magnificent condition, with the classic line Messiah seeing several ascents that day. I pointed Pete at Dave Macleod's testpiece Defenders of the Faith (fortunately only one hard pitch). To my relief, he had the decency to struggle a bit, taking a couple of falls before unlocking the crux sequence. I fared no better on second, but at least I now knew that Pete was human.

Avalanche risk dominated the crag choice for the last day too. Tim Miller and I had both done winter routes on the South Wall of Garbh Bheinn in similarly stormy and avalanche-prone conditions, so I suggested this rather esoteric venue for the finale to the week. To my relief, it was in prime winter condition and everyone was in the mood for an adventurous new route. Tim, Callum and visiting Polish climber Damien spotted the obvious crack system of the summer route Scimitar, which gave an excellent five-pitch VII,8. I pointed out another obvious winter line approximating to the line of Gralloch, and again Pete stepped up to the challenge. It turned out to be rather more challenging than I expected – what looked like accommodating pick-width cracks higher up turned out to be flared or blind, so progress depended on a tenuous series of steinpulls and laybacks with poor slopey footholds. Pete pulled off one of the most impressive leads I've ever seen, completing the route in one big pitch. It was certainly a good bit harder than Defenders the day before – Pete reckoned M8+ or M9 above spaced gear, and although I've never climbed Tech 10, I reckon IX,10 is probably a fair Scottish grade. I'm very keen for someone strong to repeat it and let us know.

The week came to a close with dinner in Aviemore and a talk from Guy Robertson. I have to confess I was too knackered to stick around for much of the party afterwards, but it was brilliant to exchange stories with all the other climbers and hear the enthusiasm and respect that all of the guests had for Scottish winter climbing and the scene around it.

I'd like to say a huge thank-you to: Simon Richardson and Al Todd for coordinating the event; Chris Huntley, Dave Broadhead, Robin Clothier and the Hawthorn clan for taking such good care of us in the huts; Mountaineering Scotland for hosting the meet; the SMC, Alpine Club, BMC and Salewa for supporting it; and, all of the other hosts and guests for being a brilliant bunch of folk to spend a week with and for making good decisions to get everyone back safe. See you all next time!

100 YEARS AGO – THE CLUB IN 1920

(*Italics* indicate quotation from the Journal or other named source.)

THIS WAS A PERIOD of high unemployment, poor living conditions for many and an economy decimated by four years of war. Against this background, the 31st AGM was held on Friday, 5 December 1919 at St. Enoch's Station Hotel, Glasgow. The usual sort of club business was discussed and W.Ling was appointed the new President. The meeting was followed by the annual dinner which was attended by 58 members and 24 guests. The retiring president, Dr. Inglis Clark, gave a heartfelt speech about *the delights that draw us to the mountains.*

The Journal

The April edition contained the usual general articles, illustrations, poetry, club proceedings, obituaries, excursions and notes. There were essays about the Cairngorms, Loch Etive Side and Ben Cruachan. Barlow and Steeple described a wintry first ascent of *The Chasm of Sgurr nan Eag* at Easter 1915 and a summer repeat in August 1919.

One of the obituaries was to Charles Pilkington, one of the club's original members. Along with his brother Lawrence he made the first ascent of the Inaccessible Pinnacle in 1880 and the first ascents of several other summits of the Cuillin *when there were no maps or guide-books.*

There was an article, which at first I thought was a spoof, about *The Scottish Cassiterides.* I was intrigued by claims that the Hebrides had *considerable and widespread deposits of surface tin, while there are also traces of silver, lead and copper.* It was suggested that these could be the fabled 'tin islands' that once provided the ancient Greeks with tin and whose whereabouts were kept secret by the sea-faring metal traders? Despite the tempting arguments it seems, like the islands themselves, a rather remote possibility, although Raasay did have a productive iron-ore mine at Inverarish at the start of the 20th century.

The October edition followed the format as detailed above. Joseph Stott (the first Journal editor) describes in evocative terms *Climbing in Dalness and Mamlorn* in 1884. He noted that a popular excursion was to travel by steamer from Connel to the head of Loch Etive, then horse-drawn coach to the Kingshouse hotel and down Glen Coe to Ballachulish where a steamer would transport them to Oban or Fort William. In 1883 approximately 2500 people completed this Victorian equivalent of our execrable North Coast 500.

Stott and friends caught the train to Tyndrum and *footed it up to Inveroran.* Mine host of the comfortable inn entertained them with *the strains of his splendid violin ... and the soul-stirring music of his pipes.* The following morning they crossed the *lonely solitudes of* Blackmount by the old drover's road to the Kingshouse. Then more foot-slogging down Glen Etive to Dalness, *once one of the royal hunting grounds of Scotland. It is utterly bare of wood but in bygone years oaks and magnificent pines flourished in its glens.* Then they took to the steep flanks of the Buachaille, *in a stormy sea of drifted snow,* only to be hit by a stupendous blizzard. They eventually reached the summit and then faced a tricky descent and long walk back to Inveroran. And that was just the first day of their weekend.

My God, these were arduous outings by tough men! No parking in a convenient lay-by and a quick dash to the summit. For example, Murray Lawson describes leaving Edinburgh on the night train and getting no sleep, arriving Aviemore at

Newly elected President W. Ling on Ben Lui, 1 January 1920. Photo: MacRobert collection.

0430hrs, an intended traverse of Braeriach, Monadh Mhor and Beinn Bhrotain disrupted by atrocious weather and rivers in spate before arrival at Inverey at 2000hrs. I can recommend that you try to read their accounts for yourselves rather than for me to attempt to retell them.

Other articles feature, guess who? Yes, Harold Raeburn. *The Exploration of the Historic Cave at Fastcastle* is described by W. Douglas. The ruined remains of this historic coastal fortress in Berwickshire were reputed to have a staircase cut out of the rock which led to a large sea-cave. Douglas could make no progress until joined by Sang and Raeburn, who swam across a deep inlet to gain access to the cave. Unfortunately, *there was not the slightest appearance of an aperture in its roof nor was there any trace of cut steps on its walls. So that alluring tradition is now smashed and the idea that there was ever a passage from the cave to the castle must be abandoned.*

Perhaps the most significant account, in mountaineering terms, was that of the first winter ascent of Observatory Ridge by Raeburn, Goggs and Mounsey in early April, 1920. Raeburn led, naturally. No crampons, short axes, ice-screws or pitons but just tweed clothing, a long wooden axe each and 100ft of rope. Remarkable, especially given that it took them a little under six hours.

Although the hills of the Southern Uplands may seem gentle by comparison, they do provide the opportunity for long walks over rolling hills, often steeped in history. In *Moffat in the Seventies*, Scott Moncrieff Penney describes such a 42-mile tramp, which was completed in a little over 11 hours.

W.W. Naismith describes *How to Stop a Fall on Hard Ice or Snow* and reviews a book by none other than that man again – Harold Raeburn. *Mountaineering Art* was published in 1920 by Fisher Unwin. The original manuscript to the book, and the fruit of several years' assiduous labour, had earlier been lost. This must have been a soul-destroying set-back but Raeburn agreed with his publishers to rewrite the book, which he accomplished in three months. Whilst never given to great introspection, Raeburn usually wrote about his exploits in a very readable way and was often amusing and perceptive in his comments and observations. The uninspiring writing in his book is not typical of his contributions to this Journal, for example. Perhaps this is an indication of the haste required to compile the work anew and that it was really a book of guidance for prospective mountaineers – a sort of instruction manual – with no great literary merit in itself. Lesser men may have evaded giving advice about technical matters which questioned the accepted norms (for example, the perennially thorny issue about the best shaft length for ice-axes) but Raeburn is quite adamant in his views. W.W. Naismith confirms this when he diplomatically states – *In this book Mr. Raeburn is downright and natural, and while we read it we can almost hear him speaking to us in his own quietly emphatic tones. He is absolutely fearless in challenging erroneous notions ... with the hearty goodwill of an iconoclast, he upsets many idols of popular climbing belief.*

In the *Geographical Journal*, another reviewer was more forthright, writing that some of Raeburn's uncompromising counsel would *give cause to ponder among the elders, accompanied perhaps with here an opening of the eyes, and there a shaking of the head.* Although middle-aged, Raeburn was no climbing fuddy-duddy and some of his opinions clearly outraged the 'old-guard' .... *Mr. Raeburn has the temerity to excuse his well-worn vice of climbing alone if he cannot find a suitable companion.*

Raeburn made it clear that his primary aim in writing the book, *after consulting almost every published work on climbing and mountaineering, in English, and in the principal continental languages*, was to encourage safety. In terms of book sales, however, the timing couldn't have been worse, for also in 1920 Methuen published Geoffrey Winthrop Young's book *Mountain Craft*. It was largely drafted before the war with specialist help from several other mountaineers, such as Oscar Eckenstein, Norman Collie, Cecil Slingsby, Tom Longstaff and Raeburn himself, who contributed a chapter about the Caucasus Mountains. Young, the more cosmopolitan by far of the two respective authors, and thoroughly at ease with the new sociability of the climbing scene south of the Border, was clever enough to sound out and incorporate the ideas and opinions of the other leading-lights of the day, and to recognise the commercial advantages that this would bring.

The two authors knew each other although there is nothing to suggest that there was any great degree of kinship between them. They came from completely different backgrounds and upbringings, but it is clear that they had a relationship of mutual respect. Young liked to party in the convivial company of intellectually stimulating companions, most of whom were younger than himself. Raeburn, his senior by eleven years, was more puritanical, self-contained and matter-of fact, a typical son of *that land of Calvin, oatcakes and sulphur*, as Sydney Smith described Scotland. Although Young's book did not really reflect his poetic artistry, it out-sold Raeburn's work and was eventually reprinted four times.

Howard Somervell, another remarkable man, joined the SMC in 1920 having previously attended club meets as a guest. He was born in Kendal and the horror of his experiences as a surgeon during the war had a profound effect on him, turning him into a pacifist. Known as a mountain artist and member of the 1922 and 1924 Everest Expeditions, he contributed a note to the Journal about the timings of his traverse of the Cuillin (a little under 11 hours, rests excluded).

There are several accounts of members' trips to the Alps and a note that Raeburn had travelled to India. It would have been entirely characteristic for Raeburn to have wished to explore the challenging peaks of the Himalaya, so he travelled to the Sikkim region to reconnoitre and possibly make an attempt on Kangchenjunga (28,170ft or 8586m), the third highest mountain in the world and highest in India. Following in the footsteps of fellow-SMC member Alexander Kellas, who had made three pioneering visits to Sikkim, he *was fortunate enough to be able to carry out a project long thought of and planned, to make a reconnaissance of the southerly access to Kanchen. I had another project, and that was to get as near as was politically possible to the world's highest peak, Everest.*

Raeburn wrote these words in a full account for the Alpine Journal. The matter-of-fact way in which he describes the difficulties, for example, of the 8-day descent of the Talung (or Rinpiram) River with his porters can be well appreciated by reading H.W. Tilman's account of the same journey, particularly given the latter's drily understated style of writing. Tilman made his descent in April, 1936, as part of a trip to try out some porters for his forthcoming Nanda Devi expedition, and makes it clear that the journey was a gruelling test for the strong party, which included Pasang Kikuli, a magnificent mountaineer who perished with two other Sherpas on a brave rescue attempt on K2 in 1939. As an example of the atrocious terrain, it took them nine hours to travel barely a mile. It was in an account of this trip that Raeburn wrote …*Our only loss was a severe one to me. My ice-axe, a*

Ling leading a party on the Mittaghorn above Saas Fee in 1922. Photo: SMC Image Archive.

faithful friend of a dozen years, doubly valued as a gift of the late Harry Walker,
A.C., was swept away by one of these flooded torrents.

The whole expedition of several months was an exceptional effort driven by
the resolve and energy of the 55-year-old Raeburn. Many lesser mountaineers,
in a more modern time with all its extra aids, would be more than happy to repeat
just a part of any of the trips.

Club Meets and members' excursions

There were two Club Meets: New Year at Loch Awe and Easter at Fort William
with both being very well-attended. Since I have already used up plenty of space
I don't intend to recount the trips of the various parties. Anyone interested can
look it up.

Travel to the Alps was back on the holiday agenda after the Great War and there
were seven accounts in the Journal about members' achievements. D. Clapperton
bemoaned the increase in guides' fees and other expenses, writing *that climbing
is scarcely an amusement nowadays for the "new poor"*. Nevertheless, R. Corry
noted that his party had made the first ascent that season of an icy Zmuttgrat on
the Matterhorn. Today, it remains a challenging climb and is one of the great ridge
climbs of the Alps.

Finally, W.Ling was, as usual, as active as ever. His diaries (books 13 & 14)
reveal that he had outings in almost every month of the year as well as two long
visits to the Alps in April/May and August.

Mike Jacob

200 YEARS AGO

MANY OF US WILL know that the approach to Salisbury Crags is called the Radical Road, but not so many will know why it bears this name. 1820 was a year of political turmoil. There was a new King on the Throne – George IV, and an Election produced an increased Tory majority for Lord Liverpool. Unrest followed the disturbances in the previous year at St. Peter's Field, Manchester in which a charge of mounted troops with drawn sabres caused a large crowd (gathered in protest over various social ills) to stampede with loss of life and widespread injuries. In London the Cato Street Conspiracy sought to assassinate the Cabinet, while in the West of Scotland a radical movement spearheaded by weavers sought to establish a breakaway republic. Both were firmly dealt with after government *agents provocateurs* were inserted into the groups. These spies stirred up the revolts and arranged for them to be mopped up. The leaders were hanged and beheaded in May (London) and September (Glasgow and Stirling), and the

James Wilson leads a group of 23 dissident weavers from Strathaven under their famous banner.

captured radicals in Scotland were put to construct a road around the base of Salisbury Crags – the Radical Road.

Many 'tourists' had visited Scotland before 1820, and recorded their experiences, but the only work that might be called a Guidebook up to this date was Mrs. Aust's (Sarah Murray) *Companion and Useful Guide to the Beauties of Scotland* (1799). This was a guidebook suitable for the rich visitor. However, by 1820 a useful network of passenger steamers had grown up, linking Glasgow and Edinburgh with the West Highlands and Islands, as well as with major English towns. These vessels could keep to reasonably dependable timetables. James Lumsden's *Steam-Boat Companion* (1820) provided a guide to the Highlands and Islands and description of the means by which they might be explored by steam-boat and stage-coach. Tremendous sales, and annual revised editions, marked a growing swell of native tourists. For the first time, the ordinary burghers of Glasgow and Edinburgh could experience Walter Scott's 'Caledonia, Stern and Wild', visit the mountainous areas, and build second homes in the islands of the Clyde. *The Companion* had no serious rival until *Black's Picturesque Tourist of Scotland* appeared in 1840.

So far as mountains were concerned, the Companion didn't offer great encouragement. Ben Nevis, for example, should only be attempted with a guide, and would take 7 or 8 hours to climb, 'Indeed the traveller, if he has not vigour of body, as well as strength of mind to support him, in so very arduous an

undertaking, and to render him steady in many perilous situations to which he
may be exposed, ought not to make the attempt; for no stranger can have the most
distant notion of the difficulty of succeeding in it.' However, it is conceded that
'if strength and courage enable the traveller to surmount it, and if he arrive at the
summit of the mountain, with a clear atmosphere, and a telescope in his
possession, he will have a view which no pencil can delineate nor language
describe.' On Skye, after an obligatory visit to the Great Spar Cave, 'the gloomy
mountains of Cuthullin, that rise in majestic grandeur in its neighbourhood, are
objects not unworthy of admiration', and the traveller 'should cross Strathaird to
Loch Scavig, where the sea view is extremely fine; the dark ridge of Cuthullin,

*Jumnotree, the source of the River Jumna. Plate 20 of Fraser's Views of the Himala
Mountains. British Library. Photo: Author.*

with its numerous spiry and serrated projections, being flanked by the equally dark and lofty ridge of Blaven.' But only viewing and perhaps admiring these gloomy mountains was recommended. The traveller is encouraged to climb only Goatfell, Ben Lomond, Ben Ledi and Mealfourvonie – then thought to be more than 3,000 feet high, an 800-foot overestimate that would wait until late in the century for correction.

The patient reader will have found the mountaineering content of this report disappointing. There are several reasons for this. William McGillivray's reports of his continuing explorations (of the Deeside mountains for example) were consumed by a house-fire in Australia, although I suspect that some scraps could be gleaned from studying his *Natural History of Dee Side and Braemar*, and his multi-volume *History of British Birds*. The promising start made by Thomas Colby and the Ordnance Survey mentioned in last year's review was interrupted by Colby's advancement to replace William Mudge as head of the Survey and the Board of Longitude – Mudge died in office in April of the year – and was not resumed for many years.

However, we are able to end with something of a bang. This was the year of publication of James Baillie Fraser's *Journal of a Tour through Part of the Himala Mountains and to the Sources of the Jumna* [Yamuna] *and the Ganges, and of his Views of the Himala Mountains*, a set of beautiful watercolours converted to coloured aquatint engravings by Robert Havell – a book of extraordinary rarity and value. Fraser (1773–1856) belonged to an Edinburgh family which had a country house at Reelig near Moniack to the west of Inverness, and he was brought up there. After a varied early life, Fraser joined his brother William in northern India in 1815, aged 32. William was an officer of the East India Company, at that time working as a political agent pursuing the Company's interests in the war with Nepal. James became engrossed with the mountain country and with sketching it, and went off on a tour to Uttarakhand to explore the sources of the Yamuna and Ganges rivers. Above the source of the Yamuna is a range of peaks known nowadays as the Bandarpunch, and Fraser attained a height of around 17,000 feet exploring it – Bandarpunch I is 6,316m. The illustration accompanying this text shows Bandarpunch II.

Fraser had a considerable reputation as a watercolour painter, but none of his works appear to have been presented to public collections or offered for sale by dealers or auction houses, so that his work is only known through Havell's prints. He was taught by the well-known English artists William Havell (a nephew of Robert Havell) and George Chinnery. Fraser went on after his Himalayan adventures to make a number of important tours in Persia, paying for his keep by working as a spy against Russia for the Foreign Office. He died at Reelig in 1856.

It is a curious coincidence that two of the people mentioned in this short review of 1820 – William McGillivray and Robert Havell – should have collaborated on the most famous illustrated book of the 19th century, John James Audubon's *Birds of America*. Havell and his son (also Robert) made the plates from Audubon's drawings, and McGillivray supplied the text. A copy of the folio edition was sold recently for more than 8 million dollars.

Robin N Campbell

A VERY SPECIAL MUNROIST

ONE DAY, MUCH TOO long ago, I was coming off a remote Munro when I met up with an oldish man who, it turned out was after compleating a second round of the Munros in his retirement, having romped Munros and Tops, when young, in 1939 (Munroist No.8). We chatted away as hillgoers do and he offered me a lift in his car, parked just below on a track (private?) while my camper was away down on the main road. He lifted the boot and lit an old Primus to bring the dixi to the boil; the first time I have ever seen a brew-up carried out in a Rolls-Royce. I used to visit Cram thereafter at his home in Edinburgh.

He must have been a Rolls-Royce man (or was it the same one?) for he and his wife Isobel had once driven a Silver Shadow overland from Kenya to India and thence overland to the UK. One thing we had in common was both being in Kenya during the time of the Mau Mau in the 1950s. I was a humble airman, aged 20, doing my National Service, he was a sort or prosecutor/judge involved in the Emergency, who was to blow the whistle on the moral rottenness of what was going on. He compared the Kenya camps to those of the nazis in World War Two – and he should know – he was a POW of the Gestapo, ending in Dachau[1] and, ironically, becoming a judge at the Nuremburg War Trials. The same horrors were being connived at and committed in Kenya.

After unhappy Kenya he was a judge in Malawi for seven years and the couple were tempted to retire in sunny Africa, but Scotland called them home; so we had our encounter and friendship. He talked little of what he had done in an extraordinary life but all his days, at every chance, he'd be off to whatever mountains possible. The SMC Journal over the years would bear entertaining notes on Mulanje or the Chimanimani Mountains and such unvisited African ranges but also Alps, Australia or Himalayas; he explored widely. (Thanks to him I'd climb summits from Cape to Kenya in 1971/72.) Only in 2018 was there a book published: D.M. Guss: *The 21 Escapes of Lt. Alastair Cram*[2]: his unique tally in a much more serious World War Two game. Well worth reading.

His second round of the Munros was completed in 1978. He died in 1994. A very special Munroist.

Hamish Brown

NEEDLE'S EYE GULLY
West Face of Aonach Dubh, Glen Coe

A WONDERFUL SET of manuscript diaries by Pat Bell (née Style, wife of the redoubtable James H.B. Bell) passed through my hands two years ago. These had ended up with Anne Murray after Pat's death, and Anne passed them to Pat Ransley and thence to me. I deposited them in N.L.S., indicating that they should be regarded as the property of the L.S.C.C. The diaries cover the years 1935 to her death in 1989.

[1] Apparently not in Dachau but in Prague, according to Guss. (Ed.)

[2] MacMillan, 2018, hardback, 432 pp, £18.99. See also the obituary by GJF Dutton and WH Murray, *SMCJ*, 35/186 (1995), pp. 745–8, and the review of Guss's book by Graeme Morrison, *SMCJ*, 2018, pp. 283–5. (Ed.)

One of these diaries 'Holidays with J.H.B.B. 1945–47' begins by describing her initial involvement with Bell, beginning with a trip to Glen Coe in 1940, five years before their marriage, along with Ilse Bell – his sister – and Nancy Forsyth, a well-known lady climber who died roped to Brian Kellett on or above the Cousins' Buttress of Ben Nevis in 1944. Bell sends Pat and Ilse to tackle a feature of the West Face of Aonach Dubh described as the 'Needle's Eye':

'We agreed to split up and Nancy being the better climber went with J. Ilse and I decided to go up No. 4 Gully by the Needle's Eye into the Amphitheatre. J. gave me instructions about the gulley, and told me when we came to the Eye to climb a chimney to the right of it […] All went well until we got to the Eye; here it looked as if the route should go up through the Eye, and I climbed up some distance, and it looked quite difficult. So, remembering my instructions I looked for a chimney, and found that down the only thing resembling one a waterfall flowed. However having great faith in the great man I spent half an hour trying to climb it and got thoroughly wet, which was more than tiresome as I had the curse and wanted to keep warm. So cold and miserable I sat in the only patch of sun and we ate our sandwiches. By this time I was far too cold to try again or to attempt the Eye, so we started a retreat.'

In fact they were in No. 5 Gully, not 4, and Bell had misdirected Pat into a horrible unclimbed pitch of the main Gully, despite the route through the Needle's Eye being his own, and made only 5 years before. His original description appeared in *SMCJ*, 21/121 (1936), pp. 50–52, and I give it below:

On 24th November 1935 C. M. Allan and I set out to do some exploration among the gullies and buttresses of the western front of Aonach Dubh [. . .] We made for No. 5 Gully from below. As we approached the waterfall at its base, and before we came too close under the rocks, we could see high above us, where the gully narrows at the middle tier of precipice. a curious hole in the rock on the left side of the gully (ascending) looking like a needle's eye. We resolved to investigate this.

At the base of the waterfall it was obvious that a traverse was necessary. We tried up to the right, and got on to a bad place on vegetatious rock with the joints. the wrong way. We were thus able to overlook an unclimbable pitch in No. 6 Gully. We returned to the base of the waterfall, climbed up interesting rocks to the left, and so traversed upwards to the foot of a subsidiary gully, pretty narrow, which went well for 60 feet or so to the foot of a dripping overhang. On our right was a 20-foot smooth slab, nearly vertical. The leader went out to the right and up on vegetatious rock, then back and across the upper part of the slab on very small holds; a very delicate pitch. Thereafter an upward escape to the right became possible, and all went easily onwards up a grassy buttress with one or two trees. On the right one sees two more rather impossible looking pitches in No. 5 Gully.

We soon reached the foot of the 'Needle's Eye', a 40-foot porphyry chimney, about 3 feet wide and roofed by a huge boulder. The chimney is very awkward near the top, where it is necessary to transfer to the right wall from the left (ascending). Above this point it would be easy to get into the upper amphitheatre of No. 5 Gully, in the upper part of which is a fine knife-edge arête or buttress, probably that climbed in 1898 by Clark, Inglis, and Maclay. We, however, climbed interesting rocks on our left to a ridge which later joined another ridge on the left, forming the southern bounding wall of the amphitheatre, which is the collecting corrie for No. 4 Gully.

In the accompanying photograph the chimney and chockstone enclosing the

'Needle's Eye Gully'on the West Face of Aonach Dubh. Photo: Davy Gunn.

Needle's Eye is marked in red. Plainly what we have here are parallel No. 5 gullies: a shallow gully on the left topped by the Eye pitch, and the deep chasm of the main gully on the right. For some reason, the Needle's Eye version of No. 5 Gully was lost sight of for a while, but it reappeared in Bill Murray's guidebook (1949) as *Original Route, F Buttress* graded Very Difficult, and has remained with this misleading name ever since.

On the journey home from Glen Coe, Pat remonstrated with Bell:

'I then told Jim just what I thought of those who gave bad instructions for a climb; he didn't say much but filled his pipe […] Ilse subsequently told me we had been misinformed about the route – It does go through the Eye.'

It is difficult to know why Bell should have sent his future wife and only sister into a place of dire peril. Perhaps Pat misunderstood his instructions, to give him the benefit of the doubt. However, it is also difficult to know why our editors should have described an obvious gully as a buttress climb, through several generations of guidebooks, instead of giving it the obvious name *Needle's Eye Gully*. And perhaps this note might encourage more visits to what is plainly an intriguing feature of the West Face of Aonach Dubh. UKClimbing logs record no ascents of the summer line and only one of the winter version, which was climbed by a party led by Hamish MacInnes in the bomber winter of 1969.

Robin N Campbell

THE SCOTTISH MOUNTAINEERING TRUST – 2019

Scottish Charity Number SC 009117

The Trustees met on 5 April and 27 September 2019. During the course of these meetings, support was given to: Mountaineering Scotland – Student Winter Skills; J Irving – Mill Cottage; Edinburgh University Mountaineering Club – Glen Lichd House; Skye Mountain Rescue Team – Storage Facility; Jonathan Conville Memorial Trust – Scottish Winter 2020; Scottish Mountaineering Club – Journal Digitisation (Phase 3); D McCallum – The Ledge; Scottish Mountaineering Club – SMC Journal; Scottish Mountaineering Club – Weather Station; R Crawford – Dundee Mountain Film Festival; Dave MacLeod – New Sport Crag; Scottish Mountaineering Club – Journal Digitisation (Phase 4); N Morrison – Aberdeen Bolt Fund; Outdoor Access Trust (D Baird) – Ben More.

The present Trustees are SM Richardson (Chairman) (*Ex Officio* immediate Past President of the SMC), DN Williams (*Ex Officio* Convenor of the Publications Sub–Committee), PJ Biggar (*Ex Officio* Editor of the SMC Journal), JRR Fowler (*Ex Officio* President of the SMC), R Aitken, D Broadhead, R Chalmers, JRG MacKenzie, E Riley and IM Young. JM Shaw is the Trust Treasurer and JD Hotchkis is the Trust Secretary.

The Trustees wish to record their appreciation to Stan Pearson and to John Hutchinson who each retired by rotation in December 2019 for their service to the Trust during their respective periods of office. John Hutchinson has continued to provide valuable input to the Trust in the design and the implementation of the Trust's new website.

The following grants have been committed by the Trustees during 2019:

Mountaineering Scotland – Student Winter Skills	£1470
J Irving – Mill Cottage	Grant of £2500– and Loan of £2500
Edinburgh University Mountaineering Club – Glen Licht House	£2000
Skye Mountain Rescue Team – Storage Facility	£5000
Jonathan Conville Memorial Trust – Scottish Winter 2020	£1500
SMC – Journal Digitisation (Phase 3)	£325
D McCallum – The Ledge	£10,000
SMC – SMC Journal	£6000
SMC – Weather Station	£2166
R Crawford – Dundee Mountain Film Festival	£1000
Dave McLeod – New Sports Crag	£1500
SMC – Journal Digitisation (Phase 4)	£400
N Morrison – Aberdeen Bolt Fund	£1500
Outdoor Access Trust (D Baird) – Ben More	£15,000

James D Hotchkis (Hon. Sec. SMT)

MUNRO MATTERS 2019

By Alison Coull (Clerk of the List)

This report covers 1 January to 31 December 2019. The five columns below give number, name and year of Compleation of Munros, Tops, Furths as appropriate. *SMC member, ** LSCC member.

6465	Fiona Miller	2018		
6466	Ian Allison	2018		
6467	Peter Wakefield	2018		
6468	Mary Laird	2018		
6469	Alan Waugh	2012		
6470	David Bell	2017		
6471	Robert Tully	2017		
6472	Jamie Thin	2018		
6473	Michael James	2015		
6474	Rob Howard	2019		
6475	Sion Pickering	2019		
6476	Derek Macfarlane	2006		
6477	Martin Carey	2017		
6478	Stephen Bennett	2017 2017		
6479	Joss Smale	2018		
6480	Peter Watson	2018		
6481	John McBarron	2019		
6482	Christopher Sangwin	2019		
6483	Gavin Theobald	2009 2019		
6484	Andy Philip	2019		
6485	Richard Legate	2014		
6486	Michael McCormick	2019		
6487	Ian Hopper	2019		
6488	Andy Prentice	2019		
6489	Jamie Johnston	2019		
6490	Ryan Manson	2019		
6491	Rachel Bracha	2019		
6492	Averil Lamont	2019		
6493	Pete Riedel	2019		
6494	Nigel Ward	2019		
6495	Dawn Gourlay	2019		
6496	Norman Gourlay	2019		
6497	Stephen McInnes	2019		
6498	Pamela Fraser	2019		
6499	Gary Fraser	2019		
6500	Ben Rowlands	2018		
6501	Cheryl Ross	2019		
6502	Jim Hunter	2019		
6503	Ian Simpson	2019		
6504	Iain Mitchell	2019		
6505	Richard Holdsworth	2019		
6506	Matthew Smith	2019		
6507	Jeremy Goodyear	2019		
6508	Jim Fothergill	2002 2019 2002		
6509	Niall MacPherson	2019		
6510	John McAllister	2019		
6511	Paul Marginson	2019		
6512	Julie Bowler	2019		
6513	Thomas Mooney	2018		
6514	Alan Findlay	2019		
6515	Malcolm Keats	2019		
6516	Andrew Eccles	2019		
6517	Jodie Mulligan	2019		
6518	Howard Andrew	2019		
6519	Richard Maxey	2019		
6520	Iain Atkinson	2019		
6521	Malcolm Wylie	2019		
6522	James Nimmo	2019		
6523	Samantha Baker	2019		
6524	Geoffrey Curnock	2019 2019		
6525	Jackie Shipley	2019		
6526	Paul Shipley	2019		
6527	Cat Trebilco	2019		
6528	Karl Markham	2019		
6529	John Cameron	2019		
6530	Naomi Watson	2019		
6531	Mike Mason	2019		
6532	Diane Munro	2019		
6533	Lois Noble	2019		
6534	Debbie Robertson	2019		
6535	Marta Panek	2018		
6536	Neil Wilkie	2019		
6537	Ewan Thomas	2019		
6538	Duncan MacPherson	2019		
6539	Tom Cardwell	2019		
6540	James Sandeman	2019		
6541	Graham Yarr	2019		
6542	Lesley Gleave	2019		
6543	Maya James	2019	2019	
6544	Edward James	2019	2019	
6545	Jim Magee	2014		
6546	Belinda Garland	2019		
6547	Steve Garland	2019		
6548	Kenneth A Roy	2019		
6549	David Pudney	2017		
6550	Eileen Holttum	1989		
6551	Andrew Govan	2019		
6552	Janet Arnison	2019		
6553	Toby Thurston	2019		
6554	Michael Brooke	2019		
6555	Jean Hammerman	2019		
6556	Steve Nicoll	2019		
6557	John B.M. Wood	2019		
6558	Marjon Van der Pol	2019		
6559	Matthew Brettle	2019		
6560	Iain Hall	2019		
6561	Bruce Greenshields	2019		
6562	Martin Lawton	2019		
6563	David Stevenson	2019		
6564	Angus Pattullo	2019		
6565	Tom Miller	2019		
6566	Ewen Cameron	2019		
6567	Alan James	2019		
6568	David Longworth	2019		
6569	Mark Hodson	2018		
6570	Stephen Walter	2019		
6571	Stan Campbell	2019		
6572	Steve Griffin	2019		
6573	Helen Homer	2019		
6574	Jason Bostock	2019		

6575	Roel Bouwman	2019
6576	Gerry Rennie	2019
6577	Andy Rennie	2019
6578	Rosalind West	2019
6579	Andres von Kanel	2019
6580	David Freeland	2019
6581	Paul Norman	2019
6582	James Selfe	2019
6583	Dave Linnett	2019
6584	Kenny Daye	2019
6585	Adrian Westbury	2019
6586	Christian Heintzen	2019
6587	Malcolm Davidson	2019
6588	Michael O'Haire	2019
6589	Caroline Mackie	2019
6590	Neil Cuthbert	2019
6591	John Morrison	2019
6592	George Molyneaux	2019
6593	John Jeffries	2017
6594	Derek Johnstone	2019
6595	Ian F Russell	2019
6596	Nick Tomkinson	2019
6597	James A. Westwood	2019
6598	Richard Davies	2019
6599	Stuart D. Hamilton	2019
6600	Cat Newsheller	2019
6601	Julie Kate Nelson	2019
6602	Alexander Nelson	2019
6603	Richard Moseley	2019
6604	Hugh Willie Munro	2019
6605	Colin O'Neill	2019
6606	Peter Eslea Macdonald	2019
6607	Shirley Park	2019
6608	Jim Park	2019
6609	Dominic McGinley	2019
6610	Mike Jacobs	2019
6611	Jim Holt	2019
6612	Graeme Rogers	2019
6613	Alastair Sinclair	2019
6614	Allister Mckenna	2019
6615	Carl Rice	2018
6616	Cha Hannaway	2019
6617	Martin White	2019
6618	Simon Kail	2019
6619	Isobel Davies	2019
6620	Michael Irving	2019
6621	Wilf Williams	2019
6622	Janice Baird	2019
6623	Angela Mamwell	2019
6624	Brian Fergie	2019
6625	Hilda Hunter	2019
6626	Alun Davies	2018
6627	David Thompson	2019
6628	Lucy Prins	2019
6629	Phillip Thompson	2019
6630	Jon Mackenzie	2019
6631	Glen Pyper	2019
6632	Philip Green	2019
6633	Peter Carr	2019
6634	George Ian Dyball	2019
6635	Alastair EM Barclay	2019
6636	John Bacchetti	2019
6637	Emma Dowman	2019
6638	Anatole Beams	2019
6639	Lenny McArthur	2017
6640	Martin Kelly	2019
6641	Derek Stuart	2012
6642	Philip Dawson	2019
6643	Stewart Houston	2019
6644	David Reay	2019
6645	Pamela Beattie	2019
6646	Fergus McDonald	2019
6647	Colin McDougall	2019
6648	Catherine Cook	2004
6649	Clive Buckley	2019
6650	Derek Lawson	2019
6651	Samuel J. Brewster	2019
6652	Donald Mackenzie	2019
6653	Heike Funke	2019
6654	Guy Dodgson	2019
6655	Will Graham	2019
6656	Peter Chippendale	2019
6657	Jillian A. Ferguson	2019
6658	Paula Hubens	2019
6659	David Morrish	2019
6660	Mike Hunter	2019
6661	Kenny Primrose	2019
6662	Philip William Power	2019
6663	Andrew Mackenzie	2019
6664	Ray Kemp	2019
6665	Elvyn Haigh	2019
6666	David Jermy	2019
6667	Roger Tiffin	2019
6668	Brian Healey	2019
6669	Mac Wright	2019
6670	Mark Hale	2019
6671	David Wilson	2019
6672	Stephen Allan	2019
6673	Roy Paterson	2019
6674	James McNaught	2019
6675	James Cameron	2019
6676	Dawn Ashford	2019
6677	Andrew McInally	2009
6678	Anne Nimmo	2008
6679	Ian Nimmo	2008
6680	Scott Lawson	2019
6681	David Buchanan*	2019
6682	Joanne Hird	2019
6683	Neil Hird	2019
6684	Nicholas J.R. Dougan	2019
6685	Graham Callander	2019
6686	Louise Close	2019
6687	Steve Vaughan	2019
6688	Lynda Watson	2019
6689	James Watson	2019
6690	David Orr	2019
6691	James A Slaven	2019
6692	Colin Craig	2017
6693	Keith Ferguson	2019
6694	Ian Stewart	2019
6695	Andrew Ogilvie	2007
6696	Stuart Greig	2019
6697	William A Parker	2018
6698	Graeme Ross	2019
6699	Judith Barnes	2019
6700	Lilian Middleton	2019
6701	Emily Scott	2018
6702	Douglas Ratcliffe	2019
6703	Mike Howard	2019
6704	John Douglas	2019

6705	P.J. Conlon (Josie)	2018	6725	Sam Shortt	2019
6706	David Hume Brown	2019	6726	Teresa Peddie	2019
6707	Ian McTeer	2019	6727	Bryn Roberts	2019
6708	Ian Welding	2019	6728	Andrew Scarfe	1988
6709	Bill MacKenzie	2019	6729	Christopher Smith	2019
6710	David Connolly	2019 2019	6730	Celia Vince	2019
6711	Paul Handley	2019	6731	Peter Farrington	2019
6712	Ian Scott	2019	6732	Martin D Robertson	1995
6713	William A. Manders	2005	6733	John Ashford	2019
6714	Rachel McIlhatton	2019	6734	Andrew Duff	2006
6715	Trevor McIlhatton	2019	6735	Mark D Spicer	2019
6716	Darren Soutar	2019	6736	Ian Parkin	1996
6717	Richard Middleton	2019	6737	Michael Souter	2019
6718	John Thorndycraft	2019	6738	Elizabeth Kennedy	2009
6719	Cameron B Gair	2019	6739	Kris Stutchbury	2019
6720	Chris Wood	2019	6740	*Alison Coull	2000 2018 2019
6721	Alison M Harper	2019	6741	Edward Brown	2019
6722	Stewart Walker	2019	6742	*Neil Adams	2019
6723	Stuart Stronach	2019	6743	Donna Ryan	2019
6724	Alan Murray	2019	6744	John Birtill	2019

Comparing this year's data with last year (in brackets): New Munroists 279 (184); females 20% (23%); resident in Scotland 64% (59%); couples 5% (9%); average age 55 (54): average completion time 26 (27); Golden Munroists 14 (12).

In 2018 the average Compleation summit party was 14. Not enough Munroists gave me this information to allow a meaningful statistic. Of those that did provide details most were either solo or accompanied by up to 15 companions. Kenneth Roy (6548) had a massive 64 friends and family on his compleation day on Meall Chuaich. He told me that amongst the party were two friends, husband and wife refugees from Syria climbing their first Munro.

Mac Wright (6669) and his Springer spaniel, Ghengis had 60 friends on Sgùrr na h-Ulaidh. Ghengis compleated the Munros with Mac. Anne Butler, President of the Munro Society tells me that she knows of 12 previous dog compleations starting with Hamish Brown's dog Kitchy in 1971.

The most popular finishing Munros were: Ben More (M) 23, Beinn na Lap (17), Ben Lomond (16), Ladhar Bheinn (12), Schiehallion (11), Slioch (9), Sgùrr Dearg (8), Meall Buidhe (8), Blàbheinn (6). Sgùrr Dubh Mòr (5), Ben Hope (4), Ben Vane (4), Ben Wyvis (4) A' Mhaighdean (4), Maol Chean Dearg (4) Ben Challum (3) Ben Lomond and Ben Nevis were the most popular first Munros.

A Time of Change
Dave Broadhead, the SMC's long serving clerk handed the reins over to me from 1 January 2019. Dave had been clerk of the list since August 2007. During this time the number of registered Munroists increased to 6464 – almost doubling. Dave has written about the role of the Clerk of the list – see 'The SMC's Clerk of the List, A short history', *SMCJ*, 2019, pp.123–5. See also Sunday Post <https://www.sundaypost.com/fp/mighty-feat-of-making-munros-countclimber-reveals-his-statistical-labour-of-love/>

I am very grateful to Dave for his assistance over the year in helping with a smooth transition, keeping me right and offering valuable assistance. Dave remains a great source of information about Munroists. Many Munroists ask me for information about previous compleations. The simple fact is that Dave will inevitably know the answer. If Dave doesn't know the answer then Dave Hewitt of Hill Informed will – so thanks to him too. Thanks also to the SMC webmaster Mike Watson for resolving various IT glitches. These usually come with the response – 'You shouldn't have been able to do that but I have sorted it now'. Also to Robin Campbell for help with some particularly obscure historical queries, Keeper of the Regalia Chris Huntley and David Stone for uncovering a picture of Percy Donald against all the odds.

A Time to Celebrate

2019 saw the centenary of the death of Sir Hugh Munro and this was marked with a number of events. On 13 March 2019, the Scottish Parliament led by MSP Liz Smith debated the motion:

That the Parliament recognises that March 2019 marks the centenary of the death of Sir Hugh Munro; acknowledges that he was a founder member of the Scottish Mountaineering Club, eventually becoming the club's president; understands that Sir Hugh was the first person to publish a list of all of the mountains in Scotland with a height exceeding 3,000 feet in the club's journal in 1891, which are now known as Munros; notes that it remains a popular hobby among hillwalkers to aim to climb every Munro in Scotland, and recognises that over 6000 individuals have achieved this feat to date.

SMC member Rab Anderson (5070) went up Ben Lawers with STV reporter Laura Alderman to record a windy tribute to Sir Hugh.

The Munro Society organised an excellent Munro Legacy Exhibition at the AK Bell library in Perth to celebrate the life of Sir Hugh and the legacy he left behind. Sir Hugh also featured in the Oor Wullie Big Bucket Trail – a nationwide public art trail of Oor Wullie sculptures. Local artist Siobhan Lynagh used a mix of carefully chosen acrylics to capture the colours of the traditional Victorian-era clothes Sir Hugh Munro might have worn. The tartan used for Wullie's trousers was Munro tartan. Munro Wullie was on top of Dundee Law.

Hugh Munro compleats on Slioch. Photo: Alan Rowan.

Famously of course Sir Hugh never actually compleated the Munros. In August Hugh William Munro (6604) rectified the absence of a Hugh Munro on the list by registering his compleation after finishing on Slioch. Hugh set out to compleat in 2019 when he realised that nobody called Hugh Munro was on the list. Among his companions that day was Iain Brooker, son of the late Bill Brooker former SMC President, Journal Editor and Clerk of the List.

A Time of Loss

2019 was unfortunately a very sad year with the loss of 3 significant Munroists – all SMC members. Andy Nisbet (107) and Steve Perry (3114) died in a climbing accident on Ben Hope on 5 February 2019. Martin Moran died in an avalanche in the Himalayas in May 2019. Andy and Steve's achievements were documented in the obituaries in the 2019 SMC Journal, and Martin's life is celebrated in this edition.

Andy compleated his first round age 18 and arguably this might still be the youngest independent compleation. He compleated another 4 rounds, the last in 2015. Andy's 5th round was done by emulating each of the days he had done in his first round which resulted in some impressively big days and a very tired Andy. Steve made a continuous winter round of the Munros on foot, an incredibly arduous achievement that has not been repeated. Martin Moran (383) compleated the Munros in winter 1984/5 starting on December 21 and finishing on 20 March. His account of this in The Munros in Winter is a Munro classic and has inspired many Munroists over the years.

A time to Savour your Round

This year's 14 Golden Munroists are; Fiona Miller (6465) 58, Iain Mitchell (6504) 56, Howard Andrew (6518) 80, Malcolm Wylie (6521) 61 Geoffrey Curnock (6524) 52, Debbie Robertson (6534) 56, James Sandeman (6540) 62, Michael Brooke (6554) 50, Alan James (6567) 51, Stephen Walter (6570) 52, Rosalind West (6578) 51, Ian F Russell (6595) 65, Elvyn Haigh (6665) 55, Peter Farrington (6731) 52.

Fiona was my first Munro registration and coincidentally I was an accidental participant on her compleation on 24 November 2018 on Càrn a' Chalmain with 30 people. I arrived at the summit around the same time as most of Fiona's party on my way to the deleted Munro top on the North summit.

Howard compleated age 80 on Sgùrr Dubh Mòr. His penultimate Munro was Ruadh Stac Mòr in Fisherfield in the company of his son Jamie, the well- known quadruple amputee and SMC member. Howard commented that an 'Octogenarian-quad amputee' team must be unique and that 'Jamie is much faster than me on the hill'.

Ian's compleation is technically a golden round as he climbed his first Munro aged 6 or 7. Hill running took over so he regarded his 'compleation' round as officially starting in 2004. He was joined by his 3 grand-children aged 4, 11 and 13.

A Time to Travel

A number of Munroists compleated from further afield. Roel Bouwman (6575), Netherlands, Andres von Kanel (6579) Switzerland, Stephen Walter (6570) Canada, Cat Newsheller (6600), USA, Mike Jacobs (6610) Canada, Wilf Williams (6621) Australia, Derek Stuart (6641), Heike Funke (6653) Germany, Paula Hubens (6658) Netherlands, Andrew McInally (6677), Norway.

Roel started in 1991 and commented that by 1999 it became an annual event.

Andres said that it didn't take him long to get 'addicted to these beautiful and dramatic landscapes.' Stephen started on the Scotsman bus as a student at Edinburgh University but moved to Canada in 1972. Retirement eventually provided the opportunity for some more extended trips to Scotland. Wilf started his Munro journey living in Kent but the final 148 were done travelling from Brisbane. He now plans to do the demoted summits and to repeat An Teallach and Stob Diamh so that he will have done all 282 Munros in the same pair of re-soled boots! Heike finished on A' Mhaighdean with a beautiful yoga pose on her summit photo.

A Time to Remember
All hill walkers were shocked at the death of Isobel Bytautas struck by lightning in the Mamores in a tragic accident. Isobel was a member of Linlithgow Ramblers and Hillwalkers and was a keen Munro bagger. I was told she would dearly have loved to achieve a Munro round. Derek Lawson (6650) was the first member of the club to compleat since that 'terrible day.' Derek dedicated his completion on Schiehallion to Isobel's memory. Colin McDougall (6647) paid tribute in his letter to his mentor and enthusiastic friend Ian Angell, killed on A' Chrois in 2006. Keith Ferguson (6693) wrote a very moving letter about his completion on Sgurr a' Mhaoraich. Keith had started the Munros with his friend Mike both reaching a total of 250 in 2018 and planning completion in 2019. Unfortunately, in 2018 Mike got knocked off his bike by a car and ended up in the spinal cord injury unit, able to walk a little with crutches. Mike encouraged Keith to continue and let him know which hills he was doing so that he could follow Keith and they could talk about the hills he had done. Keith's last Munro was done solo as he said it didn't feel right to have anyone else there if Mike was not able to do it.

Lynda Watson (6688) and James Watson (6689) compleated on 3 August on Slioch as a tribute to Lynda's mother whose birthday would have been that day. Lynda's mother had died on 27 June and she had followed their Munro journey up to 281. James also recounted a mishap on Mullach nan Dheiragain when he fell and dislocated his shoulder on a cold sleety day with a strong driving wind. His arm was dangling and his shoulder was somewhere it shouldn't be! James rather luckily and possibly foolishly managed to pop it back to compleat the hill and the other two on the round.

A Time to Register
It is never too late to register. Derek Macfarlane (6476) finished in 2006 and was prompted to register by his grandchildren. Eileen Holttum (6550), member of the Edinburgh Mountaineering Club registered her 1981 completion on Lochnagar along with her Corbett and Graham Completions in 2009 and 2018.

Andrew Ogilvie (6695) belatedly registered his Munro round of 2007 enclosing the letter that he had written on 1 September 2007 to Dave Broadhead but had never sent! In that letter he recounted being caught in an avalanche in January 1995 sustaining severe injuries and hypothermia and surviving only after the brave efforts of Ewan Robertson his partner that day. Andrew spent 13 weeks in hospital and 6 weeks on crutches. Later that year his climbing partner James Turner was killed in the Alps. Andrew said he carried memories of James on every hill after that. On Schiehallion he carried a memento that James' parents had given him after his funeral and in his mind he symbolically compleated James' round too. Andrew said that he was motivated finally to send the letter 13 years later as he would like his family to be able to find his name on the list.

Andrew Scarfe (6728) was registered by his daughter Eleanor who told me she had been subtly working to get all the information needed so she could get a certificate to present to him at Christmas, 31 years after he compleated in 1988.

Ian Parkin (6736) was motivated to register his 1996 compleation after attending the funeral of a friend who had compleated in 2009 and seeing how proud his friend's family had been of the achievement.

A Time to Achieve

All Munro compleations are of course achievements in their own right. Some of the more distinct compleations registered were David Bell (6470) who did a non-stop round of the Munros in 2017 starting on 15 March 2017 and finishing on 12 August 2017 during a break in work contracts. Joss Smale and Peter Watson compleated in 106 days in 2018. Emily Scott (6701) compleated in 2018 in a self-propelled and self-supported round over 4 months from May to September, cycling between Munros, canoeing across Mull and using a paddleboard across Loch Lomond to finish on Ben Lomond. Emily covered 2,600km and 35,000 ascent on the bike and 2,200km with 160,000m ascent on foot. Shirley and Jim Park (6607) and (6608) compleated on the Inaccessible Pinnacle aged 75 and 76 and said 'We've loved every minute of it'.

David Thompson another member of the Edinburgh Mountaineering Club finished on Bidean nam Bian. David is deaf and has written an Article about the challenges that deafness poses to a keen hillwalker. David also persuaded me to do a short sign language video with him to promote registration on the list for Deaf Hillwalkers. This was an interesting experience and required a little more than one take.

A Time for the Environment

Gavin Theobald (6483) is a rare compleationist who does not drive. Gavin wrote that the majority of his hills were done by public transport and the occasional expensive taxi. Gavin mainly backpacked and camped, hitchhiking home and adopted the tactic of going to an area and doing all of the hills there. Gavin compleated the Munros, Tops, Corbetts and Grahams on the same day (Beinn Sgritheall, NW Top, Beinn na h-Eaglaise and Beinn a' Chapuill). Gavin has compleated the Munros twice and is also ticking off Scottish 'Simms'.

Neil Cuthbert (6590) told me that he had been driving hybrid cars since 2011 and went fully electric in 2016. He says that with proper planning it is quite straightforward to access even remote mountains with an electric car.

A Time to Compleat Together

Marjon an der Pol (6558), Matthew Brettle (6559) and Iain Hall (6560) compleated together on Ladhar Behinn. George Dyball (6634), Alistair Barclay (6635) and John Bacchetti (6636) compleated on Ben More and sent me a wonderful summit photo of the three of them which summed up the pure friendship of the journey. Not quite a compleation together but Angela Mamwell (6623) compleated on Ben Lomond on Saturday 1 September followed by her friends Lucy Prins (6628) and Phillip Thompson (6629) on Ben Vane on Sunday 1 September. All of them are members of the Whanney's Climbing Club. Life-long friends from primary school in Bristol Paul Norman (6581) and James Selfe (6582) compleated together. Roger Tiffin (6667) with two artificial joints (knee and hip) compleated on Braeriach with his two sons and daughter with his wife and dog coming half way and meeting them on their return. Cameron Gair (6719) also made it a family affair compleating on Ben More with his son and 16 month old grandson. John Thorndycraft (6718) compleated on Ben Hope 35 years after starting and coincidentally met another person on the summit who was compleating after 35 years.

A Time to Persevere

Edinburgh taxi driver Andy Philip (6484) recounted a Munro journey largely without incident except for falling off one of the Tors on Ben Avon fracturing his ankle. He managed to hobble 6.5 miles back to his bike, another 6 miles back to the car and drove home.

Malcolm Keats (6515) had 10 Munros to compleat but had a heart attack in 2017, 2 days after celebrating his 60th birthday. After a year of regaining fitness he finished his last 10 Munros in 6 weeks with his niece Sally. Iain Atkinson (6520) finished over 3 years from 2016 to 2019 and is a liver transplant recipient. He wrote that doing the Munros felt like a way of honouring his donor who had died aged 17.

Helen Homer (6573) also had a delayed compleation after being diagnosed with cancer in 2018 when treatment reluctantly had to take priority over bagging. Helen and her husband told me about their tradition of singing at the summits 'Another Munro bites the dust'. In July 2019, the final Munro bit the dust.

A Time to Reflect

I was struck in the many letters I received at how much the hills provide companionship and a release from everyday life. Ian Hopper (6487) wrote about '...my need for Scotland's hills and the peace they have brought into my life…' Matthew Smith (6505) referred to '…a very long journey that has brought me a great deal of joy and fulfilment.' Debbie Robertson (6534) talked about walking in the hills bringing '…a sense of perspective and inner calm often needed in modern life...' Jim Magee (6545) said that at age 70 'I'm addicted more than ever to this special wild country we have and feel privileged I have it on my doorstep.' Gerry and Andy Rennie (6576 and 6577) from Cornwall finished on Skye aged 70 a big challenge for 'a lady who fears exposure'. Gerry said 'There is something about mountains that is spiritual and healing for the soul, a wonderful experience for mind and body.'

Isobel Davies (6619) referred to gaining '…a sense of perspective on life that only the mountains can give you.'

A Time for Interesting Mementos

Andrew Govan (6551) received a framed outline of Scotland, created using all the names of the Munros on his compleation with friends from Polmont Mountaineering Club. Tom Miller (6565) received a cake with 284 chocolate buttons. Sadly Tom reported that the champagne that was carried up ended up spread generously over Loch Sloy and the rest of the adjoining hills.

Michael O'Haire (6588) of the Pill Ptarmigans learned shortly after compleating that his daughter had given birth to twins.

Whisky is always a favourite compleation tipple. Richard Davies (6598) received a bottle of Glenglassaugh Malt for his compleation, a Malt from a distillery near where he had taken family holidays on the North East Coast of Scotland.

Cathy Cook of Edinburgh Mountaineering Club who registered her 2004 compleation received a beautiful pottery plate decorated with a picture of Gleouraich. Cathy's chose this hill as one with a good stalkers path so that her parents could come. She also remembers it as one of the last hills done with her friend Lesley Armstrong (2207) who died the following year. William Alexander

Manders (6713) who compleated on Slioch in 2005 has a picture of Scotland with Slioch highlighted on the map and his compleation date tattooed on his arm.

SMC Compleators

Jamie Thin (6472) compleated on Beinn Dearg in Dec 2018 with his wife. This was Jamie's second Munro celebration party as he had a joint last Munro party in 2015 on Sgùrr na h-Ulaidh but decided he was not quite sure if he had reached the summit of Beinn Dearg a long time previously in white out conditions. At the time Jamie thought the trig point might have been buried. His companion on that day was the Rev David Bartholomew of the map making family. David being from a family of geographers and map-makers was never convinced they had reached the top and planted the seeds of doubt in Jamie's mind. David Buchanan compleated on 25 May 2019 on Càrn a' Mhaim. Plans to finish on his 70th birthday were thwarted by his wife's hip replacement but he still managed to finish when he was 70. Neil Adams (6742) of the SMC and Edinburgh Mountaineering Club compleated on Beinn Sgritheall on 30 December 2019 in better than expected weather and possibly the last compleation of the year. As Clerk I decided I had better write a letter to myself before the year ended and register my own Millenium compleation on 1st January 2000 on Ben Wyvis.

A Time for Storms

A recent trend with the naming of storms is for reference to be made to this in the letters I receive. Storm Erik was responsible for delaying Cat Trebilco's (6527) compleation from February to June 2019. Alun Davies (6626) got back to his car after finishing on A' Mhaighdean just before the driving rain and gale force winds of Storm Hector. Replacement certificates were requested from another compleator due to flood damage from a named storm.

A Time for Ingenuity

Bill MacKenzie (6709) compleated on Beinn na Lap. His sons sent me the family report of his penultimate Munro, an ascent of Ladhar Beinn. Unknown to Bill this was against the clock as friends from New Zealand had booked to be in the Highlands for compleation. Bill had an aversion to using bothies and the family eventually decided on an approach by canoe for 4 passengers, fitted with a 25kg 4HP engine. A dry run took place in the garden to ensure smooth transitions. The canoe would reach a speed of 12kmph and reduce the four hour walk in to 50 minutes. With a high tide the decision was taken to go further up Barrisdale Bay to save a couple of hours of walking. Bill insisted that the canoe be carried to high ground for safety. On return with the tide out this meant the team (under Bill's supervision) carrying 80kg plus through sinking sands but the mission had been successfully accomplished.

A Time for Other Random Notes of Interest

One of my favourite stories of 2019 was the request I had for a Munro brooch on behalf of Sheila Murray (449) for her 99th birthday. The badge or brooch was designed by Gordon McAndrew (450). Coincidentally Sheila was a good friend of Gordon's and climbed her last Munro with him. Sheila's friend sent me a lovely photo of Sheila wearing the brooch on her birthday.

Mark Hodson (6569) could not remember the exact date of his first Munro but brought some memories back for me reflecting that it was 1984 during the Olympics. Adrian Mole was on Radio 4 and Daley Thompson was winning the decathlon.

Sheila Murray (449) on her ninety-ninth birthday with brooch. Photo: Anne Pinches.

Donald Mackenzie (6652) is the nephew of Peter Macdonald, past SMC President. He says his uncle took him up his first Munro and inspired him to start having adventures. Donald recounted one of his Munro days on Slioch where he and his friend had canoed across Loch Maree, stashing their canoes in the bushes. On the way back they saw people going into the bushes and ran down to try and stop the canoe being pinched. As he burst through the bushes he startled a couple of women having a skinny dip. He said he did not want to be called a voyeur and so the only thing to do was to join them…

2019 was during the height of the Brexit debate. Registering compleations was thankfully largely a Brexit free activity. However, Brexit did feature in one Munroist's letter to me. David Orr (6690) asked for details of the brooch commenting that Brooches seem right in at the moment. This was just after Lady Hale's Spider Brooch was much commented on when she delivered the Supreme Court's judgment against the Prime Minister's decision to prorogue Parliament.

AMENDMENTS

No.	Name	M	T	F	C	G	D
88	R.W.G. Wood	1969	1971	1976	2007	2007	
		2018					
342	Alice Simons	1984					
		2019					

No.	Name						
343	Tim Simons	1984					
		2019					
375	Robert H. MacDonald	1984	2008	1989			
		1987					
		1990					
		1992					
		1995					
		2002					
		2007					
		2011					
		2015					
		2019					
433	*Brian Shackleton	1985	2009		2005		
		2019					
619	Anthony Kinghorn	1988	2007		2008		
		2018					
640	Matthew Bramley	1989		1990			
		2019					
709	James W. Stewart	1989	1989			1998	2008	2009
743	Ian Turner	1990	1991	1990			
798	**Margaret Graham	1990	2013	2019	2004	2014	2019
		2014					
802	Neil G. Spalding	1990	2019				
856	Ivan Young	1983	1989	1989			2019
975	Alan R. Munro	1991	1991	2003	1998		
		2004					
1045	Steve Fallon	1992	1993	2010	2013		
		1994					
		1995					
		1996					
		1997					
		1998					
		1999					
		2000					
		2001					
		2002					
		2003					
		2004					
		2006					
		2010					
		2012					
		2019					
1076	A.W. Ridler	1992		2016	2011		
1114	Colin H. McNab	1992			2010		
1137	Mike Weedon	1989	2003	2004	2002		
		2019					
1143	Stephen P. Evans	1993	1997				
1237	Heather Coakes	1993			2012		
1258	Michael Hanlin	1993	1998	2013	2019		2008
1273	G. Fraser Ritchie	1993			2014		
1314	Neil S. Dunford	1994			2019		

No.	Name						
1609	Robert J. Ferguson	1996	1996		2004 2019	2014	2016
1680	Elizabeth Carnduff	1996			2002	2010	2019
1681	Peter Hastie	1996			2002	2010	2019
1801	Lindsay Boyd	1997 2000 2002 2008 2010 2017	2002		2004 2009 2019	2009	2010
1891	Dave Marshall	1993 2010 2014 2016 2018	2015 2019	2018	2014	2018	2019
1911	Martin J. Almond	1997 2006 2016 2019	1997	2014	2012	2015	2013
2019	Norman Veitch	1998	2000	2003			
2057	Alan J. Murray	1998 2007		2005	2018		
2125	James Henderson	1999 2011			2008	2014	2015 2019
2209	Anthony B. Cresswell	1999 2019					
2268	Susan Henderson	1999 2014 2019	2014	2005	2004	2010	2010
2269	George Henderson	1999 2014 2019	2014	2005	2004	2010	2010
2272	John E. McPherson	1999		2018	2015	2019	
2344	Ian Baines	2000		1983			
2345	Graham Phillips	2000	2000	2001	2013	2019	
2433	Alan Rowan	2000 2011 2015	2019	2011	2009	2019	2019
2454	** Mary Webster	2000 2014	2009		2005	2016	2019
2475	Alan Sewell	2000	2019	2002	2013		
2501	Niel Craig	1997			2017		
2574	Paul Houghton	2001			2019		
2610	Tony Smith	2001	2001	2001	2010	2016	2019
2844	Norman Keith Fraser	2002			2007 2010 2013 2019	2019	
2845	Alan Green	2002 2011			2019		
2871	Peter Hamilton	1992 2002 2008	2017	2002	1997 2011	2019	

No.	Name						
		2015					
2994	Iain Walton	2003			2008	2014	2019
3076	Nick Barr	2003					
		2019					
3112	Bert Barnett	2001	2002	2002	1998	2000	2013
		2001	2009	2007	2007	2009	2017
		2009	2015	2015	2013	2018	
		2012			2019		
		2016					
3136	Richard Speirs	2004	2004	2002	2019		
3147	Rosalyn Clancey	2004			2017		
3196	Jim Wallace	2004			2008		
		2019					
3481	Rick Salter	2005		2007	2013	2016	
3497	Richard Knight	2005	2017		2010	2019	2011
		2014					
3523	Jenny Hatfield	2005		2007	2013	2016	
3535	David Jeffery	1999	1999		2013	2019	
		2019					
3577	Michael D. Alexander	2006			2019		
3600	Ian J Hawkes	2006	2006		2017		2019
3627	Colin Donald Walter	2006	2006		2019		
		2011	2011				
		2019	2019				
3783	Alan Taylor	2006		2016	2009	2013	2019
3954	Richard E. Braithwaite	2007			2019		
3987	Colin Lees	2004	2012	2013	2019		
		2007					
		2011					
		2016					
3990	Christine Gordon	1998	2000	2007	2017	2019	2013
4003	Bill Cook	1990					
		2019					
4068	Mark Helie	2008			2019		
4120	Frank Johnstone	2003	2019	2016	2011		2019
		2013					
4122	Kennedy Hamilton	2008					
		2015					
		2019					
4174	Mark S. Crawford	2008	2019				
4224	Roger Mitchell	2008		2019	2017		
4262	Iain Dow	1992					
		1999					
		2019					
4308	Geoff Forman	2004	2004				
4328	Dorothy Stirling	2009	2019	2019	2010	2016	2014
		2011					
		2012					
		2014					
		2018					
4445	Andy Gray	2009					
		2019					

No.	Name						
4488	Andrew Rathbone	2005	2019				
4590	Peter K. Lang	2009					2019
4591	Paul Webster	2010			2018		
4597	David Chapman	2010	2019	2012			
4653	Arthur Greenwood	2010		2018	2017		
4710	John McGill	2009			2015	2019	
4803	Susan Low	2011			2019		
4824	Sheona York	2008					
		2019					
4856	Jonathan Richards	1996	1998	2011	2019		
		2010	2009				
5013	Theresa McIntyre	2012			2019		
5057	Robert Phillips	2012	2019	2017	2013	2014	2015
5069	Chris Anderson	2012	2012			2016	2015
5070	*Rab Anderson	2012	2012			2016	2015
5290	Steve Taylor	2013	2019				
5330	Richard H. Thomas	2013		2019			
5359	Ross McEwan	2013			2019		
5361	Fiona Clark	2013			2015	2019	
		2017					
5362	Stuart Clark	2013			2015	2019	
		2017					
5408	John King	2013					
		2019					
5420	Phil Wilson	2013	2019				
5474	Elizabeth Willars	2014		2018			
5505	Allison Robertson	2014	2018	2017	2015	2017	2017
		2018					
5506	Alistair Deering	2014	2015	2017	2015	2017	2016
		2018			2019		2018
5568	Derek Hepburn	2014			2019		
5670	Graham Haley	2014					2019
5792	Kevin Woods	2013					
		2015					
		2019					
5896	*Iain Thow	1984	2004	1994	2004	2007	2004
		2008	2018	2019			2019
		2018					
5946	Dan Cornell	2016		2018			
6242	Dianne Scolari	2017		2019			
6299	Eilidh F. M. Henderson	2017		2019			
6330	Tzvetie Erohina	2018					
		2019					
6471	Robert Tully	2017			2019		2019
6508	Jim Fothergill	2002	2019	2002	2016	2016	
6524	Geoffrey Curnock	2019	2018				
6543	Maya James	2019		2019			
6544	Edward James	2019		2019			
6550	Eileen Holttum	1989			2009	2018	
6612	Graeme Rogers	2019					2011
6738	Elizabeth Kennedy	2009			2019		

In 2019 I heard from 113 (91) Munroists requesting amendments to entries on our Lists (last year's figures in brackets) as follows: New Munro Rounds 33 (24); Tops 19 (10); Furths 21 (8); Corbetts 43 (36): Grahams 24 (13); Donalds 19 (14): Full House 8 (9) The total number of SMC Full Housers is now 63.

Richard WG Wood compleated his second set of Munros on the Inn Pinn on 3 June 2018. Richard is Munroist no 88 compleating in 1969. Richard's friend Bert Barnett also send me a detailed spreadsheet of Richard's many Munro (8290) and Corbett (3648) ascents. The numbers of certain individual hill ascents are notable in their own right, e.g. Sròn a' Choire Ghairbh with 1227 and Ben Tee, 1081. Richard has also compleated the Marilyns apart from three of the St Kilda sea stacks.

New Full House compleaters were: Dorothy Stirling, Robert Philips, Dave Marshall, Tony Smith, Alan Rowan, Christine Gordon, Margaret Graham and myself. Tony was accompanied by 3 Full Housers on his compleation on Pykestone Hill. In compleating the Grahams on Mullach Buidhe, Arran, Richard Knight concluded that whilst the Donalds is the easier of the lot, the Munro, Corbett and Graham rounds are near enough equal – the ability to do multi-Munro rounds on well-trodden paths versus the lower but un-pathed and often more remote nature of the Grahams and Corbetts level the playing field.

SMC member Brian Shackleton compleated a second round of Munros 34 years after the first round. Norman Fraser finished the Grahams and said in his letter that he had always promised himself he had no intentions of ever climbing them. However he managed to compleat them all in more or less a two year period once he got going. Norman has done the Corbetts three times and told me about two random encounters he had with Bert Barnett and Rhona Fraser – also at that time three time Corbett compleators.

On random encounters I was surprised to get a letter from John McGill recording his Corbett and Graham compleations. John asked if I was the Alison Coull who used to play chess saying that the last time he met me was at Aviemore Scottish Chess Championships in 1997. John was bemused about the fact I was off bivvying in the Cairngorms and neither he nor I had any conception at that time that he would be doing the Munros a decade later.

Bill Cook also a chess player compleated a second round of Munros accompanied by fellow chess player Dave Hewitt. I had a separate query from Margaret Squires (3211) whose husband Roger Squires (2959) remembered me from St Andrews Chess Club. Question – how many registered Munroists have also had a Scottish chess grading? I think I now know of seven including me.

Sheona York from London compleated a second round of Munros on Beinn Tulaichean at New Year 2018. Sheona makes many of her trips by Sleeper. Her first attempt at compleating in the preceding July was to be an ambitious walk to Beinn Bhuidhe from Crianlarich, back to Crianlarich and then up Beinn Tulaichean. The weather did not play ball and Sheona described getting to 800m of Beinn Tulaichean unable to see anything in a 'Dome of Disappointment', spending the rest of the day in her tent drinking Laphraoig, eating nuts and berries and reading her kindle until the sleeper arrived. In the sleeper the door to the dining carriage was jammed and the train crew had to 'jemmy it open with an axe before I could get any proper dinner…'

Multiple list compleator Bert Barnett compleated a 4th round of Corbetts on Morrone suggesting it might be his last request for amendment. Robert MacDonald compleated his 10th round of Munros with his final hill being Beinn

Fhionnlaidh, his 8th compleation on this hill. Robert will now be 80 and insists that he has no plans to commence round 11. His friends are not so sure.

Another multiple list compleator SMC member, Iain Thow recorded a second round of Donalds and a second round of Furths. Iain also finished visiting every British Isles Top over 900m with a separate contour 50 foot contour ring which he christened the SCRANs (single contour rings above 900m). The irrepressible Steve Fallon compleated his 16th round on Beinn Bhuidhe. Steve also registered an earlier Corbett compleation.

A note of caution for anyone doing the Furths. Steve Evans unusually requested a deletion from the list of his Furth compleations. He had been using Paddy Dillon's book *The Mountains of Ireland*, which lists 12 peaks missing out Knockoughter – the peak on the ridge between Carrauntoohil and Beenkeragh. Steve says he took a photo of the connecting ridge without realising the significance of the peak but he would not have had time to do it that day anyway.

Peter Hamilton registered his Graham compleation but only after diligently revisiting Doune Hill. Peter had read the survey report for the hill and was uncertain if he had visited the newly designated summit marked by a small cairn. Peter found the cairn as shown in the survey report had been reduced to three flat stones barely visible in the long grass. Maybe someone disagrees with the survey or doesn't know about the findings.

Possibly my oldest correspondent this year was Colin McNab who registered his Corbett compleation from 2010 on Clisham. Colin is now 84 and said he was 17 summits through the Grahams and Donalds and that 'It must surely stop sometime! Hopefully not in disaster!' LSCC Members Margaret Graham and Mary Webster compleated the Donalds together noting that they had a combined age of 155. Margaret's compleation made her the 62nd Full Houser.

Niel Craig of Glasgow JMCS registered his Corbett compleation from 2017 with the possible ulterior motive of trying to establish information about compleators of different hill lists from the Glasgow JMCS. Niel intended to incorporate this on a trophy and was looking for details of dates and names of compleator's hills. Unfortunately I was not able to help him very much as the SMC does not retain these details. It is necessary to look through the individual letters that are held in the SMC archive in the National Library of Scotland. I was able to point Niel in the direction of Dave Hewitt who has analysed all the data up to 2016. Dave helped Niel with most of the missing details. The Trig Point Trophy is a scale model of a Trig point which includes a secret compartment with a trap door containing a small summit book – currently recording 73 compleations by 52 members. Niel sent me a copy of the article in the JMCS newsletter with the full Trig Point Trophy Story. It was well worth reading and starts a remarkable new club tradition. Niel also contributed an extensive analysis of the JMCS compleators which included a very amusing 'peer review' by SMC member Colwyn Jones.

Registration to our six Lists is done by writing to Alison Coull, 258/1 Ferry Road, EDINBURGH, EH5 3AN or emailing SMCmunroclerk@smc.org.uk. For a Munro or Corbett compleation certificate please enclose an A4 sae (with correct postage – large letter). Check www.smc.org.uk for further details and to view the picture galleries of compleatonists celebrating their final summit.

Enjoy your hills.

Alison Coull (Clerk of the List)

SCOTTISH MOUNTAIN ACCIDENTS 2019

Mountain Rescue in Scotland is coordinated by Police Scotland. Police Scotland receive the initial callout through the 999 system and if appropriate, contact the local Mountain Rescue Team (MRT). Each MRT is an independent organisation who submit their reports to the Statistician of Scottish Mountain Rescue (SMR), the representative body for the majority of MRTs in Scotland. There are 28 voluntary civilian Mountain Rescue Teams in Scotland, of which 24 are members of Scottish Mountain Rescue. This report for 2019 is compiled from information received from the 24 civilian and 3 Police Scotland teams that are members of Scottish Mountain Rescue.

This annual report covers the calendar year from 1 January to 31 December 2019. As usual, MRTs were involved in significant numbers of non-mountaineering incidents but in what follows here only mountaineering incidents are considered. (It should be noted that three important mountain rescue teams, Cairngorm, Glencoe and Lochaber are not members of SMR. Accident Reports from Cairngorm MRT appear later).

TYPE	No of Incidents	
	2019	2018
Rescue	179	217
Search and Rescue	128	114
Search	94	116
Medical Emergency	33	46
Police Investigation	22	16
False Alarm	15	21
Body Recovery	9	13
Animal Rescue	8	12
Other	7	9
Technical Rescue	3	5
Water Rescue	3	1
Civil resilience	1	16
Search – water	0	2
TOTAL	502	588

ACTIVITY	Number	
	2019	2018
Hillwalking (summer)	188	151
Hillwalking (winter)	41	75
Rock climbing	7	6
Scrambling	2	2
Snow/ice climbing	5	5
MRT activity	0	0
TOTAL	243	239

GENDER	Number	
	2019	2018
Male	141	164
Female	132	98
Unspecified	38	27
TOTAL	311	289

AGE	2019		2018
	Number		%
0–16	12		6
17–25	50		15
26–35	66		20
36–45	34		16
46–55	29		15
56–65	23		14
66–75	22		10
>75	4		4
TOTAL	240		100

CAUSE	Number	
	2019	2018
Slip or trip	**79**	106
Navigation error	**39**	43
Lost	**38**	38
Fall	**24**	27
Missing kit	**21**	22
Overdue	**17**	21
Reported missing	**14**	12
Medical	**11**	18
Cragfast	**8**	15
Exhaustion	**8**	6
Benighted	**7**	8
Technology reliance	**6**	6
Other	**6**	0
Weatherbound	**4**	10
Natural avalanche	**1**	0
Belay failure	**1**	0
Cornice collapse	**1**	1
Kit failure	**1**	0
River crossing	**1**	0
Food	**1**	1
Blown over	**0**	1
Lightning	**0**	1
Rockfall	**0**	1
Separated	**0**	5
TOTAL	**288**	342

INJURY TYPE	2019 Number		2018 %
Fracture	59		45
Sprains	14		17
Fatal	9		9
Other	7		8
Bruising	6		4
Lacerations	6		9
Hypothermia	3		1
Multiple injuries	3		1
Heart	2		4
Hyperthermia	1		1
Illness	1		1
Minor cuts	1		0
Asthma	0		1
Internal	0		1
Seizure	0		1
TOTAL	112		

INJURY SITE	2019		2018	
	Number	%	Number	%
Ankle	31	32.6	46	35.4
Lower leg	20	21.1	17	13.1
Chest	7	7.4	13	10
Head	5	5.3	16	12.3
Shoulder	5	5.3	4	3.1
Spinal	4	4.2	3	2.3
Pelvis	4	4.2	0	0
Thigh	3	3.2	6	4.6
Foot	3	3.2	0	0
Other leg	3	3.2	4	3.1
Back	2	2.1	0	0
Upper arm	2	2.1	1	0.8
Elbow	2	2.1	2	1.5
Knee	2	2.1	9	6.9
Neck	1	1.1	2	1.5
Wrist	1	1.1	3	2.3
Abdomen	0	0	1	0.8
Hand	0	0	1	0.8
Lower arm	0	0	1	0.8
Other arm	0	0	1	0.8
TOTAL	95		130	

TEAM	2019		2018	
	Callouts	Hours	Callouts	Hours
Aberdeen	13	730	16	990.5
Arran	30	1838.8	24	849.4
Arrochar	22	1211.5	26	1137.1
Assynt	16	652	13	1095.0
Braemar	36	778	24	1159.0
Borders	26	1014	19	1019.4
Dundonnell	41	3123	33	1284.5
Galloway	14	599	22	773.6
Glenelg	4	100	3	107.0
Glenmore Lodge	2	53	3	47.5
Hebrides	8	236	17	2973.0
Killin	34	1674	34	2452.0
Kintail	4	161	6	266.5
Lomond	37	1224.1	38	1512.1
Moffat	9	489	35	2013.0
Oban	19	1037.4	15	383.7
Ochils	17	779.4	30	1331.7
Skye	70	2399.9	49	1372.7
Torridon	12	774	27	1635.0
Tweed Valley	50	2276	61	2151.0
Police Scotland (Grampian)	42	530.5	26	525
Police Scotland (Strathclyde)	110	3479	123	2102.5
Police Scotland (Tayside)	44	711.5	54	1009.9
SARDA (Scotland)	30	628	50	830.6
SARDA (Southern)	36	382.3	10	62.5
SARAA-Scotland	4	53	1	4.0
Scottish Cave Rescue	0	0	1	3.0
RAF Kinross	0	0	0	0
Other	0	0	0	0
Total	730	26934.4	760	29091.2

MOFFAT MRT Accident reports 2019

I am very grateful to Chris Huntley of Moffat MRT for supplying these reports. (Ed.)

Feb 17 Male in early twenties at Brattleburn bothy cut into his ankle with an axe. Unable to walk out. Evacuated by team, utilising stretcher supported on inflated wheel, to awaiting ambulance.

Mar 03 Team on standby at Moffat Base to assist Police Scotland locate missing person. In the event, no further action required as missing person gave himself up to the police.

May 26 Evacuation of casualty from illegal rave in the region of Harestanes windfarm. Particularly poor weather. Team remained on standby for the next 24 hours in case of any further incidents.

Jun 08 Call out to assist Police Scotland in locating missing person whose car was believed left on the outskirts of Moffat, since the first week in May. On June 10, decision made to check seven of the bothies in Moffat area. Report of possible sighting at Over Phawhope bothy and indication that mp was likely to be heading eastward. Jun 23, mp located in Greensykes bothy by local Police Constable, also team member. Mp safe and well, now heading back to Moffat.

Jun 23 Missing male called Police Scotland having become lost while descending Criffel. He was, however, able to find his way down before the team were deployed.

Jul 31 The team were called out by Police Scotland to assist the Scottish Ambulance Service to evacuate a female walker with an ankle injury from Criffel. A Coastguard helicopter was also in attendance and team members assisted in winching the casualty on board.

Aug 06 Team on standby to assist Police Scotland search for mp near Dumfries. Sadly, further inquiries found deceased had taken his own life.

Sep 16 Team assisted casualty with ankle injury on path beside Grey Mare's Tail. Casualty recovered by helicopter to ambulance waiting at car park.

Oct 13 Call out to assist evacuating injured male with suspected ankle fracture on Tinto. Coastguard helicopter already on route but feared that low cloud would prevent them from reaching casualty. However, they did reach the casualty and the team were stood down on route.

Nov 21 Call out to assist Tweed Valley. Stood down short while later when issue resolved.

Dec 23 Local resident became concerned when lights seen on path down from summit of Criffel disappeared abruptly from view. Team called out to confirm but nothing untoward found. Well intentioned false alarm.

SKYE MRT Accident reports 2019

I am very grateful to Ben Wear of Skye MRT for providing these reports.
Note: expressions like R948 refer to a specific Rescue Helicopter. SAS= Scottish Ambulance Service. (Ed.)

There were no accidents reported during January or February.

Mar 21 Following a report of four overdue walkers in the Loch Coruisk area, small group of MRT, plus R948 were deployed. Party had completed

Dubh ridge on the 20th and returned late to tents after route finding difficulties. No mobile signal until 1300 on Mar 21 from Druim Hain. R948 checked they were OK and able to continue. Returned to Sligachan 30 mins before full team call-out. 10 hours.

Mar 27   Call out to near Lochan na Saile. One of two walkers suffered suspected cardiac arrest and companion raised alarm using mobile phone. Seven team members were deployed. However, SAS and police were able to locate casualty just 500m north of public road. Casualty evacuated by helicopter as MRT arrived roadside. Remaining party walked to roadside by police and SAS where met by MRT. 21 hours.

Mar 31   Older local man reported missing on Isle of Raasay in fine but freezing conditions. MRT members conducted a search. 101 hours. No further information.

April 1   Search by sixteen team members. 212 hours. No further information.

Apr 2   Search by thirteen team members. 140 hours. No further information.

Apr 5   Two male hillwalkers cragfast on Sgùrr Dubh Mòr were given advice by two team members and evacuated by R948. 3 hours.

Apr 5   Solo male reported overdue, possibly lost on Cuillin ridge traverse. Two team members on stand-by. False alarm. 2 hours.

Apr 15   R948 provided transport and assisted fourteen team members in search for two German females reported overdue on the Quiraing 'loop'. 70 hours.

Apr 16   Young American female with lower leg fracture, evacuated from the Old Man of Storr by thirteen team members and R948. SAS also in attendance. 52 hours.

Apr 19   Search for three young male backpackers from Cheshire aiming to camp at Coruisk, on a round trip from Sligachan via Glac Mhor. Went up Coire a' Tairneilear instead of Mhadaidh, climbed screes to crest of the spur, and could not go forward or back. Evacuated by R948. 24 hours.

Apr 21   Search for two London based foreign nationals lost in cold, windy, and dense misty conditions on hill path above The Old Man of Storr (which they had missed in the fog). Phoned for help but link for phone-find not possible. Located by whistle, safe and well in upper Coire Scamadal. Both well equipped, but no map or compass. 52 hours.

Apr 21   MRT search for two young German backpackers on 1st leg of Skye Trail. Female exhausted by heavy bag, terrain, and cold, misty, and windy conditions. Phone-find clicked but problems converting Lat/Long. Eventually found approx. 3 kms south from MRT start point near Bealach Chaiplin on Trotternish Ridge. Evacuated by Polaris ATV to Glen Hinnisdal. 54 hours.

Apr 23   Casualty with a suspected ankle fracture, stretchered from the Fairy Pools to the car park by MRT. 32 hours.

Apr 29   Two team members deployed to assist female lost in Glenbrittle forest. Weather was fine and she was able to walk out. 4 hours.

May 11   Female slipped at The Old Man of Storr and was carried off by team members to waiting ambulance. 27.5 hours.

May 17   Eight team members attended at the Old Man of Storr, where an older Australian female had suspected lower leg fracture. She was given morphine, stretchered off in a casualty bag then evacuated by R948. SAS also in attendance. 20 hours.

May 22   Using a mobile phone, one team member assisted a walker on Sgùrr a' Mhadaidh, in cloudy, wet conditions. Team on stand-by. 0.5 hours.

May26   Call out to the Fairy Pools where a male was stranded on rock surrounded by fast flowing water. On arrival found that SFRS and Coastguard already on scene. Team stood down. 4 hours.

May 31   Team called out to Bealach nan Coisichean. One of three German males, attempting the Skye Trail reported having injured leg after a slipping on steep ground in wet conditions and unable to walk. 60 hours.

May 31   Swiss female attempting the Skye Trail required assistance from the Bealach Leacaich in wet weather and poor visibility. 2 hours.

June 1   Two Lebanese males lost in mist at the Quiraing called for help but managed to find their way off as MRT arrived on the scene. 6 hours.

June 12   Quirang. Elderly US male slipped from main path, falling approx. 20m down steep ground injuring elbow, pelvis, and shoulder. Team administered morphine prior to airlift by R948. 21 hours.

June 18   Neist Point. Casualty with ankle injury uplifted by R948 and taken to waiting ambulance at car park. Team on stand-by. 0.5 hours.

June 18   Team attended an American male at Bealach Banachdaich. He had taken a stumbling fall sustaining suspected spinal injury. Morphine, paracetamol, Entonox, and oxygen all administered at scene. Following stretcher carry to lower corrie, below cloud base, casualty airlifted by R948 to Broadford, then Raigmore hospital. 207 hours.

June 26   One team member deployed to a search on the Glen Sligachan Path. 1 hour.

June28   Six team members taken by R948 to search Coire a' Ghrunnda where female hill walker had slipped on steep rock. Casualty located and evacuated. 24 hours.

June 28   Female with lower leg fracture stretchered off by team, from Old Man of Storr to ambulance at roadside. 24 hours.

July 2   SAS requested MRT assistance to stretcher older male with ankle injury from the Fairy Pools to ambulance at roadside. 12 hours.

July 13   American female in early 20s with lower leg fracture, required stretcher carry from Old Man of Storr. 8.5 hours.

July 14   Stand-by to assist SAS at Fairy Pools for stretcher carry of female with ankle fracture. Team stood down. 0.5 hours

July 19   Male swimming at Fairy Pools suffered fatal cardiac arrest. MRT, local doctor, coastguard, and heli-med all in attendance. 40 hours.

July 19   Quiraing, American female slipped and trapped leg crossing stile at NG 446689. Suspected compound fracture of lower leg. R948 airlifted four MRT to site. Casualty splinted, stretchered to R948 and onward to Western Isles Hospital.

July 22   Search for two young Belgian males lost in cloudy wet, windy conditions on Meall na Suiramach, Quiraing. Located as per phone-find grid reference near summit trig. point and walked down off hill to upper Quiraing carpark. 42 hours.

July 25   MRT called to assist SAS at Fairy Pools for German female with lower leg injury and stretcher carry back to main carpark. 17.5 hours.

July 26   Team on stand-by for male reported with knee injury between Boreraig and Suisnish. R948 tasked to recover casualty. 2.5 hours.

Aug 1   Coire Lagan. French female sustained lower leg injury on path below Lagan Lochan. Uplifted to hospital by R 948. 12 hours.

Aug 6	Team on standby. Lone UK male walker, cragfast on steep ground, at Bealach a' Gharbh-choire in cloudy dark conditions, with shelter and warm clothes, called police in panicked state to request assistance with route finding. MR and police unable to call casualty back. Decision made to locate casualty and walk him off hill. Casualty called police (21.37) to report he had found path and was making his way down and no longer required assistance. R948 already on route and continued to casualty's location but not seen. Casualty made his own way off hill. 12 hours.

Aug 6	Search for male English walker reported missing, having taken boat to Coruisk at 9am and failed to return to B&B in Elgol on foot, as planned. Last reported sighting at head of Loch Coruisk. Missing person found early next day at head of Loch Scavaig waiting for boat having spent an unplanned night in the hut. 74 hours.

Aug 9	Old Man of Storr. Female Chinese national, lost north of Storr close to Coire Scamadal, walked off by team members. 9 hours.

Aug 9	Team deployed to Bealach na Glaic Moire, where one of a party of two French rock climbers had fallen, dislocating his shoulder. Picked up by R948. 60 hours.

Aug 10	Standby. A party of 4 twenty-something males from Dundee area got into difficulties on Banachdaich. One of them Facebook messaged his mum asking her to call MR on their behalf. After investigation it turned out that they had made it down. Two were traced to their tent at Glenbrittle campsite. The other two, one of whom had a suspected broken collarbone, were on route to Broadford Hospital. False alarm. 0.5 hours.

Aug 11	Stretcher Rescue of female with broken ankle from Old Man of Storr. 36 hours.

Aug 13	Old Man of Storr. French female with broken ankle, stretchered off hill to ambulance. 3 hours.

Aug 14	Team deployed to search for male Polish walker overdue from walk in Coire a' Ghreadaidh. Located and walked off. 5.4 hours.

Aug 16	Search and rescue of two female Canadian walkers attempting Trotternish ridge over two days. They requested assistance after one reported having leg injury and unable to continue, also having difficulty with navigation. Casualty given ibuprofen for sprained knee. Both walked off to Loch Cuithir. 49.5 hours.

Aug 17	Search and rescue in poor weather for overdue Spanish male separated from party after walking up Blàbheinn. Last seen near south top after telling group he was off to scout a route down from north top. As he failed to return, group made their way down (the way they came up) and once back at carpark, reported him missing at neighbouring house. Communication was made with missing walker and his grid reference obtained from phone-find putting his location on the west face of Blàbheinn close to Willink's gully. Team assembled and made way to grid ref. Updated that casualty mobile and walking in confused and exhausted state, also reported by Dundee police control as having been unconscious. New grid reference obtained, and casualty eventually located close to original grid on very loose ground. Made way back to top of Blàbheinn with some effort and assistance before eventual descent to car park. 180 hours.

Aug 17	'Weatherbound', German couple rescued from Beinn Edra, unable to pitch tent in poor conditions. 12 hours.

Aug 21   Dutch lady lost and exhausted in dark cloudy weather, attempting walk from Kilmarie to Portnalong via Glaic Moire. Located using phone-find near Coire a' Mhadaidh/Coire na Creiche. Walked off hill. 32 hours.

Aug 24   German female slipped, fractured ankle near Fairy Pools. Team administered morphine. Airlifted by R948. 32 hours.

Aug 25   Search and rescue of two Spanish walkers lost/cragfast north of Coire Scamadal, after setting off from Storr car park. Location given via phone-find. MRT located party and walked them off hill. 10 hours.

Aug 27   Three team members deployed to Glen Eynort, where crofter's dog stuck on ledge. Animal retrieved! 12 hours.

Aug 27   Search around Coire a' Ghrunnda in cloudy wet, dark conditions. for hillwalker lost on descent after summiting Sgùrr Dubh Mòr. He was planning to spend the night in Sgumain cave but probably became lost on descent from Sgùrr Dubh na Dà Bheinn to corrie. Called 999 from ridge before descending towards corrie and was found sheltering behind rock when mist cleared. Walked to base at 01.30. 77 hours.

Sept 2   Old Man of Storr. Young German lady slipped on path in wet conditions suffering unstable tib. and fib. fracture. Given morphine and Entonox, before being stretchered to helimed for evacuation. 21 hours.

Sept 7   Search and Rescue of two young Scottish females who became cragfast after scrambling on west face of Sgùrr a' Ghreadaidh. Prolonged technical rescue supported by R948. 57 hours.

Sept 7   Two team members deployed to investigate reports of shouts for help heard at Old Man of Storr. False alarm. 6 hours.

Sept 16   Coire na Creiche. Russian male, on holiday, walked to Fairy pools from carpark and proceeded to drink a bottle of 18 year old Talisker single malt. Last memory reported as jumping into the pools with everyone cheering. No injuries and in good spirits. Lost trying to find his way back to carpark and reported by passer-by as not moving for an hour someway off the path. Five MRT attended. Russian walked off hill and driven to Sligachan hotel. 15 hours.

Sept 17   Two MRT investigated reports from four different callers having seen flashing lights. Assumed lights were seen at Bealach Sgumain, probably of person(s), in distress or not, bivvying in Sgumain cave. False alarm. 3 hours.

Sept 20   Team deployed to rescue at Great Stone Chute where man reported as having fallen 100ft and unconscious. 33 hours.

Sept 23   Male attempting to walk from Storr to Quiraing – (very poorly equipped with jeans and umbrella, no map or compass), became lost around Carn Liath after dropping rucksack over edge. Walked off by MRT. 28 hours.

Sept 25   Male, lost, descended into Lota Corrie from Sgùrr nan Gillean. Followed waymarks (from Walk Highland) up and down SnG. No map. Location found using phone-find and casualty talked off hill. 3 hours.

Sept 26   Bearreraig Waterfall below Storr Lochs. Male took approx 15ft fall into shallow pool whilst abseiling on photo shoot. Fracture of knee and multiple minor cuts to head and neck. Given Entonox and morphine by MRT before being stretchered to suitable location for airlift by R948. 48 hours.

Oct 3   Evacuation from Loch Langaig, Quiraing by MRT of an older Korean lady who fractured ankle on guided walk. 21 hours.

Oct 3   British male, with guided party in Coire a' Bhasteir, tumbled on scree, sustained cuts, bruises, and aggravated an old ankle injury. Retrieved by R948. 12.5 hours.

Oct 13   Fairy Pools. Call-out to assist SAS. Stood down on arrival. 9 hours.

Oct 13   Call-out to base of slabs on Coire Lagan path. Scottish male walker had slipped and tumbled five metres sustaining open knee injury, bump on head, minor fractures, cuts, and bruises. Given Entonox by paramedic/winchman, leg and both arms splinted, then stretchered 50m downhill to R948 and evacuated to Raigmore hospital. Older lady and two children escorted from hill to base by MRT. 38 hours.

Oct 19   Male, Scottish, slipped on descent from Coire Lagan. Suspected fractured heel. 26 hours.

Oct 27   Female walker, knee injury. SAS went on hill before MRT got there, found casualty, and treated her. Dark when MRT arrived – took some time to get a location from SAS before a chopper could be tasked. 25 hours.

Nov 2   Scottish female walking near Ullinish point tripped. Suspected ankle fracture. Box splint applied. Morphine and Buccastem given then stretchered back to road-side and taken to hospital by friend from party. 25 hours.

Nov 10   Party of two on top of Sgùrr na Stri, one reporting chest pains radiating to neck and left arm. Suspected heart attack. R948 tasked to pick up casualty and transfer to Western Isles Hospital. Other party member walked back to car at Kilmarie. 2 hours.

Dec 28   Call out to assist male walker near Glenbrittle in dark, freezing, windy conditions. Walked off hill. R948 also in attendance. 76.5 hours.

————— • —————

There are no overall statistics for the non-SMR civilian teams, though Cairngorm MRT provided the following reports.

CAIRNGORM MRT Accident reports 2019

I am very grateful to Willie Anderson, Leader of Cairngorm MRT, for providing these reports. (Ed.)

The team was involved in 27 incidents which took 1561 Man Hours.

Jan 3   Two males without map, lost on Munros north of Glen Banchor. Despite the dark, they managed to get off the hills themselves. 12 hours.

Jan 19   Male fell on Stag Rocks. injuring ankle. Not broken but unable to weight bear. Airlifted off by Rescue 951. 25 hours.

Jan 25   Lone female lost on Ben Macdui. Located and taken to Glenmore Lodge by Rescue 951.20 hours.

Jan 27   Male sets off Personal Locater Beacon from near Ben Macdui. Stretchered off. Big team effort to get him off the hill. Taken to Raigmore by Rescue 951. 243 hours.

Jan 30   Climber falls on Doctor's Choice, sustaining leg fracture. Airlifted to Raigmore. His partner abseiled off and was walked out by CMRT. 52 hours.

Feb 25   'Guide' overdue near White Bridge. Blamed the dark, too many stones and lack of signs for the error. Turned up safe and well. 12 hours.

Feb 28   Mountain biker overdue from Strath Nethy. 2 hours.

Mar 2   Worried mother reports her son overdue. He was safe and well in Ryvoan bothy. 6 hours.

Mar 9   Two walkers without map or compass lost on Macdui. They manged to return to car park. 51 hours.

Mar 10   Male with an injured leg became separated from friend near spot height 1141. Turned up safe and well. 10 hours.

Mar 16   Ski tourer with dog became lost. Sheltered in his bivvy and called for help. 115 hours.

Apr 4   Two males trapped at Faindourain bothy by deep snow spent an extra night there but needed an airlift out due to depth of snow. 951 assisted with this. 63 hours.

Apr 8   Male lost above Glen Doe. Found safe and well. Airlifted to roadside by 951. 255 hours.

Apr 27   Two Females lost returning from Macdui. Found at Cairn Lochain safe and well. 75 hours.

Apr 27   Elderly lady, deemed high risk, lost near River Spey at Grantown. Found safe and well.20 hours.

May   No recorded incidents.

Jun 1   Walker collapsed at Loch Avon. 951 airlifted him to Raigmore. 4 hours.

Jun 16   Person threatening suicide. Hiding/ done it before. 57 hours

Jul 1   Polish couple lost on Cairngorm overnight. Walked out to Braemar the next day. 20 hours.

Jul 7   Female on Macdui path, tripped breaking femur. Airlifted to Raigmore by Bristows. 8 hours.

Jul 15   Walker injured ankle on plateau. Made it to ski area then taken off by Cairngorm Mountain staff. 4 hours.

Aug 6   Biker lost on Bynack More during wet night, required rescue. 90 hours.

Aug 7   Some team members went to recover the bike from above. 24 hours.

Aug 31   Female, deemed high risk, missing in Carrbridge area, not found at the time of writing. 136 hours.

Sep 4   Three males with two dogs become lost on plateau. One of the dogs dies. Males recovered safe and well. 84 hours.

Oct   No recorded incidents.

Nov 4   Male and female overcome by weather on plateau. Recovered safe and well. 52 hours.

Nov 15   False alarm for 2 overdue climbers. 40 hours.

Dec   No recorded incidents.

(I am most grateful to Lisa Hutchison for her help in editing the reports from all the teams. Ed.)

IN MEMORIAM

DAVE AMOS j. 2008

DAVE DIED IN SEPTEMBER 2019, at the age of 71, after a fall at an indoor climbing wall. When I heard the news it took me some time to get my emotions in order. Anger at the triviality of what he was doing when his fatal accident occurred tended to dominate and exclude more appropriate feelings. Now, I think, I have just about got things in perspective – any form of physical activity above big drops has risks, and history is full of skilful climbers who were taken when they were not anticipating danger. Death is no respecter of persons or occasions. We have to celebrate the life, not resent the manner of its ending.

Dave was born and educated in Edinburgh then went abroad for ten years or so, working in Australia and the Far East. Returning in his late twenties, he spent the rest of his life in Edinburgh, working for Edinburgh Council until retirement in his early sixties. He had a lot to do with organising the gritting of the roads in winter. No one ever thanks the Council for a well gritted road, but there are plenty of complaints, and some of the qualities which came to the fore in Dave's climbing, including patience and good humour, must have been useful in dealing with the public.

Rather remarkably for someone who went on to do so much at such high standards, Dave only took up roped climbing in his mid to late forties. Before that his main activity was judo, and I suspect that the physical fitness and mind control which served him so well when he climbed may have originated in that sport. His ability at climbing must have been apparent from early on – he told me of Martin Moran guiding him on an Alpine nordwand in a 24 hour epic on one of his first ventures abroad, and I can't believe Martin would have done that with just anyone. In Scotland Dave was a client, then a friend, of Andy Nisbet and they did new routes together.

Dave's physical abilities were such that well into his sixties (and only now, getting there myself, do I realise how remarkable it was) he went up the hill like a train, not needing walking poles to add uphill impetus. In winter he would still be bare handed when I was on my second pair of gloves. I would happily do routes with him knowing that I was relying on him to lead the crux – he was the built-in safety margin.

But Dave's performance on the hill is not what I recall most clearly about him. It is invidious to rate climbing partners for companionship, but he was among the best for me, and I know lots of people feel the same way. For such a quiet guy, not at all a party animal, never putting himself or his abilities to the fore, he was constantly in demand as a climbing partner. The reason was not only his climbing ability but his modest, generous, resilient, utterly dependable character. What you saw was what you got, right to his very core.

Dave was active in summer and winter, both at home and abroad in the USA and Europe. He developed a particular affection for climbing in Italy and put serious effort into learning Italian, the better to enjoy his visits. In addition to the SMC, he was a member of the Climbers' Club and the Edinburgh JMCS and had regular partners from all three clubs. Fairly late on in his climbing career he had a couple of unfortunate accidents, causing a broken ankle and then a broken arm. The latter in particular involved a long recovery period, but he came back from both seemingly as strong as ever and developed a new interest in ski-ing after realising how pleasant it was to be in the sunshine on the slopes above Rjukan rather than stuck in the gloom of the valley below.

Most of my own climbing with Dave was done in the Scottish winter and (other than professionals) he was the best winter climber that I have ever been out with. Mixed or ice, it didn't matter which, he just got on and climbed it.

Of course there were inevitable mishaps along the way, which Dave overcame unflappably. He tended to shed a crampon from time to time; he ruefully confessed to me that he once had had to hop up ten metres of the crux of Rubicon Wall (on the lead, of course). There was the International Meet when he and his overseas companion got lost in hideous conditions in the Cairngorms and spent a night in a trench in the snow – although he was back on grade Vs on the Ben a couple of days after the helicopter lifted them from Strath Nethy. There was the time with me on the Ben when he went off route on Caledonia and put in an epic lead on desperately thin ice, with never a wobble, to reach safety – I seconded and wobbled all the way. He also had an on/off relationship with cars – one ended up in someone's front garden after he fell asleep driving home in the early hours on return from a sun rock trip, and another was written off in a collision with a taxi as he crossed Edinburgh to come to pick me up in the early morning, en route for Creag Meagaidh.

On the day of the taxi incident we were very delayed in getting away, having to wait for insurance and garage arrangements to fall into place, but we got there in the end and climbed the Last Post in wonderful conditions with the mountain to ourselves. We walked off the plateau together in the gloaming and, inspired by exhilaration from the climb and our overcoming of adversity, coupled with the beauty of the fading purple to the east and the glowing embers to the west, I said to him something along the lines of how I knew that my intense experience of the pleasure of this moment would rapidly fade, and how I wished I could bottle and preserve it. I can't remember exactly what he said in reply, but it was accompanied by that characteristic shy grin of his, expressing agreement, appreciation, fellowship and contentment. Oh Dave, how I wish I could have bottled that too.

David Small

Stewart Bauchop writes: for those of us who climbed with him Dave Amos will be remembered for his laid back approach and cool head, whatever the situation. Quiet by nature, but with a sharp wit in understatement, Dave excelled in the drama of winter and would inspire confidence when most would be talking retreat. Stories of all night drives through closed roads, strung out leads on thin Nevis ice and seemingly effortless progress in marginal conditions, all dispatched without incident and retold with a wry smile. In winter Dave's style of climbing was just as his character, laid back and gentle – seemingly effortless with the occasional wild scart of a crampon revealing just how delicate the climbing might be.

I climbed on and off with Dave over 20 years and whilst never allowed to skip a lead I did feel very much the apprentice. We worked our way through the mid-grade classics, often in Glen Coe, and on to the bigger routes on Ben Nevis and further afield. Zero gully in a storm, the Wand collapsing in a thaw, Fluted Buttress verglassed and buried under powder, and many straightforward days just enjoying being out.

My earliest encounter with Dave's ability to kick it up a gear would be around the back of the millennium, off route on a climb called the Sphinx in Stob Coire nam Beith. We had lost the line and climbed ourselves into a cul-de-sac high up on the cliff where we were faced with a 4 metre wall, an impasse, daubed with thin smears of bullet hard water ice. With the sun going down and the Aonach Eagach Ridge lit up in alpenglow it was all very scenic but with the prospect of a long cold night in store. Facing benightment or a long retreat in the dark Dave opted to make a desperate lead edging up the wall on tips, even apologizing for hooking an old peg halfway up but ultimately leading us through.

Lots of folk will have their own stories climbing with Dave Amos, maybe further afield in the Alps or America but for me his spirit will be blowing in the spindrift, quietly whispering encouragement around the Winter corries.

BRIAN A. CLARK j. 1973

BRIAN, A NATIVE OF Dundee passed away peacefully on 7 October 2019 after a short illness, aged 81. He is survived by his wife Davena, son Neil and grandson Laurence whom he adored. Brian was from a family of five boys, he was a Joiner to trade and retired as Chief Clerk of Works with the Dundee City Council. After doing his National Service in the Parachute Regiment, he became a member of the Carn Dearg MC, Dundee in the nineteen fifties, he served on the committee and was Meet Secretary and President. In his early years he climbed extensively in Glen Clova, Cairngorms and of course throughout Scotland. He joined the SMC in 1973 and was a keen member for 46 years attending most AGM's and Dinners. His skills were key to the building of the new Carn Dearg MC hut at Braedownie

Attending the 100th Anniversary Dinner at Blair Castle, May 1989. Photo: Graeme Hunter.

Brian opening the CDMC Braedownie Hut April 2017. Photo: Graeme Hunter.

in Glen Clova which he opened in April 2017. Brian was Treasurer/Secretary to the Scottish Ex-Parachute Association who gave a guard of honour at his funeral.

I remember as a teenager, with Brian we traversed the Five Sisters of Kintail in superb Alpine conditions at Easter 1964, a long and memorable excursion. Again, in 1969 but with Neil Quinn, Brian climbed NE Buttress on the Ben in full winter conditions, in traditional style. Again, a classic and memorable experience. Brian completed his Munros on Ben Lomond in 1994.

Brian was of cheery disposition and a most trustworthy and dependable partner in any situation, he will be greatly missed.

Graeme Hunter

DAVE 'SMILER' CUTHBERTSON j. 1998

So MY OLD PAL Smiler (Dave Cuthbertson) has passed away. His death came suddenly on 2 May 2019 after being admitted to hospital with pneumonia, lung cancer, and auto-immune arthritis. He died within a week of admission. His funeral was held at the village of Dores near Inverness where he had lived for the past twenty-three years. A church service included some heartfelt tributes, and was followed by an open air buffet lunch at the village pub, in glorious sunshine, looking out peacefully over Loch Ness.

I first met him when I joined the Wolverhampton M.C. in the late 1960s. It was like meeting a bouncy young dog, full of energy, enthusiasm, and friendliness to all. His nickname says everything. He always had wide climbing interests. He once alarmed some policemen in the West Midlands by his night-time ascent of a disused brick-built factory chimney. Of course, his good-natured charm soon won them round, and the route was completed without further ado.

He was chairman of the Wolverhampton M.C, later becoming president of the Climbers' Club, a stalwart of the Alpine Climbing Group/Alpine Club, a member of the Scottish M.C. and FRCC, and an international mountain guide.

We climbed together throughout the 1970s when he led me struggling and cursing up many hard Welsh and Lakes rock routes, my successful seconding being encouraged by his stream of bubbling optimism, plus an occasional tight rope. Forays north of the border for Scottish ice led to the roles being reversed. Ours was a complementary team. His notable alpine ascents included the Bonatti Pillar, the Walker Spur, the Matterhorn North Face and after several abortive attempts, the Eiger North Face.

I had a season with him in the Bernese Oberland, resulting in ascents of the Mönch, Lauterbrunnen Breithorn (first British ascent of a route on the north face) and Ebnefluh (a new route on the north face). After this, we sadly drifted apart. He moved into the guiding profession and relocated to Scotland, whereas I concentrated on lightweight trips to the Karakoram, which he was unable to join being committed to summer guiding, and impecunious compared to me. His guiding activities included the UK, the Alps, Nepal, Peru, East Africa, and many more locations around the world. More recently, he organised a series of ice climbing visits to Rjukan in Norway for the Climbers' Club.

The author Ernest Hemingway once said that there are only three sports: bull fighting, motor racing and mountaineering – the others are just games, referring to the need to put one's life on the line. This quotation underlines an essential feature of our 'sport', the danger involved, which poses the question of where lies

Photo:
Ian Smith

the right balance between courage and foolhardiness. This is a matter which all climbers must decide for themselves. What is clear with Smiler is that anyone who employed him as a guide would be less subject to the sort of excessive rule-bound practices followed by some other guides, and would have an active and enjoyable experience, also a fulfilling and exciting one.

Smiler's choices of climbing venues, and styles of climbing show the width of his interests. The sport of athletics has many differing disciplines: sprints, middle and long distance running, and various jumping and throwing activities. Likewise, our sport also has many disciplines: single and multi-pitch climbing, ice climbing, Alpine and Himalayan mountaineering, and many more, each with its own set of challenges and flavour. Smiler revelled in most of these, so could be likened not to a sprinter or marathon runner, more to a decathlete.

He was one of climbing's great characters, and one of its most charming. Those who were guided by Smiler, climbed unguided with him or just met him in the pub, all delighted in his company, and he will be sorely missed by me and all in the climbing world who knew him.

Dave Wilkinson

David Whillis writes: Smiler was born on 26 May 1948, in Wombourne, near Wolverhampton. Educated at Ounsdale school, he left to pursue a career in Mechanical Engineering and toolmaking in Wolverhampton. But by this time an interest, perhaps better described as an obsession, with mountaineering had manifested itself, particularly in the mountains of North Wales. Scotland was an obvious draw, especially in winter. On an early winter trip to Creag an Dubh Loch, his older companions elected to climb Labyrinth Direct. The 'youth' was placed at the back. When the team realised the extreme nature of their aspirations, the 'youth' was persuaded to lead it. He later found that it was the ninth known ascent.

He found employment in North Wales, manufacturing climbing equipment. His engineering skills subsequently took him abroad, initially to Germany and on another, separate occasion California, where he worked for the well-known climber Yvon Chouinard. But he was consistently drawn back to the British mountains; not even a tempting offer from Chouinard could keep him.

As well as his main occupation as engineer/toolmaker, Smiler was also employed teaching rock climbing in various outdoor centres. This was in addition to his regular climbing trips to Scotland, the Alps and the greater ranges including, of course, the Himalaya. So, it is no surprise that Smiler cut loose from his manufacturing career, and in 1990 qualified as a British Mountain Guide.

In 1996, Smiler relocated from North Wales to Loch Ness, to be nearer the Scottish mountains, which is where he would be working all winter anyway. A number of new climbs in the Loch Ness area bear his name. Ben Nevis was his favourite mountain: he once guided Point Five Gully on two consecutive days. Smiler enjoyed many happy years teaching climbing in Scotland, with occasional forays back to North Wales, and of course every summer in the Alps, never mind trips elsewhere. One of the achievements that he was most proud of was helping to set up a climbing school on the slopes of Mount Kinabalu, in Borneo. He guided a group of climbers up Mount Elbrus, the highest peak in Russia, and therefore continental Europe. He lost count of the number of times he had climbed Mont Blanc, but it was probably about forty. He was a member of the Climbers' Club, indeed a past President. He was an elected member of the Scottish Mountaineering Club.

He could write. His anecdotes can be found in several climbing anthologies. In 2014, Smiler retired from his role as a Guide, but somewhat inevitably continued working at the local climbing wall in Inverness, initially as a technical advisor, and subsequently as an instructor, where his natural enthusiasm, good nature and infinite patience was put to good effect in teaching the next generation of climbers.

It was at about this time that he developed an inflammatory condition of his joints, affecting especially his hands, which seriously curtailed his climbing activities. Treatment of this condition proved difficult, but Smiler, when well, continued climbing, including organising regular Climbers' Club winter meets to Rjukan, and climbing trips to Spain. He died on 2 May 2019 after a short illness.

Geoff Lowe writes: Smiler loved to talk, he was a very sociable man; he was full of enthusiasm, ideas and things would happen; as Smiler would have said, 'just do it'. I had a few trips with him to Spain, Norway and around Scotland.

An experience of an event in Spain was written up in his clubs' Journals, both SMC and CC, when Smiler and his friend Richard Jolley went to do Magical Mystery Tour on the Toix Sea Cliffs. Smiler went past the exit route and continued on the traverse, going too far. He retraced his steps and exited the crag via a rickety old metal ladder and a desperate move onto rock at the end. (See 'Hot Rockin' in the Costa Blanca', *SMCJ* 2017 pp. 64–72 Ed.)

On another occasion Smiler, Ian Innes and I went to Latheron Wheel. Smiler was unwell at this time and walked in with a folding chair, he sat at the top of the crag directing operations and taking photographs, that was Smiler, determined not to miss the fun no matter what.

JOHN DUNN j. 1988

JOHN DUNN, BORN 15 JUNE 1962, was one of Scotland's most senior prosecutors, an enthusiastic climber and excellent companion, he died September 18, 2019, aged 57.

I first met John at an economics lecture in 1979 but was to get to know him better via the mountains. John was introduced to the hills by his uncle at an early age whilst still at school. Born in Glasgow he was educated at St Aloysius College. He developed his interest in the hills at university where it broadened into climbing and mountaineering. This became an anchor in his life along with his partner and wife Sandra. John and Sandra were together for thirty nine years, thirty two of these years married. As well as meeting his wife at university he established a close group of climbing friends that continued after university particularly through the Rannoch club. His death at a fairly young age is a shock for all those that knew him.

The Rannoch was a loose affiliation of people who were based around Glasgow in the early 1980s, who were adopted by some older climbers who offered a focal point around a hut in Glen Coe in the days before climbing walls and mobile phones. The hut offered an ideal base for climbing, shelter from the midges and the rain, a venue for card sessions, a little drinking perhaps, tall yarns, competitive games, the opportunity to meet many likeminded people and was any easy hitch from Glasgow. The group also offered an introduction to the SMC that John enthusiastically embraced. He joined the club in 1988. In his own words: 'The punk rockers were coming through the system to respectability'. John always like to dance and had an eclectic taste in music never quite losing his punk influences.

He undoubtedly achieved professional respectability but he always managed to retain a mischievous twinkle that hinted at a bit of fun and not taking himself too seriously. He had a lightning wit, fast analysis and generous heart.

John, affectionately known by many of his friends as JD, enjoyed a typical progression from hillwalking to winter mountaineering and rock climbing. He had a fairly conventional apprenticeship for the time in the Alps and Pyrenees climbing with people like Roger Webb, Alan Shand, Gavin Mitchell and the late Bish McAra but he had a greater focus on the Scottish hills. He completed his Munros in 1995. He was a core member of the Rannoch club that offered many climbing partnerships and excursions and he formed a particularly strong climbing partnership with the late Colin Grant. Latterly this tended to be rock climbing in the UK, visits to the North west and a whole range of venues for the annual holiday in Europe and further afield, scheduled around work and family commitments.

John was never particularly attracted to new routes but rather a good day out with friends. He was a great companion on the hill even if there was always a competitive urge. He had a long standing and enduring enthusiasm for the mountains that he was keen to share. He did have a competitive streak that was usually evident as he demonstrated superior fitness on the hill. He was equally happy to introduce friends to the hills and organised many excursions for work colleagues that were widely appreciated.

Having qualified as a lawyer from Strathclyde University he then attended Pembroke College Oxford before joining the Procurator Fiscal Service in 1985. At both the Fiscal service and the Scottish Crown office he enjoyed an outstanding career. For instance, he was intimately involved in gathering evidence, building the case and seeing through to trial the Lockerbie bombing of flight Pan Am 103 between 1991 and 2000 and was seen as instrumental in the conclusion of that case. There were many other achievements as he held a variety of senior positions in different parts of the country often at least appearing to have two roles on the go at the same time. He was heavily involved in the reform of the Scottish criminal court at all levels and in his last role as Deputy Crown agent was responsible for over 1000 colleagues in courts across Scotland. Inevitably such a successful career put some constraints on his climbing but he was always keen to get out and great company whatever the day involved. His house in Arran provided an ideal base for many years that fitted with work commitments.

John's death was all too sudden. It was only a few years after initial diagnosis of cancer to his untimely death but he faced his illness with great dignity, humour and humility. He is survived by his wife Sandra and his siblings Barbara, Kenneth and Helen.

Stan Pearson

ANDREW FRASER j. 1962

LIKE MANY, ANDREW FRASER had a life-long devotion to the outdoors, mountains, and adventure but if his time in the limelight of Scottish rock climbing was brief, it was astonishingly bright.

Andrew was brought up in Cramond, Edinburgh, into a family with a culture of adventure. His parents, Barclay and Janet, met on a walking trip to the Spanish Pyrenees in the 1930s; Barclay was a keen mountaineer and a Club member, and

was on expeditions to the Andes as well as accompanying Hamish Brown on trips to The High Atlas Mountains, while Janet was an independent spirit taking off each summer for European walking expeditions with her women pals in the family Dormobile. Living beside the River Almond, Andrew's early passion was dinghy sailing.

On leaving school in 1955, Andrew had intended to study languages, but a spell in hospital for an operation to repair knee ligaments, following an unsuccessful attempt to teach himself how to ski on the Pentlands in the days before tows or releasable bindings, inspired him to change to medicine. The repair was, by today's standards, crude, and later his patella was removed but his knee caused Andrew considerable problems in later life. He duly enrolled at Edinburgh University in 1955 and continued his sporting activities by joining the sailing club but switched to climbing, joining the EUMC in 1957.

It was propitious that in the late '50s and early '60s Edinburgh experienced a tremendous flowering of mountaineering activity, with the covert leadership of Jimmy Marshall and the legendary Robin Smith, the latter another new entrant to the EUMC. Robin soon recognised Andrew's ability, and the pair were kindred spirits becoming climbing partners and revelling in each other's intellect and love of wordplay – Robin nicknaming Andrew as 'Phraser'. At the same time Robin linked up with Dougal Haston and the Currie Boys, with Dougal also joining the EUMC. Other good climbers appeared, including Robin Campbell, Neil McNiven and Arthur Ewing. It has to be noted that the EUMC or 'Yummicks' remained an all-round mountaineering club open to rock-climbers, mountaineers and hillwalkers alike. Andrew and most of the other top men took part in all club meets and activities, while also going on other expeditions to pursue their own interests like exploratory climbing. Andrew's parents' Dormobile was in great demand for forays to Glen Coe, the Ben and beyond.

With the imminent production of a new guide to Glen Coe, Andrew and Robin focused on new routing on The Buachaille, where there was an intense rivalry with Glasgow based climbers. In June 1958, during indifferent weather, Robin and Andrew put up new routes such as July Crack (HVS) on Great Gully Buttress and Dwindle Wall (E1) on Creag na Tulaich, but their focus was very much on a new line on the Creagh Dhu's bastion of Slime Wall. Andrew's account of events on Shibboleth were published in this journal and the EUMC journal and by Hamish MacInnes in various books. In the first period of settled weather the pair put up the first ascent of Shibboleth, The Original Finish. However, they felt that although their finish was a more direct line than that of their initial intention, the original plan to exit to the right was both more challenging and more aesthetically pleasing, therefore they returned the next weekend. On the crux second pitch Andrew spent a long time and a lot of energy in an awkward position struggling to remove a peg, the only one used on the whole route, and when leading the fifth pitch, which he had climbed the week before without a problem, exhaustion from his exertions and seven hours on the cold damp wall set in. As his strength was waning he managed to place a single strand of baby nylon into a crack before peeling off and falling 30 feet; fortunately the nylon held, protecting the belay and saving Robin but not Andrew's leg, which suffered a double leg fracture. Robin escaped by traversing off and gathered a collection of the great and good, or perhaps the great and bad, of Edinburgh and Glasgow climbers. The rescue was possibly even more audacious than the climb, and is said to have influenced Hamish MacInnes to set up the Glencoe Rescue Service, ultimately resulting in Scottish Mountain Rescue. Amongst the seventeen rescuers was Hugh Currie, a Daily Record journalist and the Monday morning headline was 'Seven Inches from Death'. Another of the rescuers was the great John MacLean who teamed up with Robin the following year to complete The True Finish. It is fitting that it was a Glasgow-Edinburgh partnership that completed the climb which had been the stage for a combined east-west rescue.

Andrew returned to climbing and partnered Robin on EUMC meets to the Lake District and North Wales, where he and Robin tackled the great Brown/Whillans classics, yet both were also happy to lead and encourage lesser climbers on easier routes. Andrew was involved in another 'rescue', this time as one of the rescuers when on an EUMC meet to Loch Ossian he used his medical skills to diagnose acute appendicitis in Howard Andrew (joint author of this obituary) and organised the emergency evacuation of the patient to The Bridge of Earn Hospital for emergency surgery. As there were no trains on a Sunday this required club members bearing the stretcher seven miles down the railway line to Rannoch Station where a doctor awaited to take him the rest of the way.

EUMC members were venturing into the Alps in the summer holidays, usually after earning money labouring in pea canning factories in Kent. But enthusiasm for bigger and better things unfortunately had a downside. In 1959 two EUMC members, Jerry Smith and Jim Rourke were killed in the Alps. Jerry Smith died abseiling when descending with Andrew from the Aiguille Noire de Peuterey after a successful ascent of the South Ridge (TD/TD+), leaving Andrew alone and off route on a complex descent without any ropes; he eventually managed to link up with a German party who helped him back to Courmayeur. Neil Macniven was also killed some years later, from a freak rock fall on the Walker Spur. During Andrew's presidency of the EUMC in 1961 a young fresher called David Hall was killed in a fall on a club winter meet in Glen Coe, and Andrew had to arrange recovery of the body and later have a meeting with the grieving parents – a hard time, but worse was to come. Just over six months later, while on honeymoon in Turkey with Bobbie Fraser (née Cocker), Andrew learned of Robin Smith's death in the Russian Pamirs when a ferryman, on learning they were Scottish, showed them a piece from a local newspaper.

One of Andrew's passions was the Levant and this along with the work pressures of a junior doctor and responsibilities of marriage as much as the deaths of friends were factors that moved him away from hard climbing. His trips to the Levant were significant adventures. In 1961 travelling by train to Istanbul and travelling overland through Turkey, Lebanon, Syria, Jordan and Israel; and then in 1962 honeymooning by taking the Orient Express to Istanbul; this was not the glamour showcased by Agatha Christie but crowded carriages packed with a range of characters worthy of The Pilgrim's Progress, and their time in Turkey was not in a hotel resort but camping in their orange canvas tent and exploring antiquity in remoter and wilder parts of Turkey. Leaving Britain, Bobbie could not understand why her rucksack contained all the communal goods such as the tent, stove etc. but Andrew's, though more compact, was even heavier – the reason being that his was full of scholarly guides to the region, many of them were in French and other languages.

In recognition of the standard and range of his mountaineering abilities and achievements Andrew was elected to membership of the SMC in 1962. Andrew never lost his love of the hills, and he still managed to fit in some climbs after he left university, and in later years he had a few forays into rock climbing. A Crowberry Ridge ascent was notable because of a chance meeting with a group of Andrew's students at the top of the route, who watched in awe as Andrew at the final belay brought up not only his twelve-year-old son and ten-year-old daughter but lastly his father, whose shock of white hair was matted with blood from a 'minor' stone-fall injury. There were also trips for easier mountaineering in the Alps and Pyrenees and trekking trips to the Himalayas, but always intermingling architectural tourism in adjacent cities. Andrew's last rock climb was the Cioch Nose with his daughter Sally, in 1995

Andrew and Bobbie had a holiday cottage in Arnisdale which they used as a base from which to explore Knoydart and Kintail. He 'compleated' in 2001 (Munroist number 4052) on Sgùrr a' Mhaoraich, accompanied by large gathering of family and friends, who travelled back to Arnisdale by various routes and means including car, boat and by-foot to a party in the cottage where during a whisky-fuelled evening Andrew demonstrated his EUMC party-piece of doing a handstand on the back of a dining room chair. Andrew took great pleasure in introducing others to the pleasures of mountaineering and many have great memories of days out with Andrew, especially Beinn Sgritheall, and the surrounding hills. His last years were marred by knee problems, prostate cancer and Parkinson's disease, but he continued to push himself to enjoy his deep love of the mountains. The final example of Andrew sharing his infectious enthusiasm for mountains was in 2019 when he was able to facilitate his carer's first Munro, joining a family trip up Beinn Sgritheall. He sat patiently despite being in some discomfort waiting their return, but what mattered to him was not only that his carer completed her first Munro but that she was enthused and inspired to do more.

Andrew graduated MB ChB in 1962, becoming a senior lecturer in Medical Microbiology at Edinburgh University and NHS consultant but throughout his life Andrew had many other fields of interest – which inspired a remarkable rare book collection. In addition to studying bacteriology, his well-informed enthusiasms included the Levant, architectural history and conservation, including that of Edinburgh and especially the University, which resulted in dedicated work over many years for the Architectural Heritage Society of Scotland and the Old Edinburgh Club. In 1989 he published the definitive history of The Building of Old College of the University of Edinburgh. His many other interests included collecting Art Nouveau artefacts, a gift for languages, and a particular love for Italy and its architecture.

To sum up his character – Andrew was self-effacing but quietly confident. He would speak with authority and passion on subjects on which he was knowledgeable but was nevertheless unassuming and approachable in conversation. He had measured, thoughtful and informed views on a whole range of matters yet was also mischievously funny and (allegedly) never swore, not a characteristic of most climbers!

Andrew is survived by his wife Bobbie, son Simon, daughters Sally and Vicky and seven grandchildren. Due to the Covid-19 lockdown the funeral was family only, so friends were asked to light a candle and 'partake of a dram' in his memory. The family hope to hold a celebration later. In the many cards sent to Bobbie several people mentioned 'a twinkle in Andrew's eye'. Let us remember him that way.

Mick Park and Howard Andrew

GRAHAM KING j. 1961

TRAUMATIC AND EXCEPTIONAL EXPERIENCES shape every life. Aged six, Graham's father was lost at sea. An event that led to a strong bond developing with wider family at Taynuilt in the 1940s, where his relationship with the Scottish Highlands grew and helped form the foundation of the rest of his life. As a teenager, his much older cousin drew a pencil line on the map to depict the route to the summit of Ben Cruachan. A remarkable summer's day to the summit followed by a brief swim in the glen burn, which Loch Cruachan now covers, was a key milestone. Graham kept this map for his life and it is beside me as I type. None of his family were mountaineers, however Graham had caught the 'bug' and pursued it. Another lifelong keep was his diary from mountaineering training at Glen More Lodge when he was a senior school pupil. His week or so there, referred to from time to time, clearly made a positive and lasting impression as well as giving him skills from those in the know. Reference to early rises, runs and cold showers before breakfast, followed by a full day's learning on subjects such as navigation, mountain craft and rope work abound.

Soon after Glen More, during the winter of his last year at school, he was involved in a mountain rescue while staying at Loch Ossian Youth Hostel. This

clearly had a significant impact on him, having just turned seventeen, but was not mentioned much until a few months before his death. The trauma of having to help carry one of four bodies off the hill perhaps helped to shape his careful approach to all mountaineering pursuits, nevertheless he did not shy from adventure. In amongst all his formative years he developed a quiet and strong Christian faith. He enjoyed Creation on land and sea. In his lifetime he forgave and saw the futility of the war that taken his father. A good friend, Graham Park picks up the story:

'Graham and I knew each other from when we were sat together at Primary School aged five, and we both attended Glasgow High School, but we were in different classes there and only really became friends on his return from the Outdoor Course at Glenmore Lodge. I was recruited into his small band of climbing friends from the Glenmore Club but many of our early trips were just by ourselves. We would walk into town and take the train to the Trossachs or cycle from home. Numerous cycle expeditions were made with our tent and camping gear on our bikes. Once he wanted to visit his uncle in Taynuilt, so we cycled up there, stayed the night, and cycled back the following day. On another occasion, I was to spend a family holiday at (I think) Cullen on the Buchan coast, so Graham cycled up there with me and cycled back the following day – just for the ride, he said. He did the same in reverse at the end of the holiday!

'Graham was immensely strong. He always insisted on carrying the climbing rope (much heavier in these days) and would take quantities of tinned food on these trips – especially tinned stew – his favourite. He never worried about the weight – I once put a large boulder in his rucksack on the way up a steep slope to see if he noticed the difference, but he didn't!

'Our climbing trips continued when I went to Glasgow University and lasted until I left for England in 1960. One of our most memorable excursions was at Easter 1954. My climbing diary gives a flavour of these early excursions using public transport. I note that I got up at 2 a.m. on a Thursday, caught a bus into town at 3 a.m., met Pat (one of our regular companions) at the station, took the Aberdeen train to Perth, changed there for the Inverness train, then changed again to the Kyle of Lochalsh train at Inverness, and alighted at Achnasheen where we met Graham. We then took the postbus to Torridon, stopping at Kinlochewe for 'provisions'. The three of us camped in Coire Mhic Nobuil and the following day climbed Beinn Alligin. On Saturday it was blowing a gale and our tent was damaged, so we booked in at Alligin Youth hostel while Pat repaired the tent. On the Sunday we climbed Liathach along 'a very interesting ridge reminiscent of Aonach Eagach' and I note 'a tricky descent' in 'a gale-force blizzard of frozen snow'! On the Monday, we missed the bus so walked to Annat, got some more food and walked back to the Youth Hostel. On the Tuesday we caught the bus to Kinlochewe where we camped and climbed Slioch. The following day Graham and I climbed Beinn Eighe by walking round to Coire Ruadh Staca and climbing a gully to the summit. On Thursday we set off to return home, but the bus did not appear so we started to walk towards Achnasheen! We eventually got a lift to the station and returned home. Graham would plan all these trips – the rest of us just followed his lead!

'By 1955, I had passed my driving test, and we decided things would be much easier by car, so we pooled our resources and bought an old pre-war Hillman for the sum of £38. Graham performed some engineering magic on the engine and made new mudguards (remember mudguards?) to replace the old rusted ones. They would have looked more suitable on a steam locomotive but served the purpose.

'Graham had a prodigious memory – he had filed away in his head the names of all the boys in his class at school, and also the teachers, of course, and could remember the words of the songs in the school musical that we had taken part in – we would to sing them on the way down from a climb. Until the last few years, he remembered the dates of all the expeditions we had shared and would regale me with amusing details which I had completely forgotten about!'

Mountaineering adventures continued in his twenties and thirties, in 1965 he married Heather who was an active member of the LSCC. A year later he completed his Munros and is recorded as number 70 by the SMC. While he went on to complete two more rounds and then the Corbetts in 2009, he baulked at the expression 'bagger'. His life reflected his love of being in wild places, whether walking the west coast of Lewis to Harris, climbing in Norway, visiting North America, sailing in Hebridean waters, or taking friends on the Cuillin. Alongside these was a strong affection for Mechanical Engineering and Steam Locomotives. In 1963 he was part of a team who purchased Caledonian Railway 828 and to his death he was involved with storage at Glasgow Transport Museum and then, in the early 1990s, restoration and running at Strathspey Railway.

Graham King locomotive enthusiast on the right.

Many stories abound: Graham on the Basteir Tooth in mist and wind almost being taken out by a high speed large bird; singing Psalms whilst battling with a climbing boot losing its sole during a 'fresh air' ascent on the Cuillin; turning up at Sourlies late after a day out only to find the food was in the car; using greaseproof paper to trace a rough map from the OS map glued to the club hut wall when the party had planned a day and discovered there was no map.

Perhaps like us all, stories of mishaps stand out. While not remarkable in terms of wild climbing exploits, they do indicate something of Graham. A group of friends on the Mamores enjoying debate and blethers as much as the view realised they had descended the wrong side. This necessitated a taxi from Kinlochleven to Glen Nevis. Graham, a tall chap, was in the front. The taxi driver let slip he was a retired steam locomotive driver. Deep, technical conversation followed. As did a puncture, rusty wheel nuts, Graham's mechanical engineering muscle and then more railway anecdotes. On arrival at the top of Glen Nevis the taxi driver had 'inadvertently' switched off the fare meter.

Nine years ago, Graham was staying with family in the North. An ascent of Fionn Bheinn, Achnasheen, was planned. Graham turned up at breakfast in waterproof trousers. No comment was made at this hitherto unknown practice; however, he clearly felt a need to explain to his daughter-in-law and let slip that he had left his climbing trousers at home. 'Not to worry' he said, as pyjama trousers with waterproof ones on top would be grand. And grand they were, when a few hours later he was at the summit fondly remembering alighting from the train and catching, with his friend Graham Park, the Torridon postbus driven by Alec. While he enjoyed days out for a few more years, this was to be his last Munro summit.

Heather pre-deceased him in 2018. He leaves two sons, both who thought it normal to be brought up visiting club huts for outdoor adventures through all seasons of the year and inevitably went on to catch the 'bug' themselves...

Iain and Alan King and Graham Park

W. ALLAN McNICOL j. 1985

ALLAN McNICOL WAS BORN in Glasgow in 1928. His father John McNicol owned a successful electrical engineering business which he had established in Anderston at the end of the First World War, specialising in the installation and repair of electric motors and generators. The family home was in Jordanhill and Allan attended Glasgow Academy before going on to study electrical engineering at what was then the Royal College of Science and Technology, now Strathclyde University. He graduated with Honours in 1950 and after serving an apprenticeship in his father's firm he joined the Merchant Navy as a junior engineering officer, which gave him his first taste of foreign travel, visiting far-off lands from America to Japan. His interest in boats and in the great outdoors had been kindled during his boyhood when he was in the Scouts and would go off with them to crew in sailing boats on Loch Lomond. In due course he became a fully competent sailor, chartering boats for voyages in the Baltic, the Mediterranean and the Atlantic.

After two years in the Merchant Navy Allan returned to join his older brother, Ian, in their father's firm. He joined the JMCS and escaped to the hills regularly, walking and climbing with his brother and various members of the SMC. Ben Nevis was a favourite destination and in 1951 Ian and Allan were with Tom Weir on the first ascent of Continuation Wall on Raeburn's Buttress. There is a well-known photograph taken around that period showing the interior of the CIC Hut, with Allan sitting in front of the old stove and Graham Macphee in the background surrounded by an array of drying clothes, obviously after a good day on the hill. His main activity though was ski-mountaineering which he pursued sometimes but not always with a guide, making numerous trips to the Alps and elsewhere. In 1977 he traversed the High Level Route from Argentiere to Zermatt in the

Allan seated in the CIC, Graham Macphee behind.

company of several SMC members, a demanding trip in less than ideal conditions (see *SMCJ* 1978, p. 315).

In 1956 Allan married Dr Evelyn Camrass, a past president of Glasgow University Mountaineering Club who had recently returned from the successful first all-female expedition to the Himalaya. In due course their son Martin and two daughters Sula and Erica arrived and were introduced to the hills, all of them becoming proficient skiers. During their long marriage Allan and Evelyn led an extraordinarily adventurous life, travelling the world together with further ski trips to the Alps, exploring Greenland, trekking in the Himalaya, dog-sledding in Spitzbergen, Kamchatka and Hudson's Bay and of course sailing. They were both on the classic steam yacht Carola during the famous SMC Centenary Yachting Meet of 1997. Shortly after that they moved to Fintry and they also acquired a cottage in Glen Feshie where they hosted a wonderful barbecue every summer for almost thirty years, a great annual gathering of their many friends. They also joined the Loch Morlich Sailing Club.

Allan joined the SMC in 1985 and gave service to the Club as Convener of the Western District for more than ten years. His brother Ian had joined in 1954 and he died in 2017. Both their sons followed them into the family business which is now into its second century and still going strong in Anderston.

In 2016 Allan and Evelyn moved to Inverness and were welcome additions to our Northern District group as well as keeping up with the LSCC of which Evelyn has long been a prominent member. Allan was delightful company and even as his health deteriorated, he was always interested in other people and what they were up to on the hills. I wish I had known him longer. He died on 3rd December 2019 in his ninety-second year. He will be greatly missed, especially by Evelyn and their children and grandchildren to all of whom we extend our condolences.

Peter F. Macdonald

MARTIN MORAN j. 1988

ON 26 MAY 2019 we lost my father, Martin Moran, in a Himalayan accident alongside seven other climbers. They were ascending a new summit in the Nanda Devi range, Garhwal Himalaya. My father is well known for his work as a mountain guide as well as being a pioneering climber at home in his local Scottish mountains, as well as Norway the Himalayas. First ascents in remote areas were his lifeblood and he often took clients with him to share the adventure, stand upon virgin peaks or ascend new ice lines in the Norwegian Fjords.

Born in North Shields in 1955, my dad soon found the mountains with his parents, walking in Northumberland, the Peak and the Lakes on family holidays. From a young age with the venture scouts, he was always looking for adventure in the hills; the mountains quickly became his passion and obsession. As a boy he became captivated by maps and would collect them, spending his evenings reading them by torchlight under the covers. As he himself admitted 'I was lost to mountaineering at a very early age'.

My Dad married my Mum, Joy, in 1976 and their shared love for the outdoors continued throughout their marriage. After graduating from Cambridge University in 1977 with a degree in Geography, Dad qualified as a Chartered Accountant in 1980 and began a short-lived, office-based, career. In 1984 the pull of the mountains became too strong and they soon sold their house and belongings to dive into the unknown in a campervan bound for Scotland.

My father first gained notoriety with his continuous round of the Munros in winter. Endlessly supported by Mum, who accompanied him on many of the Munros, he completed the round in 83 days. This record, followed by his qualification as a British Mountain Guide in 1985, allowed the couple to launch a guiding business in the wilds of the North West Highlands. Settling in Lochcarron gave my parent's clients unfettered access to beautiful mountains and a more adventurous style of course, a theme which would continue throughout Dad's guiding life. The Moran Mountain courses soon gained many lifelong fans who returned time and again to be guided by Dad and experience the home comforts provided at base camp by Mum. As a guide Martin would receive a huge amount of pleasure and stories from days out with his clients and it is clear that the feeling was mutual. Dad's dry sense of humour would shine through as he recounted tales of the clients over dinner. His fondness for his students was always clear.

Dave Sharpe (BMG) Writes of days guiding for Moran Mountain:
There were very few 'easy' days working for Moran Mountain in Scotland. The

area is wild and generally quite inaccessible necessitating big walk-ins off the back of early starts and late finishes. This did however mean it was rare to see many (if any) other folk on the hills and we often had the crags to ourselves. Miles and miles of Torridonian monoliths, as far as the sea.

Martin saw these points as key to his business model, ever keen to get away from the crowds and an easy sell to clients looking for something special. Martin built and demanded something extra from both his Guides and clients and was never happier than when groups came back off the hill having had to put in a 'little extra' (often a few savage extra hours descending safely off the hill in appalling weather). His eyes would light up at such information: mission, achieved!

He would only ever give you just enough information (never all the pieces of the jigsaw), to go off and have a total adventure. Information is key and Martin was always keen to keep the uncertain element of any outdoor forays. This was Martin's nature through and through, always looking to give folks the 'full' experience and nothing less. If you just wanted to 'tick' the box, this was not the course or the place for you…

In 1986 and 1990 respectively, I and Hazel were added to the family and promptly taken around Europe as Mum and Dad ran their guiding business from the Alps and further afield. Every summer would be spent on a campsite crowded with climbers and their families while Dad took clients to even greater heights. I remember as a child the buzz of the chalet life in the Alps. Guides and clients coming and going with tales of dawn views from jagged peaks, multiple pitches of clean granite and sleepless nights spent in bivouac huts. All of these adventures played out from our valley base amongst the alpine flowers to the jangle of cowbells under brilliant blue skies. Looking back now it was a very special place for both clients and guides alike; a hub of activity for all things mountaineering with an atmosphere of endless enthusiasm which my father always brought to any mountain experience.

Andy Perkins writes of his time guiding with Martin in the Alps:
In the late '90s when I was approaching the alpine section of the British Mountain Guides' training scheme, the given wisdom to accumulating those precious "quality mountain days" for one's logbook was simple and short: go work for Martin. Asking around, it seemed as though everyone had been to Evolène at some stage in their career. I hardly knew where Evolène was (having misspent much of my alpine youth in Chamonix), and all I knew of Martin was that he'd written a book about Scottish winter mountaineering and had done all the alpine 4000'ers.
    So it was with some curiosity that I rocked up to the chalet in Evolène in July 2000 for my first alpine work. The fact that I worked for him almost every summer since and have continued to do so with Graham and Janine Frost, who bought the alpine part of his successful business a few years ago, speaks for itself. Guiding for Martin Moran is the kind of work I enjoy.
    Rather than necessarily being strapped to the 4000m list, technical terrain was sought after. If you returned to the chalet with tales of it being a little bit more difficult than anticipated, or perhaps a few hours longer, Martin was plainly delighted. His enthusiasm for the Valais and the Oberland, wilder than nearby Chamonix, was clear. If you came up with a cunning plan for something off the beaten track, his eyes would light up, and then he'd make a couple of suggestions or give you some beta, having clearly been there a few years ago. One of my finest achievements in guiding was to return from Besso in the Val d'Anniviers and hear him say "I must get there some time". What? I've climbed something Martin hasn't done in the Valais?" BOOM – as the young people say these days.
    He was a wise, kind and gentle man with phenomenal enthusiasm and drive. He was always a delight to spend time with, whether on the hill, in the hut or in the chalet. He had a profound influence on my life as a mountain guide, and I will miss him greatly.
    Whilst introducing the joys of the hills to people was a large part of his life, Dad found his true creative outlet through personal challenges and first ascents. A keen runner in his early days, he set a new Cullin Ridge record in 1990 with a time of 3 hours and 33 minutes. In 1992, with Simon Jenkins, he embarked on a continuous, self propelled "round" of the 4000m alpine peaks. They completed the 75 peaks in 53 days. In recent years, Dad was still overcoming serious mountaineering challenges with his 2016 solo traverse of the Cullin in winter alongside an unplanned bivouac in the valley below. He spoke to me of this with the glint of adventure in his eye which never left him throughout his life.
    I strode into the blackened glen, dreaming I would see an array of parked cars at the hut, but alas, apart from the green glow of the fire safety light, the place bore no sign of life. I was too worn mentally to particularly care. The entrance offered a porch to keep me out of the wind and a bench seat provided a semblance of insulation. I loosened my boots, put on my down jacket, and stretched out in triumph. I had actually done it! (SMCJ, 2016, p. 132)
    Alongside his guiding and personal climbing, Dad was an eloquent writer and avid diary keeper. His Munros in Winter and Scotland's Winter Mountains titles have encouraged countless people to get out into our wilderness areas and

challenge themselves. His additions to the climbing and guide book catalogues of mountaineers around the world will be a lasting legacy of inspiration. You only really die when your name fades from memory, and as long as there are mountaineers striving to push themselves amongst the mountains of Scotland, the Alps, Norway and the Himalaya, Dad will be there through his inspiring contributions to these ranges. In his own words: Mountain climbing, in its finest guise, is a triumph of human spirit over the shackles of convention.

The mountains were where Dad and I had our closest moments. Climbing with Dad gave me my most terrifying but rewarding climbing days out. He could be an uncompromising climbing partner at times but always encouraged me to realise my potential. Some of my fondest memories are of our last Himalayan expedition to Satopanth in the Gangotri Valley. The expedition was difficult and excessive snowfall forced us down from the peak before the summit. Despite all of this we were a strong team and relished the opportunity for adventure together. Even after a month spent at 5000m in a Vango Force Ten tent, there were only shared jokes and mutual support for each other.

Technically, Dad was a strong climber and it was in his winter climbing that he found the apex of his ability. Like the painter of a canvas, he had an eye for a strong line and added many, now classic, climbs to the imposing cliffs in the North West. In 1993, he climbed Blood, Sweat and Frozen Tears (VIII, 8) on Beinn Eighe. Never one to miss out on a first ascent, his partner on this, and many of his early winter forays, was Andy Nisbet. Blood, Sweat and Frozen Tears is now a sought after test piece for those wanting to break into the 8s.

His most notable addition to the unrelenting steepness of the Beinn Bhan cliffs was The Godfather (VIII, 8). Climbed in 2002 with leashed, straight shaft tools and a near benightment on the final pitches it saw him and Paul Tattersall adding a four star classic to this seldom travelled area. As Dad entered the period of life in which many slow down, his technical climbing only increased in pace; he knew his time for operating at the highest level was running out.

Enlisting, among others, Robin Thomas, Pete Macpherson and Murdoch Jamieson's unending enthusiasm, he added several cutting edge lines to remote mountains such as An Teallach at the grades of IX and X. Wailing Wall (IX, 9) is a notable example; hard and tenuous climbing in the remote amphitheatre of An Teallach.

Robin Thomas sums up his nature well in this passage:
There are numerous incidents and anecdotes that stand out from the various climbs and days of work we did together that illustrate to me the nature of the man I knew. There was the route we climbed one winter on Beinn Eighe, Martin was on the last of ten days 'sponsored famine' (living on £1 a day in aid of the Haiti earthquake victims). He carried out the whole climb including leading a very steep and difficult pitch completely on-sight on no more than a handful of peanuts. Late in the day (probably around 10pm) whilst climbing on the last pitch by head torch light Martin fell and swung wildly across the wall, after half an hour of fiddling with the ropes he was able to join me on the ledge. He never once mentioned the horrific fall. Later on still, after making a rapid descent of the mountain by bum slide it became apparent that one of Martin's ice axes was missing, he declined my offer of food (even though the midnight official end of his famine was now long since passed) and proceeded to climb the 500 vertical metres back to the top to find his axe. All this from a man well into his fifties and just before starting work with a new group of clients a few hours later.

Whilst the Scottish hills were where Dad made his home, a piece of his heart always lay in the great Himalayan mountains. An avid proponent of the path less travelled, he encouraged exploration away from the honeypots of the high peaks which draw so many. Writing in an article entitled The Joys of the Unknown Dad writes:

Ever since the first ascents of the highest peaks of the world, the mainstream media has presumed that there is nothing worthwhile left to explore in the Himalaya. How wrong they are! ...Mountaineering in the Himalaya has been an active sport for 125 years, yet many peaks of lower altitude are still unclimbed. Leading expeditions to the Himalaya over the last 35 years, often twice in a year, he has ascended many untouched summits, often in the company of clients. Whilst he would remain humble about these achievements, they read as an impressive list of Himalayan exploration in line with his early heroes such as Eric Shipton.

Martin Welch writes:
Towards the end of one expedition Martin was excited at the prospect of traversing over an unclimbed col into another valley where he thought he knew where it might go, so he persuaded another team member to join him and off they went with the agreement to meet him at some obscure roadhead in 3 days time, allowing us the chance to head back down the valley and climb the mythical path of 10,000 steps,hewn into the rock walls and disappearing up into the mists and to who knew where. Three days later we all met up again with great tales of excitement and adventure. He was the magician who simply provided the ingredients for the magic to happen.

Highlights in India included the first ascents of the West Ridge on Bagarathi 1, 1983, the South Face of Nanda Kot, 6,861m in 1995 and the West Ridge of Nilkanth, 6,596m in 2000, along with many other pioneering ascents. Still going strong in 2015, Dad and his long term climbing partner Ian Dring made another first ascent.

Ian Dring writes:
Out of the blue in 2015 Martin emailed asking if I would like to join him on an expedition to the Miyar Valley in India the following year. We organised a trip to Hoy where we climbed the Old Man and routes on Rora Head including the classic Roring Forties – it wasn't said but I was clearly being checked out. It was a great few days, Martin was excellent company, the passion for climbing and adventure was still fiercely present. The box ticked that I could still climb, we firmed up our objective –the stupendous looking north spur of an unnamed and unclimbed 5,755m peak located at the junction of the Miyar and Jangpar Glaciers, an ambitious objective for a team with a combined age of over 140 years. We gave the route an ED1 grade and named the mountain Marikula Killa – the citadel of the goddess Marikula, a local ancient devi who keeps a maternal watch over the inhabitants of the valleys of Lahaul.

My Dad's last expedition was also to break new ground with a group of keen clients. They were ascending a still unnamed peak 6477m in the Nanda Devi region. Right up until his last breath, he was following his passion and inspiring others to do the same.

Having gone through my father's writings from the last 45 years, I would like to leave you with excerpts from a letter reflecting on his life and motivations, which he wrote in September 1995 at Pindari Base camp, in the valley where he died. The title of this letter was The Back of Beyond:

I marvelled at the play of mist and evening sunlight on the heather-clad hills with all the thrill that I remember as a boy. These, the hills of my wildest dreams thirty years ago, are now the hills of home. I've moved to them, grown to them and am now inseparable from them.

Here I am today, with a business to run and a family of two. The final resolution of tension between a buccaneering adventurous spirit and deep love of Joy, Alex and Hazel is essential to my future happiness and indeed to theirs.

Martin on the summit of Panwali Dwar, Nanda Devi in the background. Photo: Moran Collection.

The time has undoubtedly come to disconnect from the headlong careerism that takes climbers to K2 and Everest (and often leaves them there) and realise that the essence of my love for the mountains can be realised by dreaming of them, looking at them and writing about them.

The hills of home are no less beautiful than when I saw them as a boy. My travels to mountains all over the world have been exhilarating but they have revealed that there is no ultimate fulfilment in ever looking for larger and bigger horizons. By such an attitude, one is rejecting and discarding the horizons which moved the spirit, the outline of the Lakeland hills, the Scottish peaks, the Chamonix Skyline or the Pindari Valley. To achieve oneness with nature that will carry the soul beyond its mortal span one must return to one's roots and there be content. My roots are at home in Achintee, my blood is Alex and Hazel, my love is Joy and my hills of home need my care and attention. The restless spirit must eventually realise where its home lies, and I am in the process of coming home to stay.

It is in the shadow of the mountain goddess Nanda Devi where his remains now lie in the ever-shifting snows of the Himalaya. A poignant resting place for a man who gave so much of himself to the mountains and the community which finds solace within them.

Alex Moran

Jonathan Preston writes: as a friend, climbing partner and colleague I'd like to pay tribute. Martin meant many things to many different people from all walks of life. First and foremost he was a devoted family man and my heart goes out to Joy, Alex and Hazel: his nearest and dearest.

I knew Martin initially as a colleague, a fellow member of the British Mountain Guides. We first worked together in 1995 in Switzerland and India, and then over a prolonged period of over twenty years in Scotland and Norway as well. He soon became more than just a work mate as we climbed together all over the Highlands in summer and winter. His motivation, geographical knowledge, technical ability, meticulous planning and organisational skills were legendary. I found him totally inspiring and whatever we were doing and whatever the weather we always had a good time.

His contribution to the development, nurturing and mentoring of young British Mountain Guides cannot be underestimated. He took fresh faced climbers under his wing and gave them the opportunity to work alongside him in Scotland and the Alps. Not one or two but countless generations of Trainee and Aspirant Guides owe him a great debt for allowing them to practise their skills and learn their trade here in the NW Highlands and in the mountains of the Swiss Valais.Many of today's talented Guides living and working full time in the Alps started out working in Lochcarron and Evolène.I certainly learnt a lot from Martin and relished the chance to climb classic routes with him and his clients both at home and abroad, as well as exploring more esoteric quarters of the globe.

Martin was a real pioneer. He had a great skill for mapping out new challenges. He had a good eye for a line on a crag or a remote peak. His legacy of fine first ascents in Scotland, Norway and India bear testament to this.

I find it extremely poignant that to this day his body and spirit reside in an area that he loved and to which he was drawn back time and time again – the peaks along and around the Nanda Devi sanctuary.

Now we mourn his passing, but everyone who knew him can be thankful and grateful for having spent time with such an incredible character, one whose like we shall not see again; Martin was truly special…

ANNE B MURRAY

ANNE MURRAY died in a care home in Elderslie in April. She was of course known to SMC members as Bill Murray's wife, but Anne was a considerable mountaineer, poet, and passionate defender of Scotland's mountain landscapes in her own right. Originally from Glasgow, she trained as a physiotherapist and worked in Dundee in the early 1950s, when she went out with both the Carn Dearg and the Grampian Clubs. She used to reminisce that the Deargs regarded the Grampian Club as a bunch of softies, who took travelling rugs for comfort on the Club bus.

Anne was no kind of softie. She joined the LSCC in 1954 and in 1956 traversed

Anne Murray belaying in Glen Coe.

the Cuillin Ridge en cordée féminine with Anne Littlejohn and Betty Stark. She was a loyal and very active member of the Ladies' Club, becoming President in 1986-88. Members recall her with affection as a strong mountaineer and an encouraging companion on the hill, with a notably sharp wit, on occasion employed to devastating effect against unwarily condescending male climbers.

Anne shared Bill's concern for Scottish mountain landscape, and expressed that sensitivity very effectively in her poetry. I cannot recall anyone so fiercely and vocally passionate in that regard. When I was Chair of the old Scottish Countryside Activities Council I would tremble when the LSCC trio of Rhona Weir, Irene Addie and Anne appeared together at our general meetings, to make it plain that SCAC was being far too mealy-mouthed in our response to the latest outrage being perpetrated against our mountains, and to add steel to our resolve.

Bill and Anne met in the hills, and married in 1960. Their honeymoon, an extended camping tour of the Highlands in mostly dire weather while Bill undertook the survey work for Highland Landscape, was to typify their close-matched partnership in life, letters, and mountains. It was in the nature of Bill's work that while composing his books he undertook a good deal of ghost-writing, editing and reviewing to help keep the wolf from the door. Anne, with her own highly evolved feeling for words and their use – "I love dictionaries" she told me once – had developed such an intimate awareness of Bill's style and language that he trusted her not only to draft material for him, but even, when he was hard pressed, to write it herself under his name.

Being married to Bill for 35 years, Anne enjoyed the wife's prerogative of not always treating W.H.Murray with the unadulterated admiration that most outsiders conferred on him. But she was a veritable tigress in protection of Bill's writings and his reputation. When, after his death, she undertook the painstaking and heart-wrenching work of editing his incomplete autobiographical text into The Evidence of Things Not Seen, I found myself in the invidious position of go-between in a sustained struggle over content, style, and presentation with Anne on one side and Ken Wilson for Bâton Wicks on the other. Each of these redoubtable characters independently confessed to me in the course of interminable phone discussions that they'd never dealt with such a difficult person as the other. That was Anne: a formidable force, not always comfortable, but utterly engaged with mountains. An unforgettable personality.

Robert Aitken

REG PILLINGER j. 1972

REG PILLINGER died in August last year at the age of 88. Reg was a lifelong enthusiast for climbing and for mountain country, from pioneering hard climbs on grit, at Lawrencefield and Millstone Edge in the Eastern Peak in the 1950s and early 1960s, to compleating his Munros in 2002 in a goodly company of friends on Schiehallion, before going on to add the Furths in 2007. The years between included several alpine seasons in the late '50s and '60s, and a spell in Kenya in the later 1960s when he made multiple ascents of the main tops of Mt Kenya and their satellites, with Ian 'Pin' Howell among others.

Reg had climbed in Scotland in summer and winter from the 1950s on, but he joined the Club during a period when he worked in Glasgow and lived in Bearsden, at one point just down the road from Donald and Anne Bennet. A man of endless good humour and social warmth, at different times Reg climbed with a quality selection of SMC members, including Donald, Morton Shaw, Ken Crocket, and Colin Stead. It was Colin who proposed Reg for membership. He recalls a typical Reg occasion when, driving to Craig-y-Barns through the Sma' Glen, they collided with a pheasant, which was not killed but took off up the hill above with Reg and Colin in hot pursuit. It duly made it safely to the pot.

Reg's main rope-mate at that time and afterwards was his fellow Climbers' Club member Ted Maden. In his spell of ardent activity north of the Border his climbs ranged from Arran and Ardverikie to Carnmore, but he also indulged his tireless capacity for huge long-distance walks, stravaiging across much of the country in pursuit of Munros.

Reg's stay in Scotland was relatively short: by 1979 his work as a University technologist and a company director in the paper and packaging industry had taken him back south to Quorn in Leicestershire. From there he retired in 2000 to Stratford-upon-Avon, but maintained his SMC membership and his contagious enthusiasm for Scottish mountains and wild country, despite being sadly housebound over the past two years. Following his death a memorial appeal was set up for donations to the John Muir Trust, specifically in respect of Schiehallion. Everybody who knew and climbed with Reg recalls him as a man of infinite good cheer and good companionship.

Robert Aitken

PROCEEDINGS OF THE CLUB

At the committee meeting in October 2019 the following were admitted to the Club. We warmly welcome:

ANDREW APPLEBY (29)
RORY BROWN (28)
WILLIAM BURNSIDE (53)
WILLIAM HASTIE (27)
ANDREAS HEINZL (48)
ALASTAIR ROSE (38)
JOE TROTTET (29)

And at the April 2020 meeting:

TOM BELL (42)
STEVE HOLMES (38)
ZÖE STRONG (37)
FINLAY WILD (35)

The One-Hundred-and-Thirty-First AGM and Dinner

30 November 2018

A return visit to The Carrbridge Hotel seemed very popular. The AGM was well attended and the Dinner almost the busiest I've known.

The first attraction to the weekend was the afternoon talk given by Robert Durran on the climbing opportunities in Wadi Rum, Jordan. Robert explained that this was a venue for all standards of rock climbing and was truly an adventurous venue where competent climbing was a necessity, even if not at the highest standard. Certainly, the descents from some of the summits looked like they took a certain amount of route finding skill. To follow up on the talk Robert had already arranged a club meet in Spring 2020. (Alas, one of many events to fall foul of Covid-19. Ed.)

The 2019 AGM followed a short while later. As in previous years, the office bearers are able to send out a lot of information by email in advance of the AGM. This means much of the discussion is responding to that information and there may be a few extra points of information added by the Office Bearer. The secretary explained that the Members' handbook (which gives member addresses and contact details) should not fall foul of General Data Protection Regulations as it is deemed to be for a legitimate club purpose and useful to members. The club website is being updated although a concern was raised that older, invaluable historical information was no longer available. All agreed this should not be lost and would be reinstated. The club congratulated Brian Shackleton on his appointment as the new President of Mountaineering Scotland. Our Convenor of the Huts Sub-Committee informed the club that actions were continuing to permit the club to purchase land for a new highland hut. However there are some issues with Crofting Restrictions that still need to be resolved before a purchase could be completed.

An innovation with reciprocal rights for huts was announced such that during one weekend in 2020, the SMC will have sole access to the Cairngorm Hut at Muir of Inverey and the Cairngorm Club would get sole use of the CIC hut. The Meets secretary said he thought that more hut exchanges could be arranged with other clubs.

The final significant action for the AGM was to vote on changes to the length of time in office for the senior committee positions. As explained to the club, it seemed desirable to ensure committee positions were for shorter defined periods which meant that there could be a steady change-over of members in positions and should mean more people are involved with the running of the club. The proposal from the committee was passed. With this vote over the AGM finished and we moved to the bar ready for the Dinner.

During his address to the Club, the President, John Fowler, listed some truly outstanding climbs by current members in Scotland and abroad, but also recorded the club's shock at the loss of three of the most active members, namely Andy Nisbet, Steve Perry and Martin Moran during 2019. Our guest speaker was an inspired choice. Murdo MacLeod is a photo-journalist who comes from the Isle of Lewis. Murdo most elegantly intertwined his climbing experience, his upbringing in Lewis, his knowledge of the striking overhanging cliffs of Sròn Uladail and added the possibility that he surely must be related to another MacLeod of the Dave variety.

With bright and dry weather predicted for Sunday, the President's walk had many takers. The chosen route was a walk up Creag Dubh near Newtonmore. Many photos were taken on the top as we relaxed and continued the social aspect of the Dinner weekend. Then much to our surprise a young eagle flew in to see what it was that had attracted over 20 folk to the summit. It actual flew in from below the summit so we had no warning of its appearance. It hovered so low that you felt you could almost touch the talons. Its arrival took us all by surprise and hardly any of us took a photo.

Chris Huntley

Photo: Noel Williams

*...apart from
the eagle-eyed President!*

Photo: John Fowler.

MEETS

Lakes Meet, Robertson Lamb Hut, Langdale
6 –7 September 2019

A full turn out in late summer sunshine made for a splendid meet. Indeed, it was so warm on the Saturday that the sluice was closed on the beck at the side of the hut. It is a splendid contraption, looking like a converted printing press, with oak sluice gates across a narrowing in the stream. It is a vernacular construction in laid slate blocks, bigger than a bath, smaller than a swimming pool, but nonetheless a refreshing, pre-prandial tonic. Not everyone succumbed. Note – if attending Lakes Meets in future bring swimming togs. The Hut has also had a recent upgrade done and meant comfort for all. Some early arrivers had done routes on nearby crags such as Black Crag above Wrynose Pass. It is worth getting there early for a Friday's cragging if the weather forecast is good.

Saturday saw folk keen to get out and go beyond the immediate confines of the valley. Several parties headed up to Gimmer. Tom Prentice and Geoff Cohen did Crow's Nest Direct while Duncan Reid and Alix Hery did Kipling Groove. Trying to translate the pun in the latter route name, to a French climber probably proved to be the most difficult part. I forgot to ask Duncan Reid whether the peg I had clipped forty years ago was still there. Brian Shackleton and Helen Brown also went up to Gimmer and enjoyed the route-finding conundrums of 'C' Route before electing to finish with the rather more direct 'D' Route.

Back standing row: Stuart Murdoch, Dave Broadhead, Geoff Cohen; Fraser Reid (guest).
Front standing row: Tom Prentice; Brian Shackleton, Simon Fraser, Chris Ravey, Kenny Robb.
Back seated row: Bob Reid, Jayne Murdoch, Lisa Hutchinson, Fay Brown (guest), Helen Brown (guest), John Fowler.
Front seated row: Duncan Reid (guest) Alix Hery (guest).
Photo: John Fowler Collection.

Quite a few members indulged in a nostalgic visit to Middle Scout Crag recalling first trips made half a century ago. It is a bit of a wee gem – an unassuming, rounded dome of really clean rock amidst the tumble of Whyte Ghyll's lower slopes. Just about all the routes on the crag were climbed by various parties, including the President, over the weekend.

The descent from Raven Crag proved to be something of a trial for various parties on the Sunday. After completing routes, the usual scramble down the east of the crag was shut due to rock fall risk. The easy alternative to just keeping climbing up and up till it was possible to descend the gully bounding the west of Middlefell Buttress was 'interesting' to say the least. Several teams headed up Whyte Ghyll and Pavey Arc as well. Team Reid/Hery climbed the bold Forget Me Not, E1 5b, just right of the upper slab routes.

On Sunday Alison Coull and Tricia Gill did Poker Face E1 on Pavey Ark. Just after Alison and Tricia left the hut Geoff Cohen asked Kenny 'does Alison know the first pitch doesn't exist now'. Luckily, after a lot of looking and trying to make things fit the guidebook, Alison and Tricia decided there was nothing that looked climbable. The alternative start is p.1 of Golden Slipper. Tricia got the excellent crux pitch. Alison wisely diverted onto the final pitch of Golden Slipper on p.3. UKC makes interesting reading on that one and the guidebook says this is the original and more 'pleasant' way.

Geoff Cohen on the crux of Crow's Nest Direct (HVS), Gimmer. Photo Tom Prentice.

As usual, plenty of Wainwrights and Marilyns were also ascended. A splendid hut curry was also enjoyed by all on the Saturday night – and the meet organiser would like to record his thanks to all those who helped.

Route List:
Tom Prentice & Geoff Cohen – D Route (S), Crow's Nest Direct (HVS).
Bob Reid & Fraser Reid – Route 1 & Route 2 on Upper Scout & Evening Wall on Raven Crag.

Duncan Reid & Alix Hery – North West Arete (VS), Kipling Groove (HVS), Forget Me Not E1 5b.
Jane Murdoch, Stuart Murdoch & John Fowler– Longscar & Black Crag. – 5 routes (including Katie's Dilemma, Sharp as Glass, Jolly Rodger).
Brian Shackleton & Helen Brown – C Route (S), D Route (S) on Gimmer.
Alison Coull & Kenny Robb – Black Crag & Long Scar (inc Hold On, Blind, Sharp as Glass).
Dave Broadhead & Fay Brown – Round of Mickleden.
Simon Fraser – Round of Duddon (Marilyn); two lovely pubs; so quiet compared to Langdale.
Lisa Hutchison – Ill Crag/Broad Crag/Helvellyn Striding & Swirral Edges in foul weather with Simon on Friday.

Attenders: Lisa Hutchison, Andrew James, Geoff Cohen, Stuart Murdoch, Jane Murdoch, Brian Shackleton, Helen Brown (guest), Dave Broadhead, Fay Brown (guest), Simon Fraser, Kenny Robb, Alison Coull, Chris Ravey, Fraser Reid (guest), Duncan Reid (guest), Alix Hery (guest), Tom Prentice, John Fowler and Bob Reid.

Bob Reid

Welcome Meet, Lagangarbh, Glen Coe

25–26 October 2019

The final weekend of October found a dozen new members of the Club at Lagangarbh for a Welcome Meet hosted by the President and Vice-Presidents.

L-R: David Myatt, Gordon Lacy, Sophie-Grace Chappell, Stan Pearson, Bob Reid, Iain Smith, Tim Miller, Steve Addy, John McKenna, Forrest Templeton, Dave Strang, Jon Ascroft, Tim Taylor, James Hotchkis, John Fowler (President). Photo: Tom Priestley.

While not everyone could get away for the Friday evening, those who did quickly introduced themselves and got down to some serious drinking, aided by the President's bottle of malt, which somehow was empty before morning.

Saturday was blustery with snow showers blowing through on a strong wind, giving an early taste of winter. Clearly not cragging weather but all ventured out. While the established members must have been feeling anti-social and went out alone, the Aberdeen team of Dave Strang, Steve Addy and Forrest Templeton took a walk up Sgor na h-Ulaidh from the Glen Coe side and only saw two other walkers during the day. None had done this hill before. Tom Priestley and Iain Smith did Stob Coire an Albannaich and Meall nan Eun, while John McKenna and Tim Miller scrambled up The Nose on Gearr Aonach and were met by Gordon Lacey and Tim Taylor who had done the Zigzags. All four had sufficient energy to then go to the Ice Factor in Fort William.

In the evening we were joined by Jon Ascroft, Sophie-Grace Chappell, Stan Pearson and James Hotchkis, all of whom had been unable to get away the previous day, and then everyone settled down to a communal three course meal and a selection of beer and wine. Surprisingly, not all the drink went, which could have been a reflection on the Friday night session.

On Sunday the weather was slightly warmer but just as damp and some found a reason not to go on the hill and left for home or headed to the Kingshouse to watch the Rugby World Cup semi-final. Jon and Steve went up Beinn nan Aighenan and Glas Bheinn Mhor in Glen Etive and Dave and Forrest took a walk up Beinn Fhionnlaidh from the Etive side but were so busy gassing on the walk in that they were half way up Sgorr na h-Ulaidh again before they realised! This was actually a fortunate mistake as the climb up Fionnlaidh was more interesting on the craggy west facing side. Finally, on the way home, Tom Priestley did Meall nan Tarmachan and the Tarmachan Ridge.

Despite the mixed weather, the Welcome meet was considered worthwhile and we hope to repeat it in 2020 and beyond.

Members present: John Fowler (President), Steve Addy, Jon Ascroft, Sophie-Grace Chappell, James Hotchkis, Gordon Lacy, John McKenna, Tim Miller, David Myatt, Stan Pearson, Tom Priestley, Bob Reid, Iain Smith, Dave Strang, Tim Taylor, Forrest Templeton.

David Myatt

Ski Mountaineering Meet 2020

8–9 February, Lagangarbh, Glen Coe

With a remarkable annual consistency, the 2020 date decreed by our hard-working Meets Secretary was the weekend that the anthropomorphised Storm Ciara duly arrived on our shores. The coordination of meets imposed by the aforementioned secretary, also allowed me to enjoy the arrival of the baptised Storm Dennis at the CIC hut club meet the following weekend! This consistency is in no way a criticism of our Meets Secretary, it simply allows a mention of the climate crisis issue of global warming in this meet report.

Modern technology in the form of accurate weather forecasts and phone embedded computer chips, allows almost universal access to forecasting websites, and this inspired Ann and Colwyn to attempt a summit on Friday 7 February. The hill was a modest climb (664m), a Graham named Uamh Bheag (translates as Little Cave NN687111).

The hill lies just south of the Highland Boundary Fault and they approached from the A84 trunk road going towards Callander from Stirling. At Bridge of Keltie, immediately before Callander, they took the Dalvey road which climbs to the end of the public road next to a waterfall where there was adequate space for a couple of cars to park. A polite request was made to the passing farmer to seek approval to drive further up the private track to park, but he was having none of it, citing damage to car mirrors from cattle as the reason for denying permission!

The weather was fine and there was even some watery sunshine as they set off to walk first to the rambling buildings of the farm (Easter Brackland), then on up the well-formed track to a substantial area of hardstanding at around the 350m contour.

From the hardstanding there were the usual stalking related saturated quad bike tracks leading up the hill and shortly they were able to follow one, then an ancient grassy moraine which was thankfully dry underfoot. On reaching the col west of the main summit they turned to follow the ridge to the large flat summit, marked by an untidy cairn close to the intersection of three sheep fences. The ordnance survey triangulation station was not on the true summit but about 500 metres further east at an altitude of 662 metres. A geocache box carelessly hidden nearby was unearthed.

There was little wind at the summit allowing a pleasant luncheon to be enjoyed. However, the sky darkened, the sun was now hidden, and the wind was picking up. So they packed quickly and, with the positive help of gravity were soon back down on the approach track and safely back at the car thereafter.

In sharp contrast to the early weekend activity of these two members, the majority of SMC members who had seen the forecast of the arrival of Storm Ciara, decided to stay at home. Therefore, only the most hardy elite members of the SMC appeared at Lagangarbh in 2020 or perhaps not! Friday night was spent in a warm fug at our club hut in Glen Coe as the wind strengthened and the rain started.

On Saturday morning Bob Reid joined Ann and Colwyn to walk up the Devil's Staircase to the highpoint of the West Highland Way (550m) where, in the buffeting wind, they temporarily enjoyed a fine view of the Mamores. The overnight precipitation had produced a vague mantle of snow above the 600 metre contour but there was not enough snow to ski, even if they could have stayed upright!

After (late) morning coffee in the relatively new Kingshouse Hotel, Bob headed to Glasgow while Ann and Colwyn endured the stiff headwind to walk back to Lagangarbh. It was noted that the footpath on the north side of the footbridge was being eroded by the fast-flowing burn which flowed down from the A82, and which might shortly make access to the cottage problematic. Amy and Eric arrived shortly thereafter. Saturday night was spent in warm comfort at our club hut as the wind strengthened further and the rain continued.

On Sunday morning, there was a dusting of snow at the hut being washed away by the driving rain. Everyone remaining at the meet either travelled home or diverted to visit friends on the way.

Members: Colwyn Jones (Convener), Amy Goodill, Bob Reid, Ann MacDonald. Guest, Eric Lang.

Colwyn Jones

Skye Winter Meet, Glen brittle Memorial Hut

6–8 March, 2020

The summit of Glas Bheinn Mor with mist shrouded Blaven behind. Photo: Roger Robb.

Four members attended. The weather was mainly poor but at least, this year, there was some snow. Pete Biggar and Roger Robb were fortunate in coming a day early. En route to the hut they ascended Glas Bheinn Mor above Loch Ainort on a day with reasonable gaps in the showers. Then on Friday, although the main Cuillin were swathed in cloud and rain, they went north and climbed Beinn Edra from Glen Conon in mixed weather but with some clear spells giving fine views of the Quiraing.

Appalling weather prevented much further activity, although Dave Broadhead walked up into Coire Lagan on Sunday. Noel Williams carried out research in connection with Cuillin History.

PJB.

On the descent from Beinn Edra looking towards the Quiraing. Photo: Roger Robb.

Just how appalling the weather was on the Saturday can be judged by the state of the River Sligachan. Photo: Noel Williams.

All the meets planned for later in the year – including the 2020 Easter Meet – were cancelled as a result of the Covid-19 lockdown.

JMCS REPORTS

Edinburgh Section: our former secretary opened this column last year by commenting on 'what an odd year it has been'. Little did we know what was to come in 2020. The tragic COVID-19 pandemic has hugely curtailed our activities, with many members' mountaineering pursuits consisting of fingerboard sessions, online climbing films and daring ascents of Arthur's Seat.

Inevitably, we had to suspend club meets and events in March and close our two much-loved huts – The Smiddy in Dundonnell and The Cabin in Laggan – until further notice.

With most hills and crags off limits, some frustrated club members resorted to scrubbing the cobwebs off some long-neglected brick walls in Leith, jamming fists and feet into the concrete roof cracks beneath a Murrayfield bridge and even returning to Dougal Haston's old haunt, Currie Wa's. Others made do with socially-distanced walks in the Pentlands, where the fine weather often allowed tantalising views to out-of-reach Stùc a' Chroin and Ben Vorlich.

The five-mile travel limit allowed plenty of scope for my own long-term battle to continue with my slippery nemesis, the Black Wall Traverse at Salisbury Crags. Doing my bit to aid its transformation into glass.

It seems like a lifetime ago, but before all this our members had been beginning to enjoy the late arrival of good winter conditions, including some pleasingly busy weekends away together at the Cabin. We had been looking forward to a packed itinerary of evening and weekend meets, especially as we welcomed quite a few new, younger members to our club this year. I hope they've not been put off by this strange, isolated start to their time with the Edinburgh JMCS.

We will return to the Cairngorm Hotel in Aviemore for our AGM on Saturday 21 November 2020, provided Scotland's new normal allows such gatherings. Member Oli Warlow is all set to talk us through his amazing Classic Rock By Bike adventure.

We had a very enjoyable AGM at the same venue last November, with many members arriving at the dinner fresh from grand winter days out in the Cairngorms above a stunning cloud inversion.

Our member Stan Pearson gave a brilliant after-dinner talk about his adventures on the sea-cliffs of Ireland. Stan's stories had us all considering booking summer trips to the Burren, Donegal and Fairhead. Fingers crossed such frivolous excursions will again become possible in the not-too-distant future.

Our president Thomas Beutenmuller paid tribute at the AGM to long-time member Dave Amos, who tragically died in an indoor climbing accident in September 2019. Dave's friends David Small and Stewart Bauchop also wrote touching obituaries to Dave in our 2019 winter newsletter, recalling memorable days together on big routes and paying tribute to his 'modest, generous, resilient, utterly dependable character'. Dave is missed by all who knew him.

That same newsletter contained a diverse array of articles detailing our members' exploits, from epic Alpine tales of derring-do to my own fumbling about on damp Skye sea cliffs. As always, the newsletter is available to download from our website.

Hopefully by the time you're reading this, our huts and meets will be back up and running again, so do keep an eye on <edinburghjmcs.org.uk>. The huts are available for booking by kindred clubs by contacting the custodians whose names are below.

If you are interested in joining the Edinburgh JMCS, we're a friendly bunch and always welcome new faces. We have Monday and Wednesday night activities – mainly indoor in winter and outdoors in summer when the weather allows. Pop an email to membership secretary Nils Krichel in advance, just to check there's not been a change of plan: <nils.krichel@gmail.com>.

Present Committee – Honorary President, John Fowler; President, Thomas Beutenmuller; Vice-President and Smiddy custodian, Helen Forde <helen.forde1@btinternet.com>; Treasurer, Bryan Rynne; Cabin custodian, Ali Borthwick (01383 732 232, before 9 p.m.); Secretary, Danny Carden <secretary@edinburghjmcs.org.uk>; Membership Secretary, Nils Krichel; and ordinary member, Catrin Thomas.

Danny Carden

Glasgow Section: the club has enjoyed a full and active mountaineering year during 2019. We welcome new members and guests to our regular meets.

The 2019 Presidential dinner was an excellent event at the recently refurbished Kingshouse Hotel in Glencoe on Saturday 9 November 2019. At the 2019 AGM that evening it was reported that there are 85 current section members in total, 43 ordinary members and 42 life members. The club had one new member recorded as joining in 2019. There were three new life members (awarded after 25 years of continuous membership). The evening of the presidential dinner was completed with an address from our guest speaker, Alan Rowan, aka the 'Munro Moonwalker,' who told us the entertaining and inspiring story of his own compleation project, a moonlit Munro ascent during all of the full moons, achieved in 2018.

The section organised a full schedule of more than 20 weekend meets in 2019 including successful weekends at all of the five SMC huts. There are meets every two weeks throughout most of the year, but only a single meet in August. The meet venues vary each year, which cover the whole of Scotland and occasionally beyond. In the late spring and summer there are midweek evening meets to various central belt rock climbing venues. There are also midweek indoor climbing meets in The Glasgow Climbing Centre at Ibrox throughout the year.

One of the most popular meets with Glasgow JMCS members is the late May bank holiday workmeet to the club hut at Coruisk on the Isle of Skye. The spectacular boat trip from Elgol to Coruisk (free to workmeet attendees) perhaps contributes to that popularity. The hut itself continues to be busy at weekends with overseas clubs now making regular bookings. Despite inclement weather during the 2019 workmeet, the hut received the necessary routine maintenance. Coruisk has become a recognised wedding venue, although a large number of couples simply use the Coruisk landing stage as the setting for that most important day of their lives! If any SMC members are planning to stay on Skye (or perhaps even get married there) please contact the hut custodian directly <coruisk@glasgowjmcs.org.uk> or via the Glasgow JMCS website:<www.glasgowjmcs.org>.

The Glasgow JMCS newsletter remains a surprising and entertaining read which continues to thrive under the editorship of Dr Ole Kemi. Four issues are published per year and circulated via the JMCS website in February, May, August and November. The newsletter welcomes contributions from all authors, not only JMCS members, and we welcome all ideas and contributions for future issues.

The winter season 2018–19 was, as this audience will know, a season of many starts and many stops – long stops. The weather generally did not play ball. The cold spell in early February allowed two members to make a long-awaited winter ascent of the barrel buttress on Quinag via the route Badajoz, which it was felt deserves classic status.

The winter route of the season was undoubtedly Postern on The Shelterstone by our current president and his climbing partner (an ex-president) in March. Having backed off the year before due to warm conditions, they finally completed the ascent and it was the walk out that was problematic. A storm hit and blasted them, especially their eyes. The president reported that he was nearly blind for a week afterwards. However, more was to come when, between the Shelterstone and Hell's Lum, they suddenly, found themselves being carried downhill uncontrollably for 80 –180m (subsequent GPS analyses showed). Luckily, when the avalanche stopped both were on the surface. Less eventfully, club members also climbed Monolith Grooves on Beinn an Lochain; Cutlass on Ben Nevis; Lomond Corner, a very nice climb so close to home on Ben Lomond; Fallout Corner and Overseer Direct in Coire an Lochain; and Pinnacle Arete and Lost the Place, again on Ben Nevis.

The President was skiing in Lyngen, Norway during Easter, and was lured into the Vasarrennet cross-country ski race, which he completed. However, we can assume he didn't win, or no doubt we would have heard about it. In April two retired JMCS presidents, accompanied two SMC members and two others, on the fine Tour de Soleil ski tour, Switzerland from Binn to Realp/Engleberg.

One highlight of the domestic summer season was climbing the two sea stacks; Atlantic Wall (Am Buachaille, where they met two SMC members) and Diamond Face route (Old Man of Stoer) in one weekend up in the north-west. Other routes that members climbed were Minus One Direct on Ben Nevis (almighty exposure confirmed on that pitch), The Needle on The Shelterstone and the Fhidleir's Nose Direct.

On a hot day in August when psyched up for cracks, a party having just returned from endless crack climbing in Norway, on Buachaille Etive Mor blitzed Mainbrace Crack (including the Direct Finish), White Wall Crack, Hangman's Crack, Gallows Route, and North Buttress in descent.

Direct Direct and A Crack in the Clouds, were climbed with a superb onsight lead by an ex-president on the latter, without crack gloves. A rarely attempted crack climb in an obscure place on The Cobbler, but which was recently cleaned. Two excellent routes, and they were back down that day in time for ice cream in Arrochar. On a blustery day in September, two members enjoyed an ascent of King Kong on Ben Nevis, and even managed not to get lost (uncommon, apparently).

The mid-week meets included a visit to Dun Leacainn with ascents of Mutation, Devil's Elbow, and Dominator Direct. The advice is to get out there and climb on the crag before the trees grow again.

Norway saw three members climbing for almost two weeks in glorious weather, with the first rain appearing when they were flying home. Too many climbs to recount in full, but highlights included the South Pillar of Stetind, The English Corner in full and subsequent traverse of Eidetind, a joined up traverse of Kuglhornet and Sildpollentind ridges, The Goat in Svolvær, and West Pillar Direct on Presten, Henningsvær. All routes which are highly recommended.

Two retired presidents had an extended summer trip to Switzerland walking/climbing 32 peaks in 42 days, finishing with two 4000m peaks: the Nadelhorn(4327m) on 30th August 2019, then 4 days later they summitted the

Colwyn and Ann on the Dom; the Mattertal below and the Matterhorn in the background. Photo: Jones Collection.

Dom(4545m). Two members completed their rounds of the Munros in 2019 bringing the club total of Munroists to 52, and of these 6 have also completed the Corbetts.

President, Ole Kemi; the position of Vice President is currently vacant; Secretary, Phil Smith; Treasurer, Justine Carter; New Members Secretary, Dave Payne; Honorary President, Neil Wilkie.

Colwyn Jones

Lochaber Section: In 2019 the main event for the club was the meet to Slovenia at the end of June and start of July, with seven members making the trip by various means and routes. Summer conditions were in force which allowed for lighter packs with excellent hot, sunny weather during the first week or so and more predictable afternoon or late evening thunderstorms every other day during the latter part of the trip. We opted to stay in the small village of Trenta, located almost at the heart of the Triglav National Park, with all staying at the campsite, Kamp Triglav, which was ideally suited in terms of access to the mountains and also for excellent facilities in the campsite, as well as friendly local restaurants nearby.

Outings to the hills could be gained direct from the campsite, or via a good local bus service to the top of the Vrsic Pass (Highest road in Slovenia) where shorter days or alternative routes can be achieved. Slovenia has in excess of 150 mountain huts and shelters with a number of good quality huts in the surrounding area of the Trenta Valley. Staying at the huts during normal weekdays is usually easily achievable, however at weekends it would be better to book ahead as the huts can fill up, especially ahead of a good weather forecast.

Slovenia's highest Mountain, Mount Triglav, is accessible direct from Trenta which we completed over two days and staying at the Koca na Dolicu hut, which entailed a 17km and 1500m ascent over well made paths dating back to WW1 with fantastic scenery all round. The hut provided meals and bedding, so only equipment for the day was required. A further 700m of ascent gained the summit with some nice and easy scrambling on the top 300m. There were a number of slightly exposed sections where a fixed cable provided some protection, should this be required. Via Ferrata routes of varying grades are located across the mountains which can be linked to access different huts in a high mountain traverse. Although we opted to drive to Slovenia, fly/drive travel arrangements could be made, with Trenta only two hours drive from Ljubljana airport, or half that time to the more popular North side.

The club also held the usual weekend meets to Kincraig, Crianlarich and Dundonnell as well as our winter evening slide show by former Club member Ian 'Suds' Sutherland. The year ended with our annual dinner and AGM at the Nethy Bridge Hotel.

President: Ken Scoular; Treasurer: Ken Scoular; Hut bookings: Ewen Kay; Hut Custodian: George Bruce; Secretary: Iain MacLeod
<ia.macleod@btinternet.com>

Iain MacLeod

London Section: our programme took place predominantly in North Wales. Inclement weather was a factor. Camping meets elsewhere were re-arranged to take advantage of our hut in Bethesda. A soaking on the hill is less important when there is the prospect of a hot shower, warm dry hut and a pint or two in the pub around the corner. We did, however, meet twice in the Lake District, in Scotland, in Pembroke and on the Costa Blanca in Spain.

Where did the winter go? It seemed to appear briefly and then melt away fast. We missed it. There was almost no snow in the Cairngorms in late February and early March when the Section stayed in the Milehouse for a week. You pack ice axes and crampons and end up climbing Ardverikie Wall. But it was nice to see the view from the tops. So often at this time of year, when bent double by the wind, all you see is the inside of a cloud. As ever on our winter meet the food, drink and company were excellent. We are grateful to Nigel Charlesworth who has taken over from David Hughes as Chef on this meet. How we can eat and drink so well and still make a small profit for the Section is a mystery.

At least it didn't rain on our meets in the Lake District in May and June. In Borrowdale we stayed in the excellent Climber's Club hut. In Eskdale we camped. Both venues provided classic rock routes and long days out.

September saw us rock climbing in Pembroke and mountain biking in the Afan Forest on the way there. A group of us also went sailing in the Hebrides though strong winds kept us mainly in coastal waters. In October, our hut got a good 'deep' clean. We would welcome more visitors. If you fancy a weekend doing some of the classic routes in Snowdonia do give our Hut Custodian a call.

A dose of winter sun is now a regular feature of our programme so in early November we gathered in Calpe on the Costa Blanca. It's a great place to go when it's wet and windy at home. You draw back the curtains and there is hardly a cloud in the sky. And there is something there for everyone – great climbing, walking, scrambling on the limestone ridges and even some Via Ferrata. We climbed on the Penon de Ifach, Puig Campana, in the Mascarat Gorge and at Sierra de Toix.

The year ended with our annual dinner and AGM at the Heights in Llanberis. On a sad note, we lost four dear friends during 2019. This is lot for a small section to bear but perhaps inevitable when you grow old together. In April, we lost Roy Hibbert: climber, biker, sailor, always ready to cock a snook at the young pretenders and mischievous to the end. In May, it was Dawn, wife of Dave Edmonds, a former Treasurer. Dawn was our neighbour in Glanafon Street and always had such zest for life. In June, David Hughes passed away. David was our Treasurer for 20 years. He organised our winter meets for most of this period. Our "curry meister" fed us well and was a dab hand at finding good red wines at a very reasonable price. As a young man David was on the first ascent of Yo-yo with Robin Smith. David's memory was remarkable. You could always rely on his advice on routes and how best to get to crags. In August we said goodbye to Robin Watts, a former Treasurer and Secretary of the Section. After a career in the Army, Robin settled in Snowdonia. He was never happier than when out on his beloved local hills with various dogs. All, will be sorely missed.

President, Trevor Burrows; Secretary, John Firmin <john.firmin3@btinternet.com>; Treasurer, Gordon Burgess Parker; Hut Custodian, David L Hughes <davidlewishughes@hotmail.com>.

John Firmin

Perth Mountaineering Club: it was the year when ropes remained on shelves and boots walked new paths closer to home. Climbers swapped carabiners for paintbrushes and quickdraws for garden tools. Adventures and plans were put on hold but memories of past exploits, climbs and achievements were remembered and shared. Regular friends and companions became distant with club activities stopped but we will meet again don't know where yet or when!

2020 got off to an excellent start again with our annual Burns Weekend Meet at the Ochils Mountaineering Club Hut at Crianlarich where we enjoyed the ambiance of the facilities. Once again the camaraderie and willingness of people to make it a good weekend was exceptional with an excellent communal meal, Burns traditions followed, sword dancing, guitar playing, dance, poetry and song. Weather prospects for the weekend had been very pessimistic with high winds forecast so several members opted for the comforts of The Ice Factor on the Saturday, some sports climbing and others honing skills on the ice wall for future expeditions. Four set off for the Gordon Bothy at Achallader and had a pleasant day. A group of three relying on a different forecast and good route selection to account for wind direction chose a winter climb on the Central Buttress of Bidean nam Bian. They were having a rewarding and successful day until one member glissaded and tore his leg badly on a hidden rock resulting in a difficult descent to the road and a trip to Belford hospital for stitches. Sadly they had to have their supper after midnight and missed the Burns celebrations.

In March just before lockdown we were lucky to have a social meet to say farewell to our German Club member who was returning to her homeland but leaving some of her heart in Scotland, a country she had come to love. It is nice to have memories of what was our last club gathering and of meeting friends prior to the social distancing rules.

Reflecting on PMC successes since last year's report. The club trip to Cortina D'Ampezzo went ahead in early July with eleven members. Weather once more presented a challenge as, after Europe being hit with a 40 degree heatwave, the

Dolomites bore the brunt of the disturbed weather with daily violent thunderstorms. A good selection of Via Ferrata were still sampled and enjoyed along with the historical aspect of their origins. A particularly memorable day was following on from an ascent of the Col Demi Bos, exploring the Lagazuoi tunnels and Martini Ledge, the entire area having been a scene of the mountain war fought between the Italians and Austrians.

Nine club members attended the annual climbing trip to Kalymnos. Old favourite crags were visited as well as new ones explored. Four members were delighted to complete Wings for Life, the multi pitch epic which follows a buttress along a giant cave on the island of Telendos. The following day a relaxing sea kayak trip out of Vathy was planned along the coast to several beautiful remote beaches.

In July two members had a quick trip to the Alps where they climbed Pollux and completed the Breithorn traverse. The club was also very active closer to home with several Tower Ridge ascents from different parties and a complete Skye Ridge Traverse from three members.

The June Meet at the wonderful location of the Coruisk Memorial Hut was exceptional with superb weather allowing a good selection of climbs on the adjacent crags and wild swimming in the loch and sea. Three members took the opportunity to climb the Dubhs Ridge and Grahame and Raymond climbed the obscure summit of Sgùrr Coire nan Lochan, reputed to be the last summit climbed in the British Isles. This required a long scramble, an abseil then short climb to the top. A party also climbed at Suidhe Biorach getting two routes done, *Fertility Right* (S) and the awesomely exposed *Hairy Mary*, (HVS), prior to getting the ferry across to Coruisk.

Other meets included Elphin, another weekend of bad forecasts when several members pulled out. Only five members attended the Naismith hut but two members set off to try the scramble on the SE side of Cul Mor while another group ascended Ben Leoid from the East.

Throughout 2019 and prior to lockdown the club has met regularly on Wednesday evenings and other wet days at the Perth College Climbing Wall where we have continued to attract new members. The wall staff must be commended for their frequent route setting presenting us with regular challenges of great variation.

In 2019 monthly pub nights also became a feature of the PMC calendar with The Venue in Perth being the first choice and then opening it up to allow people to share a local in their own area.

The annual PMC dinner was held at the Chatni Indian restaurant where due to excellent club attendance we were able to book exclusively. Having a local venue allowed more members to attend, meet up and enjoy a very sociable night. We were also able to celebrate our club's ninetieth birthday and the achievements of one member who not only had reached the fit age of 70 but also had many other numbers to his name. 52 Alpine Summits over 4000m, Munro's 282 x 2, Corbett 222 and Punros, the Pyrenean version of Munro's but a hell of a lot higher 129. Respect to our Club member Jeff Harris and a good example to our younger members of what is out there and can be done. The club benefits greatly from the sharing of experience and knowledge among members and the wealth of different skills and qualities within its membership.

Amongst the struggles that Lockdown has presented we must celebrate the good news of the elevation of the Mountain hare to protected species saved at last from the carnage of culling. Looking to the future, I feel sure the club will gradually resume activities in the phases the government introduces. It is pleasing that even during lockdown we have continued to have enquires from prospective members. It can be certain that the mountains and our freedom will be all the more appreciated just as having witnessed the transformation from Spring to Summer I have appreciated the emergence of each new flower on my local walk. PMC is strong, healthy and hopefully can continue to be so despite the challenges faced in recent months.

President, Wendy Georgeson; Vice President, Catherine Johnstone; Secretary, Tim Storer.

Wendy Georgeson

SMC ABROAD

South-East Alaska – Stikine Icecap

The Stikine Icecap straddles the USA-Canada border and lies between the Stikine River and the coastal waters of Frederick Sound in South-East Alaska. Spectacular granite peaks rise from a myriad of glaciers that cover an area equivalent in size to Wales. It would be the perfect alpinist's playground if it were not for the weather, which is truly atrocious. To the west lies the Gulf of Alaska, a malevolent, tempestuous sea responsible for most of the precipitation that strikes the Pacific Coast of North America. Consequently the Stikine is one of the wettest places on earth and has been described as a 'rain icecap'. Unsurprisingly this makes climbing in the area extremely challenging, and the Stikine Icecap is rarely visited by climbers. It is one of the wildest and least known mountain ranges on earth.

The Devil's Thumb (9077ft) is the most celebrated mountain in the Stikine Icefield, and sees two or three visits a year. The rest of the range is almost completely neglected. Approximately 25km to the north-west of the Devil's Thumb, at the head of the North Baird Glacier, lies the impressive Oasis Peak (7925ft). This little visited spire has only been summited once. Together with The Devil's Thumb and its satellite Burkett Needle, it is considered to be one of the most spectacular mountains in South-East Alaska.

Mark Robson and I have made several trips to the Coast Mountains of British Columbia and were keen to visit the Stikine. Our plan was to make the second ascent of Oasis Peak via a new route from the north. This had been attempted a couple of times in the 1970s, but our tactic was to visit in the spring (early May) hoping to find more stable snow, ice and mixed climbing conditions than those encountered by the previous teams in mid summer. We flew into the North Baird Glacier from the fishing village of Petersburg by helicopter on 30 April 2019. As far as we could tell, we were the first documented climbing expedition to visit the glacier for over 40 years.

As soon as we arrived it was immediately clear that any technical climbing was out of the question. All the mountains were heavily snowed up, draped with enormous cornices and unstable snow mushrooms. But more significantly, it was not freezing at night and there were (literally) hundreds of avalanches. So after a week we abandoned plans for Oasis Peak and moved our camp down glacier to where we could access the North Arm of the North Baird Glacier.

Finally, on 9 May, the weather improved enough for us to climb through the icefall guarding entry to the North Arm. We were probably the first mountaineers ever to visit this part of the icecap and were surrounded by over a dozen unclimbed peaks. The big prize however was P7180 (also known as Hyder Peak), which lay 8km away at the head of the adjacent Dawes Glacier. This massive and isolated mountain, with a steep rocky summit triangle, lies on the western edge of the range. We made the 5km long and 1200m ascent the following day during a brief 24-hour weather window via a combination of post-holing through deep snow, skiing where possible and then mixed climbing on the summit triangle. The view from the precarious and massively corniced summit looking east to all the major peaks in the range was breathtaking. During the trip we were also successful in making first ascents of P5910, P5720, P5800 and the shapely P5919 before flying out on 12 May.

Overall, we only had three days when it was not raining and the visibility was good enough to climb. Snow conditions remained soft throughout, avalanches

Stikine, 12 May 2019, Mark Robson traversing above the clouds during the first ascent of P5919 in South-East Alaska. Photo:Simon Richardson.

took place constantly and we experienced considerable cornice difficulties. Despite all of these challenges, it was an extremely rewarding expedition. The climbing was rarely technical, but picking safe lines and negotiating the beautiful corniced summit ridges made it very exacting. We had one huge cornice collapse, but fortunately we both stayed upright on the solid side of the fracture line! And above all, when the rain stopped and the fog lifted, we were treated to some of the most beautiful and pristine mountain landscapes either of us had ever seen.

Alaskan climbers are notoriously modest about publicising their achievements, but there are no records of previous ascents of any of the peaks we climbed. Hyder Peak was one of the highest unclimbed summits (with over 3000ft prominence) in South-East Alaska.

Canadian Rockies – Mount Phillips

29 Sept. 2008 The North Face of Mount Phillips in the Canadian Rockies. The North Spur takes the lower rib then goes through the headwall to finish on the West Ridge just right of the summit. Photo: John Scurlock.

It all began with a photo. Flicking through the Internet one evening, I came across John Scurlock's beautiful image of the north side of Mount Phillips. The compelling, sharp-cut North Spur dividing the north-east and north-west faces of the mountain was a feature that simply had to be climbed!

I met Canadian climber Ian Welsted on the 2016 International Winter Meet. We share a love of wild places and arranged to do some exploratory alpine climbing in the Canadian mountains last summer.

When I was packing my bags in Aberdeen I was concerned that an unusually large high pressure system anchored over Alaska in June and July had directed unsettled weather over the Canadian mountains, and wondered whether our primary objective would be in condition. Almost on a whim, I printed off the photo of Mount Phillips hours before I boarded the plane to Calgary.

When I showed the photo to Ian he was similarly inspired and the route seemed a safe option as the late Rockies spring transitioned into summer. Timing is key when it comes to alpine climbing, and we hoped to take advantage of cool conditions on the back of a passing front. Neither of us had heard of Mount

Phillips before, but a quick Google search revealed it was a 3246m-high peak just to the north of Mount Robson. Phillips' 600m-high north face appeared to be unclimbed. Ian contacted local climbers Jesse Milner and Dana Ruddy in Jasper, who said they knew about the line, but generously said they would be delighted if we gave it a go.

On 21 July 2019, we left the Berg Lake trail just above Emperor Falls and bushwhacked through forest that opened out to meadows of wild flowers with the Emperor Ridge of Robson towering behind. Scree and snow slopes led to a comfortable bivouac on the right flank of the Phillips Glacier. We rose at 12.30 a.m, anxious to become established on the route before snow on the east flank of the spur softened in the morning sun. A two-and-a-half-hour approach over the col east of the mountain saw us crossing the bergschund at dawn, and we moved quickly up the lower spur on mixed snow and rock.

Our pace slowed at two-thirds height where the spur abuts the steep headwall. I had hoped for a hidden ramp leading right to the west ridge, but instead we were forced into the 'jaws', a narrow ice gully that cut deeply into the headwall. It appeared to end in an impasse, but fortunately an icy ramp led left to easier ground. It was now midday and the sun was softening the snow at an alarming rate. Every time we dropped a rock it precipitated a huge surging avalanche down the face below. We were perfectly safe—but thankful for our alpine start. The next pitch across the snow band to reach the final part of the west ridge should have been a straightforward romp across a 45-degree slope, but instead Ian was forced to make a bold and demanding lead on dark shattered limestone covered in a wet layer of snow. I marvelled at his skill placing knife blades and finding the perfect location for our precious single Pecker.

Then, suddenly, it was almost over. A broad ledge on the west ridge gave way to three exposed and intricate pitches up the sharp arete to the summit. It was 5.00 p.m. The weather was good; there was no need to hurry. Robson towered 700m above us and behind we could see down the Rockies chain to Mount Clémenceau and beyond. To the north the view was even more intriguing. Steep and jagged peaks stretched all the way to the horizon, holding countless possibilities for more adventures to come.

Our climb is the third route on Phillips, but needless to say the SMC had already left its mark. The mountain was first climbed by Norman Collie and Curly Phillips in 1923.

Canadian Coast Mountains – Mount Waddington

The primary objective for Ian Welsted and me during the summer of 2019 was the first complete ascent of the West Ridge of Mount Waddington. Somehow, in the chase for more technical objectives, the central spine of the highest peak in the Coast Mountains had been overlooked. And there it was, Waddington's unclimbed Upper West Ridge marching boldly across a double page spread in Don Serl's guidebook – a sharp 1500m-long pinnacled crest rising up to a fine snow arête and the summit plateau.

The Mundays' pioneering route up Waddington climbed the lower 3.5 km of the West Ridge to 3300m and then followed the natural line of weakness up the Angel Glacier to the Northwest Summit. It was a logical line and hugely committing for 1928. Unfortunately the Mundays did not have the firepower to continue to the main summit, which had to wait until 1936 when Bill House and Fritz Wiessner summited via the South-West Face. This bold and committing

16 Aug. 2016 Mt. Waddington from the north-west, with the West Ridge on the right skyline and the massive icefall of the Scimitar Glacier flowing down to the right. The west-east traverse of the mountain started at Fury Gap, off-picture to the right, and finished with Waddington's summit towers (from right to left): False Summit, Northwest Peak, and the Summit Tower. Photo: John Scurlock.

undertaking was the most difficult alpine route in North America at the time and comparable with the advances being made in the European Alps on the Eiger and Grandes Jorasses.

Our plan was to traverse Waddington starting from Fury Gap at its western end. We would follow the Munday route to the foot of the unclimbed Upper West Ridge, climb this and go on to bag the False Summit (3980m), North-West Summit (4000m) and Main Summit Tower (4019m) before descending the Bravo Glacier route to complete our 12km journey at the eastern extremity of the mountain at Rainy Knob.

Mike King dropped us off by helicopter at Fury Gap (2500m) on 3 August 2019. We felt rather exposed to be in the deep in the heart of the Waddington Range with just light alpine packs, but with no further ado we set off up the snow slopes above towards Fireworks Peak, the first minor summit on the Lower West Ridge. The snow was knee deep after days of storm and it was slow going. Ian's famous trail breaking power saved the day and we stopped to bivouac at 2 p.m. a little after Herald Peak. It felt ridiculously early, but we were not going to make the start of the West Ridge that evening, so there was no point in pushing too hard.

Next day we traversed over the two Men At Arms summits and followed a spectacular corniced ridge over Bodyguard and Councillor peaks. The going continued to be tough in the deep snow but we were hopeful that the Upper West Ridge had been scoured by the wind and the snow consolidated in the sun and the terrain would firm up. Once again we had a leisurely mid-afternoon bivouac near the start of the ridge.

On day 3 were up and away before dawn, and sure enough conditions on the Upper West Ridge were excellent and provided fast climbing on hard snow and

12 Jan. 2007 Waddington's Upper West Ridge from the air. Photo: John Scurlock.

easy ice along a ramp running below the south side of the crest. We moved together, with the occasional belayed pitch, until a hidden gully led up onto the previously untrodden Epaulette Glacier that sits astride the central section of the ridge.

We couldn't believe our luck that it had all gone so smoothly, but we were soon confronted with the sting in the tail. As we left the glacier, the ensuing snow ridge narrowed to a knife-edge draped in delicate cornices. I traversed a cheval along the wafer-thin crest and belayed by excavating a deep hole in the snow. Our situation was precarious, but there was no option other than to continue across the steep and heavily loaded slope on the north side of the crest to gain the upper ramp leading to the Northwest Peak.

Ian made a long and committing traverse, manfully digging deep to find ice screw runners, but the snow on my pitch was too deep for screws. I ploughed a sideways trench for 30m until a blind three-metre jump into a bergschrund brought us back into contact with more reasonable terrain. That afternoon we tagged the False and Northwest summits before descending a linking route called The Stroll to gain the broad terrace below the main summit.

Day 4 was another beautiful day but we were nearly turned back on the Summit Tower due to falling rime ice. As the sun moved behind the Tooth the onslaught abated, and we enjoyed a succession of excellent mixed pitches up the icy central chimney. The weather was completely different to when I climbed Waddington in a storm in 1997, but the climbing was similar, and reminded me of icy mixed on the Ben. On the summit we took in the 360-degree panorama looking north-south along the spine of the Coast Mountains and west to the Pacific Ocean before making a series of abseils back to our bivouac tent.

Before the trip, Don Serl had warned me that descending the Bravo Glacier might be the crux of the whole route. We awoke at 3 a.m. and set off down steep

05Aug. 2019: MountWaddington's 200m Summit Tower viewed from the Northwest Peak on Day Three. Photo: Simon Richardson.

névé slopes through the dawn to gain the Bravo Headwall. How things had changed in the intervening 22 years! Instead of deep snow flutings it was now a broken rocky slope and we carefully abseiled down to the Bravo Glacier icefall.

We soon became lost in a maze of huge crevasses and serac walls. After an hour we reached an impasse and tried three different routes without success. We were resigned to re-exploring the first option when Ian spotted some old footsteps in the distance on the lower glacier below. This gave us the incentive to force a way through and soon we were following a wanded trail left by a US team several weeks before. Unfortunately they had been unable to find a way up to the Bravo Headwall, but their tracks saved our day.

We reached Rainy Knob at 11 a.m. but were not ready to break the spell. We lounged on a huge flat slab of granite drinking coffee and taking in the magnificence of the surroundings and enjoying the deep glow that comes when you achieve something that you have set out to do. Eventually we reached for the radio and within minutes we heard the throb of the helicopter. Our adventure was complete.

Simon Richardson

REVIEWS

Journals of Kindred Clubs: Climbers' Club Journal, No. 128 (2017–18); MAM Journal, 9/1 (2017–18); Ladies' Scottish Climbing Club Journal, No. 8 (2018).

At a time when conventional newspapers are going to the wall, it is reassuring to receive each year an undiminished assortment of mountaineering-club periodicals. Perhaps we should seek an explanation in the age profile of a typical club's members. Is it likely that an association of teenagers would issue a printed journal each year? Indeed, would they even band together in the first place? Whatever the reason for their survival, these publications provide a tangible record of their members' adventures, leavened in varying proportion with articles of wider interest. Long may they continue!

The Climber's Club Journal maintains its customary high standard, with articles on climbing around the globe and just a slight Welsh bias. Nigel Barry contributes a survey of 'Classic Scottish Rock up to Severe', and controversially dares to propose for each route a 'realistic modern grade': thus *Afterthought Arête* on the Stag Rocks gets Very Difficult instead of the customary Moderate, and North-East Buttress is Severe, 4c. Barry's selection is difficult to fault, though his advice that a bicycle offers no advantage when approaching *Integrity* (VS 4c, by the way) is surely redundant. Poetry is well represented too, and there is even some fiction. (At least I hope the events in 'Betrayal on the Badile' were fictitious, or the Swiss police should be investigating a murder in the mountains.) Steve Andrews's '21 Years an Officer' is compulsory reading for any club member minded to volunteer as a hut custodian, while a survey of 'The First Ten Years of the Climbers' Club' is one of several interesting historical pieces. Its author, Ian Wall, traces the club's roots to C.E. Mathews and his founding of The Society of Welsh Rabbits in 1870. 'This band of explorers rapidly multiplied, as rabbits do,' and the more soberly styled Climbers' Club was constituted in 1898.

Even more prosaic in name is the Midland Association of Mountaineers, dating from 1922, whose hundred-page journal contains several readable and informative pieces. By coincidence both that journal and the CCJ carry personal accounts of Munro-bagging campaigns that spanned several decades and entailed many trips to the Highlands. I especially enjoyed Roger High's unpretentious 'Chance Encounters of a Munro Kind' in the MAMJ, in which it is the plants and birds, the Brocken spectres and human encounters, that he relishes as much as the hills themselves. A sparkling photograph of his daughter on Sgùrr nan Gillean adorns the back cover, while Rick Allen's shot of the Mazeno Ridge of Nanga Parbat is on the front.

Both the CCJ and the MAMJ devote a sobering portion of their pages to obituaries. Despite their choice of pastime, the members commemorated have died mostly 'in a good old age, full of days, riches, and honour,' so it is a shock to discover, amongst the grey-bearded late worthies of the Climber's Club, the blithe faces of Rachel Slater and Tim Newton who perished in their twenties, the victims of an avalanche in Observatory Gully. I hope their end was swift.

Like most club periodicals, the CCJ and MAMJ are hardy annuals or biennials. By contrast the slender organ of the LSCC is an *amorphophallus titanum* among climbing journals, coyly emerging at intervals of several years. Indeed, this is only the eighth issue in the club's 112-year existence, with the consequence that some of the accounts are of exploits a decade or more ago. The boundary between reportage and history is accordingly blurred, and the photographs accompanying 'West Greenland 1998' have captured the démodé cagoules and bunnets of an earlier age. Successful expeditions to Ladakh in 2000 and Bolivia in 2008 are described too, and more recently we find Koon Morris completing her first 8a route at Craig a' Barns.

The histories of the three LSCC huts are related in three well-researched articles, with Pat Brown identifying Milehouse's former residents through the 1861 census. What would those humble labourers and woodcutters have made of the cottage's 21st-century occupants? And who bestowed on the old Post Office at Aultbea its new name, 'Ronnan'? (We are given a clue.)

Graeme Morrison

Mountaineers — Great Tales of Bravery and Conquest: the Alpine Club in association with the RGS (Dorling Kindersley, 2019, hardback, 360pp, ISBN 978-0-24129-880-0, £25).

This recently updated book is the product of a collaboration between the Alpine Club and the Royal Geographical Society. Originally published in 2011, it provides a sweeping history of the events and stories, triumphs and tragedies, that arise when men, women and mountains meet. It is broad in its scope, beginning in 3000BCE with the unfortunate Ötzi the Iceman, finally freed from his icy grave in 1991, and ending with Alex Honnold and his free-solo ascent of El Capitan in 2017. Along the way it embraces science, religion, archaeology, geology, art and literature, all seen through the prism of mountaineering.

The book is organised in six sections: The Early Mountaineers; Climbing for Art and Science; the Golden Age of Alpinism; Beyond the Alps; and the Age of Extremes. Each section begins with an illustrated time-line of the significant events and actors in that section, set out in a tabular format. The majority of entries in each section are confined to just two facing pages, though some of the more significant characters, such as de Saussure, Whymper, Mummery and Mallory, extend over four pages. Each entry is a combination of text and a variety of illustrations: engravings, paintings, photographs, maps and mountain topographies. This extensive use of illustrations prevents the overarching organisation of the book becoming repetitive; it is visually rich and no two pages are the same. Interspersed in this overall organisation are entries under four further headings: Mountaineering Innovation, which traces the development of mountaineering equipment; Mountain Portraits, which provides descriptions of the major mountains in the Alps, the Himalaya and North and South America; Mountain Lives, which provides accounts of those who live in, or by means of, mountains; and Experiencing Mountains, which describes the ways in which the experience of mountains has been recorded, for example in literature, photography and film.

Although the book is visually rich, it is not merely a picture book; the text also is excellent. Whilst a number of writers and editors are acknowledged in the preface, there seems to have been just one principal author, Ed Douglas, the current editor of the Alpine Journal. There is certainly a consistency of style across the texts that suggests a single author or at least good editorial control. The writing is lucid and condenses often complex stories and time-lines into concise, lively prose that carries the reader along. The text is often peppered with wry observations and quotations that bring the various characters vividly alive. For example, in the eighteenth century we meet one William Windham who is described as having '…an utter abhorrence of restraint' and who, when in the mountains above Chamonix, was '...extremely entertained by continual echoes caused by cracking a whip or firing a pistol'. Lucy Walker, in making the fourth ascent of the Eiger, was 'fuelled by champagne and sponge cake to beat her chronic altitude sickness'. Her American contemporary, Meta Brevoort '…was assertive and spoke her mind; when she witnessed mule-drivers beating their animals, she beat the mule-drivers'. Willi Unsoeld, who together with Tom Hornbein made the first traverse of Everest, 'saw deep spiritual value in mountains and wasn't shy about spreading the news'. And finally, Anderl Heckmair, after being introduced by Leni Riefenstahl to Hitler, found himself 'unimpressed by the Führer'.

This book, then, is an ambitious project that is well realized. It is perhaps not a book to be read from cover to cover but rather to be dipped into with a cup of coffee to hand, though you may find your coffee cold before you put the book down. Most of the stories and characters in the book, certainly from the mid - nineteenth century onwards, will be familiar to most of today's climbers. But a good story never suffers from a retelling and the men and women mountaineers and their adventures that mountaineering has spawned are well served here.

David Stone

Scotland's Mountain Landscapes – a geomorphological perspective: Colin K Ballantyne (Dunedin, 2019, hardback, 174pp, ISBN 978-1-78046-079-6, £28).

The author is Emeritus Professor of Physical Geography at St Andrews University with an illustrious academic career stretching back 40 years. He is also a keen hillgoer who knows his way around the Highlands having compleated the Munros (three times) and the Corbetts. If anyone is qualified to write about the landscape of our mountains it is Professor Ballantyne.

He gave an excellent talk to the Northern District earlier this year about the Ice Age in Scotland. I was fortunate to join him for the pre-talk meal in Inverness and was able to thank him in person for the use of one of his diagrams in *Skye Scrambles*. However, I also discovered that I now have to amend the story about the type of landslides that took place in Trotternish. The talk was extremely well attended and afterwards Colin had a small number of copies of his book for sale. I was fortunate to get a copy, though many were disappointed.

There is certainly great interest in the mountain environment as the sales of *Hostile Habitats* testifies. This book is aimed at the interested amateur wanting to learn more about the processes that have sculpted the Highlands over vast tracts of time. It is an attractive book with numerous coloured illustrations. The author has included a clear introduction to each topic and has deliberately avoided the worst excesses of technical jargon.

There are ten chapters in total covering events before, during and after glaciation. The introductory chapter discusses geology, weathering and dating. The latter includes a mention of TCN dating (terrestrial cosmogenic nuclide exposure dating – if you must ask), a relatively new technique which now helps date when rocks were first exposed after glaciers melted and also when landslides occurred.

The shaping of our mountains was obviously hugely influenced by the repeated glaciations of, geologically speaking, recent times. The author paints an interesting picture of how the landscape must have looked prior to glaciation. The summits would have been more rounded, very few lochs would have existed, and instead of fjords on the west coast there would have been shallow inlets.

The author is well aware that our ideas about landscape evolution inevitably get updated and modified as new research is carried out. He mentions the classic caldera origin for the volcanic pile on Ben Nevis, though there has been a recent suggestion that instead it is a roof pendant and no collapse took place.

Many topics are inevitably only touched on and some additional details would have been welcome to aid understanding: a photograph or diagram to show what varves look like, a diagram to explain how roche moutonnées are formed, an additional sketch map to show the origin of the middle Parallel Road in Glen Roy, inclusion of cone sheets (important features in the Cuillin) and maybe even caves and potholes. This book certainly whets the appetite for further information. My only wish is that the author now writes a much more comprehensive book on this complex and fascinating subject for which he is exceptionally well qualified.

In summary, this book is an excellent introduction to mountain landscapes, and is a sure to appeal to the market it is aimed at.

Noel Williams

Chasing the Dreams: Hamish Brown (Sandstone Press, 2019, paperback, 320pp, ISBN 978-1-91224-078-4, £8.99; ISBNe 978-1-91224-079-1, ebook, Kindle £4.07).

With some books, especially those with numerous, short narrative descriptions, I like in the first instance to flick through the book, picking out pages which have caught my eye. Akin to sniffing a wine's bouquet if you like. In this book, Hamish's follow-up to *Walking the Song* (2017), I had chosen a dangerous route, as it often drew me in like some sucker at a carnival, beguiled by the barker's sing-song. Happily, unlike the carnival experience, the narratives from Hamish were invariably interesting.

In his foreword, Brown briefly lays out the line of the book, with sections of related themes and interests. Much of it is of course autobiographical, and has been published before, though I very much doubt if many have read all that is in this collection. Hamish writes that he had taken more to heart Dr Johnson's admonition to Boswell, '...when we travel again let us look better about us.' I disagree: Brown has the valuable knack of descriptive writing that is easy to follow and often fun to read; he has his diaries for fact-checking, and I would predict that adding any more detail to his tales would lead to readers switching off. Sometimes it's what you leave out which makes it work.

In other cases, I catch myself wondering just how Hamish knows some facts he mentions, such as when, on Ben Nevis, he spots climbers on routes on Càrn Dearg Buttress, including *Centurion* and *Caligula*. Now, how and where did he acquire the knowledge to recognise these rock climbs? The former classic route I could believe, as it takes such a prominent line and has been around for a considerable time, but *Caligula* is the province of hard climbers, and our man does not sup there.

The book divides the essays into eight sections, with for example the first having the title 'Tramping in Scotland.' As noted above, the sections have related themes, giving the reader a choice of how to approach the book. My choice was to vary the reading as much as possible, typically choosing one from a section then going to another section for the next read. Alternatively, should you be interested in the young Brown (and as you know, he's no chicken!), then you can wade through his youthful author section, or the overseas stories and so on.

There are some interesting nuggets of information to be found here and there, much like a block of stone studded with various xenoliths. So in his very first essay, on tackling winter Munros on ski, Brown observes, using his log books or diaries, that as the years advanced, so did the altitude of the snowline, hill-for-hill, time-of-year for time-of-year. 'You would need to be mental', as he writes here, 'to deny climate change'. There are two longer articles, one on the Ben Nevis Meteorological Summit Station and the other on Sheriff Nicolson of Skye, both well covered.

In another walk, Brown relates how memory can be patchy, but in this case he was able to recall the story of how Gairloch became Mackenzie land. He was quite proud of his memory. This is another instance where my curiosity got the better of me and off I went to read up the sorry tale. You can find it related in a marvellous book by John H. Dixon. (*Gairloch in North-West Ross-shire* [1886]. Chapter 7 has the title 'The M'Leods of Gairloch'. The entire book is available at <electricscotland.com/history/gairloch/g2ndx.htm>, and a very bloody story some of it is too.) I would always be careful however of someone's memory (and that includes my own!). Even if backed up by a diary entry at the time, it is possible to forget either partly or entirely, an event in the past.

Brown intersperses his text sections with the occasional short poem, saying or proverb (including some of his own) for example, 'Hills and seas neither love nor hate us / But they have the notion yet to try and break us.' —Anon.

It should be a mark of how interesting is this collection of Brown's that I was frequently tempted to spend more time truly reading it than simply tasting it. This comment should be tempered by the fact that I have read little of his output over the years, his material not being infected by the vertical stuff. Perhaps his many fans would hesitate before a purchase if they thought it was a reheating of old dishes. I certainly have little hesitation in recommending this book as a thorough insight into the adventures the outdoors in Scotland can offer.

There is one possible thorn here, however: much of his wanderings were done decades ago, when the hills were lonely. He does not provide the dates the articles were written, so it is my conjecture that many of the places and sites he writes about could now be spoiled by crowds. You have been warned!

Having written the above paragraph, I have to note that we are currently in an unprecedented situation throughout the world with the appearance at the end of winter 2020 of a new virus that rapidly became a pandemic. This prompted many countries, including the UK, to call a virtual halt to hillwalking and other games. This review was written during March-April of that year, and the countryside has never been quieter, giving the reading of this book an air of melancholy. It has also given me, and hopefully other readers, added yearning for more of the outdoors.

Finally, and I almost say that with reluctance as I could go on with more promissory notes on his material, I once asked Hamish, in one of our very rare and very short conversations, whether he had ever felt bored on a walk up a hill. As you might expect the answer was a definite No. This takes enthusiasm, and he has been successful here in imbuing his collection with that same feeling.

(The text in this collection was edited by fellow SMC member Bob Aitken, who also prepared the articles into their final form).

Ken Crocket

Sannu Bature — The Climbing Life of Des Rubens, SMC: edited by Geoff Cohen (Upfront Publishing, 2019, hardback, 353pp, ISBN 978-1-78456-667-8, £16.99).

This book is a splendid celebration of the life of our late and much-loved Past President, Des Rubens. It has been put together by his great friend Geoff Cohen with whom he shared many adventures over more than forty years, forming one of the most successful climbing partnerships in the history of the SMC. About half the book consists of selected entries from the diaries which Des maintained up until 1986 (when family responsibilities took over) and these are supplemented by articles written by himself and others for the *SMCJ*, the *Alpine Journal* and the *Scottish Mountaineer* magazine. Also included are the moving tributes and obituaries which followed his untimely death on the Finsteraarhorn in June 2016.

For me the most absorbing passages are the diary entries, particularly those from his early days with the EUMC. Des was a fine writer and his diary is no mere catalogue of ascents but a series of vivid descriptions of the whole mountain experience, punctuated with his own inimitable, dry humour. Whether climbing steep rock or ice or tramping through the rain over boggy moors, his enthusiasm for the hills in all their moods shines through. Many obvious epics are understated, such as his bold solo ascent of the final pitch of *Big Top* when his second was unable to follow. After reaching the top, 'I found a bod, borrowed his rope, and abseiled down to Mitch twirling gaily in space. Three 150-foot abseils took us to the foot of the climb and I returned the rope to its rightful owner.' As simple as that. In contrast, he describes in great detail a wonderful week's walking through Knoydart with his wife Jane in the spring of 1975. The diversity of his interests is exemplified by a later, long weekend in the Cairngorms when he spent the first day ice-climbing above Loch Avon, the second rock-climbing on a roadside outcrop and the third ski-touring on the Great Moss.

Des's early Alpine seasons are described by Dave Broadhead (including their ascent of the Walker Spur, summed up in just three sentences) and the later ones by Geoff Cohen and Stan Pearson. Des himself tells the story of his ascent, at the age of 60, of Mont Blanc by the Peuterey Ridge which he achieved with Geoff in 2013, surely one of the highlights of their partnership. Then of course there were the expeditions; for Des was a natural explorer, and his travels, all in the best light-weight tradition, took him to the Karakoram, where in 1985 he made a notable attempt on Gasherbrum III — again with Geoff — as well as to the Caucasus, China, Peru, Canada and the Yosemite valley. These are recounted in a number of previously published articles all of which make engaging reading regardless of the success or failure of the expedition in its objectives.

In his professional life Des was a highly respected Outdoor Education Teacher, and this aspect is covered in an enlightening chapter contributed by Jane as well as in a tribute by a former pupil of Craigroyston High School in Edinburgh where he worked for many years.

The book is lavishly illustrated with superb photographs and is worth having for these alone. Not all good climbers are also good photographers but Des was very obviously both. Happily, so are several of his friends and the results include some nostalgic pictures of the man himself. The front cover shows him in his element on a Californian rock-climb but I much preferred the later portrait beside the title page, taken on the Obergabelhorn in 2010 at the time of his Presidency.

This book is a fitting memorial to a man who lived life to the full and seemed to embody the spirit of Scottish mountaineering. It is well presented with a good-sized font for the text, excellent quality for the photographs and the chapters in a roughly chronological sequence with short editorial introductions where appropriate. It is a book that can be read through or dipped into at random, for each episode is a good tale on its own while also being part of a much greater story. The title is derived from the Hausa language and was often quoted by Des and his friends, meaning simply 'How are you, my friend?' He was a friend indeed to many, and Geoff is to be congratulated, along with the other contributors, for producing what should be an essential addition to all our bookshelves.

Peter F. Macdonald

Crazy Sorrow: Grant Farquhar (Atlantis, 2019, paperback, 260pp, ISBN 978-1-99996-005-6, £20.67).

Crazy Sorrow is a significant book. It documents the life of Alan Mullin, who stands alongside Raeburn, Patey, Smith and Nisbet as one of great innovators of Scottish winter climbing. Grant Farquhar should be congratulated for not only describing the life story of this important pioneer, but also for capturing the spirit of a key period in Scottish climbing history.

Alan Mullin made an unconventional entry into the world of climbing. He joined the army at the age of 16, and spent eight years on active service before he retired owing to an injured back. Without the constraint of a full-time job, he was able to turn his considerable energy to Scottish winter climbing. After experimenting with some of the easier routes in the Northern Corries, he was leading difficult Grade VI within 12 months. He formed a strong partnership with Steve Paget, and in October 1998 (Alan's third season), they made the second winter ascent of *The Needle* (VIII,8) on the Shelter Stone.

The following year Mullin and Paget upped their game a notch further and returned to the Shelter Stone to make the first winter ascent of *The Steeple* (IX,9) with the *Dusk till Dawn Variation*. The route was climbed in a single 24-hour push by climbing continuously through the night. Two weeks later, Mullin was in the headlines again with the first winter ascent of *Rolling Thunder*, an E1 rock climb on the Tough-Brown Face of Lochnagar. This was the first (and only) time a new Grade VIII had ever been soloed. It stunned the climbing world, not least because no other party made it into the corrie that day as the weather was so bad. Niall Ritchie's long distance shot of Alan climbing the route, with avalanches crashing down either side (reproduced in the book), remains one of the most iconic winter climbing photos ever taken.

The impact of these routes on the Scottish winter climbing scene was electric. It normally takes years of experience to acquire the spectrum of skills necessary to climb high-standard winter routes, so how could a relative newcomer operate at the highest standards of the day? The answer partly lay in Alan's rigorous training regime, but mainly in the total focus and unswerving determination he applied to his routes. As someone new to the Scottish winter game, Alan was unencumbered by the weight of history, and almost unknowingly smashed his way through psychological barriers. Many other climbers realised that they could also increase their performance, and over a couple of seasons in the late 1990s, average standards rose a full grade. No longer were Grade VIIs the province of the elite, but they were accessible by weekend climbers too.

Despite the inspiration Alan provided, he had an uneasy relationship with the climbing community. He claimed to respect no other climber's achievements, but in effect he deeply craved recognition by his peers. At first this was forthcoming, but eventually it became increasingly withheld as it was realised that the majority of his ascents were flawed. Several of his routes were climbed when not fully in condition, and others used a point or two of aid. Whilst Alan was always honest about the manner of his climbs, his enthusiasm to describe the intensity of his experience meant that he sometimes forgot to immediately relate all the details.

Alan was on a quest to find a Scottish climb that was comparable in technical difficulty to the hardest bolt-protected climbs elsewhere. In November 2002 he fulfilled his dream when he made the first winter ascent of *Crazy Sorrow*, a difficult E3 6a on the Tough-Brown Face of Lochnagar, with Steve Lynch. The route goes through a huge roof on the second pitch, with scant protection. Alan graded it X,11, renamed it *Frozen Sorrow*, and suggested it was a contender for the hardest traditional mixed climb in the world. Unfortunately the gloss was taken off this remarkable lead by allegations that he had inspected the route beforehand, and climbed it when it was out of condition. Once the photos were published it was clear that the route was in *bona fide* winter condition, but once again Alan's impatience had got the better of him and he had abseiled off after the crux pitch and failed to complete the route.

Frozen Sorrow was the last of Alan's great climbs, and he announced his retirement soon after. He was clearly disenchanted with the climbing world for not recognising his achievements on his terms, but his body was also taking the toll from his intense training régime, and he was living with a series of chronic injuries. Alan found it impossible to control the demons that had driven him so hard during his short but remarkable climbing career, and tragically he took his own life in March 2007.

Grant Farquhar has made an important contribution to Scottish mountain history by pulling together this account of Alan Mullin's all too short and turbulent life. *Crazy Sorrow* is based on Alan's writings, contemporary accounts by other climbers and more recent interviews. Grant skilfully adds colour to the climbing narrative with accounts of Alan's tough upbringing and brutal time in the army that sets the context for his later climbing career. Grant is a professional psychologist and is well placed to explain the internal conflicts that Alan faced at the end of his life.

Crazy Sorrow is not a comfortable read, but it documents a vibrant and important phase of Scottish climbing. The tragedy of the Alan Mullin story is that Alan never recognised his profound influence on the climbing world. If he had, his life might not have been so troubled, and perhaps he would still be with us today.

Simon Richardson

The Uncrowned King of Mont Blanc — The Life of T. Graham Brown, Physiologist and Mountaineer: Peter Foster (Bâton Wicks[1], 2019, paperback, 205pp, ISBN 978-1-89857-382-1, £14.95).

The story of Graham Brown – as he was called by all who knew him in Edinburgh – is told here by Peter Foster, alpinist and consultant gastro-enterologist, who has

---

[1] Bâton Wicks is an imprint of Vertebrate Publishing, which VP purchased from the late Ken Wilson.

written articles about Brown for the Alpine Journal and for our own Journal[2]. The book has been ably reviewed at length in the AJ, by Ed Douglas, and on the Footless Crow blog by Dennis Gray[3], so it is useless for me to repeat their excellent commentaries. It is sufficient here to note that Foster covers Brown's early life in Edinburgh, his physiological work at Liverpool in Sherrington's laboratory, his war work and the early stages of his professorship at Cardiff[4] in five careful chapters, before turning to his mountaineering career. Although the hook of mountaineering was set in 1914, when he was 32, the war intervened, and it was not until 1920 that he became devoted to it. Thirteen chapters then deal with Brown's climbing career in Britain, the Alps, Alaska and the Himalaya. A final three chapters cover Brown's stint as Alpine Journal Editor, his contributions to Alpine historical literature, and his years of retirement in Edinburgh.

It is unlikely that Foster's book will be the last word about Brown. His voluminous archives in the National Library of Scotland, although accessible to the public, are subject to severe limitations where photography is concerned, and reproduction by the Library is prohibitively expensive except to scholars with large grants. And of course there are substantial archives elsewhere, notably at the Alpine Club, as well as Brown's many contributions to mountaineering journals and his books – in all, a prodigious mountain of material. Foster's biography is however a thorough piece of research, with admirable pains taken to describe Brown's scientific work, and to be fair to Brown's achievements –which have often been overlooked because of his difficulties in managing personal relations. Even his scientific work, which encompassed a breakthrough in understanding of the rôle of centres in the spinal cord in the control of locomotion, suffered neglect because of his unfortunate decision to publish his most important papers in German, just before and during WWI.[5]

Foster has two main threads in his evaluation of Brown's mountaineering: the lack of recognition given to Brown's tremendous achievements in the Alps, and the flaws in his character that led to endless disputes with Frank Smythe about the Brenva routes, to fallouts in the Himalayas following the 1936 Nanda Devi expedition and during the 1937 Masherbrum expedition, and to quarrels with Geoffrey Young and Tom Blakeney during his tenure of the Editorship. There seems little doubt that Brown was much disliked: only Edwin Herbert (later Lord Tangley) and Charles Houston seem to have had much liking for him, and he fell out with Houston after Nanda Devi and Tangley had the miserable job of sacking him from the Editorship. It is always difficult for an editor to know when to go, and Brown had done five journals, so Tangley may have done him a favour by saving him from further undermining attacks by Young and his friends.

Brown's Alpine career spanned the period 1924–1937 with some seasons after the second War, and encompassed *grandes courses* on all the major peaks of the

[2] 'The Brenva Feud' (with Gareth Jones), *AJ* 2014, 223–30; 'The Vagabond Professor,' *SMCJ* 2015, 423–7.

[3] *AJ* 2019, 330–35; footlesscrow.blogspot.com August 2019.

[4] For his later career at Cardiff, see the wonderful account by Gareth Jones (2011), 'Thomas Graham Brown (1882–1965): Behind the Scenes at the Cardiff Institute of Physiology,' *J. Hist. Neurosciences*, available on researchgate.net.

[5] 'Die reflexfunktionen des zentral-nervensystems, besonders von standpunkt der rhythmischen Tätigkeiten beim Säugetier Betrachtet,' Ergebnisse der Physiologie 13: 279–453 and 15: 480–790.

chain. Foster characterizes 1933 as his annus mirabilis. This was the year in which, climbing with the guide Alexander Graven, he achieved his dream of a third route on the Brenva Face, the *Via Della Pera*, which was a triumph of research and route-finding by Brown. 'In an extraordinary fortnight, he climbed Mont Blanc six times, making three new routes, two of which were at the highest standard of difficulty for the period. In addition, he made half a dozen first ascents on the peaks above Zermatt and in the Dauphiné (p. 84).' The Mont Blanc fortnight was only an episode in a very long season: 'In just under eight weeks .... [he] had only five days of rest: three were enforced by bad weather, and two were spent in travelling between regions (p. 96).' Foster concludes, 'Nine years after his first visit .... aged fifty-one, [he] was the foremost alpinist in Britain (p. 98).' I am sure that Foster is correct in this judgment. Brown had even contemplated ascents of the north faces of the Eiger and Grandes Jorasses, visiting Kleine Scheidegg and the Leschaux Hut (twice) to inspect them. Yet he did not prosper within the Alpine Club, being refused the Vice-Presidency twice and never considered for the Presidency.

There is no doubt that Brown's approach to mountaineering was excessively scientific: many of his companions ridiculed his habit of continuous photography and meticulous note-taking on major climbs. But there is nothing wrong with making notes and taking photographs. Many of us must wish, as I certainly do, that we had done more of that sort of thing. If George Mallory had taken better care of his camera and made some notes in 1924, we would not 100 years on still have to wonder where he got to on Everest. It must surely be that Brown's companions deplored the waste of time and the incompatibility of such bureaucracy with the romance of mountaineering. Yet Brown was not without romance; the source of his interest in the great Brenva Face and perhaps in alpinism was an early reading of the romantic novel *Running Water* by A.E.W. Mason, which filled his mind with potent fantasies. As Edwin Herbert remarked, Brown's was a very complex personality, and of course there is a case that these two elements – a strong imagination allied to meticulous experimentation – are crucial components in scientific progress.

Brown's talent for diplomacy may be assessed at zero. Time and again Foster describes him falling into unnecessary squabbles with key figures in the Alpine Club and elsewhere. But I wonder if many of these squabbles were more or less inevitable. In the period of Brown's involvement the Alpine Club was dominated by an elite forged by Geoffrey Young at Pen-y-Pass, and mainly composed of the products of the favoured English public schools and Oxbridge (in the main, Cambridge). Brown was Scottish, of course, and a product of Edinburgh Academy and University, remote outposts in a barbarian land. The spiteful attitudes of Young and his crony Claude Elliott are well described by Foster around pages 166–7. I used to believe that it was just Scots in the Alpine Club who were subject to back-stabbing and prejudice (thinking of poor Raeburn – who, before and after WWI, was the foremost alpinist in Britain) but now I think that English mountaineers not part of the *jeunesse dorée* had just as hard a time before the cleansing rise of the ACG. So I wonder if Foster, educated at Westminster and Christ Church, Oxford, becomes just a touch too comfortable in the final chapters with the common tendency within the Club to find flaws in Brown's character. Perhaps not: George Ingle Finch, so like Brown in temperament and background, would be a possible contradictory case, although he (like Brown) left his papers to the NLS rather than to the Alpine Club. And of course I am myself prejudiced, having enjoyed the pleasure of Brown's company in the last few years of his life, and having found him at all times amiable and agreeable.

A final word about the layout of Foster's book. On cover and title-page 'Mont Blanc' is headlined and capitalized, whereas 'Graham Brown' is not, just as in Tony Smythe's biography of his father Frank, 'Everest' is dragged onto the title page for no good reason. These are market-driven impulses of the publishers rather than the authors, I suspect. There is a useful bibliography and index, and every chapter is meticulously referenced in a manner pleasing to the shade of Brown, although all are shovelled to the end of the book, which would not have pleased him; and, for a decrepit reader like me, a magnifying glass is required to read these appendices, which rather demeans their importance.

Robin N. Campbell

Paul Preuss, Lord of the Abyss — Life and Death at the Birth of Free-Climbing: David Smart (Rocky Mountain Books, 2019, hardback, 247pp, ISBN 978-1-77160-323-2, £19.95).

Paul Preuss (1886–1913) was one of the finest climbers and alpinists of his age. He was the Alex Honnold, or Julian Lines, of his day – someone who could solo rock at the highest level. Indeed he preferred soloing to climbing with a partner; his purist philosophy regarded not just pitons but even ropes as detracting from the moral worth of a climb, and thus he even looked askance at abseiling. One of his most famous achievements was the 1911 first ascent, solo, of the East face of the Campanile Basso. When we climbed it with plenty of modern gear I felt it deserved about E1 and was very happy to take a belay below the steepest section!

This well-researched biography by David Smart (editorial director of Canada's climbing magazine *Gripped*), documents in detail Preuss's climbs in the Eastern Alps (and a few in the Western Alps) but also presents a fascinating picture of the climbing scene in Austria in the decades before the first world war. We get a feel for the style and difficulty of the climbs pioneered by Preuss and his contemporaries, for their clothes and equipment, the state of the huts, what they ate and drank, their social life in the cities, how the alpine clubs functioned and what the numerous alpine magazines were like.

Preuss was 'almost ritualistically fastidious about his clothes': his sister 'noted that although he often returned from a climb with his suit in tatters, everything from his tie to his vest remained in its proper place.' Perhaps unusually for his time, Preuss often climbed with women, and although not without chauvinism he penned an article on 'Climbing with Women' for the climbing press. Once he had become well known he lost interest in his doctoral studies in plant biology, and became almost a full-time lecturer on climbing, skiing and alpinism: between 1912 and 1913 he gave over 150 presentations.

Although there are sections about his sorties from Zermatt and on the south side of Mont Blanc, and a couple of longer chapters about his climbs in the Dolomites and Kaisegebirge, much of the climbing takes place in a part of Austria that is probably less familiar to many British climbers. Altaussee, southeast of Salzburg, was where Preuss spent much of his adolescence and first began to climb alone in the mountains of the Gosaukamm, Totes Gebirge, Dachstein and Gesause ranges. Unfortunately the book lacks any detailed maps of these mountains. So, for example, when one reads (p.49) a list such as 'the Hochtor, the Planspitze, the Tamischbachturm, the Grosser Buchstein and the Rosskuppe' one is little the wiser, especially as the few mountain photographs are black and white ones of the period with generally poor resolution. While some of the contemporary photos convey beautifully the atmosphere of the period and the dress, equipment and bearing of the protagonists, there are some that are just too blurred and small to be of great interest. They are also arranged in a confusingly random order, whereas the text as a whole is arranged in a logical historical sequence. Although it may have been considered too jarring with the originals, it would have helped to provide some clear modern photos of the main mountain faces described in the text.

The introductory chapter covering Preuss's family background and early years is set in the late Austro-Hungarian Empire. Preuss's father, a musician, was Jewish but assimilated; his mother, a Protestant from Alsace, converted to Judaism. I was surprised to discover just how many of the climbers in Preuss's coterie were Jewish, though Preuss himself converted to Protestantism at the age of 22. Smart devotes a fair number of asides to considering how Preuss's Jewish background, along with the prevailing anti-Semitism in the Austria of the times, affected his approach to climbing. Preuss often climbed with Sigmund Freud's daughter Anna and son Martin, and Smart considers what the psychoanalyst might have discovered : 'Would time on Martin Freud's father's famous couch have exposed a system of insecurity behind Paul's self-confidence? ... He had been sick as a boy but survived [polio], although his father had died, giving him a sense of immortality and a bond with his mother by removing the Freudian rival. Had Paul's personal struggle been sublimated into climbing ethics?'

Pen portraits of some of Preuss's famous climbing contemporaries make a valuable addition to the book. For example we learn that Hans Dulfer was highly musical and wanted to compose 'an Eroica on rock'. He apparently wrote: 'It seems strange to me that the majority of climbers know only one urge, which is to go on bagging one summit after another.' Not a Salvationist, then! I warmed too to the anticlerical socialist Tita Piaz, who was expelled from school for refusing to make his confession and failed his guide's test which he described as an exercise in servility. While both these brilliant climbers acknowledged Preuss's even greater brilliance, they were less extreme in their attitudes to protection. A debate on this topic in the climbing magazines of 1911–12 is illuminated in an interesting chapter. Preuss felt that you should only climb up that which you can also safely climb down. He enunciated six fundamental 'theses' among which were: 'The piton is an emergency reserve and not the basis for a method of working. The rope is permitted as a relief-bringing means but ought never be the one true means for making the ascent of the mountain possible'. According to Smart, 'his theses put the climber's vulnerability to failure and even injury or death at the existential core of climbing.'

As an illustration of his prowess, in 1908 Preuss took time off from a short-term tutoring job in Zermatt to solo the Matterhorn by the Hörnli ridge, descend the Italian ridge, and after a cold bivvy return to Zermatt via the Breithorn. Not a bad two-day excursion! Although largely remembered for his amazing rock climbs he was also an avid ski tourer, and was enthusiastic about 'enchainments' even in winter. In all this there is much that prefigures modern approaches. Preuss met his fate on a solo attempt on the unclimbed North ridge of the Mandlkogel. It is not known exactly why he fell, but Smart carefully considers all the hypotheses that have been proposed. It was a cold October day, the rock was very suspect and he had only partly recovered from a fever.

This is a book very well worth reading for its thoughtful coverage of a vital period in the evolution of rock climbing as well as its rounded picture of an outstandingly talented and complex climber. There have been previous biographies in Italian and German but it is the first in English. With lively writing and meticulous bibliography Smart offers the monoglot British climber an opportunity to gain a much deeper understanding of the history of continental climbing in the decades leading up to the First World War.

Geoff Cohen

Alpenglow: Ben Tibbetts (self-published, 2019, hardback, 320pp, ISBN 978-1-91612-310-6, £50).

This is a sumptuous volume of artistic and photographic images of routes in the high Alps, researched, climbed, photographed, drawn, written up and published by the author himself. Much more than a coffee-table extravaganza, it is both an historical and a personal account of 4000m peak ascents by Tibbetts over the past ten years. He has climbed all the routes he describes; indeed, he was the second Brit to complete all the 82 UIAA 4000m peaks, as a qualified Alpine guide resident in Chamonix (lucky so-and-so!).

Tibbetts opens his heart in the writing, revealing with honesty when he has been scared witless; or was thrilled with a night sky on torch-lit climbs, his photographs exulting in dawn panoramas with partner concentrating on the way ahead, not posing, but looking well to each step. We feel the reluctant 2 a.m. starts, the sleep deprivation, the hypoxia of altitude, the doubts and hesitations along the way; but also the watchful discipline demanded by changing conditions, where an awkward decision might need intuition as well as intelligence, insight born of hard experience. He admits that '... sometimes just good luck ...' keeps the show on the road; with crowded routes, a dislodged boulder 'thirty metres above us ... the size of a football ... coming directly for us ... bounced once ... glancing blow ... I was shaking uncontrollably ... finally out of the terror zone.' He admits to the doubts and insecurities of the night before a route, that cold chill of uncertainty with deteriorating weather and the crux still ahead, thunder throwing up overhead, and lightning fizzing with energy.

What of the routes chosen? The Lauper route on the Mönch, the North-East Ridge of the Jungfrau, *Cresta di Santa Caterina* on Nordend, *Cresta Signal* on Signalkuppe, the North Ridge of the Weisshorn, and of course the Zmutt on the Matterhorn. Big routes. And the evocative pre-dawn pools of light on snow; and cream-cake cornice edges. Then the expedition-sized routes on Mont Blanc, namely the *Peuterey Intégral*, *Cecchinel-Nominé* on the Grand Pilier d'Angle, and the long and adventurous *Brouillard Intégral* direct from Val Vény. And more modest routes for normal mortals, throughout the Alps, occasionally bumping into the celebrities within our Alpinism. Aspirational, all of them. No need to take that long-haul flight to a far-away continent; it's all here in Europe.

There are moments too of transcendence, after he has snapped his photographic fill, when he can gaze out across a vast landscape and reflect that 'making drawings and photos in these savage landscapes ... gives my life purpose'. Here at last his humanity and humility become at one with nature. He reflects that '... moments in the mountains are so often far more potent than any words, photographs or memories...' And thus we the readers once again find ourselves heading back there, if only because we have now armchaired our way through photographs that reminded us of profound experiences we yearn to repeat.

John Allen

I had been following Ben Tibbetts's fine photographs on Facebook for some years. I was impressed. They are beautiful. I knew that Tibbetts was in the process of climbing all the 4000-metre peaks in the Alps, and that he was working on a book about them. I'm a little unclear about the numbers. But then I'm not very good at counting, or ticking. How many 4000-metre peaks *are* there in the Alps? Martin Moran and Simon Jenkins climbed 75 of them in a single push in 1993, as recounted in *Alps 4000: 75 Peaks in 52 Days*. Will McLewin only lists 53 in his magnificent book, *In Monte Viso's Horizon: climbing all the Alpine 4000m Peaks*. It seems the number of Alpine 4000ers fluctuates in much the same way as the number of Munros in *Munro's Tables*. In the contents pages of his book, Tibbetts lists 73 summits (if I've counted right). Searching online, one site says that although there are 85 'tops' above 4000 metres, there are just 50 'principal peaks'. Happily, the numbers aren't the point. 'For me,' Tibbetts says in his introduction, 'the summit is like a punctuation mark in the story …'

Tibbetts's book was announced for 2019. I knew he was self-publishing. I subscribed, to secure my copy. I had been expecting a large-format coffee-table book stuffed with beautiful photographs — what I disrespectfully refer to as 'mountain-porn'. *Alpenglow* is indeed a large-format coffee-table book stuffed with beautiful photographs. But it is much more than that.

In the lead-up to printing, Tibbetts had been requesting help from publishing professionals. Oh dear, I thought, perhaps he's taken on more than he can chew. Producing a large-format coffee-table book stuffed with beautiful photographs requires a lot of investment, both in terms of money and in terms of editorial, design and production skills.

When my copy eventually arrived — there had been some trials and tribulations with the printer, something to do with creased dust-jackets I think — I opened the package with some trepidation. Was it going to be a rather embarrassingly amateur mess? It wasn't. It isn't. Not only are the photographs beautifully shot; they are beautifully printed. And the design is first-rate. There are also a number of useful diagrammatic drawings by the author. But the real surprise, to me at least, was the excellence of the writing.

Tibbetts has read widely in the historical accounts, not just those of Victorian pioneers such as Sir Leslie Stephen, but also those of less familiar figures such as Hans Lauper, the first ascensionist of the 1921 route on the North-West Spur of the Mönch. He also provides much practical advice regarding conditions, approach, route, descent and equipment. But it is his accounts of his own ascents that give this book its real quality. In his introduction Tibbetts says that photographs can only tell half the story, if that. Photographs can be thrilling, beautiful, uplifting, he says, but the full experience of climbing a long and serious Alpine route — the fear, strain, effort and uncertainty — can only be conveyed in words. 'Many of the experiences in this book,' Tibbetts says, 'represent my internal struggle between my desire for adventure and my darkest fears. Although this emotional interplay could define much of human experience, alpinism in particular requires its faithful to subject themselves to an extremely high baseline of risk …'

Tibbetts is scrupulously honest about his experiences. Having suffered a number of near misses, he is ever aware of his fallibility and mortality, always anxious about the safety of his partners. At one point, teetering along a narrow ridge of snow and ice, he writes: 'The promise of feeling liberty, joy and oneness with the mountain environment was negated by the simple fear of falling.' This is not Gaston Rébuffat, perfectly poised on the crest, chin up to the summit. Tibbetts frequently questions his own motivations, often contemplates turning round and retreating. He is not afraid to show us that he is not a mountain god; just a human like the rest of us — aspiring, perspiring, weakening, sometimes terrified.

Tibbetts rarely ascends his 4000-metre peaks by the *voie normale*. If he does, then it is combined with something meatier: for example, the ordinary route on Castor (one of the very few peaks in this book I have climbed myself) is followed, on the same day, by the traverse of the entire summit ridge of neighbouring Lyskamm. At the other end of the spectrum, there are modern test-pieces such as the *Colton-MacIntyre* on the Grandes Jorasses, and the author's own new line on the Aiguille du Jardin. In between, there are a host of challenging classics, from the North Ridge of the Weisshorn and the Zmutt Ridge on the Matterhorn to the *Cresta di Santa Caterina* on Nordend and the *Peuterey Intégral* on Mont Blanc.

For the armchair mountaineer — as we all must be during lockdown — this book is manna from heaven. Stuck within our four walls, we are privileged to accompany an experienced and thoughtful guide via his words and pictures up some of the most glorious and demanding routes in the Alps, sometimes concentrating on a small patch of snow or rock, sometimes revelling in the beauty and warmth brought by the dawn, sometimes contemplating our modest place beneath the immensity of the entire, star-filled sky.

Ian Crofton

Scottish Island Bagging: Helen & Paul Webster (Vertebrate, 2019, paperback, 256pp, ISBN 978-1-91256-031-8, £17.99).

Most people would agree that islands have a particular charm and attraction over and above the basic fact they stand separated from adjacent land masses, surrounded by water (depending, of course, on how you define 'an island', of which more later). Islands have long sparked the creative imagination, evoking romance, fantasy, mystery, tragedy, notions of paradise, utopia and dystopia, across all of the arts. In literature, for example, Goodreads.com lists no fewer than 858 novels set on islands. On the silver screen, Wikipedia lists hundreds of films located on an island (with a special sub-category of films set on uninhabited islands!). There's even a sub-genre of reality TV specialising in islands — think of 'Castaway' or 'Love Island. And let's face it, 'Desert Mainland Discs' might not have captured the public imagination quite as well as its island counterpart. Hamish Haswell-Smith, author of the definitive work *The Scottish Islands*, wondered whether it might be 'because an island is of human scale, easy to comprehend, safe and defensible when the world beyond is big and terrifying.'

There is, to quote Helen and Paul Webster, the authors of *Scottish Island Bagging*, an 'indefinable magic' about islands, not least the ones that surround the Scottish coastline. Scotland apparently has over two-thirds of the total UK coastline, some six thousand miles in all, and around it lie an immeasurable number of islands and islets, skerries, reefs and stacks, mostly on the west coast. The variety of maritime and mountain landscapes and geology, the rich natural and social history, and of course the weather, conspire to create a unique character. Haswell-Smith goes as far as to contend 'there are few parts of the world which possess such magic and mystery'.

Before getting on to island *bagging*, we should first we say what we mean by the term *island*. The 1861 Scottish Census defined an island as 'any piece of solid land surrounded by water which affords sufficient vegetation to support one or two sheep, or is inhabited by man', understandably (for census purposes) overlooking an awful lot of Scotland's rocky and/or uninhabited landmasses. More recently, Haswell-Smith applied what he described as 'very restrictive rules of classification' in drawing up his list of 162 islands, excluding any that were bridged (e.g. Skye), smaller than 40 hectares, or not completely surrounded by water at 'Lowest Astronomical Tide' (e.g. Oronsay, reached across The Strand from Colonsay at low tide). The Websters took a pragmatic approach in this guide, and focused on '99 islands that have regular trips or means of access for visitors', along with an additional 55 that have no regular transport but are still of 'significant size or interest'.

So what's this 'island bagging' (a term that's likely to raise the hackles of some readers) all about? The analogy with Munroing is obvious; the annual reports in this journal are testament to the many ways in which people 'compleat', and so too with island bagging. The Websters start by reminding us that, at the very least, you have to visit the place!

Yorkshireman Andy Strangeway went one step further and, over a period of four years in the mid-2000s, slept at least one night on all Haswell-Smith's 162 islands (no mean feat). However, given the range of features that distinguish one island from another— or as Haswell-Smith put it, in this 'serene yet chaotic landscape….every isle has a distinct personality. Each is an individual' — the Websters suggest that there is no single 'correct' way to 'bag' an island. To quote the authors, 'Which island experience you choose is entirely up to you.'

What of the guide? Well for its size it is a fairly lavish publication, nicely laid out, well written, and illustrated with high-quality photographs that complement the text. The guide is divided into geographical clusters, with, for each island, details of access and accommodation (if available), a description of its key features (geological, historical, and cultural), then, depending on its size, one or more paragraphs outlining particular things to do or see. For example, there are descriptions of walks to summits and key viewpoints, along with plenty of references to things cultural, be they historical, musical or gustatory. The recommendations made for islands with which I am well acquainted seemed, on the whole, appropriate. It is not a climbing or mountaineering guide, and understandably any references to climbing are made in passing: Pabbay gets half a paragraph (Mingulay none!), the Skye chapter somewhat cringeworthily includes a 'Conquer a Cuillin' section, and so on. But although it is not written for climbers, there are plenty of suggestions for walks and scrambles, some of them quite challenging, for example the 128 km-long Skye Trail. The guide is well indexed and the only thing that grates is the inevitable tick list ('In the Bag') at the end of the book.

There is always a danger that waxing lyrical about beautiful and wild places might encourage people to visit in large numbers, at best crowding them out, at worst perhaps even destroying them. One only has to look at the unintended negative effects that the hoards undertaking the 'North Coast 500' have had on local communities. Having said that, island economies depend crucially on tourism and most would likely welcome and could probably accommodate increased traffic (more than ever, one expects, after COVID). Further, singing the praises of some of the islands in this guide is unlikely to boost visitor numbers overmuch as they are especially challenging to access. For example, to get onto Boreray, one of the St Kilda archipelago, Andy Strangeway had to find someone willing to take him, wait six weeks for the right tide and, once landed, was faced with a scary scramble to the summit (it's quite steep!). Indeed to visit most of the 55 islands that do not have routine access you will have to charter a local boatman.

I should declare my hand. I am an island addict, mainly hooked on the Scottish islands, though not exclusively. (We have a friendly rivalry with another family, with whom we have enjoyed many a hearty Hebridean holiday over the years, triggered whenever one of us visits a 'new' island, wherever it may be on the planet.) As with all addictions it started innocently enough: a Victoria Weekend trip to Skye with the Edinburgh University Mountaineering Club in 1971. We approached by fishing boat from Mallaig, and camped at Loch Scavaig. It rained virtually the whole weekend. We trudged up to Sgùrr MhicCoinnich on two consecutive days and started out to climb, but were rained off, in succession, and in descending order of difficulty, *King Cobra* (two pitches), *Dawn Grooves* (one pitch), *Crack of Dawn* (half a pitch) and *Fluted Buttress* (a few moves — until the sleet started). Tents flooded, we eventually decamped to the hut to the chagrin of two Club members 'of a certain age', but luckily we had a couple of members in our ranks to defend our actions. On the last night the rain stopped, the stars came out and we had a bonfire with a backdrop of the serrated ramparts of the Cuillin — how could I not crave for more? Arran and Mull followed, then from the '80s onwards most family vacations were island holidays. I have visited brochs and stone circles, quirky tearooms and folklore museums; circum-perambulated on foot1 and cycle; sploshed across strands at low (and occasionally not-so-low) tide; marvelled at the sight of the wild flowers on the machair, the call of the corncrake and the clownish antics of the puffin; shared vast shimmering beaches with grazing cows, seal colonies and otters; and gasped in awe at stunning coastal scenery. New routing on Coll and Colonsay, long sea-level traverses on many an island, and the sea cliffs of Mingulay and Pabbay have given some of the best climbing experiences of my life.

So, yes, I'm a devotee and this guide has without doubt further whetted my appetite. I would recommend it as an interesting and useful addition to the bookshelf of anyone visiting the isles and wanting to look beyond the climbing. But be warned: as the authors point out, island bagging may be more dangerous than Munro bagging. Unlike the Munros there will always be more islands to visit. 'Once started there is no cure.'

John Spencer

The Equilibrium Line – poems inspired by climbing: David Wilson (Smith/Doorstop, 2019, paperback, 87pp, ISBN 978-1-91219 -674-6, £9:95.)

It was said of oil painting that the greatest effect was best produced by the least amount of material. One could echo this about poetry also, and this first collection by David Wilson reveals his ability to uncover in a few intense words and phrases his interests in mountaineering from indoor climbing to bouldering, traditional rock climbs in the Lake District and Yorkshire, winter climbs on Ben Nevis, and trips to the Alps. Within these aspects some definitive strands within his work emerge: he displays a strong interest in the history of the sport and the people who have framed it. The opening line in his first verse, *Lines of Ascent — To W. H. Murray, 'Mountaineering in Scotland'* runs: 'Your book was a tent I slept in each night' and discloses the awakening dream of the teenager later experimenting at Harrison's Rocks with aspirations for an Alpine future. Elsewhere George Mallory, Don Whillans, Walter Bonatti, and Wanda Rutkiewicz are acknowledged in his verses, and Rébuffat, Lachenal and Terray are all referenced in the contours of his verses.

Another sinuous line to emerge from this volume is his fondness for place and the special qualities of mountain landscape. Areas are visited and revisited as he concedes openly 'I need my old familiar hill.' Climbing days at Stanage Edge and Almscliff are remembered for more than the quality of rock and the difficulties of crux moves. Walking in Snowdonia, the Dales and the West Highlands are warmly celebrated in all weathers and seasons. Within this theme he finds the names of hills and crags have a power contained in them to recall events, and he celebrates them for the achievements they brought and also 'those times you were gripped.' His commemorations run from Mont Blanc to Pen-y-Ghent, from the Central Pillar of Frêney to the *Left Unconquerable* of Stanage.

The conclusive topic that emerges, one immediately recognisable to us all, is his relationships with partners, other climbers and those who have shared his hill days. From two lost in an avalanche on Ben Nevis 'knowing they were somewhere beneath us', to rope partners in the Alps and Yorkshire crags, the collaborations and companionships are recalled. Alongside this the chance meetings in mountain huts that make the incidents and accidents of our climbing days are also recognised and admired.

What Wilson offers us is not only a careful meditation on the many aspects of mountain activities but also a gentle probing inquiry into what happens to us in the process. How we meet the challenges, cope with loss, and reflect on our memories of mountain days. The treasury of sight and colour whether of place or the seasons; the number of hills a daysack has summited with you, and how odd bits of kit can suddenly remind you 'about couloirs bulging with fat blue ice' are all noted and enjoyed. These are the mature reflections of an experienced climber who honours all the joys of involvement in mountaineering and acknowledges the sorrows we may undergo along the way.

Donald M.Orr

The Andes – A Guide for Climbers and Skiers: John Biggar (Andes, 5th edition 2020, paperback, 352pp, ISBN 978-0-95360-876-8, £ 34.00).

Author John Biggar (no relation of our Hon. Ed.) is a professional mountaineering instructor based in Castle Douglas, Kirkcudbrightshire. For the past 25 years he has been running a business which specialises in mountaineering, skiing and ski-mountaineering expeditions to South America. Written, published and printed in Scotland, we should all feel proud of this, the only complete guidebook to the peaks of the Andes, now in its 5th edition. Previous editions have been translated into French, Spanish, Polish and Czech, so this is clearly a popular and successful publication. The first two editions received enthusiastic reviews in this Journal (*SMCJ* 1997, p. 454 and *SMCJ* 2000, p. 477), and this reviewer is equally impressed. Packed into 352 pages and covering seven different countries, there is route information for all 100 of the major 6000m mountains plus over 300 other peaks, accompanied by over 200 diagrams, 270 photographs (mostly colour) and 80 maps, all in an attractive, sensibly sized paperback.

In his Introduction the author shares his enthusiasm for this 'ideal destination for experienced mountaineers aspiring to greater heights or remoter peaks without the bureaucratic problems of a Himalayan expedition.' He goes on to give lots of up-to-date and useful advice on Where to Go and When to Climb, Travel to the Andes, Altitude and Acclimatisation, Planning Mountain Expeditions, Climbing Conditions and Hazards, Equipment, Tips for High Altitude Expeditions, Environmental Impact and Responsible Tourism, and finally a section on Ski-

Mountaineering. The book is worth buying for these 30 general pages alone, but the nitty-gritty of what follows is invaluable. Divided into geographical areas, for each peak described there are details of Times, Heights, Grades, Grade Variation, GPS Coordinates and Maps. In his review of the original guide, Grahame Nicoll used the term 'honest', and this still shines through. This is not just a collection of bland descriptions and nice pictures. The author draws on his considerable local knowledge and experience to give concise, helpful information, with reference to other guidebooks and better maps where appropriate. In 2016 I had a very enjoyable visit to the Cordillera Blanca (*SMCJ* 2017, p.312), and I could not fault his descriptions of the valleys we visited and the peaks we climbed.

The author warns of discrepancies between the heights given on traditional IGM maps and more modern satellite digital elevation data, so I was disappointed to learn that my highest peak, Tocllaraju, has been downsized from 6043m to c.5990m, a small dent to my pride but not as upsetting as the re-heighting of some of our beloved but recently demoted Munros. For the benefit of baggers there are useful Appendices with lists of The 6000m Peaks of the Andes, The Highest 5000m Peaks, plus A Brief Mountaineering History of the Andes, a brief note on The Inca Mountaineers, a short Bibliography, and some English-Spanish Vocabulary.

So, if you are a bit jaded with our crowded European Alps, do crack on with the Spanish lessons, get a copy of this excellent guidebook, and start saving up and planning a trip to South America.

Dave Broadhead

Scottish Rock, Volume 2 (North), Third Edition: Gary Latter (Pesda Press, 2020, paperback, 480pp, ISBN 978-1-90609-571-0, £29.99).

Scottish Rock Vol. 2 now has an updated third edition to replace the second edition which was published in 2014. It describes over 2500 of the best rock climbs north of the Great Glen, including Skye, the Outer Hebrides and Orkney, while its sister volume describes the area further south. It has the same clear presentation as previous editions, and with some improved photographs and new photo diagrams it is sure to inspire.

In terms of content, numerous minor changes have been made and three more significant 'new' crags have been included. The book is of identical size and length to the previous edition, so to provide space for this new material several minor crags have been deleted and the history at the start of each section has been removed.

Creag nan Cadhag (sport climbing at Stone Valley Crags) has been added, with 25 routes from F5+ to F8a+. Also new is Super Crag Sport which is the right side of Loch Maree Crag — some fine looking bolt-protected routes here for those climbing at F7a and above. At Diabaig a new diagram of the South Wall (just beyond the main wall) reveals numerous routes in the VS to HVS grades that will be attractive to those operating at that grade. 'Super Crag Trad' near Lochinver (which bears no relation to 'Super Crag Sport') is the final major new addition, where there are some fantastic looking climbs for those operating in the extreme grades.

My local and popular sport climbing venue, Moy Rock near Dingwall, has not been included, and for some reason Creag Ghlas with its superb *Salamander* and other fine routes is described in Volume 1, South. There are other worthy crags that could have been included, but route selection for such a book is always going to cause debate and this is often what keeps it interesting — you may well discover something new to go and climb!

Overall the guide is well laid out and easy to use, with a good selection of routes and photographs. If you wish to climb on one of the newer venues described, or do not have a copy of the previous edition, I would recommend this book.

Andy Tibbs

Hard Rock – Great British rock climbs from VS to E4 4th edition: Ian Parnell (Vertebrate Publishing, 2020, hardback, 256pp, ISBN 978-1-91256-029-5, £39.95).

Most, if not everyone, reading this review will be familiar with Ken Wilson's Hard Rock. First published in 1974, it saw instant success and quickly became recognized as the authoritative representation of rock-climbing in Britain. Ken's aim was to present examples of the best climbs from all across the country at the upper end of the grade range, and routes that show-cased different types of climbs — mountain routes, sea cliff routes, outcrop routes, aid routes, traverses, a sea-stack (The Old Man of Hoy) and a gully (*Raven's Gully*). He wanted to encourage climbers to travel and experience the climbing to be had away from their familiar haunts. I am sure Scotland would have been a mysterious place to many climbers south of the border pre-1974.

I saved up and bought my copy around 1977 when still a teenager and just getting into climbing. I remember being transfixed and inspired by the writings, and poring over the photos for hours at a time. Lines like 'Arran moves like a vast steamer up the Clyde' and 'Beinn Trilleachan's side has lost a patch of skin' are permanently imprinted on my mind.

An inevitable consequence of the book's success was that the routes became collectors' items, and people would go on special trips just to notch up another tick. My own first *Hard Rock* route was *The Great Prow* in 1978, and over the years I've ticked off 54 of the 60 routes, which is a respectable tally. Yes, I admit to being one of Wilson's 'puerile tickers'! Very few have ticked the whole book — about half-a-dozen, the first being SMC member Stephen Reid — although I believe a number have done them all except *The Scoop*, the big stopper route.

A second edition of *Hard Rock* was published in 1981 and a third in 1992. This new book, compiled by Ian Parnell (Ken Wilson died in 2016), is the fourth edition and although it follows the same format it incorporates some major revisions. Comparing it with my old first edition a number of changes are immediately apparent: firstly, it has grown in size and its weight has increased (from 1290g to a hefty 1730g), a true coffee-table book; secondly, all the photos have been replaced with new colour images; and thirdly, controversially, the list of routes has been altered. *Deer Bield Buttress* in the Lake District collapsed in a rockfall in 1997 and for a long time *Totalitarian* was earmarked as its substitute; more recently *North Crag Eliminate*, also in the Lakes, suffered the same fate, *Nimrod* on Dow Crag being its replacement. These are both excellent choices (particularly as I've already climbed them both).

Parnell has then taken a bold step and decided to remove the two aid routes The Scoop and *Kilnsey Main Overhang*. These now go free at E7 and F8a+ and are too hard for inclusion in Hard Rock. (*Main Overhang* was renamed *Mandela* because it was thought that it would never be freed!) These routes are still climbable as aid routes, and indeed the SMC *Outer Hebrides* guide has both free and aid descriptions for *The Scoop*; the author however wanted to avoid 'the potentially damaging process of aiding free climbs,' and I suspect also judged that aid climbing is just no longer popular. The essays for both these routes are included in an Appendix (without photos), which is a nice touch as both are worthy historical records.

In another bold move, eleven additional routes have been added to the book — eight from the now popular sea-cliffs of Pembroke, Lundy and Swanage, and three from Scotland. *Angel Face* on the Far East Wall of Beinn Eighe with its improbable line and hidden holds is a brilliant route from an area not previously represented. The account by Martin Moran of a March ascent is entertaining and informative. *Vulcan Wall* on Sròn na Cìche is a slightly surprising choice, being an old classic — why was it not included in the original book? Kevin Howett provides a well-researched historical essay and gives Hamish MacInnes a hard time for using aid on the first ascent. *Prophecy of Drowning* on Pabbay is by far the newest (1996) climb in the book but its status is already well established, and as an Outer Hebrides route it is a fine replacement for *The Scoop*. Eleanor Fuller's write-up does it justice and evokes the excitement of climbing in such a magical place, bringing back memories of my ascent with Bill Wright. It would be interesting to know if *The Prozac Link* was considered, as it has much easier access but may have been discounted due to being a tad too difficult.

The book starts with a reproduction of Ken Wilsons's eight-page 'Development of Hard Rock Climbing In Britain' and three further pages by Ian Parnell to bring this up to date. To my knowledge this is the finest historical summary of the evolution of British rock climbing. The original essays for the original routes have been retained. These are now 46 years old and many are showing their age. For example, terms such as 'rubbers', 'moacs' and 'kletterschuhe' may not mean much to recent generations, whilst phrases such as found in Robin Campbell's account of *Swastika*, 'On these slabs is to be found a kind of climbing which, 18 years ago when the first routes were made, ...' are now inaccurate, and reference to the occasional surreptitious point of aid speaks of another era. This does not however detract from the book, but vividly transports the reader back half a century to a time when these climbs were at the cutting edge of what was possible. Most of the essays are well written, some very well. Ed Drummond's write-up of *Great Wall* on Cloggy is widely recognised as the finest piece of writing in the book — remember 'Seal-cold in my shorts I was feeling a little blue'?

The photographs are what brings the book bang up to date. There are dozens of very fine contemporary action photos, all in colour, and many full-page. It must have been a mammoth task to source some 200 quality images for the book; looking at the credits, a huge number were the work of Ian Parnell himself, who must have spent many hours hanging on an abseil rope. The superb front cover shot (by Parnell) is of Mary Birkett on the *Central Buttress* of Scafell and is particularly well chosen to illustrate the character of British trad climbing. And the colour of her bright yellow trousers has been exactly replicated in the title font colour, and here and there throughout the book — a neat design feature. It is important in a descriptive book like this that the photos should illustrate the climb rather than the climber, and there are one or two photos where I would say the climber is too much the focus of attention, for example pages 89 and 93. Another significant difference from the original *Hard Rock* is the number of women featured in the photos, although only two of the ten new essays have been written by women.

Previous editions incorporated small, hand-drawn crag diagrams. These have now gone and are replaced by photo topos, all nicely exposed apart from the Carnmore shot which is too shady. I would have liked to have seen belay stances marked (perhaps by a short break in the route line), which would have given an instant impression of the length of a route. Another minor improvement would have been to include the rock type in the route info. There are few obvious errors: I spotted that the caption for a photo of *South Ridge Direct* states that the climber is on the S-Crack, whereas it is actually the Y-Crack.

In summary, this new edition is a lavish book full of good writing and wonderful photos, and is highly recommended to anyone who doesn't already own a copy. In a world where sport climbing and bouldering are becoming ever more prevalent, it is a magnificent celebration of 'trad' climbing as we practise it in Britain. It is a credit to Ken Wilson's vision that most of the routes in the book are still recognised as 'classics': the likes of *Shibboleth*, *Kipling Groove* and *A Dream of White Horses* are still must-do routes, *Hard Rock* or not. The number of routes has now increased from 60 to 69 so the book might well be of interest to those who already own an earlier edition. My tally has automatically increased to 57 but advancing age makes completion seem unlikely, unless one of the younger members wants to lead me up some English and Welsh E3s and E4s. However, somehow it wouldn't feel quite right without *The Scoop* in the bag!

Grahame Nicoll

******

ERRATA
'This is the wandring wood, this Errour's den...'
(Edmund Spenser, *The Faerie Queene*; Canto1; xiii)

In the 2019 Journal:
Front cover   The photo should be credited to Gary Robertson.

In Robin Campbell's article p. 25 the last sentence on Hugh Grecian Williams should end '...seem to be somewhat later.' And footnote 19 should follow these missing words instead of at the end of the paragraph on the following page.

In the same article in footnote 27 p. 31, there is regrettable confusion between Horatio McCulloch and John MacCulloch. Both Donald Orr (*SMCJ* 2018, pp. 40–46) and Campbell are, in their articles, discussing Horatio McCulloch. John MacCulloch is discussed by Campbell in his Note 'Two Hundred Years Ago' (*SMCJ* 2019, pp. 246–7).

p. 81   The photo should be attributed to David Medcalf.
p. 153 top   Tom's Gully should be Consolation Gully.
p. 242 line 6 '...we might be more reluctant…'
p. 274   Robertson Lamb Hut, not Lang.
p. 291   Bill Sproul died on 4 July 2018 (not 2017).
p. 297   Almscliff, not Almcliffe.

(These errors and any others detected have, as always, been corrected in the archived version of the Journal.)

ORDERING THE SMC JOURNAL

Members should automatically receive a copy of the Journal when it is published. Members wishing to order extra copies or non-members wishing to place a regular order should contact the Distribution Manager, Dave Broadhead, by **e-mail** <journal.distribution@smc.org.uk>.

SMC JOURNAL BACK NUMBERS

Back numbers of the Journal may be obtained from Clifford Smith:
16 House o' Hill Gardens, Edinburgh, EH4 2AR.
e-mail: <journal.archive@smc.org.uk>
tel: 0131-332 3414   mob: 07748 703515

The following years are available: post and packaging are extra.

	Year			Year
£5.00	1972		£12.95	2000
	1977			2001
	1978			2002
	1979			2003
	1980			2004
	1983			
			£13.95	2005
£5.50	1985			2006
				2007
£5.70	1986			2008
	1987			
	1989		£14.95	2009
	1990			2010
	1991			2011
	1992			2012
				2013
£6.95	1993			2014
	1994			
	1995		£16.95	2016
				2017
£8.95	1996			2018
	1997			2019
	1998			
£11.95	1999			

SCOTTISH MOUNTAINEERING CLUB HUTS

Bookings can be made to stay at any of the five Club Huts by contacting the relevant Custodian.

CHARLES INGLIS CLARK MEMORIAL HUT, BEN NEVIS
Location: (NN 167 722) On the north side of Ben Nevis by the Allt a' Mhuilinn. This hut was erected by Dr and Mrs Inglis Clark in memory of their son Charles who was killed in action in the 1914–18 War.
Custodian: Robin Clothier, 35 Broompark Drive, Newton Mearns, Glasgow, G77 5DZ.
e-mail <cic@smc.org.uk>

LAGANGARBH HUT, GLEN COE
Location: (NN 221 559) North of Buachaille Etive Mor near the River Coupall.
Custodian: Bernard Swan, 16 Knowes View, Faifley, Clydebank, G81 5AT.
e-mail <lagangarbh@smc.org.uk>.

LING HUT, GLEN TORRIDON
Location: (NG 958 562) On the south side of Glen Torridon.
Custodian: Patrick Ingram, 119 Overton Avenue, Inverness, IV3 8RR.
e-mail <ling@smc.org.uk>.

NAISMITH HUT, ELPHIN
Location: (NC 216 118) In the community of Elphin on the east side of the A835.
Custodian: John T Orr, 8 Fleurs Place, Elgin, Morayshire, IV30 1ST.
e-mail <naismith@smc.org.uk>.

RAEBURN HUT, LAGGAN
Location: (NN 636 909) On the north side of the A889 between Dalwhinnie and Laggan.
Custodian: Clive Rowland, Inverene, Links Place, Nairn, IV12 4NH.
e-mail <raeburn@smc.org.uk>.

SCOTTISH MOUNTAINEERING CLUB GUIDEBOOKS
Published by SCOTTISH MOUNTAINEERING PRESS

HILLWALKERS' GUIDES
The Munros
The Corbetts and other Scottish hills
The Grahams & The Donalds
The Cairngorms
Central Highlands
Islands of Scotland including Skye
North-West Highlands
Southern Highlands

SCRAMBLERS' GUIDES
Highland Scrambles North
Highland Scrambles South
Skye Scrambles

CLIMBERS' GUIDES
Scottish Rock Climbs
Scottish Winter Climbs
Scottish Sports Climbs
Inner Hebrides & Arran
Ben Nevis
The Cairngorms
Glen Coe
Highland Outcrops South
Lowland Outcrops
North-East Outcrops
Northern Highlands North
Northern Highlands Central
Northern Highlands South
Skye The Cuillin
Skye Sea-Cliffs & Outcrops
The Outer Hebrides

OTHER PUBLICATIONS
Ben Nevis – Britain's Highest Mountain
The Cairngorms – 100 Years of Mountaineering
A Chance in a Million? – Scottish Avalanches
Hostile Habitats
The Munroist's Companion
Scottish Hill Names – Their origin and meaning
Mountaineering in Scotland: the Early Years
Mountaineering in Scotland: Years of Change

APPS
SMC guides to the Northern Corries and Polney Crag are available on the Rockfax App <https://www.rockfax.com/publications/rockfax-app/>.

E-BOOKS
Please see <https://www.smc.org.uk/publications/ebooks>

APPLYING FOR MEMBERSHIP OF
THE SCOTTISH MOUNTAINEERING CLUB

The following notes are provided outlining the principles by which climbers may be admitted to membership of the Club.

The Committee does not lay down any hard and fast rules when considering applications but considers each case on its own merits. Candidates must be over 18 and have experience of mountaineering in Scotland in both summer and winter. This experience should have extended over a period of at least four years immediately prior to application and should not be confined to just a single climbing district.

The normally expected climbing standards include:

- Experience of winter climbing including several routes of around Grade IV standard and the ability to lead climbs of this level of difficulty.
- Rock climbing experience including climbs of Very Severe (4c) standard and the ability to lead routes of this level of difficulty. In considering applications, emphasis will be placed on multi-pitch climbs in mountain locations.
- The ascent of at least 50 Munros of which at least one third should have been climbed in snow conditions.

In short, the candidate should be able to show – by producing a detailed list of climbs – that they are competent to lead a variety of outings in the mountains of Scotland in both summer and winter. The technical standards specified refer to applicants currently active and may be varied at the discretion of the Committee for older candidates provided that the applicant's routes reflect a reasonable standard for their time. Climbing in the Alps and elsewhere is taken into consideration. Candidates who do not fulfil the normal qualifications listed above but who have made special contributions to Scottish mountaineering in the fields of art, literature or science may receive special consideration.

It is essential that each candidate, before applying, should have climbed with the member proposing the application. It is also desirable that a candidate should be introduced to a member of the Committee before the application is considered. Application forms must be obtained on behalf of candidates by members of the Club who may not propose or support candidates for election during their own first two years of membership. The annual membership fee is £40.00 (£30.00 for those aged 65 and over) which includes the Club Journal.

A fuller version of these notes for members wishing to propose candidates is available from the Club Secretary who is happy to advise candidates and members on any aspect of the application process. Please contact Tom Prentice, Honorary Secretary at:

e-mail: <tpoutdoor@aol.com>
tel: 0141-6321333.

OFFICE BEARERS 2019–20

Honorary President: Neil W. Quinn
Honorary Vice-Presidents: Robert T. Richardson and Robin N. Campbell
President: John R.R. Fowler
Vice-Presidents: Stan Pearson and James Hotchkis

Hon. Secretary: Tom Prentice, 43 Thorncliffe Gardens, Glasgow, G41 2DE.
Hon. Treasurer: J. Morton Shaw, 7 Kirkbrae Terrace, New Deer, Turriff, AB53
6TF. **Hon. Membership Secretary**: Geoff Cohen, 198/1 Grange Loan,
Edinburgh, EH9 2DZ. **Hon. Meets Secretary**: David Myatt, Blairhill Gardens,
Rumbling Bridge, Kinross, KY13 0PU. **Hon. Editor of Journal**: Peter J.
Biggar, Ceol-na-Mara, Fasaig, Torridon, Achnasheen, IV22 2EZ. **Hon.
Librarian**: John C. Higham, 9 Balfleurs Street, Milngavie, Glasgow, G62 8HW.
Hon. Archivist: Robin N. Campbell, Glynside, Kippen Road, Fintry, Glasgow,
G63 0LW. **Hon. Custodian of Images**: David Stone, 30 Summerside Street,
Edinburgh, EH6 4NU. **Hon. Reporter on Accounts**: David Small, 5 Afton
Place, Edinburgh, EH5 3RB. **SMC Website Manager**: Michael P. Watson, 57
Mortonhall Park Crescent, Edinburgh EH17 8SX. **Convener of Publications
Sub-Committee**: D. Noel Williams, Solus Na Beinne, Happy Valley, Torlundy,
Fort William, PH33 6SN. **Convener of Huts Sub-Committee**: Andrew M.
James, 41 Urquhart Road, Dingwall, IV15 9PE. **Information Officer**: vacant.
Rep. to Mountaineering Scotland: Stan Pearson, 5 Greenhill Park,
Edinburgh, EH10 4DW. **Committee**: Neil G.F. Adams, David Myatt, Graeme
Morrison, Fiona Murray, Christine Watkins and Viv Scott.

Journal Information

Editor:	Peter Biggar, Ceol-na-Mara, Fasaig, Torridon, IV22 2EZ. **e-mail** <pjbiggar149@btinternet.com>
New Routes Editor:	Simon Richardson, 22 Earlswells Road, Cults, Aberdeen AB15 9NY. **e-mail** <newroutes@smc.org.uk>
Photos Editor:	Ian Taylor, 15, Pulteney Street, Ullapool, Ross-shire, IV26 2UP. **e-mail** <itandtf@hotmail.com>
Reviews Editor:	Graeme Morrison, 42 Orchard Drive, Edinburgh, EH4 2DZ. **e-mail** <g.d.morrison@btopenworld.com>
Distribution:	Dave Broadhead, 17 Drumdyre Road, Dingwall, IV15 9RW. **e-mail** <journal.distribution@smc.org.uk>
Back Numbers:	Cliff Smith. **e-mail** <journal.archive@smc.org.uk>

INSTRUCTIONS TO CONTRIBUTORS

The Editor welcomes contributions from members and non-members alike.
Priority will be given to articles relating to Scottish mountaineering. Articles
should be submitted **by the end of April** to be considered for inclusion in the
Journal of the same year. Material is preferred in electronic form and should be
sent by e-mail direct to the Editor. Most common file formats are acceptable.

Illustrations not relating to an article should be sent to the Photos Editor. All
images should be high resolution and have explanatory captions including the
source. Books for review should be sent to the Reviews Editor by the end of April.

The Editorial team reserves the right to edit any material submitted.

INDEX OF AUTHORS

INDEX OF PEOPLE

Bold numerals denote an article by the person; *italic numerals* denote an image of the person.

INDEX OF PLACES & GENERAL TOPICS

Italic numerals refer to a picture; *fn* indicates a footnote.
FA = first ascent; FWA = first winter ascent.

INDEX OF PHOTOGRAPHERS & ARTISTS

INDEX OF REVIEWS
(Reviewer in parenthesis)